Between the Balance Sheets

Tales of corporate financial behaviour

Robert Willott

Illustrated by Rebecca Cother

Foreword by
Sir Martin Sorrell

By the same author
GOING PUBLIC (Editor)
CURRENT ACCOUNTING LAW AND PRACTICE
GUIDE TO PRICE CONTROLS 1977-78
THE ENCYCLOPAEDIA OF CURRENT ACCOUNTING LAW AND PRACTICE
THE PURCHASE OR REDEMPTION BY A COMPANY OF ITS OWN SHARES
(with Peter Wolstenholme)
REBUILDING BLOCKLEY
SHOP! (with Pamela Readhead)

Published by Fintellect Publishing Ltd
Vine House, High Street, Blockley GL56 9ET, United Kingdom

© Fintellect Ltd 2022
ISBN 978-1-5272-5887-7

British Library Cataloguing in Publication Data:
A catalogue record for this book is available from the British Library

Printed and bound in the UK by Biddles Books Limited, Castle House, East Winch Road, Blackborough End, King's Lynn, Norfolk PE32 1SF

Between the Balance Sheets

Tales of corporate financial
behaviour

Contents

Foreword

As we all know, advertising and marketing services is an industry not exactly immune to hyperbole and occasionally outrageous claims. In the pages of *Campaign* and *Advertising Age*, agency leaders have seldom missed an opportunity to talk up their latest wins or put a positive gloss on their P&L. Bob Willott is someone who has always been resistant to swallowing the BS the industry comes out with. A qualified accountant, over many years he held the industry to account both literally and figuratively, digging into the Companies House records of individual agencies and providing forensic analysis of balance sheets, cashflow statements and remuneration schemes – often to the extreme embarrassment of those involved.

Initially as launch editor of *Accountancy Age* and latterly as the editor of *Marketing Services Financial Intelligence* (his accountancy firm also provided annual league tables of agency profitability for *Campaign*), Willott would uncover the kind of hidden truths in those company accounts that frequently gave lie to public pronouncements and were certainly what the financial director had hoped that nobody would notice. This book is a compendium of some of his best pieces written over 50 years, each prefaced with a retrospective commentary that is often equally insightful, and certainly more entertaining than the original, since his published reports were written in the dry, dispassionate prose of a professional number cruncher.

The period covered by this collection saw marketing services grow up from a cottage industry to an international, eventually global business with many publicly-quoted agency groups whose shareholders could rightly expect to receive reliable and accurate information about their investment. It was also a period over which the perceived value of agencies was subject to vagaries of sentiment and enormous variation. So it's quite right that Willott and his ilk were putting those deals and share prospectuses under the microscope, bringing transparency where obfuscation was too often the default mode. From his early tussle with Robert Maxwell on the inflated value of Pergamon Press, right through to his recent appraisal of Dentsu's bid for global status, Willott uses his technical knowledge of accounting to unearth errors and inconsistencies, but also to suggest lessons that should be learned, ways in which the codes and standards could be improved to provide better account-ability.

Of course, I have a personal interest in this. I've been involved in the industry for almost the entire period Willott writes about, firstly with Saatchi & Saatchi, then as founder of WPP and today as executive chairman of S4 Capital. So I'm pleased to say that I have only two mentions in the index of *Between the Balance Sheets* – I will take that as an endorsement that I haven't done too much wrong! As someone who was once described as a 'bean counter' I'm only too well aware of the importance of sound financial reporting in our industry – alongside such equally vital capabilities as creativity and innovation. There's much to discover in these pages that will prove just as relevant to industry leaders going forward as it has been in the past.

Sir Martin Sorrell
Founder & Executive Chairman
S4 Capital plc

Preface

My aim in writing this book was almost entirely sentimental. By the time I finished, it had become something more. Having written a number of reports on the financial affairs of various companies over the past half century, I thought it might be useful and instructive to gather them together in one volume. This was particularly so in the case of the more recent reports that had been published only in digital format and left me without any tangible and readily accessible version to revisit in my old age[1].

The book brings together 31 tales of companies' financial behaviour, spanning 50 years. Most of the core material has been derived from reports I wrote for *Accountancy Age* – the first publication I had the good fortune to edit from 1969 - and *Marketing Services Financial Intelligence* – the final publication I edited before fading into retirement for a third time in 2019. Each tale is prefaced by an explanation of its timing and context, and supplemented with a commentary on related subsequent events.

As my task progressed, some common themes emerged. Among them was the natural human desire displayed by some company executives to portray an excessively favourable impression of the state of their business, made all the easier by a mixture of shortcomings in company law and a contentious financial reporting regime. Fortunately there are also plenty of examples of excellent business conduct — some evidenced in the chapters that follow — which serve to highlight the contrast between the good and the bad.

Looking first at the current state of corporate law, the book notes a number of improvements that have been introduced during the period under review, but it also identifies various aspects of corporate behaviour that merit further attention in the statutes. For example, the law should be updated to:

- impose significant penalties on companies that fail to file particulars of shareholders and their shareholdings in accordance with section 853F of the Companies Act

---

[1]. *Fortunately the History of Advertising Trust has kindly retained a copy of the digital content of "Marketing Services Financial Intelligence".*

2006, perhaps in the mistaken belief that it is sufficient to refer the public to the company's register *(see p.212)*.

- amend section 442 of the Companies Act 2006 to state that the due date for filing accounts following a change in accounting reference date shall be the later of (i) the date by which accounts would have been filed in the absence of a change in reference date and (ii) three months after the changed accounting reference date *(see p.271)*.

- require that, where (a) a public company enters into a transaction with another company, and (b) a person who has been a director (or shadow director) of one or both such companies at any time within 12 months preceding the transaction is also a related party to one or both companies, there shall be disclosed in the accounts of each such company the amount of gain or loss accruing to such person directly or indirectly as a result of that transaction *(see p.363 et seq.)*.

- make it unlawful for a person who has been a director of a company at any time during a period of twelve months prior to that company being declared insolvent to (a) be appointed a director of any company that acquires or has acquired a business from that insolvent company, or of any of its subsidiary companies, for a period of five years from such insolvency declaration, and (b) hold any shares directly or indirectly in a company that acquires or has acquired a business from that insolvent company or of any of its subsidiary companies during a period of five years from such insolvency declaration *(see pp.134 and 253)*.

- exclude from the definition of a company qualifying as a micro-entity (and thereby entitled to file micro accounts) any entity that would fail to satisfy the qualifying conditions in section 384A, Companies Act 2006, when aggregated with another company or companies under common control, as defined[1] *(see p.383)*.

- amend the relevant sections of the Companies Act 2006 to reinstate an obligation on companies to provide the Registrar of Companies with the residential address of each director for display on the public file, given the responsibilities and accountability of the office held and the privilege of limited personal liability afforded to the owners of such companies *(see p.xvii)*.

Most of these proposed changes were first presented to the Depart-

---

1. *In March 2021 The Institute of Chartered Accountants in England and Wales called for a review of the micro-entities regime.*

ment for Business, Energy & Industrial Strategy at a meeting held in November 2018. Since then the Government has been consulting interested parties on a fairly extensive overhaul of company law affecting corporate transparency and the operation of the public registry at Companies House. But the Department explicitly declined to indicate which of the above matters it hopes to address in forthcoming legislation.

From an examination of the Government's initial public response, it would appear that only two of the items are being addressed – namely changes to accounting reference dates and the eligibility to file micro accounts - although further consultation is expected on other potential improvements in the financial information required in publicly filed accounts. Despite the evidence presented in chapter 30, the Government says it "does not believe there is any reason to change the provisions on residence and nationality" and makes no mention of improving the disclosure of related party transactions in the manner advocated in that chapter.

The sad reality is that there are few votes to be gained from keeping corporate regulation in good order. But surely even those politicians who favour "light touch" regulation of business would accept the need for prescribed boundaries beyond which company conduct is likely to be harmful to society. On top of that, there needs to be a leadership culture that exemplifies the attributes of integrity.

Alongside shortcomings in company law, the regulation of financial reporting has also sunk into something of a morass, overly influenced by an academic approach, as several chapters illustrate.

The current regime evolved in the wake of a major public controversy arising from the acquisition of Associated Electrical Industries (AEI) by the General Electric Company (GEC) in 1967[1]. AEI had forecast a profit of £10 million for 1967. Prior to publication, the forecast had been reviewed by the company's auditors. After the takeover, GEC published audited accounts showing a loss at AEI of £4.5 million. Much of the difference was attributed to changes in accounting policies applied to stock and contract valuations, but also to management decisions taken by GEC after it gained control. The question for the accountancy profession was this: how could such variations in accounting policy be acceptable and how could two different firms of auditors approve such variations? To make matters worse, in 1968 the accountancy profession

1. See "Takeover" by Sir Joseph Latham, Iliffe Books 1969.

was rocked by the Pergamon Press scandal that exposed Robert Maxwell's dubious business practices and, more pertinently, resulted in the publication of a report by PriceWaterhouse claiming that the audited profit of £1.5 million declared for 1968 should more appropriately have been reported as a £60,000 loss (see chapter 1).

These revelations prompted a young and articulate professor of accounting, newly arrived at Edinburgh University from Canada, to give vent to a series of criticisms of the UK accountancy profession in *The Times*[1] in 1969. His name was Edward Stamp. The article prompted the president of the Institute of Chartered Accountants in England and Wales, Sir Ronald Leach, to initiate the creation of a more publicly visible Accounting Standards Committee[2] to take responsibility for codifying accounting principles and developing obligatory accounting rules.

As the years passed, rumblings continued about how the accountancy profession conducted itself, often expressed in over-simplistic terms. One such criticism was easy to construct but harder to prove or disprove, namely that the profession was conflicted by being involved in the creation of rules governing the presentation of accounts, overseeing the conduct of its members in their preparation, and then conducting an audit.

Moves were made within the accountancy profession to separate the making of accounting rules from the policing of them. Tom Watts, a PriceWaterhouse partner who chaired the Accounting Standards Committee (ASC) at the time, instigated a review of the standard setting process. In the course of that review he spent many hours consulting with the London Stock Exchange, the embryonic Council for the Securities Industry, the Bank of England and the Department of Trade, as well as with the various professional accountancy bodies, about how they might participate in an independent policing mechanism to review non-compliance with accounting standards by listed public companies. The outcome was a proposal to set up a "Panel to Review Non-Compliance with Accounting Standards" that was included among Watts' recommendations when his report was published in 1981.

At the same time, tensions had been mounting between the six individual accountancy bodies who had previously agreed to

---

1. *"Auditing the Auditors" by Professor Edward Stamp, The Times, 11 September 1969. See also "Accounting Principles and the City Code" by Edward Stamp and Christopher Marley, Butterworths 1970*

2. *Initially called the Accounting Standards Steering Committee*

collaborate on a range of matters. Each body had to approve any new accounting rules and doubtless this lead to delays and frustrations among those seeking to improve standards. In 1985, a former ASC chairman Ian Hay Davison pondered out loud whether "the solution to the problem may lie in giving the ASC the power to promulgate standards on its own authority like the FASB in the United States", as Professor Brian Rutherford's book[1] records in some detail. This was not a new idea, but one that had been bubbling away under the surface for some years.

I think Tom Watts would have been sympathetic, but his well-tuned political antennae would probably have warned him that it was unlikely to have gained support from the accountancy bodies in 1981. Instead he agitated for a souped-up machine with a dedicated top rate Director of Accounting Standards leading a substantial technical team at a significantly increased cost. It did not require a great deal of imagination to work out that, if accepted, these changes could readily form the stepping stones towards a fully independent standards-setting organisation.

Inevitably the Watts report fuelled the divisions between the accountancy bodies, not least between the Association of Chartered Certified Accountants (ACCA) and The Institute of Chartered Accountants in England and Wales (ICAEW). The ACCA sometimes showed signs of an unwarranted corporate inferiority complex and resented the rather aloof attitude displayed by some members of the ICAEW, brought into sharp focus when the ICAEW's members rejected a plan to merge with the other professional bodies in 1970. The ACCA also resented the fact that the ASC was staffed by a technical directorate employed by the ICAEW at its Moorgate Place headquarters and that initiatives sometimes seemed to emanate from that building in a manner that left the ACCA feeling it was being side-lined.

Nowhere was this schism better illustrated than when the ACCA torpedoed Tom Watts' proposals, particularly the blueprint for a possible policing mechanism that he had worked tirelessly to achieve and which had garnered a fair degree of consensus from City regulators and Government. The ACCA also wanted the ASC staff to be separated from the ICAEW's technical directorate.

Throughout this period I was the technical director of the ICAEW which provided staff support on everything from advocating changes in company law and taxation to the development of

1. *"Financial Reporting in the UK"* by Brian A Rutherford, Routledge 2007

auditing and accounting standards on behalf of the combined accountancy bodies, as well as overseeing the ICAEW's publishing activities. For example, the Accounting Standards Committee was serviced by a team of ICAEW staff headed by a committee secretary. Alongside that I had been involved with Tom Watts' initiative in the background and was impressed by the progress he had made in gaining support for a policing body.

While the accountancy bodies were wrangling among themselves in 1980, senior members of the ICAEW decided to move ahead with proposals for the appointment of a Director of Accounting Standards as Tom Watts' report would recommend. This meant that my role would need to be split. Would I like to run the hived-off Accounting Standards Committee or remain in charge of the rump of the Institute's technical activities?

My response was to decline both, not because they would not have been interesting, but because my gut feeling was against the overall plan. Given the disagreement between the accountancy bodies over the need for an independent policing panel, and the day-to-day administrative problems of trying to serve six masters, I accepted that it was only a matter of time before the accounting standards would be set by an independent body. But in my view the removal of the accounting standards rule-making from the direct purview of the ICAEW and other professional bodies would diminish that organisation's standing and influence in Government and the wider world. And, in leaving the profession with the responsibility for disciplining its members for breaches of the accounting standards — without an enforcement body that placed responsibility for compliance on company boards as a whole — the ICAEW would quickly become the whipping boy for corporate financial failings in the future.

Naïvely or otherwise, I believed that the accountancy profession itself should remain the driving force in developing the best possible accounting standards, drawing on as a wide a constituency of participants as practicable, with an independent agency enforcing compliance as Watts had recommended[1]. Surely that was what the public would expect? Yes, the work needed to improve, with a more disciplined academic foundation (a "conceptual framework"). And standards needed to be global in their application.

It is for others to reflect on whether indeed the stature of

---

1. *As events turned out, both the setting and policing of accounting standards in the UK were removed from the accountancy profession's direct oversight when the Financial Reporting Council was set up in 1990.*

the ICAEW has been diminished by the removal of its technical rule-making role, much of which was later assumed by the International Accounting Standards Board under the able leadership of David Tweedie who was knighted for his work.

One of Professor Stamp's criticisms – probably with some justification at the time – was that the ICAEW had a heavy anti-intellectual bias: "Few of its members are university graduates", he said. Yet today, rightly or wrongly, I find myself criticising the International Accounting Standards Board for having become too academic. That is not to belittle the enormous amount of good work done and the greater intellectual discipline that was brought to the task after David Tweedie assumed responsibility, but to question whether by its nature an independent rule-making body staffed by a more academic team might become too theoretical in its outlook. As you will read, I believe the pendulum has now swung too far towards the academic in developing what I call an "as if" approach to accounting that sometimes pays little regard to the contractual substance of a transaction.

One example of "as if" accounting affects almost every company that chooses to make an acquisition where a vendor remains employed by the company. Often the transaction is structured so that part of the purchase price is deferred. That deferred element is called an "earn-out" but for reasons that will become clear the term has become misleading. Except in exceptional circumstances (and depending on how agreements have been drafted) the accounting rules require the deferred element to be treated as if it is remuneration rather than part of the purchase price.

We shall see a variant of this rule in chapter 28 where M&C Saatchi agreed to allow vendors to retain some of their shareholdings provided those shares were placed under put and call options enabling M&C Saatchi to acquire them later.

One justification for this accounting rule appears to be that the vendor is continuing as an employee of the company while being party to an agreement that renders the earn-out entitlement null and void if the employee leaves before a predetermined date[1]. Such a clause is interpreted as linking the deferred payment to employment rather than being a simple deferment of the purchase price.

Let us examine a little more carefully the nature and purpose of a so-called "earn-out" arrangement. It is to recognise the volatility of company profits, particularly in businesses that depend on

1. See International Financial Reporting Standard 3 "Business Combinations" para. 55..

the creative talents of their personnel. Typically the purchase price is calculated as a multiple of the company's maintainable profits, as would be the case for a company whose shares are traded on a public stock exchange. In valuing the company or its shares by reference to a multiple of profits, the buyer is making a judgement not only about what would provide a reasonable return on his investment based on the historic profit but also about the future rate of profit growth (or otherwise) to be expected.

Not surprisingly, if a buyer is relying on the maintainability of profits, there would be considerable merit in withholding part of the purchase price until there is some assurance that the implied rate of growth will be delivered. So, instead of buying the target company outright for a single payment based on a multiple of the historic profit that assumes a rate of future profit growth, payments are normally made by instalments using an "earn-out" formula that should result in a more reliable valuation.

Put simply, the "earn-out" takes account of the actual performance in the early years following acquisition instead of relying on an estimate. The formula usually comprises (i) an initial payment based on a prudent multiple of the past profit and (ii) one or more further payments designed to uplift the initial price by an amount that puts a value on the actual growth in profits achieved during the succeeding few years. Typically the deferred amount might be calculated by applying a multiple to, say, the average profit earned in the five years following acquisition and deducting the initial payment from it. That is not remuneration. It is a deferred component of the total purchase price.

Any agreement with a vendor to waive the deferred payment if employment ceases prematurely is intended to compensate the buyer for the risk that the company's longer term prospects may also be diminished by the premature loss of a key executive. Arguably the case for treating a deferred payment as performance related remuneration would be much stronger if it was not linked to the acquisition agreement and had no predetermined end date. An even better argument would be one that showed that the selling employee's core remuneration package had been reduced after the acquisition to a level that was no longer consistent with what would be expected for a similar job in a comparable business.

Another example of "as if" accounting arose when, with the support of the London Stock Exchange, UK public companies were permitted to promote an alternative definition of profit "as if" all exceptional, non-recurring and otherwise inconvenient items had never occurred. This massaged result is often called "headline profit" and is said to have more appeal to investment institutions, which should come as no surprise.

The Corporate Finance Institute (an organisation of investment professionals that provides courses for financial analysts and issues certificates to participants) claimed that the use of "headline earnings" as a measure provided "an accurate representation of the business performance". The CFI went on to suggest that managements "misrepresent" the financial performance of the company by including items such as extraordinary and non-recurring transactions and, if not adjusted for, they flow through to essential metrics like the price/earnings ratio widely used by investors.

The CFI omitted to mention that the relevant international accounting standard makes no reference to "headline earnings" being acceptable in calculating earnings-per-share, a position that was confirmed to me by the International Accounting Standards Board itself[1]. Nevertheless, the UK's investment professionals have succeeded in persuading the South African Institute of Chartered Accountants and the Johannesburg Stock Exchange that headline earnings-per-share should be disclosed by South African listed companies alongside the figures required by the international accounting standard. According to the CFI's definition, "headline earnings" should exclude items like:

- Gains or losses arising from the sale of assets;
- Gains or losses caused by discontinuance of operations;
- Charges caused by write-downs in the value of assets, including the amortisation of intangible assets like goodwill;
- Charges caused by reductions in the number of employees.

What the CFI did not say was that headline results enable managements to divert attention from the true outcome of their company's performance. By allowing the income statement to include this alternative measure of profit or loss, upon which public pronouncements tend to focus, companies are permitted to mislead their shareholders by giving the impression that the highlighted items are of no consequence. They may be unusual and non-recurring, but highlighted items are real and do have consequences, occasionally bringing a company to its knees.

One can sympathise with the desire to explain to shareholders what the underlying performance of a company has been,

---

1. *International accounting standard 33: Earnings per share*

stripped of unwanted distortions, but the place for any such explanation is in a note to the financial statements that can be reconciled to the statutory profit or loss. The audited statutory result is the only "true" result and the income statement should not be contaminated by the inclusion of "headline" figures within it. Let us hope that the London Stock Exchange and the UK Government will take a firmer position.

ROBERT WILLOTT
October 2022

Acknowledgements

I am pleased to have this opportunity to thank a number of people who have encouraged me, sometimes unwittingly, along the pathway of my curious career that culminated in the preparation of this book. It started 66 years ago when a teenage friend Tony Christopher drew me into amateur journalism by suggesting I might help him launch a magazine for the Boy Scout troop of which we were both members. Then, having qualified as a chartered accountant, I was intrigued by an advertisement in *The Observer* for someone to become the editor of a new weekly financial news magazine. I wrote to enquire whether the magazine would be interested in an occasional freelance contribution on accounting matters. The response to my letter destroyed any notion of a planned career.

Instead I have to thank the people at Haymarket Publishing — particularly Lindsay Masters, Robert Heller (who taught me how to write), Michael (now Lord) Heseltine and Paul Buckley — for hoisting me out of an accountancy partnership into the stimulating world of journalism and publishing, initially to edit *Accountancy Age*, and for supporting me later when my first wife was taken ill. Ann, a research chemist at Unilever, had been generous enough to back me in what seemed like a very risky career move at the time. Neither of us could have known how all-consuming that journalistic career would become and the extent to which it may have deprived my family of the time and attention it deserved.

I would also like to thank another life-long friend and fellow articled clerk Tony Hill in whose company the practice of auditing was almost enjoyable, Paul and Pepita Walker who among many kindnesses allowed me to spend weeks studying for my accountancy exams amidst the beautiful Peak District, and Janet Briffett for her support as the publisher of my first book and later partnering me in a small independent publishing venture.

Sir David Tweedie, when technical director of the Institute of Chartered Accountants of Scotland, brought intellect, humour, and generosity of spirit to my work as his opposite number at the ICAEW, and was clearly destined for greater things. I still remember the balloons he sent to Chartered Accountants Hall to mark my departure. When I returned to a "proper job" as an accountant at Spicer and Pegler (later subsumed into Deloitte), I found myself among partners and colleagues in a firm that genuinely had the characteristics of a family. They supported me during bereavement and later when a falling tree chopped my car in half. On top of that they were brave enough to allow me to open an office in London's West End with the unfailing and enthusiastic support of a marvellous team led by Richard Nicol - an adventure that I believe proved to be fulfilling and fun in equal measure for all of us involved.

I am indebted to the University of Nottingham, especially Professor John Coyne and the late Professor Mike Wright who, with support from Spicer and Pegler and Barclays Development Capital, established the original Centre for Management Buyout Research, produced some valuable output and honoured me as a special professor for a number of years.

In a more recent adventure, I had the good fortune to work with Amanda Merron, Graham Golding, Steve Waring and Chris Moody, all of whom took a risk with their careers by joining me when we set up the specialist accountancy practice of Willott Kingston Smith in London's West End with the support of Kingston Smith's then senior partner Michael Snyder. The practice was dedicated to serving the niche business sectors of marketing, entertainment and the professions. Along the way, Graham Beckett and his colleagues at Results International (as it is now called) shared with us their merger and acquisition expertise in a joint venture.

Life could have been very different if it were not for the many clients who went out of their way to support me in my various business ventures, notably Brian Chapman, John Bartle, Nigel Bogle, Sir John Hegarty, Peter Shilland, Nigel Maile and Mark Collier, but there are many, many more. Thanks to you all and to those who have contributed knowledge and advice during the preparation of this book, not least Matthew Rowbotham of Lewis Silkin for his input on the current treatment of earn-outs. I am also indebted to Ian Robert and Esther Carder of Moore Kingston Smith for their technical advice.

No-one reading this book will fail to notice the wonderful illustrations accompanying each chapter. These are the original work of Rebecca Cother and we were extremely fortunate to discover her talent. I am very grateful to Catrina Popham who cheerfully took on the task of proof reading over 100,000 words, and to my daughters Sian and Carys for casting their objective eyes over some of the narrative. Thanks also to our lawyers Michelmores, especially Jayne Clemens, and to Jacob Dean and Felicity McMahon from 5RB Chambers. Their collective wisdom and support over a long period was invaluable in bringing this venture to a successful conclusion.

The most stalwart supporter of this venture has been my wife Carolyn who frequently has overcome an inner desire to throw my computer out of the window. Whether that commendable self-restraint stemmed from loving devotion or from a reluctance to kill any innocent passers-by, we may never know. Thank you anyway.

RGW

1

Pergamon's Paper Profits

Most people can still remember Robert Maxwell, the Polish born former Labour MP for Buckingham, publishing tycoon and football club owner whose life came to a dramatic end when he disappeared from his luxury yacht in the Atlantic Ocean in 1991. Until then he had been the boss of a collection of media businesses, including Mirror Group Newspapers, British Printing Corporation and the US publishing house Macmillan.

But his first and most famous publishing venture was Pergamon Press which he created in 1951 and sold in 1991 under pressure from creditors. Throughout that period he had lived and worked from a mansion called Headington Hill Hall that was leased from Oxford City Council.

Pergamon had been built by Maxwell into a sizeable public company when, in 1969, he was presented with an opportunity to sell the entire business to a US company Leasco Data Processing Corporation that was run by Saul Steinberg. On completion Steinberg claimed that Maxwell had misrepresented the profitability of his business and lobbied successfully for Maxwell and his supporters to be ousted from the Pergamon board. Price Waterhouse carried out a comprehensive review of Pergamon's past accounting practices and the UK's Takeover Panel persuaded the Government to appoint inspectors – barrister Owen Stable and accountant Sir Ronald Leach - to investigate the conduct of the business.

Put simply, Maxwell's aim had been to maximise profit, justified or otherwise. The higher the accumulated profits, the better the security Pergamon could offer to bankers, the easier it was to buy other companies at a favourable price, the greater the realisable value of Maxwell's personal shareholding and the higher his personal prestige and influence. As the inspectors concluded:

> Having now investigated a large number of transactions between Pergamon and the Maxwell family private companies we have come to the conclusion that until the Leasco deal foundered the real purpose behind the transactions on which we have reported was to increase the value of Pergamon's shares in

> the stock market. The Pergamon saga and Pergamon's reputation as an exceptional "growth stock" could not have been established without the network of related private companies and without undertaking transactions such as the ones on which we have reported in this report, and this purpose is discernible through all Mr Maxwell's conduct with regard to Pergamon. It runs like a thread through all that he did up to the time when the Leasco deal went off. From the time when the Leasco deal foundered part of his energies switched to ensuring that so far as he could arrange matters the private companies were relieved of some of the special transactions into which they had entered.[1]

It would not be unfair to describe Maxwell as a dishonest bully, albeit his public persona was more that of a flamboyant campaigning entrepreneur. Despite outward appearances, there were suggestions that he also had been an Israeli spy. The Government inspectors concluded that "notwithstanding Mr Maxwell's acknowledged abilities and energy, he is not in our opinion a person who can be relied on to exercise proper stewardship of a publicly quoted company".

The Price Waterhouse report into Pergamon's past accounting practices concluded that the company lost £60,000 in 1968 instead of the profit of £1.5 million originally reported in accounts audited by Chalmers Impey. Prior year and other adjustments increased that loss to £734,000. Another £2 million was lost in the next nine months and a further £2.3 million was lost in the year after that.

Robert Maxwell in April 1971

This chapter recounts in detail the myriad ways that Maxwell contrived to misrepresent the financial condition of Pergamon. It concludes with a commentary on the revisions made to the 1968 accounts by Price Waterhouse that was first published in *Accountancy Age* during September 1971. That commentary anticipated that, if all the uncertainties identified by Price Water-

---

1 *Department of Trade: Final Report on the Affairs of Pergamon Press Ltd, paragraph 1224; HMSO 1973.*

Pergamon Press - profits and losses

	Year to 31 Dec 1968		Nine months to 30 Sept 1969	Year ended 30 September		
	As originally published	Per Price Waterhouse		1970	1971	1972
	£'000	£'000	£'000	£'000	£'000	£'000
Trading profit (loss) as reported	2,104	495	29	-684	-83	309
Tax	-1,108	-339	-18	-76	-56	-89
Impairment of ILSC		-787	-507			
Other exceptional items	534	573	-1,465	-1,579	-320	156
Minority interests	-27	-2	-30	5	-10	-61
Profit (loss) adjusted for period	1,503	-60	-1,991	-2,334	-469	315
Prior period adjustments	23	-985				
Other adjustments	313	311	-154			
Dividends paid	-554	-554				
Increase (decrease) in net assets	1,285	-1,288	-2,145	-2,334	-469	315

house were to become realities, Pergamon might turn out to have been worth absolutely nothing at 30 September 1969. Indeed the Department of Trade inspectors themselves confirmed that Pergamon still had a negligible value at 30 September 1972:

> At the 30 September 1972 the consolidated balance sheet of Pergamon and its subsidiaries disclosed net assets of £4, 000 represented by share capital and share premium accounts, aggregating £4, 525,000, less an accumulated deficit of £4,521,000. Thus virtually the whole of the share capital and reserves had been lost.

Among the many detailed criticisms made by the inspectors was one that the accounts of various Maxwell controlled companies were approved by the shareholders before the auditors had reported on them and, in some cases, were not presented to the shareholders within the statutory time limit.

Another criticism described how debts due to Pergamon of £215,938 and £45,213 at 30 June 1968 and 8 November 1968 respectively were assigned to a Maxwell controlled company for an aggregate amount of £155,213 to avoid Pergamon recognising that those debts had a realisable value of only £21,000. When threatened with removal from the Pergamon board, Maxwell gave instructions to cancel the above-mentioned debt assignments so as to avoid having to reflect in his company's accounts the write-down from book value to realisable value of the debts so assigned.

The inspectors also said that Pergamon shareholders ought to have been told that about one-third of the £2.1 million pre-tax profit reported for 1968 was derived from sales and prospective sales of back issue journals, that the whole of Pergamon's trade in back issue journals was carried on with only two customers - both of which were controlled by Maxwell or related parties - and that Pergamon faced a huge contingent liability under the agreement with one of those companies whereby reprint rights were granted (later valued at $1.6 million) in return for a 10% royalty.

The inspectors judged it "improper" for Maxwell to have included £100,000 in the Pergamon profit forecast for 1968 in respect of Spanish translation rights and to cause such a profit to be created by debiting a Maxwell family company through a journal entry in the books of Pergamon. Maxwell was accused of inducing the purchase of the rights by Pergamon's 70% owned US subsidiary Pergamon Press Inc (PPI) from a company under Maxwell's personal influence called Maxwell Scientific International Inc (MSI) by giving a guarantee on behalf of Pergamon - unknown to its board - just four days before the extraordinary general meeting of Pergamon called to consider removing Maxwell from the board.

Maxwell was criticised for not including an adequate note to Pergamon's 1968 accounts explaining that the company had created an exceptional profit of £266,000 by valuing its stock of journals for the first time, bearing in mind that, without the exceptional profit of £266,000, the profit forecast for 1968 of "not less than £2 million before taxation" made in the offer document for the shares in *News of the World* would not have been met.

The inspectors also discovered that shipping invoices prior to 1969 relating to back issues sent to MSI contained values which bore no relation to the invoiced values of the goods and that this was done to mislead the United States Customs.

Among the many critical conclusions drawn by the inspectors was one that stood head and shoulders above all others:

> In our opinion there was a serious lack of disclosure in the accounts regarding not only Pergamon's transactions with MSI Inc, but also regarding the general nature of the transactions with the Maxwell family companies and of their bearing on the accounts of Pergamon.[1]

Such was Maxwell's arrogant domineering nature that he responded to the inspectors' report at the time by publishing his own "counter report", claiming that the inspectors' findings were

---

1. *Department of Trade: Final Report on the Affairs of Pergamon Press Ltd, paragraph 1223: HMSO 1973.*

riddled with errors. We received a copy at *Accountancy Age* and I began to study it with some enthusiasm.

But then I spotted a strange inconsistency. In an attempt to disprove one of the inspectors' claims, Maxwell had attached a copy of a handwritten ledger account to support his view. The more I looked at the document the more confused I became. Then everything became clear: Maxwell had muddled up his debits and credits.

Instead of lending support to his case, the ledger account damned Maxwell and added weight to the inspectors' criticism. As a journalist, this was a line of enquiry worth pursuing. I telephoned Maxwell. He took the call, but before I could explain my line of enquiry he was bellowing down the phone: "What you need to say is...". And off he went with a string of criticisms of the inspectors. I waited patiently, muttered some vague expression of interest and then attempted to draw Maxwell back to my own questions.

"What you need to say is...", he roared again. And again I listened to the tirade before venturing to draw his attention to the ledger account. "What you need to say is...."

Whether Maxwell had any understanding of the nature of my enquiry has remained a mystery ever since. He either didn't listen or he realised he was too far out of his depth to provide a convincing response. I tried once more...

"That's very interesting Mr Maxwell, but could we look at the ledger account?"

My question was cut off in full flow. "I think this conversation has gone on long enough", Maxwell shouted and slammed down the phone. I never heard from him again. But his response portrayed everything I needed to know about the man.

Pergamon performed poorly under Leasco's umbrella and, despite the damning indictment of his past corporate stewardship, Maxwell managed to borrow enough money to buy it back in 1974. Not for nothing was Maxwell described as the bouncing Czech.

As we shall see, Maxwell's personality and his disregard for the norms of business behaviour were vividly displayed during the unravelling of his questionable business affairs. Indeed, he might be described as the master chef among the book cooks.

Among the accounting controversies that were exposed by Price Waterhouse was a habit of increasing the cover price of Pergamon academic journals. No one could quarrel with that. But they might quarrel with the way in which Maxwell applied the price increases to the book value of the piles of printed sheets that remained unsold on the shelves of his printers.

At Maxwell's direction those stocks of unsold journals ceased to be valued at cost but instead were valued at what that cost would have been if uplifted by the percentage uplift in selling price.

Thus unsold stocks of academic journals were growing in value and contributing to reported profit while taking up an ever increasing amount of shelf space at Pergamon's various printers. When Pergamon collapsed those unsold journals remained on the printers' shelves. Most of the profit reported on their cover price increases was never realised.

By an unexpected coincidence I was visiting one of Pergamon's former printing subsidiaries —Wheatons — near Exeter some time later. Our conversation wandered into Maxwell territory and Wheaton's managing director let slip a revealing anecdote. "When Pergamon collapsed", he said, "we could not find enough pulp mills in the West of England to process the quantity of unsold journals that Maxwell had stockpiled."

The 1969 accounts of Pergamon Press and the report of independent accountants Price Waterhouse & Co should be made compulsory reading for every accountant in training or practice.

The original audited accounts for 1968 showed a pre-tax profit of £2.1 million on net assets of £7 million. Then, in the summer of 1969, Leasco paid £9 million for just 38% of the company, the book value of which is now being estimated as £2.5 million at 30 September 1969.

No-one — not the auditors Chalmers Impey & Co or the reporting accountants Price Waterhouse — will express an opinion as to whether the 1969 balance sheet accurately reflected a true and fair view of the state of the company at 30 September. Among the 22 important notes accompanying the accounts (which are a remarkable example of how well complex accounts can be explained) are references to four substantial contingent liabilities which could cost the company £5 million (more or less) and contingent assets (a rarity in financial reporting) which could realise about £2.5 million (or something). If all the uncertainties became realities, Pergamon might turn out to have been worth absolutely nothing at 30 September 1969. Poor Leasco. Poor Maxwell (he still owned 27%). And poor innocent public shareholders.

Before examining the accounting practices, it is worth taking a quick look at the financial management policy of the new board. Faced with severe liquidity problems following last autumn's shake up, the board has decided to dispose of assets which are not an essential part of the principal field of activity of the group. The colour commercial printing section at Bletchley, the Layton-Sun engraving and typesetting division, the Speed-writing and Speedtyping businesses and Air Express are all potential victims of the policy.

But with stocks and debtors (£10.5 million) in the original 1968 accounts exceeding the value of sales for the whole of that year (£9.8 million), and subsequently finding that the major part of debtors related to sums advanced to part-works publisher International Learning Systems Corporation (ILSC) as working capital (now controlled by British Printing Corporation, referred to here as BPC) or to sums due from Maxwell associated companies about which there is much uncertainty, the new Pergamon board clearly had to take positive action to preserve the future of the company.

The 1969 accounts incorporated all the recommendations made by Price Waterhouse. Chalmers Impey, in a 1,000-word qualified report, does not accept that the original 1968 accounts should necessarily have incorporated all the amendments that Price Waterhouse suggested.

There are three major adjustment headings in the 1969 accounts. First, a provision of £507,000 is made for a loss on the investment in ILSC. Pergamon subscribed for 50% of the shares of ILSC at a cost of £1,008,000, when it was formed with BPC in July 1967. By December 1968, a further £1,140,000 had been advanced as working capital, but this sum had been included under the general heading of "debtors" in the 1968 audited accounts.

A note to those accounts on ILSC matters stated that Pergamon's total

investment at that date amounted to £2,030,237, of which £1,022,188 was in the form of "advances on loan and current account". By no stretch of the imagination could such a treatment of advances to an associated company be justified as a generally accepted accounting principle.

Subsequently the severe losses incurred by ILSC became apparent and in February 1970 BPC agreed to acquire a further 40% of the equity for £200,000. The investment by Pergamon at September 1969 has been valued at £225,000 (representing the original cost of a 10% holding at £200,000, plus BPC's anticipated payment of £200,000 for 40% of the equity less £175,000, being a liability under a profit warranty).

At September 1969, the cost of Pergamon's investment had reached £2,348,000 and the difference between this and the revised balance sheet value of £225,000 (amounting to £2,123,000) has been written off. Of this sum, £507,000 relates to advances in 1969 and is shown as a specific charge in that period's profit and loss account. The balance of £1,616,000 is included as prior year adjustments.

The second important heading is the charge for "exceptional items" of £1,465,000 in the 1969 profit and loss account. It would have been normal practice for some of these items to appear under the "exceptional" heading in any company. For example, there is a surplus on sale of properties (some of which relates to sale and lease-back fund-raising arrangements under Maxwell's management), re-organisation costs, expenditure on takeover bids and the

Leasco negotiations.

The *exceptional* exceptional items relate to the cost of back issues printed during the nine-month period of the 1969 accounts and the highly controversial provisions against balances receivable from certain Maxwell family companies, totalling £1,506,000.

The dealings in back issues by Pergamon had a significant effect both on the published profits of the company and on the adjustments recommended by Price Waterhouse.

Of the exceptional items charged in the 1969 profit and loss account, two (totalling £1,451,000) related to back issue transactions.

Pergamon had granted back issue dealership rights for the western hemisphere to Maxwell Scientific International Inc (MSI), and — for the rest of the world — to Robert Maxwell & Co. MSI, a US company, is owned by a Maxwell family trust (in which his children have a contingent interest) and Robert Maxwell & Co, a UK company, is controlled by Maxwell personally.

The major part of the exceptional charge concerns the balance of £1,219,000 shown in Pergamon's books as due from MSI at 30 September 1969 and which is deemed doubtful. The remaining £232,000 relates to the cost of printing excess copies of journals in 1969 for sale as back issues.

Until 1968, all printing costs for journals were charged directly against revenue in the year of publication. When back issue sales arose, the proceeds were credited in the year of receipt and effectively represented a pure profit in that year. Unsold back issues were always treated as of no value for year-end stock purposes. Because of the market potential for back issue sales, it was normal practice for Pergamon to print quantities of journals in excess of current subscription requirements.

MSI wrote to Pergamon on 6 October 1969, cancelling its trading relationship with the company, and the market for back issues is now more dubious than it had previously been. Pergamon has therefore felt it necessary to treat the proportion of printing costs in 1969 deemed to relate to back issues as an extraordinary charge of £232,000.

As an accounting practice, this is clearly open to question. While it is possible that the print order will now prove excessive (because it was influenced by a "firm" order for back issues from MSI), it is difficult — on the basis of evidence so far presented — to see how the company can assume that no back issue market now exists. There is the Robert Maxwell & Co market (a limited one) and, assuming the legal dispute over whether or not the MSI cancellation is valid is settled within a reasonable time, someone will eventually act as Pergamon's western hemisphere back issue dealer and hopefully earn some sales. On this basis the cost, so far as it is not excessive, is more ordinary than exceptional.

But the crux of the back issue controversy is the sheer size of the transactions. From January 1966 to 30 September 1969, sales of back issues to Maxwell controlled MSI totalled £1,815,000. Of these, journals to the value of £441,000 had actually been delivered to New York, the remainder (£1,374,000) being held in a warehouse shared with Pergamon and Robert Maxwell & Co at Olney, Bucks. A note by Price Waterhouse suggests that the sales value of these back issues was £1,401,000 at 30 September 1969 – leaving a small discrepancy of £25,000 unexplained. The fact remains that the vast majority of back issue sales to MSI over four years had not even left England, let alone reached customers of MSI (the estimated cost of MSI sales for the period is only £225,000).

In the light of the alleged cancellation of the trading agreement with Pergamon, and bearing in mind the quantities of back issues unsold by MSI, Pergamon has made a 100% provision against the balance of £1,219,000 shown in the books as due from MSI at 30 September 1969. It is regrettable that the components of such a sizeable balance are not explained by either the company or Price Waterhouse.

Auditors Chalmers Impey did not see a detailed order for the sales to MSI in 1969 and the firm relied upon a telex from the president of MSI (outlining back issue "requirements" for 1969) as confirmation that, for the first time, a firm order for future sales of back issues existed at 31 December 1968 and a change of accounting basis could be justified by the new situation.

This change in basis provided for a valuation of back issue stocks to be included as an asset in the 1968 balance sheet.

On the evidence available, Price Waterhouse has not disagreed with this decision. But it does point out that the presentation in the 1968 accounts as originally published is not necessarily the best.

The Price Waterhouse view is that, if the stock of back issues of £341,000 at 31 December 1968 is credited to the 1968 profit and loss account, then the comparable value at 1 January 1968 of £326,000 should have been debited. The adjusting entry would then be shown as a movement on reserves or an adjustment relating to prior years. The profit for 1968 would have been £326,000 less, but the net asset value at 31 December 1968 would be unchanged.

In the original 1968 accounts, the only note on stock valuation says: 'Stocks are valued at the lower of cost and net realisable value and include £266,416 of costs incurred in the year in respect of additional printing and reprinting of journals to meet firm orders'. This is a classic example of an explanatory note that explains nothing. The change in accounting treatment should have been clearly and specifically noted.

Turning to prior year adjustments, these totalled £2,573,000 and resulted from the recommendations of Price Waterhouse.

In August 1969 Pergamon received back from Robert Maxwell & Co books to the value of £214,000. Of this sum, £119,000 related to books sold to Robert Maxwell & Co in 1968. These stocks included the best part of £95,000 worth of books invoiced in December 1968, being a reserve stock supply sent to Robert

Maxwell & Co's warehouse. With hindsight, Price Waterhouse considers that the profit element in the 1968 sales which were returned in 1969 should be eliminated from the 1968 accounts. This profit amounted to no less than £85,000 which, when added to charges to Robert Maxwell & Co for administration expenses of £64,000 that should not have been so debited, cause adjustments of £149,000.

The major question here is whether or not auditors should make enquiries about sales to associated companies and, more important, how should they determine the need for a provision against sales returns. Did the auditors have sufficient reason to make enquiries about the substantial invoice for £95,000 rendered to Robert Maxwell & Co in December 1968? Was there any evidence that the goods might be returned?

Books held in stock were included at the lower of cost and net realisable value, as is usual. Cost meant just that. No overheads — just plain, direct cost.

However, Price Waterhouse has since discovered that certain stocks were included in the 1968 balance sheet at an inter-divisional transfer price which exceeded cost by £13,000. It is fair to ask whether this type of error is of any real significance.

But the peculiarities of publishing are exposed where net realisable value is the relevant basis of valuation. As a book gets older, its realisable value is considered to decline. Pergamon provided for this by applying a fixed percentage based on the period which has elapsed since date of publication. Surprisingly, when a book was reprinted,

the date of "original" publication was amended so that the original stocks suddenly became "new" again.

This practice is not necessarily as hair-raising as it may at first sound. If public (and not management) demand is the cause of reprinting, it is reasonable to argue that the original copies are very saleable and that their value should not be less than cost. But two things follow. First, any write-up should be credited to the year's profits in which the original write-down was charged (an adjustment to reserves, rather than current profits). And secondly, the departure from the basic formula should be noted.

The most extraordinary departure from the net realisable value basis at Pergamon was when unbound copies were bound. When printed, only a portion of the total run is immediately bound. The remainder is held as "flat stock" and Pergamon applied its obsolescence provision formula to the flat stock as well as bound copies. But when some of the flat stock was bound, the company updated the books as new and started the write-down formula again. The company would thereby produce instant profits which more accurately relate to prior years and which are contingent on the bound copies being saleable.

In two other cases, special offers of old titles (to libraries and to students) had been deemed a justification for up-valuing the copies to cost rather than realisable value. In the case of library sales, the difference in value was £88,000, but when the special offer ended in September 1969, sales were only sufficient to cover the written down value. Pergamon up-valued the stocks to cost although sales anticipated for the two years 1968 and 1969 were expected to reach only 80% of the original written down value. In the case of school titles, no provision had been made for obsolescence.

The conflict in accounting principles here seems to revolve around whether a formula should be designed to accommodate all the quirks of the business and then be rigidly adhered to, or whether the formula should be amended in some cases to relate figures to management's assessment of the market value. Price Waterhouse has taken the first view.

There were other prior period adjustments. The Speedtyping subsidiary's typewriters had been treated as stock, with no depreciation provision. And apparently account was taken of journal orders worth £25,000 as sales although cash was not subsequently received.

The final contentious subject relates to the depreciation of revalued fixed assets. Pergamon revalued certain assets at 30 September 1968 and decided that depreciation should only be provided from that date. From the balance sheet viewpoint this is perfectly reasonable. But the profit and loss account benefits artificially because, for nine months, no depreciation is charged. Clearly the revaluation should be adjusted back to the beginning of the accounting year, providing a full year's depreciation on a suitably increased asset value. The additional depreciation charge becomes £63,000.

Now the affairs of **MSI** and **PPI** remain to be resolved. And, of course, the tax adjustments. What book value is finally placed on Pergamon Press at 31 December 1968 no-one yet knows. But as an enlightening auditing and accountancy case study, it will be a long time before Pergamon is surpassed.

2

Incompetence in Excess

E xcess Holdings was a Lloyd's insurance underwriter that caught my eye solely because a stock market listed insurance broker C E Heath announced in *The Financial Times* that it had sold its minority shareholding in the business.

That was in the early nineteen seventies, when several insurance companies had already been exposed for selling policies at prices that paid inadequate regard to the likely cost of claims. The most famous example was probably Vehicle & General Insurance which became the subject of a Department of Trade investigation.

The Department of Trade report aroused my interest in the intricacies of insurance company accounting and we wrote quite a lot about Vehicle & General's shortcomings in *Accountancy Age*. Natural curiosity prompted me to wonder whether there was something similarly untoward at Excess that had prompted C E Heath to dispose of its shareholding. So I ordered copies of the previous five years' accounts.

I learned two lessons from this exercise. One was not to always assume that dodgy accounts are produced by dodgy people. They can equally well be prepared by incompetent people. And secondly, the only way to find out is to confront the people involved.

My examination of the Excess accounts raised a number of contentious issues, not least the probability that the company had underprovided for insurance claims incurred but not reported[1] and thereby overstated the apparent strength of the group's balance sheet.

In those days I had a working relationship with *The Guardian* and its City editor Charles Raw had invited me to share with him any "exclusive" stories we might unearth. This could benefit both parties as the wider coverage would enhance *Accountancy Age*'s reputation. The Excess story was certainly a "scoop", so I called Charles Raw. Slightly to my surprise he announced that he would

---

1. Insurance claims incurred but not reported (IBNR claims) are the amounts owed by an insurer on a particular date to all valid claimants who have suffered a covered loss but have not yet reported it. Inevitably this can only be an estimate and the industry has developed formulae for doing so.

travel over to our West End office straight away to have a look.

I should add by way of background that, by this time, our 5,500 word report had been reviewed thoroughly by an experienced chartered accountant Annette Rutteman (who sadly died

Excess head office

long before her time in 1978)[1] and by our lawyer the delightful, down-to-earth James Crocker.

Crocker's view was that, provided the facts had been researched from public documents and accurately interpreted, the report was fit for publication. Furthermore, in his opinion it would be unwise to confront the company as this would almost inevitably invite the threat of an injunction.

Crocker was a plain-speaking lawyer, but one who would back his client to the hilt if an item was accurate and in the public interest. In doing so he carried our libel insurers with him.

Charles Raw was impressed and wanted to run excerpts in *The Guardian*. "Had we confronted the company?" he asked. I explained that we had relied on Crocker's advice. After all he was a man for whom I had immense respect. Raw was adamant. He never published without confronting the subject company, a practice he had inherited from his days as a member of the "Insight" investigative team at *The Sunday Times*.

I thought for only a few moments. Yes, I would accept Raw's terms and publish in conjunction with *The Guardian*. That way, if Excess took us to task, there would be two defendants to finance any legal action rather than one. And I already knew that we were suitably insured.

So an appointment was made to interview Excess managing director Hugh Jago at the company's City office. Charles Raw and I met outside the office — a typically dull post-war block in Fenchurch Avenue that befitted a company that had been founded in 1894. We took the lift to the executive floor and were shown into a fairly large, but unpretentious, office. Facing us was Hugh Jago, silver-haired and seated behind a traditional large desk. To our left was the company secretary Michael Dane.

At first sight neither of them looked like a devious crook, dedicated to defrauding innocent members of the public by accepting insurance premiums in the knowledge that they could not meet potential claims. But first impressions don't always count for much.

The moment had arrived to expose the two of them. We explained what we had found and challenged the men to justify their dodgy doings. The response was totally unexpected. No bravado. No well-rehearsed, but unconvincing, explanations.

---

1. *Annette was the wife of Paul Rutteman, a widely respected partner in Arthur Young (now Ernst & Young) who often helped me to grasp the more obscure aspects of accounting principles and became a personal friend.*

"It was a mistake", said Jago. And so it transpired. The company had been brought to its knees by sheer incompetence, without the slightest desire to harm anyone or to gain anything for themselves. So we amended a few lines of our report to enable readers to realise that the story was indeed one of incompetence alone, albeit incompetence of an extraordinary scale, made easier by shortcomings in the legal framework within which insurance companies were operating at that time.

We advocated changes in the law and sent the report to the relevant Government department.

The full text, originally published on 31 December 1971, is reproduced below. Charles Raw honoured his promise and ran an abbreviated version in *The Guardian*[1]. Soon afterwards, independent accountants were sent into Excess to investigate.

Not long after that, policyholders gained a little comfort when the Excess insurance business was absorbed by an American insurance company in the Hartford Financial Services Group.

And if there were any lingering doubts about the inadequacy of the Excess balance sheet at that time, they would have been quickly dispelled by the revelation that a further £6.2 million provision was required for claims relating to the period up to 31 December 1971, not to mention a £1.8 million contingent liability for capital gains tax.

Despite improvements introduced in the 1967 Companies Act, it is still not possible to judge the strength or weakness of an insurance company from its accounts.

Aided by special disclosure privileges which are not available to ordinary companies, insurance firms are not required to highlight matters which are crucial in determining the true state of a company's financial affairs.

And, although particular regulations have been made for the conduct of insurance companies, those rules are in a number of cases imprecise.

Some of the current problems are evident from a study of the activities of the Excess Insurance group between 1966 and 1970.

What deductions can be drawn from its accounts?

It is evident that the group's premium income has frequently fallen below claims, making the company reliant on non-underwriting revenue like investment income and capital gains.

That in itself may not be uncommon among insurance companies, given the depressing claims experience of recent years. The important test is to determine what inroads have been made into reserves.

Although the Excess group's

1. *"Shortfall by Excess Insurance", The Guardian, 31 December 1971.*

accounts showed it met the Department of Trade's solvency margin with ease for 1971, its net assets took into account unrealised capital gains without provision for the contingent tax liability thereon. They ignored a provision for motor insurance claims not notified at the balance sheet date. They ignored the fact that underlying asset values of the life subsidiary fell short of the cost of the investment in that company. And a capital increase had been financed by a holding company loan stock issue.

Could shareholders and policyholders really obtain a comprehensible view of the company's financial position during that period of time? And is the insurance industry's argument that more disclosure would endanger public confidence justifiable?

Excess, a British Insurance Association member, started its business of insurance underwriting in 1894, under the management of a gentleman named C E Heath. That name is borne today by an entirely separate organisation, C E Heath & Co.

But until recently there were substantial cross-holdings between Excess and C E Heath. Then Excess bid for C E Heath, only to be thwarted by Lloyds.

Now C E Heath has shed its holding (or most of it) and another company has moved in to take a similar slab of the equity.

The strength of any company is normally measured by the value of its net assets — the amount by which its assets exceed its liabilities.

The same yardstick applies to insurance companies, except that the law stipulates by how much their assets must exceed their liabilities to satisfy the Department of Trade that they are sufficiently solvent to carry on in business.

For example, in 1971 Excess Insurance Company (the main operating company in the Excess group) was required by law to have net assets (as defined) of at least £2.1 million. That figure is officially described as the "minimum solvency margin".

The minimum solvency margin attributable to a particular insurance company depends on its general premium income received in the previous year. For a company in the size category of Excess, the margin would be calculated by adding £500,000 to 100% of its 1970 general premium income in excess of £2.5 million.

When it comes to calculating the actual surplus of assets over liabilities in a company, the law in places is incredibly vague. Assets can include tangibles or intangibles — like goodwill and deferred development costs —as they did at Vehicle & General. There is no rule about how assets may be valued, nor a requirement for the valuation basis to be disclosed.

To Excess' credit, it has regularly disclosed the valuation bases applied to its assets, although those bases changed with monotonous regularity.

Companies not engaged in insurance usually value their assets at cost, or market value if lower. The market values of investments have to be disclosed. There has also been a welcome trend towards companies introducing in their accounts, by note or otherwise, current values for many of their assets.

But insurance companies are specifically exempted from disclosing market values unless they wish to, and are permitted to create "inner reserves" which are used to write investments down, even below cost.

The Jenkins Committee on company law was "not much impressed" by arguments in favour of concealing market values of invest-ments, but conceded to persuasion by the insurance industry which pointed out the political pressures which might be imposed abroad on overseas investments if market values were disclosed.

Despite Jenkins, lately there has been a gradual movement towards market values in presenting invest-ments in insurance accounts.

On the liabilities side, insurance company law is rather more specific. It points out that, to determine whether a company meets its solvency margin, both contingent and prospec-tive liabilities must be taken into account.

Having looked at the legal definitions of assets and liabilities, how does Excess measure up?

According to the chairman, assets of Excess Insurance Company exceeded liabilities by £6.1 million at 31 December 1970. However, in its certificate to the Department of Trade, that figure was subsequently revised downwards to £5.9 million. Both those figures compare with the minimum solvency margin for 1971 of £2.1 million mentioned earlier.

The £5.9 million was arrived at after applying Excess' current accounting bases which had changed regularly between 1966 and 1970.

While the changes themselves may have been perfectly laudable and put Excess in the vanguard of accounting standards, the net assets figure might have been rather less than £5.9 million without them.

Indeed, if the 1970 accounts had been produced on the 1965 accounting basis, it is estimated that assets would have exceeded liabilities by only £1.8 million. The solvency margin would have been missed by £300,000 and the Department of Trade would be hopping with excitement. More interesting still, even in 1965 the net assets were £2.2 million, when the solvency margin was nearer £1.4 million computed on a 1967 Companies Act basis.

The accounting changes warrant closer examination.

In 1965 and prior years, the company's expenses were charged against the earnings brought into the profit and loss account for the particular year. But — quite reason-ably — Excess decided that, since results of the underwriting activities to which the expenses related were not brought into profit and loss account until two years later (under the "three—year" account system which is unique to some insurance activities), it would be fair to charge the expenses into the underwriting account in the first place so that their effect was also deferred for two years.

The effect of this accounting change was to eliminate almost all operating expenses from the profit and loss account for both 1966 and 1967, while the results of the 1966 and 1967 underwriting accounts were working their way through to the profit and loss account.

Without this change Excess would have slipped very close to its solvency margin for 1967 although market values gave a safety margin.

The new practice adopted by Excess had been widely accepted as the norm among insurance companies. But it is fair to ask whether it would have been slightly more cautious accounting if some provision had been charged in the 1966 and 1967 accounts in respect of the underwriting loss for 1966 which eventually appeared in the 1968 accounts. Unfortunately. It would have been difficult for Excess to anticipate the outcome of that year's underwriting activity in advance.

Although the change in basis may be more desirable, the chairman of Excess justified it by an entirely different explanation: "Owing to the increase in the 1966 expenses as a result of very considerable expansion in business it has been felt appropriate to vary previous practice commencing this year..."

In 1967, Excess suffered from devaluation. Its underwriting accounts were badly hit and transfers were made from reserves to ease the burden. But the reserves remained reasonably buoyant because, in common with other companies in the business, the values of overseas investment were also revised to give effect to the devaluation benefit. Some £649,000 was put back into reserves on unrealised gains.

In 1968, Excess singled out its holding in C E Heath & Co for revaluation. This 15% holding had been around for a long time and, although there is no indication of its cost in the Excess accounts, it was probably no more than par, or about £200,000. With the stroke of a pen, that investment became £1.7 million (less a provision for capital gains tax of £335,000).

While it appears that about £1.6 million was credited to reserves that year, the accounts suggest that the proceeds of revaluing the C E Heath shares did not go there. Instead Excess followed another quaint custom among insurance companies and applied the revaluation to write down other quoted investments in the balance sheet.

Michael Dane. company secretary at Excess, said that "from memory" the £1.6 million increase in reserves came from *realised* gains.

At the same time "to give share holders a clearer picture of the distribution of the group's investments", as the chairman put it, the amounts shown against the various classes of investment (British Government securities, unsecured loan stocks, etc.) were revised in proportion to their market values, although "in total the historical cost has been retained". This weird approach is a further peculiarity of the insurance industry.

In 1969, C E Heath's share price slipped a little. And there was a call for further support of the underwriting funds. Excess scrubbed the provision for capital gains tax on its C E Heath shares and, at the same time, put all its other quoted investments onto a market value, rather than cost, basis.

That change, which put Excess firmly in line with modern insurance accounting practice, produced £709,000 as an "investment reserve" which was then taken into account in computing the company's net assets. But no provision was made for the contingent capital gains tax liability.

Also in 1969, Excess capitalised the cost of new equipment and vehicles at £268,000, apparently for the first time.

The stock market continued its decline in 1970, dragging down the balance sheet values of Excess investments. It seemed likely that the so-called investment reserve, which arose on up-valuing the shares from cost to market value in 1969, would have become an investment deficit. But it almost looks as though someone at Excess bumped into the last asset of any real size - its properties.

At 1 January 1970, Excess seems to have owned only freehold property included at a cost of £621,000. At 31 December 1970, the property was freehold and leasehold "at valuation at 30 September 1970 with additions at cost". The new value, arising apparently from a group financial reorganisation, was no less than £2.9 million.

Even insurance companies are required to distinguish between freehold and leasehold properties in Department of Trade accounts (but not in shareholders' accounts) although they are excused from stating just what has happened to their values. Not Excess. A note in the subsequently published accounts only says: "'The unrealised surplus arising from the revaluation of property less the depreciation in the valuation of investments on the above (market value) basis is represented by the investment reserve."

The chairman said the revaluation of the property "clarifies" the overall position. Admittedly, the change put all major assets on to a market value basis. But in other ways the revaluation confused rather than clarified.

The 1970 prospectus for a loan stock issue explains that £1.9 million of the new value related to leasehold premises in Fenchurch Avenue, London. Thus future accounts would have to bear amortisation charges of about £60,000 each year.

Probably the investment reserve gained nearly £2 million at December 1970 on revaluing the property, which means the quoted investments fell by the best part of £1 million (or, put another way, to about £300,000 below their original cost).

Whatever actually happened, the investment reserve was given a net boost of £914,000. And there was no provision for capital gains tax on the property revaluation.

The main outcome of the various accounting changes was that by December 1970 the net assets in the Excess Insurance Company balance sheet had got as close to market value as possible. But market values can go down as well as up. And how! Between January 1969 and December 1970 the market values of quoted investments plummeted by over £3 million to a figure which was *eventually less than a "cost less amounts written off" basis.*

While current value accounting clearly gives a more useful guide to the worth of a company on a given date, it can lead to companies making inadequate provision for value fluctuations.

The main reason for the move to current value accounting has been to discourage the extensive "asset raiding" which has occurred among companies in recent years. It is a radical change from the traditional ultra-cautious practice and is academically more attractive to accountants.

Is it safe? On the basis that the Companies Act formula for computing solvency margins was created in the days before inner reserves were brought out into the open, it seems that the formula should now be revised to give a greater safety margin.

Until now the inner reserves have been a safeguard against the continuing saga of claims under-provisions. If they are now to be grossed up into the net asset figure, the solvency margin should be raised accordingly.

Hugh Jago, Excess managing director, and finance director Denis Ault agree and favour tougher standards.

There is another important issue arising from the use of market values in the Excess accounts. There has been no provision for tax on capital gains. If insurance company legislation and common sense are applied, some allowance must be made for this contingent liability. The English ICA specifically recommends that provision should be made in the accounts, or the amount stated in the notes to the accounts. The Scottish Institute does not recommend its members to provide specifically for this possible liability.

Yet the Insurance Companies Act is quite specific in requiring contingent and prospective liabilities to be taken into account when comparing net assets with the minimum solvency margin. Current thinking in the US accounting profession also favours a contingent gains tax provision. With unrealised gains totalling £1.6 million, the contingent liability for Excess could be significant.

Jago and Dane expressed complete ignorance of the Insurance Companies Act requirement. When the relevant section was quoted, Jago defended the company's action on the grounds that it was general practice in the industry and that a co-director – the eminent tax QC Charles Beattie – supported the company's current practice.

Beattie subsequently explained that his opinion had been given purely as a director, without regard to accounting principles. He favoured a note being included in the accounts indicating that a liability could arise, but without quantification. However, he had given his opinion without reference to the 1958 Insurance Companies Act with which he said he was "not familiar".

Apart from changes in accounting bases, there are other asset movements in the accounts of Excess Insurance which merit attention.

Consider its subsidiary companies. In 1968, Excess Motor Insurance was created by changing the name of a small-time subsidiary formerly known as Fencourt Insurance. The capital was increased from £100,000 to £1 million by issuing additional shares to the parent. On 1 January 1969, all the UK motor insurance business was conducted through this company.

Excess Motor acquired some of its business from the failed *Alpha* insurance group, Midland Northern & Scottish. In 1970 its premium income reached £5.6 million and subsequently it pushed up its rates by about 100%. According to its accounts, Excess Motor kept above its solvency margin by £164,000 at December 1970. But take a closer look.

After its first year of business — 1969 — Excess Motor carried forward a provision of £744,000 in respect of outstanding claims. At the end of 1970, the company indicated in a statutory return (called a "claims settlement analysis") that it still needed to provide about £791,000 to cover outstanding claims relating back to 1969. Yet during 1970, according to the claims settlement analysis, it paid out no less than £1.7 million (subject to adjustment for small sums to be met by reinsurers) in respect of 1969 business. So the total amount paid or to be paid out after the year end on claims relating to 1969 was about £2.5 million.

On the face of it, the provision for outstanding claims in the 1969 accounts appears to have been short by about £1.7 million. In percentage terms, that shortfall was about 230% of the actual provision.

These figures and their interpretation were put to Jago and Dane.

According to Dane, the recently introduced claims settlement analysis, required by law and prepared under his supervision, contained the wrong figures and was in his words "meaningless".

The errors arose from a misunderstanding of the insurance companies accounts regulations which Jago called "ambiguous". The law requires the claims settlement analysis to include all claims originating in the particular year (in this case 1970).

Excess had interpreted the regulations as meaning only those claims relating to premiums received in 1970.

Significantly perhaps, the claims settlement analysis is one of just two Department of Trade returns which do not have to be scrutinised by the company's auditors.

Without knowing about Excess' £1 million-plus mistake, a shareholder or policyholder might be forgiven for seeking an explanation in a note accompanying the 1970 accounts. The company explained: "No provision has been made for claims not notified to the company at 31 December 1970."

It was suggested to Jago that the exclusion of claims not notified did not reconcile with the requirements of the Insurance Companies (Accounts & Forms) Regulations 1968, which defined outstanding claims as including "claims the amounts of which have not been determined and claims arising out of incidents which have not been notified to the company".

In Jago's view, the note met the legal requirement that the claims should be provided for in the accounts. However, he went on to concede the error by claiming that subsequent accounts did include a provision for claims not notified at the year end.

On the face of it, Excess Motor Insurance would still have fallen short of its solvency margin for 1971 if the un-notified claims (estimated by Jago at about £200,000) had been provided for, and the claims settlement analysts "mistake" had not been made.

Jago agreed, but added: "You must take the group as a whole." He also pointed out that the motor company's share capital had been increased by £250,000 in September 1971 following a further allotment to the parent Excess Insurance Company.

Jago added that the accounts contained a "hidden reserve" because commission payments had all been written off when they arose while, under the new regulations, the unearned portion of premiums was carried forward. An attempt was made to quantify the un-notified claims by reference to the Department of Trade returns.

The average value of a claim worked out at the absurdly low figure (by industry standards) of £37, throwing further doubt on the accuracy of the published returns.

Jago said he too had been surprised by this figure. His initial reaction, he said, had been: "They've done it again!"

But it now appeared that the figure returned for the "number of claims" (which had been divided into the value of claims to calculate the average figure) might also be a "mistake". Dane admitted it could be the number of payments made in connection with claims. Since each claim may be settled by several payments, the whole exercise would have been useless.

In the balance sheet of its parent company, the value of the £1 million investment in Excess Motor Insurance would have been difficult to justify if un-notified claims had been taken into account.

The other major subsidiary is Excess Life Assurance Company. Again the underlying asset value of the company at December 1970 fell short of the £1 million issued capital by about £161,000. No provision was made, but values have risen since then.

What else was in the balance sheet?

The net assets were better off by £1.4 million following a group reorganisation In 1970. This boost came from an increase in share capital subscribed by a newly-formed holding company which offered its own shares to the public in exchange for the entire share capital of Excess Insurance. The new parent is called Excess Holdings.

After the initial share exchange, Excess Holdings invited the public to take up 10% convertible loan stock to the tune of £1.5 million with a conversion date of 1974-83 and a repayment date of 1984-85. The proceeds were used to buy one million 25p shares in Excess Insurance, its subsidiary.

Excess Holdings paid 140p per

share, putting a market value of £8.4 million on the group. Thus Excess Insurance (to which the Department of Trade directs its solvency test) increased its permanent capital out of Excess Holdings' not-so-permanent loan stock.

In theory that share issue gave Excess Insurance cash of £1.4 million, and a share capital of 6 million 25p shares at an aggregate nominal value of £1.5 million. But the 1971 annual return doesn't show it that way. That return, dated June 1971, reports that the total issued capital was 5.6 million 25p shares at an aggregate nominal value of £1.4 million. Only 620,000 shares had been issued for cash although Excess Holdings was supposed to have taken up one million.

If the annual return was correct (which seemed highly unlikely) 380,000 25p shares — which should have produced 140p each or £532,000 — had not been taken up and the assets of Excess Insurance Company had been overstated accordingly.

Again, Dane's explanation was predictable. It was another mistake.

So much for the company's assets. What about liabilities? The main item was the underwriting fund which had been built up over the years to meet outstanding claims and unexpired risks. It also contained the portion of premiums which are unearned at the balance sheet date.

Whether a company uses the "three-year account" system which is common among Lloyds underwriters or the normal one-year accounting system, the law does not require the basis for computing the outstanding claims provision to be disclosed. Thus there is no easy way by which the shareholder or policyholder can judge the effectiveness of such a provision. Fortunately, the "claims settlement analysis" introduced in the 1968 insurance company rules and effective from 1970 will eventually make the task slightly less difficult.

But it would take a further five years before the Department of

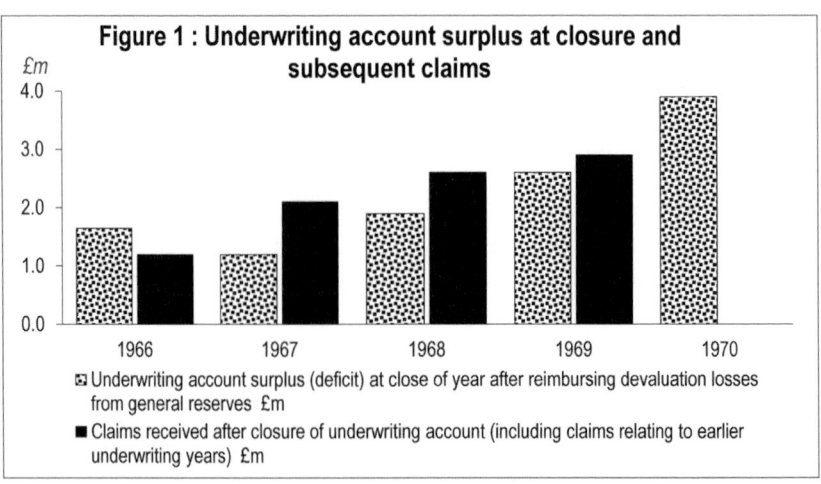

Figure 1 : Underwriting account surplus at closure and subsequent claims

£m

4.0

3.0

2.0

1.0

0.0

1966   1967   1968   1969   1970

▨ Underwriting account surplus (deficit) at close of year after reimbursing devaluation losses from general reserves £m

■ Claims received after closure of underwriting account (including claims relating to earlier underwriting years) £m

Trade would be able to draw some conclusions about the adequacy of outstanding claims provisions in a company. Further claims can flow in for some years, and so it would be impossible to estimate the precise amount of the provision required. And inflation must throw even the best estimates into confusion.

But it seems fairly safe to estimate that, after any given underwriting year has been closed, further liabilities could easily reach 25% of the claims already charged into the underwriting account before closure. Obviously the amount of the provision required to meet those claims is crucial to both the long-term performance and solvency of the company.

In every underwriting year at Excess between 1964 and 1967 inclusive, all prior years' claims received in the year after an underwriting account had been closed exceeded the surplus on that underwriting account before making transfers to or from the profit and loss account. The accompanying graph (figure 1) shows the gap between the underwriting account balance when closed and the claims paid later which refer to that particular underwriting year and earlier years. Clearly the graph is not a totally reliable guide, but it is the only guide. At least it shows an improving trend.

Unless it is made compulsory for companies to publish in shareholders' accounts the basis used for computing the outstanding claims provision plus a statement of any shortfall between claims and provisions, the public is going to remain very much in the dark. What can be deduced is that, from 1966 to 1970, claims received by Excess Insurance relating to pre-1968 totalled £9.7 million. During the same period, the reserve fund was bolstered up from an opening figure of £1.8 million to £7.2 million – an increase of £5.4 million.

Therefore, to meet prior years' claims (received or outstanding) funds of £15.1 million (£9.7 + £5.4 million) had been generated between

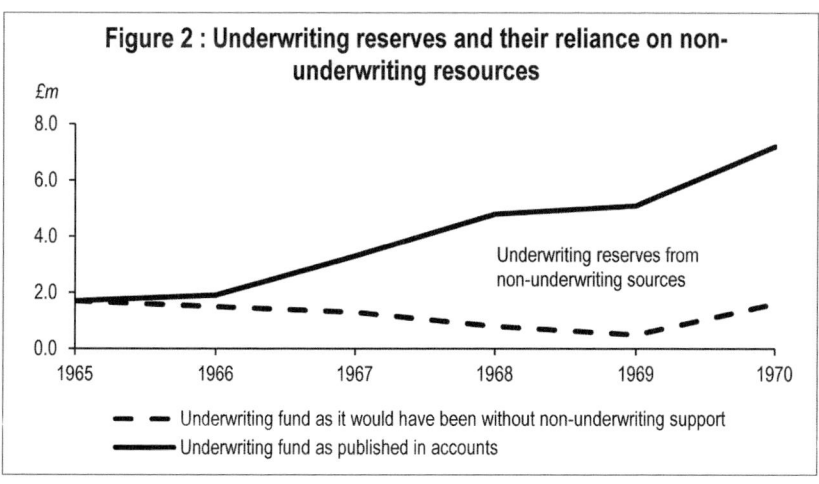

Figure 2 : Underwriting reserves and their reliance on non-underwriting resources

- - - Underwriting fund as it would have been without non-underwriting support
——— Underwriting fund as published in accounts

1966 and 1970.

About two-thirds of that sum was provided from underwriting accounts closed in the period. The balance, along with dividends paid to shareholders, was met from investment income and realisations. As a result it has been impossible to build up any general reserves during that period.

The proportion of the underwriting reserve fund at December 1970 which can be regarded as financed from premium income through underwriting accounts (rather than from investment income and other profits) is difficult to assess. Doubtless the company would have had the details. But at least £3.2 million of the 1970 fund of £7.2 million must have come from that source when the 1968 underwriting account was closed as no further claims would have been received until 1971 (after the three-year account had closed). The remainder would have come from the investment income and realised capital gains.

Another way of looking at the position is to see what the underwriting reserve fund would have looked like if no outside subsidy had been introduced (figure 2). On this basis the reserve at December 1970 would have been only £1.5 million

Figure 3 : Sources and uses of group funds 1966-70 inclusive

Sources	£	£	Uses	£	£
Operating income:			Operating losses:		
Investment and sundry income, tax refunds less expenses	5,183,000		Losses on insurance business of group other than underwriting (mainly motor)	856,000	
Exchange profits on overseas investments due to devaluation	649,000		Transfers to underwriting reserves during period including net losses reflected in published profit and loss account and devaluation losses)	5,715,000	6,571,000
Realisation of investments and sundry other adjustments	2,301,000	8,133,000			
Revaluation of quoted investments from cost to market value, less write-offs (without any capital gains tax provision)		709,000	Dividends paid to shareholders		1,723,000
Revaluation of properties (estimated to produce about £2 million increase) less depreciation in market value of quoted investments (without capital gains tax provision)		914,000	Net movement in reserves: Investment reserves (increase) Capital and general reserves (net decrease)	1,623,000 -161,000	1,462,000
		9,756,000			9,756,000

and not the £7.2 million actually achieved. But not only is it difficult to judge when claims under-provisions have arisen, it is also almost impossible to discover where the funds used to top up the underwriting provision have come from.

With the present-day company law privileges available to insurance companies, adjustments reflecting serious under-provisions in past years can be made without companies having to highlight those shortfalls in the profit and loss account or balance sheet.

One of the most important requirements which should be imposed on the accounts of insurance companies is the publication, preferably as a separate part of the profit and loss account, of all movements on reserves. In particular, each type of movement should be identified. At present, insurance companies are specifically excused from showing these movements.

In support of the present concessions, the Jenkins Committee argued that "the information required by the Insurance Companies Act to be disclosed in their revenue accounts is so detailed that it is difficult to see how substantial transfers to and from inner reserves could be made without disclosure".

Regretfully, the facts do not bear Jenkins out.

One way of summarising the Excess group's activities between 1966 and 1970 would be by a funds flow statement as in figure 3. During that period, underwriting and other insurance activities absorbed £6.6 million. Dividends absorbed a further £1.7 million, making a total of £8.3 million.

This outlay was met from investment income, tax refunds and other sundry adjustments of £5.2 million. Most of the balance came from unexplained credits to reserves of £2.9 million which may include realised gains.The remaining shortfall of £0.2 million has been funded from an effective decrease in capital and reserves during that period.

The investment reserve is created entirely from unrealised gains in property values, less any depreciation in value of quoted investments.

Excess is confident that its reserves are adequate to meet any foreseeable trend in claims. Jago refers specifically to the loading which has now been added to provisions for future claims when underwriting accounts are closed.

Moreover he says an extra £1 million was transferred from general reserves in the 1970 accounts for contingencies. That transfer is a "general" one, not related to any particular year.

Then there is a further plus point in favour of Excess. Now that its investments are published at market value, the rise in share prices during 1971 should provide a healthy bonus in the present accounting year which ends today. Nevertheless, Excess provides a salutary example of inadequacies both in insurance legislation and standards of financial reporting which need urgent attention.

3
The Ruining of Rolls–Royce

Perceived as one of the world's leading engineering companies, Rolls-Royce's collapse in February 1971 prompted a collective gasp of surprise around the world. Its strategic importance to the UK aircraft industry and the country's defence was not lost on the Government of the day and it came as less of a surprise to find the Government ready to bail out the company by acquiring its aero-engine manufacturing assets.

Rolls-Royce had been developing a large technologically advanced three–shaft turbofan engine suitable for long range subsonic transport. The engine, with blades made from a new light–weight material called carbon fibre, became known as the RB211 and the technology has since been applied to the evolving family of engines now known as the Trent.

The collapse of Rolls-Royce lead to an investigation. The Government appointed two inspectors to report to what was then called the Department of Trade and Industry, namely Robert MacCrindle QC and chartered accountant Peter Godfrey. Their report, along with a number of other studies commissioned before and during the debacle, exposed a series of shortcomings many of which have since been remedied. But not all.

After reading those reports and meeting with Sir Ian Morrow who, as we shall see, played a major role during the collapse and subsequent resuscitation of Rolls-Royce, I formed the view that it was not just the account-ants and the accounting rules that were wanting, but also the Rolls-Royce culture and its management's ability to indulge in imprudent sales projections without applying any measure of probability.

The RB211 engine

Upon the appointment of a receiver on 4 Febru-ary, the Minister of Aviation

Supply Frederick Corfield announced that the Government would take over such assets of Rolls-Royce's aero engine, marine and industrial gas turbine divisions as were deemed essential to maintain continuity of activities that were "important to our national defence, to our collaborative programmes with other countries and to many air forces and civil airlines all over the world".

"We were not prepared to accept any risk that the activities of Rolls-Royce which are vital to our national defence should stop", added the Chancellor of the Exchequer Anthony Barber when he addressed the House of Commons. "To put it bluntly, without Rolls-Royce engines many of the aircraft of the Royal Air Force would be grounded."

Barber reported that Rolls-Royce had contracted to deliver 540 RB211 engines[1] to the US aircraft manufacturer Lockheed Corporation at a price of £350,000 each at a specified time and with a specified performance. By the time the receiver Rupert Nicholson[2] was appointed, the estimated manufacturing cost per engine had risen to £460,000. And Rolls-Royce had committed itself to a contract with heavy penalty provisions which would become operative in the event of non-fulfilment.

"On the information now available, on every engine delivered to Lockheed there would have been a loss of not less than £110,000", Barber continued. "The House will see that on present estimates of production costs, the actual losses on production alone would have been at least £60 million. That is not all. The launching costs are now estimated to be much higher than was estimated only last November. A provisional estimate now puts them at £170 million at least, or at least £35 million more than the estimates of last November."

Cabinet papers reveal the extent of Government worries about, on the one hand, the cost of underwriting the continuation of the RB211 project and, on the other hand, the scale of financial penalties – estimated at up to £50 million – that might become payable if the Lockheed contract were to be breached:

> Ministers considered that, whether the RB211 project was stopped or continued, it would not be a responsible use of public funds to assume a very large unquantified commitment either by supporting the company with funds which it had no prospect

1.. *A draft White Paper presented to Cabinet on 7 December 1971 recorded that 450 engines had been ordered (three per aircraft) by Lockheed plus a further 96 engines had been ordered by airlines as spares – a total of 546.*

2. *Nicholson was a partner in accountants Peat Marwick Mitchell, now KPMG, who died in December 2000.*

of repaying or by the Government taking the company over and thereby making itself responsible for all the company's debts and obligations. If the Government were not prepared to take over the company and underwrite its large and unquantified liabilities, the board's proposals for the appointment of a receiver... would take effect. Thereafter, two choices would be open to the Government — either to take no further action, and let the receivership, and ultimate liquidation of the company, follow its normal course; or to enter upon negotiations with the receiver for the purchase of those Rolls-Royce assets which were vital to the national interest.[1]

The Government concluded that the appointment of a receiver was the only way the contract could be terminated without assuming massive unquantifiable further liabilities, even though this might lead to the demise of the RB211 project and adversely affect employees and all the other parties involved. As events evolved, the receiver was able to renegotiate the contract terms and Lockheed's custom was secured.

The development cost over-runs reported to Parliament had a number of adverse consequences, the most obvious being on cash flow. And, as the balance sheet weakened, so it would became ever harder and more expensive to attract additional capital. Whether this was the reason why Rolls-Royce changed its accounting policy for development costs twice between 1961 and 1967 is not known, but it certainly enabled the company to maintain some sort of dividend policy — important in preserving its credibility on the stock market and among the banking community.

Until 1961, Rolls-Royce had prudently written off all research and development expenditure as it was incurred. But such prudence meant that the costs were rarely charged in the same financial

The Locklheed TriStar powered by RB211 engines

1. *Draft White Paper presented to Cabinet by the Secretary State for Defence, December, 1971*

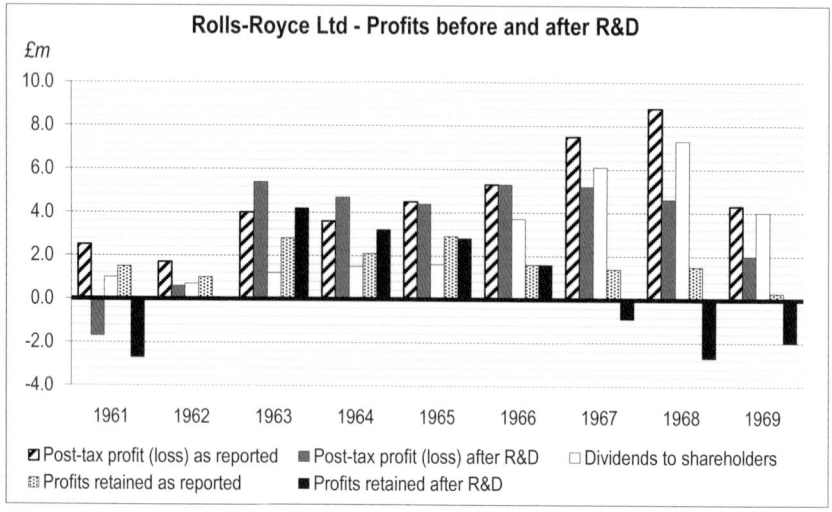

periods as when the sales revenue was achieved. Arguably current profits were being penalised by costs that related to transactions that would be completed in a future period.

So Rolls-Royce decided it would carry forward the cost of research and development that was expected to be recovered from the future sale of any engines that were in production or on order at the year end, but would deduct from that intangible "asset" any further development costs that were expected to be incurred in fulfilment of those orders.

Then, in 1967, Rolls-Royce decided its accounting policies needed further adjustments. It was these further adjustments that aroused my curiosity and later prompted the article which is reproduced at the end of this chapter.

This is how Rolls-Royce explained its decision: "These established principles are, however, not appropriate during the early years of the development and production of the RB207 and RB211 engines, for which orders had not been received at the year end. Therefore, in respect of these engines, it is intended to adopt the practice of amortising the launching costs over estimated future sales." At the end of 1967, the company had capitalised (carried forward) an extra £532,000 representing those launching costs.

But, as the Government inspectors observed rather pointedly in their report[1]: "The carrying forward of research and development expenditure does not of course solve the inherent financing problem. The cash has been spent."

1. *Dept of Trade & Industry investigation under s.165(a)(i) of the Companies Act 1948, p87.*

The effect of these two accounting changes was to add £11.7 million to reported profits over the period 1961 to 1969 inclusive, converting a cumulative profit of a mere £3.4 million to a more impressive £15.1 million. However, the story didn't end there. In its 1969 accounts Rolls-Royce had also made an additional post-tax provision of £11 million in respect of "the inevitable uncertainties as to the ultimate recovery of the research and development costs of the RB211 engine". Somewhat misleadingly, the £11 million charge was shown as an "appropriation" of profit and not as a deduction in arriving at the profit for the year.

In the aftermath of the Rolls-Royce debacle, accounting rules have been tightened up. Research and development costs may only be carried forward as an intangible asset in the balance sheet if it is probable that future economic benefits will flow to the entity from that asset and the cost of the asset can be reliably measured. In assessing its value, the asset must be examined in two parts – costs relating to the research phase and those relating to the development phase.

During the research phase it is generally impracticable to assess the likelihood of the expenditure generating any future economic benefit. So the rules state that all such expenditure should be written off as an expense when incurred and must never be capitalised as an intangible asset.

By contrast, any costs incurred during the development phase must be capitalised in the balance sheet as an asset provided the reporting entity can demonstrate all of the following criteria:

- the technical feasibility of completing the intangible asset so that it will be available for use or sale;
- intention to complete and use or sell the asset;
- ability to use or sell the asset;
- existence of a market or, if to be used internally, the usefulness of the asset;
- availability of adequate technical, financial, and other resources to complete the asset; and
- the cost of the asset can be measured reliably.

If any of the above recognition criteria are not met, the expenditure must be written off as incurred.

Once development costs have been capitalised as an intangible asset, they must be amortised over the asset's finite life. But amortisation must not begin until commercial production has commenced (thereby matching the income and expenditure in the period to which they relate).

During the year preceding the appointment of the receiver, the Industrial Reorganisation Corporation (IRC) had agreed to advance further loans to Rolls-Royce provided steps were taken to strengthen the financial controls and forward planning.

In response Ian Morrow was parachuted in as joint deputy chairman. Morrow was a Scottish accountant who possessed two of the top professional qualifications. He brought to his new task a great deal of experience and was also well regarded as a company "doctor" — a description he abhorred. He played an influential role in events leading up to the receivership and thereafter was appointed a director of the successor company Rolls-Royce (1971) where he continued to sort out the financial mess. Later he was to be knighted for his efforts.

I met with Ian Morrow at his unpretentious office in the City of London to discuss the questions I would like to ask him in a formal interview. He was of modest height but of fairly square build, clear thinking and easy to talk to. I met him again at Rolls-Royce's Derby headquarters and was surprised by how open he was in relating what he had found there.

Most commentators have blamed the collapse of Rolls-Royce on its poor budgeting and weak financial controls. But the weaknesses were not just in financial controls. As we shall see, that over-simplified explanation ignores another massively important influence. Nevertheless, it is hardly surprising that the engineers blamed the accountants and the accountants blamed the engineers.

As the IRC reported at the time: "Rolls-Royce is literally an engineers' company. The management is dominated by them." The aero-engine division alone had a board of 21 members. Only one came from finance. The other 20 were engineers. Ian Morrow told me that the management team was impervious to financial reality,

Sir Ian Morrow

although he used blunter language to make his point.

Rolls-Royce had legitimate pride in its engineering expertise and its long history of manufacturing (mainly successful) aircraft engines. Its behaviour in the years leading up to its collapse suggest that there was a widespread culture throughout the company that assumed there would always be enough buyers for its engines because they would always outclass (and therefore outsell) all of the competition.

Such was the engineers' confidence that no-one seems to have looked too critically at the size of the market for the RB211 or the share that might be gained by Rolls-Royce.

According to the Plowden Report[1], global demand for newly built (wide bodied) long haul airliners over the 10 years to 1975 was estimated at between 500 and 1,000.

In essence there were four such aircraft for which the RB211 would initially be suitable — the Douglas *DC10*, the Lockheed *TriStar*, the Boeing *747* and the European *Airbus*. Three engines would be required for each *TriStar*, plus spares. However, subsequent technological developments enabled later aircraft designs to use only two higher-powered "stretched" engines.

Put at its simplest and based on the information available to Plowden, the global market for engines with a specification similar to the RB211 and its derivatives was likely to total no more than 3,900 and probably nearer 2,500, including spares. But two other engines would become available — one from General Electric and one from Pratt & Whitney.

With three out of the four airframes being built by US manufacturers and two out of three engines being built there, the odds were stacked heavily against Rolls-Royce. Competition would be tough and even more so if corporate patriotism had any role to play.

What's more, there were other factors weighing against Rolls-Royce, not least that Pratt & Whitney had a very close relationship with the market leading US airframe manufacturer Boeing. The odds against Rolls-Royce became even more starkly evident when Boeing confirmed that it would fit the Pratt & Whitney engine into the initial version of its *747* jumbo jet.

On top of that, US engine manufacturers had been able to develop new engines for civil aircraft on the back of government financed major military aircraft programmes. Consequently the

---

1.. *Report of Committee of Enquiry into the aircraft industry 1964–65 (Cmnd 2853).*

Civil airliner engine market projection: ten years to 1975

	Minimum	Maximum
Long range airliners - over 10 years to 1975 (as per Plowden)	500	1,000
Engine sets per plane	2	3
Global market size	1,000	3,000
Allowance for spares (say 30%)	300	900
Total global market for engines	**1,300**	**3,900**

Total western aircraft designs suitable for RB211	4
Total competitive engine designs including RB211	3

Assuming **maximum** market size achieved...	Rolls-Royce market share
If RB211 were to be selected for one triple-engined aircraft on an exclusive basis, potential sales might be (3,900/4)	975
If RB211 were to be selected for 50% of one twin-engined aircraft, potential sales might be (1,000 x 2 x 1.3)/4 x 50%	325
If RB211 were to be selected for **all** aircraft and all were triple-engined	3,900

development costs allocated to each civil aircraft engine would probably be lower than those borne by the RB211, offering scope for highly competitive pricing.

The RB211 could rely only on Government launching aid to pay for a percentage of its development costs, but much of that would have to be repaid out of future sales revenue. To make matters worse, the formula devised in the early nineteen sixties for calculating the Government's levy on each RB211 engine sold was based on a share of the hypothetical profit generated. But the hypothetical profit was just that. As the article reproduced from *Accountancy Age* at the end of this chapter pointed out, it was based on assumed production costs, sales volumes and selling prices.

In reality, actual selling prices were often discounted during negotiations with hard-nosed buyers. And actual production costs would vary by reference to changes in the overall quantities required and to variances in labour and material costs. If, as a result of these variances, the actual profit margin dropped below the hypothetical figure used for calculating the Government levy, the shortfall would be borne by Rolls-Royce.

In a White Paper[1], the Government justified its approach to the recovery of launching aid in the following terms:

---

1. *Rolls-Royce Limited and the RB211 aero-engine, Cmnd 4860, 1972.*

In return, the Government receives as a levy on sales of engines and spare parts a share of the forecast margin between the proposed selling price and the estimated manufacturing cost. This margin, and the Government share, is normally fixed at the outset (subject to review arrangements in some cases). The intention behind the arrangement is that production risks, as well as the risks of a cost overrun on development should lie with the manufacturer, so that for example, if manufacturing costs exceed estimates and erode the actual margin, he should still pay the Government levy. Risk and the possibility of profit should thus remain with the manufacturer and provide a commercial incentive and a spur to exercise commercial judgements.

Then, as the development costs of the RB211 put an increasing strain on the company, the Government introduced a new formula for its sales levy from 1968. This time Rolls-Royce and the Government would divide the group's profit between them in agreed proportions after deducting a predetermined rate of dividend on its shares (some of which were classified as employee shares).

Given the highly competitive market conditions described above, Rolls-Royce seems to have taken a very optimistic view of its potential market share. A profit projection provided to the Ministry of Technology in June 1967 envisaged sales of 3,289 engines, including spares, over a ten year period. The same figures were presented to the Rolls-Royce board shortly afterwards. They assumed the engine would be used in both triple-engined and twin-engined aircraft, and that there would be an uplift of 30% to allow for spare engine sales. As the Department of Trade inspectors noted later: "The forecast was based on the hypothesis that there would be only one engine manufacturer and one aircraft manufacturer supplying this market."

Although this hypothesis is said to have accorded with industry opinion at the time, it was quickly overtaken by events. Indeed, it is hard to believe that any experienced revenue forecaster would not have envisaged a range of scenarios, at least one of which assumed that rival engine-makers from the United States would have entered the market.

By February 1972 – one year after Rolls-Royce had collapsed – orders and prospective orders for the triple-engined Lockheed

Rolls-Royce RB211 sales estimates June 1967		
	Initial thrust rating	Higher thrust rating
TriStar triple engined	892	638
Other twin-engined	528	472
Spares (30%)	426	333
Total	1,847	1,442

TriStar had reached only 178, requiring 694 engines if allowance is made for spares, but far short of the 1,530 anticipated in June 1967 (see table).

Rolls-Royce had never equipped itself with the amount of capital that would be necessary to cope with a material shortfall in its sales projections, let alone the punitive consequences of cost escalation and severe

Lockheed TriStar orders at 1 February 1972		
	First buy	Second buy
Eastern	37	13
TWA	33	
Delta	18	
Air Canada	10	
Air Jamaica	1	
L1011 OREG Ltd	-	
HAAS/Turner	2	
PSA (still being renegotiated)	2	
Sub-total	**103**	**46**
Air Holdings (not sold on yet)	29	
Court Line (letter of intent only)	[5]	
BEA	Decision awaited	
Total known potential orders	**178**	
Engine requirement including spares	**694**	

Source: Ministry of Technology evidence to Public Accounts Committee, 1972

price competition. But the company remained positive – relying on a toxic mixture of engineering self-belief and the need to retain a sizeable share of the global market for survival.

Forty-two years after the collapse of Rolls-Royce, new legislation[1] was introduced requiring companies (other than small companies) to include in their directors' report to shareholders "a description of the principal risks and uncertainties facing the company". Whether such a requirement would have caused the board of Rolls-Royce to consider more thoroughly, disclose and hopefully act upon, the risks that it was taking will never be known. But it is step in the right direction.

The quality of Rolls-Royce's sales forecasting was inseparably bound up with the manner in which the company accounted for its research and development costs and calculated its future cash requirements, as can be seen in the following article published in *Accountancy Age* in November 1970. The probability of those sales forecasts being achievable appears not to have been tested sufficiently seriously, presumably because the Rolls-Royce management didn't want to face up to the consequences.

The article appeared just as the Government pumped more cash into the ailing giant, only two months before Rolls-Royce veered into a steep dive and crashed.

---

1 *The Companies Act 2006 (Strategic Report and Directors' Report) Regulations 2013*, inserting s.414A into the Companies Act 2006

At a time when technical advance has become increasingly rapid and complex, it is hardly surprising that companies are needing substantially greater resources to finance the research and development of new products. The predicament in which Rolls-Royce now finds itself is partly, if not solely, due to the lack of capital for development, aggravated by the escalating costs involved which bear no resemblance to original projections.

Both the airframe and aero-engine industries have come under the public spotlight in Britain and abroad because, in some cases, internal resources have not been adequate to keep the companies in business. But closely linked with the physical cost of research is the manner in which that cost is reflected in the published accounts.

Sometimes, when a company has seemingly come upon hard times, research and development costs appear to be shunted forward in the hope that there will be bigger profits to support them in the future. Although good accounting practice frowns upon changes in treatment, it can often be reasonably argued that development projects today are so much bigger and take so much longer than those of yesterday that a change of basis is appropriate.

Against this backcloth, Rolls-Royce changed its accounting basis for research and development costs in 1961. Having prudently (but not necessarily logically) charged all expenditure against current revenue until then, it proved impossible to show a profit in 1961 without acknowledging that the benefit of the expenditure was mostly unearned at the balance sheet date. So Rolls-Royce began carrying forward a proportion of the costs to be set against future revenues. In presenting a more attractive set of accounts, Rolls-Royce did not succeed in magically improving its basic problem - inadequate returns on capital and inadequate resources for growth.

The fact of the matter is that no-one likes skeletons in the cupboard and, even today, Rolls-Royce would probably revert to the write-off basis if profits would stand it.

Yet many will argue that the only rational approach is to match development with earnings arising therefrom. This "matching principle" is being widely discussed in the United States (Arthur Andersen & Co is just one accounting firm which advocates such a treatment), but the theory gains no more practical support in industry there than it does here.

Among airframe and engine manufacturers in the US, General Electric and Pratt & Whitney believe in writing everything off (except recoverable design costs on government contracts) just as soon as the cheques are written out. Boeing also charges to revenue the expenses related to commercial and government projects, except on fixed-price incentive contracts. This practice, coupled with the fall in turnover, contributed to the 1969 trading loss of £14 million.

It will come as no surprise, however, to find that Lockheed (which, like Rolls-Royce, has its problems) changed its basis for government fixed-price contracts in 1968 to carry the expenditure forward and write it off against future sales. The TriStar costs have also been carried forward.

In Britain, British Aircraft Corporation applied the matching principle to the BAC111, but has written off everything else (including the BAC311 costs to date). Hawker Siddeley found its profit fell in 1969 because, like Boeing, it continued to write off all research and development costs as soon as incurred, without the immediate return.

So far, therefore. Rolls-Royce is the first British company in the field to adopt a positive carry—it—forward policy in relation to new projects. Why?

To understand the reasoning at Rolls-Royce, it is first necessary to examine the development processes in the aero—engine industry. There are three essential elements of development costs in launching a new engine.

The first is the development cost which involves expenditure right up to two years after the engine enters service. Under the present system this expenditure is carried forward and charged against sales. Development expenditure incurred after the two years is charged against profits immediately.

The second element is the tooling cost. This comprises items like production tooling and expenditure related to getting production models on to the market.

The third element is commonly described as the learner cost which is really a premium on early production models until the run settles down to a normal cost. Rolls—Royce applies this measure to the first 200 production models of a particular engine. Both tooling and learner costs are amortised against profits within about two years of being incurred.

Rolls-Royce spends much less on basic research (including the carbon fibres discovery) and most of it is financed by outside sources.

The whole system of financing development expenditure has changed radically in the last decade.

Before the Spey, most commercial engine developments followed on the back of military applications which were government aided. So the development costs to Rolls-Royce were, by present—day standards, negligible. This was certainly the case for the Avon, Conway and Dart engines. Until the development of the Spey, the Government contributed towards the first stage (the development stage) only, in return for a levy on sales. This levy varied from nil to 12.5% of the sales proceeds, depending on the extent of involvement.

On engines prior to the Spey, Rolls-Royce managed to finance the costs involved out of its retained profits and other internal resources, pending reimbursement by the Government. But the Spey — a much more expensive project — was the first case of a new engine having to depend on government support beyond the development stage. The government agreed to contribute to the development, tooling and launching costs.

This engine has proved a "winner", according to H E Trevan-Hawke, the company's finance director. It is fitted in the BAC111, the Hawker Siddeley Trident, the Fokker Fellowship and Grumman Gulfstream executive aircraft. It cost £30 million to develop, and was also incorporated in the Buccaneer military aircraft.

The levy arrangement for repaying the Government was abandoned and an almost incomprehensible formula was substituted. It had four stages and was based entirely on projections of the expected margin between estimated sales revenue (less the amount of anticipated profit) and estimated production costs. The margin was calculated and agreed in advance from the information then available. No sane man could have expected that calculation to prove accurate once the engines began rolling off the production line. But Rolls-Royce was still living in pre-Ferranti days — and so was the Government.

The new formula — applied to most government contractors in this type of work — required Rolls-Royce to repay the Government's contribution to development costs by remitting an agreed proportion of the theoretical profit margin on every engine sale. Naturally, if the actual margin was less than expected, Rolls-Royce could have found itself paying to the Government (at certain stages of the formula) more than the actual overhead recovery! To gain government support it is likely that Rolls-Royce was over-optimistic in calculating the expected "margin" only to find that, on the day of reckoning, the repayments ate into already limited resources of the company.

The four stages of the formula were simple to apply, once the margin had been agreed. The first stage provided for the recovery of Rolls-Royce's own contribution to development and launching costs. Depending on the particular contract, the company would probably pay about 25% of the "margin" to the Government until its own costs theoretically had been covered by the retained 75%.

Then stage two would come into play and the ratio would be reversed: 75% of the "margin" would be paid to the Government as each sale took place, until the Government's contribution had been cleared. But it is perfectly possible that the true margin actually proved to be less than 75% of the estimated total margin. In which case, the company would be paying out in cash to the Government more than it was actually receiving, net of production costs, on the sale.

However, the government was not concerned with actual costs. It had a deal and would stick to it. Once the Government had recovered its contribution, the "margin" was split 50/50, until the Government had received 125% of its investment. Then stage four came into force, and only 25% of the "margin" was payable to the Government on all future sales[1]

The lesson of this formula is quite clear. If, for example, a particular engine costs so much to make that the expected "margin" vanishes, the Government still gains provided enough engines are sold — at any price.

---

1. *This basis for recovering development costs was superseded with effect from 1968*

The absurd situation could have arisen, where the Government insisted that British European Airways, for example, should buy Rolls-Royce engines which were actually unprofitable to manufacture, simply because the Government would then get back its money from Rolls-Royce (with a premium) even though Rolls-Royce sinks deeper into debt. The Government, therefore, takes a comparatively negligible risk.

Fortunately, the Spey was successful. Its development cost did not exceed budget. But there were later engines which cost much more than anticipated to develop.

Alas the Rolls-Royce management chose in 1961 to amend its accounting practice on development expenditure in the light of the new government formula and increased costs involved. At the year end (although initially the assessment was made in the following April), the order book was examined and firm orders for future sales of engines and anticipated spares were quantified.

The company then used the budgeted development recovery per sale, deducted the amount contributed by the Government together with anticipated further development costs for the next three years, and capitalised the balance.

At this point the engineers in the company became over-enthusiastic, and on every project the costs escalated. Inflation played a part in this, but only a part.

The now famous RB211 engine, which is used in the Lockheed TriStar, was the cause of yet another change in accounting treatment. On the one hand, the company decided to carry forward all development expenditure and charge it off against future sales. On the other hand, it became obvious that the successful recovery of that expenditure was in doubt. So a special provision for present and future losses was created "below the line".

Unfortunately, in the 1969 accounts, the auditors recommended that the special provision relating to the RB211 should be deducted from the total deferred development expenditure relating to all projects. The effect of this treatment was simply to disguise the true position, since the costs on the RB211 at December 1969 of £10 million (net of investment grants and government participation) were much less than the £20 million provided for the ultimate under-recovery.

At the same time the auditors asked that the special provision be charged against current profits, rather than as an appropriation. But on this point Rolls-Royce won the day. So the outcome was an unhappy compromise.

If annual accounts are to be at all meaningful, then the matching principle is worthy of more support. Expenditure should be carried forward against relevant sales. But this form of accounting pays no attention to capital resources. Indeed it tends to cloud the most important single factor which can make or break a company like Rolls-Royce. Is there any money in the kitty?

And how accurately can future sales and costs be calculated? If the basis for calculating the deferment of development expenditure hinges on future events, perhaps there is no safe practice other than to write off every penny as soon as it is spent. But it is the very immensity of project which creates the accounting problem.

If all expenditure was written off immediately, the accounts would look devastatingly sick. But isn't that the real position? Isn't Rolls-Royce sick?

If there is one certain lesson to be drawn from this case, it must be that although accounts may fool the shareholders, in the end it is all a matter of cash. You either have it or you haven't. And how it is generated is a management problem to which, no doubt, Ian Morrow as the new financial adviser is directing much of his attention.

4
Interpublic's Internet Fiasco

The arrival of the internet brought with it opportunities for businesses to interact directly with existing and prospective customers using digital media like email and *Facebook*. So it was not long before those businesses saw digital marketing as a cost-effective alternative to direct mail, TV and press advertising.

In addition, the growing e-commerce space offered new retail opportunities to existing businesses and digital-only start-ups, with the added benefit of gathering increasingly valuable customer data.

However, the turn of the millennium proved to be a watershed moment for young digital marketing agencies. Having initially basked in the glory of being flavour of the month, suddenly a number of those agencies were hitting the financial buffers or struggling to pay their bills – companies like Deepend that over-reached itself internationally.

By the middle of 2002, the second largest US internet consultancy Scient had filed for bankruptcy after accumulating losses of $660 million. In the UK, Entranet went into liquidation. The Swedish consultancy Icon Medialab, in which The Interpublic Group had invested significant sums, was also reported to be rapidly running out of capital[1].

By the end of 2001 Omnicom Group's digital investments — Agency.com, Organic and Razorfish — had accumulated losses totalling more than $700 million between them and in chapter 8 we shall learn how it managed to rearrange its digital investments so as to minimise the impact of those losses on its own shareholders[2].

Other young digital agencies had already been sold to, or received investments from, larger advertising groups that were frightened of missing out on what they perceived as a burgeoning new source of revenue and profit.

No-one doubted the need to invest in digital marketing technology and the rush to acquire pushed up valuations well beyond what could be justified by the digital agencies' early perfor-

1 *See also chapter 15*
2 *See page 77.*

DIARY OF AN INTERNET INVESTMENT FIASCO	
1999	
April 27	Interpublic invests $20m in Swedish internet consultancy Icon Medialab for just under 20% of the equity.
November 12	Interpublic makes further cash investment of approximately $12m in Icon Medialab. Interpublic also restructures existing loans into convertible debt repayable on 12 November 2000
December 13	USWeb/CKS, in which Interpublic had originally acquired a shareholding in 1995, merges with Whittman Hart to form MarchFIRST to become the "largest pure-play internet professional services firm in the world".
2000	
March 30	Interpublic invests a further $20m in Icon Medialab and declares intention to become major investor in Icon Medialab's new Asia-Pacific venture.
June 13	Interpublic converts some of its Icon Medialab loans into shares and makes an extra (approx) $4m cash investment also.
October 25	Interpublic increases amount of its Icon Medialab convertible loan and extends repayment date from December 2000 to January 2002.
November 14	Another Interpublic investment MarchFIRST files notice with SEC saying quarterly return to 30 September delayed, but meanwhile announces decline in demand for services and a $920m loss for nine months to date.
November 20	MarchFIRST files delayed quarterly return confirming $928m loss for nine months to 30 September. Company needs $50m additional funding for quarter to 31 December and a further $50m in early 2001. Ability to obtain such funding on acceptable terms, if at all, will depend on factors such as market conditions and company's performance. Other problems include very big bad debt provisions and cost over-runs on fixed price contracts.

mance. Sometimes the hope value seemed almost beyond price and, sooner or later, a downward adjustment was inevitable.

The account that follows, first published in May 2001, focuses on the investments in digital agencies by The Interpublic Group and its apparent slowness to recognise the decline in their market value as the initial bubble burst in the midst of its bold attempt to

2001	
February 28	Icon Medialab reports loss of about $240m for 2000 and further major restructuring plans. "The restructuring actions taken during the fourth quarter...are insufficient to secure our position", the company says.
March 19	Interpublic announces agreed bid for True North Communications.
March 30	Interpublic files financial results for 2000. Although unrealised value of internet investments has slumped, no provision is made against profits for the year.
April 12	MarchFIRST announces it has filed for bankruptcy and has sold off certain assets.
April 18-23	MarchFIRST announces further asset sales.
April 26	Interpublic announces loss for first quarter of 2001 after charging $160m provision for impairment of investments including MarchFIRST and Icon Medialab. Chief Financial Officer states: "The write-downs are non-cash adjustments..."

acquire another major US marketing group True North Communications.

When Interpublic Group, at the time the third biggest publicly-listed marketing services group in the world, announced its bid for its US rival True North Communications in March 2001, why didn't it mention a potential $160 million write-down of its internet investments?

"The transaction will unite the resources of two of the leading diversified advertising and marketing communications firms to create the world's largest marketing communications organisation", trumpeted Interpublic.

At a stroke, Interpublic would topple world-leader WPP Group (which had recently acquired Young & Rubicam) from the number one slot.

At the time True North was on the back foot, having reported special charges of $50 million in its accounts for 2000, prompted in part by the need to write down its investment in internet consultancy Modem Media.

By contrast, within days Interpublic was adding a further gloss to its own corporate image by reporting improved financial results for 2000 – post-tax profits up from $331 million to $359 million and earnings per share up 6.3%. Then the bad news began to emerge. Interpublic too had investments in internet consultancies.

On 26 April, Interpublic published its figures for the first quarter of 2001. A loss had been incurred of $38 million following a massive $160 million pre-tax write-down of its investments in internet related businesses.

The two most significant provisions were against investments in MarchFIRST in the US and Swedish based Icon Medialab International.

MarchFIRST had filed for bankruptcy on 12 April after losing $928 million in nine months. If the investment write-downs had been reflected in its figures for 2000, Interpublic's post-tax profit for that year would have been nearer $260 million than the $359 million actually reported, and may have had a material impact on the terms proposed for the True North bid. So why was the write-down not made in the 2000 figures?

When this question was put to Interpublic by *Marketing Services Financial Intelligence*, the company offered the following explanation:

"The market for internet stocks deteriorated significantly after the year had ended...the triggering event was the bankruptcy of MarchFIRST. At that point we took another look at other investments and decided on the conservative course. The value of Icon Medialab is so far below our cost that the likelihood of our realising full value is virtually *de minimis*."

But what are the full facts? Interpublic's investment in March-FIRST stemmed from a 28% stake it had acquired in CKS Group in 1995. After a succession of mergers with USWeb and Whittman Hart, the enlarged group announced in December 1999 that it had become the "largest pure-play internet professional services firm in the world" and

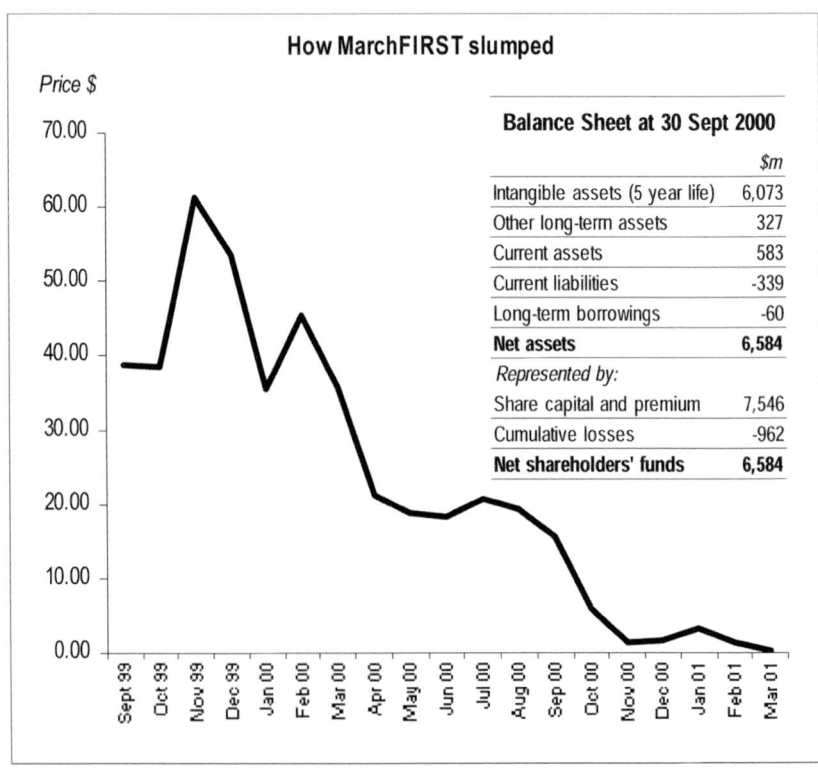

shortly afterwards adopted its new name.

Less than a year later, March-FIRST was notifying the US Securities and Exchange Commission (SEC) that its quarterly financial return would be delayed. There had been a fall in demand for its services and losses of $928 million had been incurred in the nine months to 30 September 2000.

A week later, on 20 November 2000, the full return was filed. It made depressing reading. The company needed a capital injection of $50 million to meet its financial needs for the December quarter (which had only six more weeks to run) and would need another $50 million early in 2001.

Ability to obtain such funding "on acceptable terms, if at all, will depend on a number of factors, including market conditions and the company's operating performance", MarchFIRST said. The funding requirement had been exacerbated by $100 million costs associated with the mergers, a $78 million jump in bad debt provisions (to 17% of gross debts) and unquantified cost overruns on fixed price contracts. Clearly things were not looking good.

Meanwhile there had been developments at Interpublic's Swedish investment in Icon Medialab. Interpublic invested its first $20 million in the group in April 1999, and had added to that investment periodically since. By the end of 1999 the stock market value of Interpublic's investment in Icon Medialab was a dizzy $322 million. Further funds were provided in March and June 2000.

"Icon Medialab's expansion plans are right on track and Interpublic remains an enthusiastic partner", said Interpublic chairman Phil Geier in April 2000. Soon Geier had retired, but the investing continued.

On 25 October 2000, Icon Medialab announced: "Subject to shareholders' agreement, Icon Medialab and IPG have agreed to extend and prolong the existing 80 million Swedish krona convertible which was due in December of this year. The convertible will be increased to 110 million Swedish krona and the exercise period is extended to 15 January 2002."

Thus pressure on Icon Medialab's finances was eased and coincidentally Interpublic would not have to consider the consequences of any possible repayment default in that year. Meanwhile Icon Medialab was busily trying to cut costs as its share price tumbled 93% from the 299 krona quoted in December 1999 to a mere 20 krona at 31 December 2000.

On 28 February 2001 – three weeks before Interpublic announced its bid for True North and a full month before it announced its results for the year 2000 – Icon Medialab had reported a loss of about $240 million for 2000 and further major restructuring plans. "The restructuring actions taken during the fourth quarter...are insufficient to secure our position", the company said.

As Interpublic finalised its True North bid and the publication of its own results for 2000, it noted that the overall market value of all its investments had dropped substantially below their cost. Any paper gains previously recorded in Interpublic's books had been wiped out.

So the evidence seems clear. Contrary to what Interpublic now says, it must have been as obvious to those inside the company as it would have been to those outside, that the market for internet stocks had deteriorated significantly by the time Interpublic announced its results for 2000.

The only serious question remaining was whether that deterioration should have been treated as a permanent impairment in value requiring a write-down against profits in Interpublic's accounts for 2000 or whether it was simply a temporary hiccup.

Ironically, True North itself had already addressed this very question

after undergoing a very similar experience. But True North had come to the opposite conclusion to Interpublic. True North decided it should write down its investment in Modem Media in 2000 because that company had invested in another internet consultancy Vivid Holdings when internet share prices were heavily inflated and had subsequently concluded that the goodwill value attributed to that unrealistically priced investment was "fully impaired and cannot be recovered".

Back at Interpublic, both MarchFIRST and Icon Medialab had also made major investments in other internet companies at inflated prices, giving rise to vast amounts of goodwill and other intangible assets.

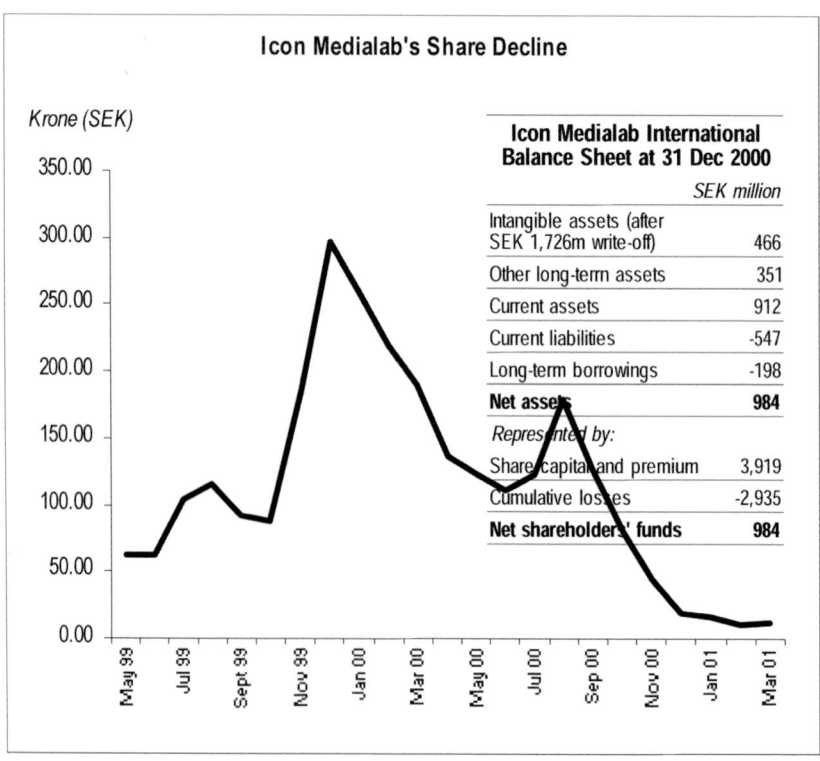

Icon Medialab's Share Decline

Krone (SEK)

Icon Medialab International Balance Sheet at 31 Dec 2000	
	SEK million
Intangible assets (after SEK 1,726m write-off)	466
Other long-term assets	351
Current assets	912
Current liabilities	-547
Long-term borrowings	-198
Net assets	**984**
Represented by:	
Share capital and premium	3,919
Cumulative losses	-2,935
Net shareholders' funds	**984**

Indeed at MarchFIRST those assets included "purchased technology, workforce in place and customer lists" which in aggregate were judged to have an average economic life of just five years. The amortisation of those intangible assets against profits had been a major — but not the only — contributor to the massive losses now being reported.

When explaining away the nature of the $160 million investment write-down at a press briefing, Interpublic's chief financial officer Sean Orr was eager to emphasise that this was a "non-cash accounting adjustment to mark the recorded values of these investments to their estimated recoverable values".

But was it simply a non-cash accounting adjustment reversing earlier "paper" revaluation gains? Clearly Interpublic had invested real cash in those businesses. So *Marketing Services Financial Intelligence* asked Interpublic whether Orr's comments meant that no provision had yet been made in respect of the significant cash amounts invested.

The company's view seems to have shifted somewhat as a result. It now tells us: "The write-downs were non-cash in that the cash was invested more than a year ago (years ago in some instances) and the current write-down would not be a cash-using event in the current quarter."

Lost cash is lost cash. It seems Interpublic still has some explaining to do.

After outbidding Havas to acquire a publicly listed UK media buying agency
WPP attempted unsuccessfully to amend its offer terms in the wake of 9/11.

5
Time Up For Tempus

The role of the "media independent" emerged in the middle of the 20th century when some of the more enterprising media buyers decided they could make a better living outside of conventional advertising agencies rather than within. Until then advertising agencies normally collected a commission of around 15% of all media spend and this was expected to cover all the creative and media buying services that the agencies provided.

By nature, media buyers had a more commercial edge to their business dealings than was to be found among account executives and creative personnel. They were (and are) traders first and foremost. So they were content to take a smaller percentage of media commission and leave the balance to the creative agency.

But being traders, the media buyers found additional ways to maximise their income, sometimes buying media space in bulk at a discounted rate as principals, accepting the risk involved, and then finding buyers from among their clients. On other occasions media buyers would earn a rebate if they achieved a high volume of bookings and that rebate was not always shared with clients (as Interpublic experienced to its subsequent embarrassment).[1]

It was perhaps inevitable that the major groups would seek to recapture the income flows that had been acquired by the media independents. Indeed, the acquisition of a media independent would also enable the acquiring group to combine its existing clients' media spend with that of the acquired media buyer, creating even more

Chris Ingram: Founder of Tempus:

---

1. *See chapter 4.*

buying power and potentially more appealing advertising rates from media owners.

It was against this backcloth that a mighty and acrimonious battle took place to acquire the publicly-owned media buying group Tempus Group in 2001. The group had been built up by Chris Ingram, one of the founding fathers of the Association of Media Independents in the UK and it was there that I first met him. Athletic in build and lifetime supporter of Woking Town football club, one might expect him to be fairly competitive.

Ingram had started his advertising career in 1960 at the age of 16 with an agency called Pictorial Publicity. Six months later the agency was taken over by John Pearce and Ronnie Dickenson, and renamed Collett Dickenson Pearce. Ingram worked in the media department, in those days a junior service department to the main creative agency.

In 1964 he joined an expansionist agency **KMP** which was floated on the London Stock Exchange in 1969 and embarked on a hasty acquisition spree. But the group was badly hit by the three-day week and Ingram left in 1976 to start his own media buying agency Chris Ingram Associates.

After a shaky start, the company gained momentum and grew rapidly through the nineteen eighties. The group was floated on the London Stock Exchange in 1989, renamed Tempus, and by 1993 was employing 2,600 people in 67 offices across 29 countries with a turnover of $3 billion.

In the meantime, WPP Group had been buying shares in Tempus and had accumulated a 25% stake by 2001. The French group Havas Advertising was also showing an interest in the company and the Tempus board took a decision in principal to sell.

Havas Advertising offered to pay Tempus shareholders 50% above the market price for their shares in the hope of deterring a counter-bid from **WPP**. Havas was Ingram's preferred acquirer, not least because he thought it would be more attractive to Tempus managers than a bid by WPP.

But that was not to be. WPP bid for Tempus, only to find that the terrorist attack on New York's twin towers in September 2001 prompted Havas to withdraw immediately, leaving WPP's bid as the last one standing. The analysis that follows was published in *Marketing Services Financial Intelligence* in August 2001 while the bid battle was in full flood. It examined the terms of each bid and pondered whether WPP would obtain value for its money.

WPP itself had second thoughts about the price it had offered. As share prices plummeted WPP took the opportunity to seek approval of the City's Takeover Panel to a cancellation of its cash offer, citing as justification a "material adverse change" in circumstances flowing from the events of 11 September. WPP also sought to argue that a general decline in economic conditions contributed to the adverse change.

On appeal the Takeover Panel concluded that "a change in general economic circumstances may legitimately be relied upon when seeking to invoke the relevant conditions, but only if and to the extent that in doing so the requirements mentioned in paragraph 16 [of the Panel's statement] are satisfied[1]".

In relation to the materiality test, paragraph 16 stated that "meeting this test requires an adverse change of very considerable significance striking at the heart of the purpose of the transaction in question, analogous, as the 1974/2 Panel Statement put it, to something that would justify frustration of a legal contract".

The Panel went on to comment on the relevance of the general economic circumstances at the time:

> The events of 11 September occurred during a period of economic decline both generally and in the advertising sector and this was known to WPP and indeed reflected in the public statements by WPP before the announcement of its offer. WPP did not rely on the general economic decline which was already apparent. They relied on the effect of the events of 11 September on economic conditions as they affected Tempus. They said these events were exceptional and unforeseeable and this is indeed correct. Views on the likely progress and length of the decline varied widely before, during and after the announcement of this bid, and markets were unusually volatile during that time. Tempus said rightly that to succeed WPP had to distinguish between the causative effects and show what were the consequences on Tempus' prospects of the 11 September events and the aftermath as opposed to what was the effect of a known general and sectoral decline existing prior to 11 September.

The Panel concluded:

> For an offeror to invoke a material adverse change condition and so withdraw its offer requires, in the opinion of the Panel, the offeror to demonstrate to the Panel that exceptional circumstances have arisen affecting the offeree company which could not have reasonably been foreseen at the time of the announcement of the offer. The effect of the circumstances in point must be sufficiently adverse to meet the high test of materiality described in paragraph 16 above and judged, at least in

1. *The Takeover Panel Report "Offer by WPP Group for Tempus Group PLC - 2001/15*

the present type of case, not in terms of short term profitability but on their effect on the longer term prospects of the offeree company. Indeed, as WPP made clear it was the longer term prospects of Tempus which had provided the strategic rationale for the offer and this seemed to the Panel to be central to the value which WPP placed on Tempus at that time.

The Panel considered the submissions of the parties and the arguments they made at the time of the hearing, including but not limited to the basis of the attempts to predict the future profits of Tempus, the longer term effects of the events of 11 September on Tempus, the general economic decline affecting the advertising industry before and after the posting of the offer and the strategic reasons for WPP's offer for Tempus. The Panel came to the conclusion — on the evidence before it — that WPP had failed to demonstrate that between 7 September and 22 October there was a material adverse change in the context of the bid such as to entitle them to invoke the material adverse change condition, and had so failed by a considerable margin. The appeal, therefore, failed.

Thus WPP's appeal was rejected and the company was obliged to follow through on its offer, eventually netting £432 million for Tempus shareholders on 6 November 2001. This is how the WPP and Havas bids compared before Havas withdrew:

At first sight WPP Group's all-cash offer of 555p per share would be sufficient to persuade both the Tempus Group management and the wider public to reject the 541p mixed offer from Havas Advertising.

If the issue was simply about the best exit terms, inevitably the most attractive offer would be the one that ensures immediate cash and the highest price. Under the Havas offer, the Tempus management team was committed to taking Havas shares in exchange for a proportion of their Tempus shares as well as accepting a lower price than the WPP cash offer. So if those managers can bring themselves to believe that a future under Sir Martin Sorrell's control will be no less comfortable and remunerative than working for Havas, their decision would be a no-brainer.

But for shareholders and prospective shareholders in the eventual winner, there is the separate question of whether the deal offers a real prospect of enhancing the value of their investment.

And the judgement on that aspect is not just about the cost to the bidder, although the Havas camp did itself no favours by apparently understating the net cost of share options it intends to buy out. On a directly comparable basis, the cost of the deal to WPP is already some £40 million or 10% less than to Havas (see table that follows), helped by the fact that WPP already owned over 16 million shares at an average cost of 240p.

At least as important is the judgement about whether either bidder will be able to achieve the two essential ingredients of a satisfactory return on that cost, namely synergistic gains (more commonly described as economies of scale) and organic earnings growth.

Assuming a target return on the capital investment would be 15% per annum, the bidders would have to deliver a lot more than just the synergistic gains they claim to be available (Havas says they are worth £12 million per annum before tax whilst WPP believes they are worth £13 million per annum). These economies on their own would only be sufficient to generate a return on the investment of around 5% (see table) which is even less than the current cost of borrowing.

To bridge the gap between that meagre return and a target 15%, Tempus would also have to deliver organic profit growth of about 20% per annum on a long-term basis if Havas wins the bid battle. If WPP wins, a lower but still challenging growth rate of about 18% per annum will be required.

So it is worth taking a closer look at whether these profit enhancements are likely to be achieved. Let us look first at the predicted synergistic gains.

On the face of it both bidders will have to work very hard to achieve the savings they seek, as they represent

How the costs of the Tempus bids compare
(at 21 August 2001)

	Havas [1]	WPP
Earnings to be acquired:	£m	£m
Tempus post-tax profit for 2000 before goodwill amortisation	11.1	11.1
Synergistic gains claimed by bidder (net of estimated taxation)	8.0	9.1
	19.1	20.2
Less: Dividend received on existing Tempus shareholding	0.0	0.7
Total additional earnings	**19.1**	**19.5**
Cost of acquisition:		
Shares purchased previously at average price of 240p per share	0.0	39.8
Offered for shares not already owned	463.3	383.4
	463.3	423.2
Less:		
Estimated spare cash in Tempus *(Note 2)*	25.0	25.0
Proceeds from exercise of Tempus share options *(Note 3)*	34.6	34.6
Net cost to acquirer:	**403.7**	**363.6**
PE based on above	21.1	18.6
Return on capital assuming no future earnings growth	4.7%	5.4%
Cost per Tempus share (net of option revenues)	471p	424p

Notes:
1. *Tempus is required to pay £4 million to Havas if Havas is outbid.*
2. *Estimated by "Marketing Services Financial Intelligence"- not reflected in offer documents.*
3. *Havas offer assumed only 3.45 million options exerciseable whereas total potential is 10.48 million according to WPP, a figure closer to that disclosed in the Tempus accounts for 2000 - Havas figures above have been adjusted to reflect the higher cost and proceeds.*

almost 10% of Tempus Group's operating and administrative costs last year. Media buyers are traditionally regarded as a fairly frugal bunch and it remains to be seen whether Tempus was an exception.

According to Havas, the cost savings will arise from rationalisation of head office functions, a reduction of overheads in markets in which both Tempus and its existing media network Media Planning Group (MPG) have operations, and cost savings associated with combining and rationalising media buying efforts of both groups in overlapping markets. The combined media buying business will adopt the name CIA Media Planning.

Culturally Havas may be less ruthless in its approach than WPP, having only recently acquired full control of the Media Planning Group. Tempus chairman Chris Ingram alluded to "similar cultures" in the offer document, adding: "We will have the operational freedom to continue to build our differentiated service".

WPP intends to dismantle the Tempus infrastructure entirely, merging the CIA Worldwide media buying operation with The Media Edge which it acquired with Young & Rubicam last year.

The group plans to move the Tempus branding businesses Added Value and BrownKSDP into its established brand identity and strategic consulting division, whereas Havas intends to keep those businesses within its enlarged MPG media operation. So not only does WPP start with an acquisition cost advantage, but it also looks likely to deliver the most synergistic gains.

In doing its calculations WPP is adamant that there was no "double counting" of any synergistic gains already taken into account when pricing the Young & Rubicam bid last year, notwithstanding the plan to merge the CIA network with Y&R's media operation. The extra £13 million represents entirely new savings, WPP told *Marketing Services Financial Intelligence.*

Depending on your assessment of which bidder is most likely to achieve the greatest synergistic gains, the second question is whether Tempus has the potential to deliver organic growth of over 18% per annum year

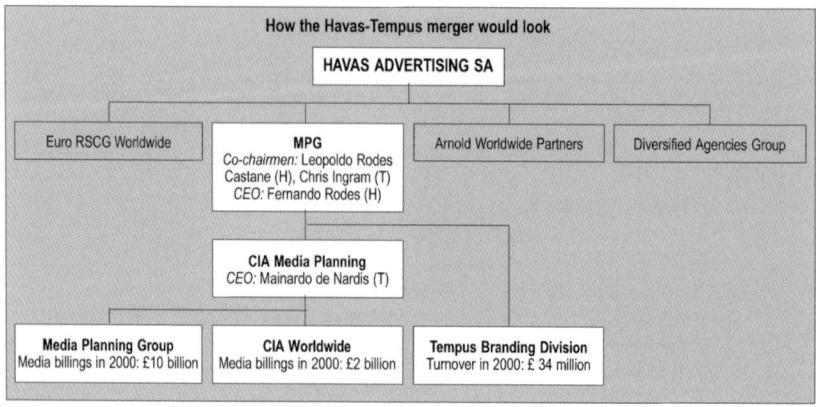

How the Havas-Tempus merger would look

HAVAS ADVERTISING SA

Euro RSCG Worldwide

MPG
Co-chairmen: Leopoldo Rodes Castane (H), Chris Ingram (T)
CEO: Fernando Rodes (H)

Arnold Worldwide Partners

Diversified Agencies Group

CIA Media Planning
CEO: Mainardo de Nardis (T)

Media Planning Group
Media billings in 2000: £10 billion

CIA Worldwide
Media billings in 2000: £2 billion

Tempus Branding Division
Turnover in 2000: £ 34 million

after year. The recent track record looks encouraging.

As the next table[1] shows, Tempus achieved an average annual growth in earnings per share of 18.5% during the last three years, but that was before excluding any inflationary element.

Net of inflation the average growth rate dropped to 16%. And although growth in earnings per share is not the same measure as organic growth in absolute earnings, in the current economic climate a question-mark must hang over the company's ability to grow organically at 18% per annum in future.

The potential for organic growth will also be influenced by the way in which the Tempus businesses are positioned by their future owner and by the confidence that positioning instils into its management.

At first glance, the Havas proposition is cleanest. The CIA brand would be preserved as part of the merged business with a continuation of the newly forged links with its branding businesses. The opportunity to build on its position as

1. See page 52

fourth largest network worldwide is likely to be grasped with enthusiasm and further organic growth should be attainable, subject only to the economy and the limited market clout of Havas advertising agencies.

At WPP the merger will form a second media network within the group, alongside the bigger MindShare operation. Both networks will come under the overall supervision of a new management team drawn from MindShare, The Media Edge and Tempus.

It is hard to decide whether WPP has a longer term objective to merge both networks — MindShare is already number one in the world and The Media Edge would be fourth largest after the merger.

On the one hand, WPP has shown itself to be perfectly happy owning competing brands — J Walter Thompson, Ogilvy & Mather and Young & Rubicam, for example.

On the other hand, such a strategy would seem incompatible with a structure that puts the competing networks under common management, as will be the case in the proposed media division.

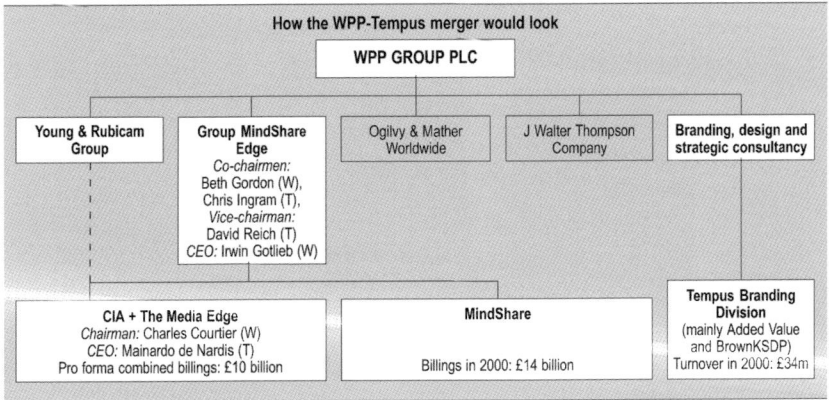

This confusion may be enough to put the brakes on the rate of organic growth that will be necessary to justify the cost of the deal. Add to that the historic links of The Media Edge with the tarnished image of Y&R and the challenge becomes even greater. All this uncertainty may also dampen the enthusiasm of Tempus managers. All in all, it is hard to believe that either bidder will achieve the rate of growth necessary if a return on capital of 15% is desired. Initially, the Havas deal may have more market impetus, but that is

essential in view of the faster growth rate it would need to compensate for paying £40 million more for its prey and being less optimistic about the synergistic savings available.

Is a 15% return on capital necessary? That is up to the bidder to decide. In doing so it must seek adequate reward for the inherent risks of running such a business as well as for the cost of capital involved.

When WPP raised more capital earlier this year it negotiated an average cost of around 6%, but the additional facility arranged for this

Tempus Group - Earnings per share and RPI movement 1997 to 2000

Year ended	Earnings per share (p)	Growth pa	Retail price index	RPI change pa
31 December 1997	9.4		160.0	
31 December 1998	10.9	16.0%	164.4	2.8%
31 December 1999	12.8	17.4%	167.3	1.8%
31 December 2000	15.6	21.9%	172.2	2.9%
Average 1997-2000	**12.2**	**18.5%**		**2.5%**
Average growth pa net of inflation		**16.0%**		

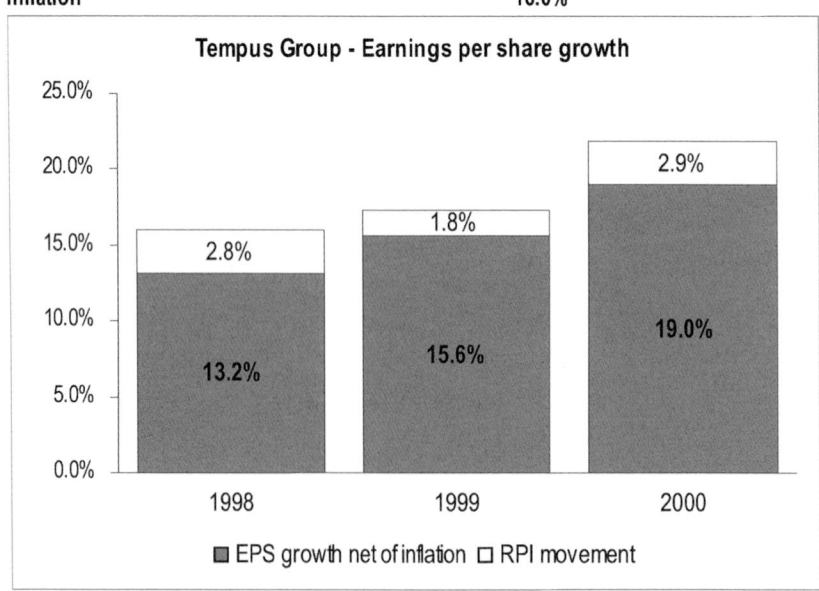

deal will probably be more costly.

Havas too will have a hefty interest bill for the £482 million facility arranged with JP Morgan and Societie Generale. The price of the "strategic benefits" is high and time alone will show whether it can be justified.

Japan's dominant marketing group's attempts to play on the world stage as domestic competition drives the company to take a more global view

6
Dentsu's Defensive Debut

Dentsu is Japan's biggest advertising agency group and it has dominated its domestic market for many years. Yet until it acquired the British based Aegis Group in March 2013 — more about which can be found in chapter 23 — Dentsu had failed to become a truly global player, despite various abortive attempts. For example, in March 2000 Dentsu entered into a strategic alliance with the US based group B|Com3 and, in doing so, handed B|Com3 control of most of Dentsu's non-Japanese businesses in return for a minority shareholding.

At that time B|Com3 was the holding company for a collection of mainly US marketing companies that included Leo Burnett (which in turn had a stake in the UK creative agency Bartle Bogle Hegarty), D'Arcy Masius Benton & Bowles and the media buying agency Starcom Mediavest.

Dentsu's head office in Tokyo's modern Shiodome Centre

Ascending one of the 70 lifts in Tokyo's Shiodome Centre to reach Dentsu's headquarters, I sensed the choice of building made a statement not only about the company's dominant domestic role among the other large Japanese advertising agencies located nearby but also about its aspiration to gain greater influence around the world.

In November 2001, with competition from foreign marketing groups hotting up in its own back yard, Dentsu sought a stock market quotation and became more acquisitive. This chapter, first published in December 2001, describes the evolution of Dentsu on the world stage and how domestic conditions drove the company to take a more global view. Later chapters will describe how the French Publicis Groupe bought out Dentsu's stake in B|Com3[1], how Dentsu then acquired Aegis[2], and how Dentsu became caught up in some costly domestic dramas[3].

For many, many years Dentsu has enjoyed the position of the dominant advertising agency in Japan, benefiting from very high profit margins and intimate shareholder relationships with the media owners.

Competition from abroad posed no threat to its cosy trading environment. But all that is changing now.

Dentsu's Japanese market domination is under challenge as Omnicom Group, The Interpublic Group of Companies and WPP Group have acquired sizeable shareholdings in its domestic competitors. The growing impact of aggressive media buying agencies owned by the multinationals may also upset Dentsu's comfortable relationships with domestic media owners, eventually driving down commissions and undermining Dentsu's magical 20% profit margin (see table opposite).

To date Dentsu has failed to build a truly global client base. Instead it has relied upon its indigenous clients and on servicing inward advertising needs of multinational clients - many of whom may gradually desert to their principal global agency networks. So far Dentsu's international achievements have been limited to little more than the establishment of a modest international delivery network

for its domestic clients. In the latest financial year only 5.3% of Dentsu's sales revenues were derived from outside Japan.

If Dentsu wants to remain among the top players it cannot afford to adopt the traditional Japanese long-term approach to building its international business, relying solely on its strong domestic trade and its equally strong balance sheet (see table). It is time for a giant leap forward. And that means buying big,

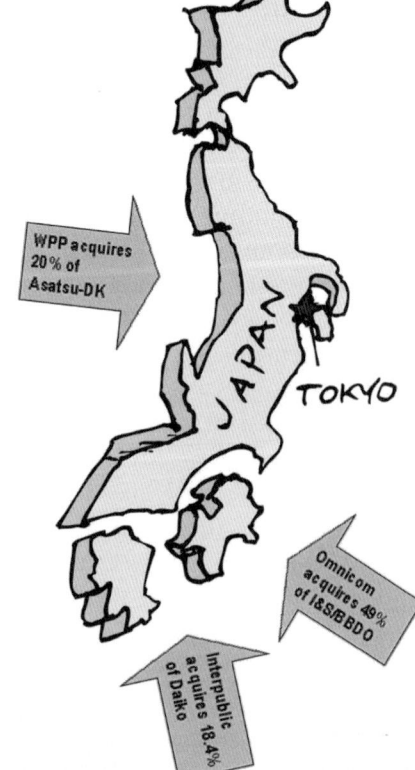

WPP acquires 20% of Asatsu-DK

JAPAN

TOKYO

Omnicom acquires 49% of I&S/BBDO

Interpublic acquires 18.4% of Daiko

---

1. See chapter 7.

2. See chapter 23.

3. See chapter 29

How the top 6 multinationals compared in 2000
(based on US accounting rules)

Company	Country of origin	Revenues (gross income)	Op profit before amort'n	Operating profit margin	Op profit after amort'n	Post-tax attrib'able profit
		$m	$m	%	$m	$m
Omnicom Group	US	6,154	961	15.6	878	499
Interpublic Group of Companies	US	5,626	785	14.0	673	359
WPP Group [1]	UK	4,149	513	12.4	376	186
Dentsu [2]	Japan	2,537	524	20.7	521	403
Publicis [3]	France	1,662	205	12.3	174	32
Havas Advertising [4]	France	1,543	154	10.0	108	28
Average of the above:		**3,612**	**524**	**14.5**	**455**	**251**

1. Includes only three months' results of Young & Rubicam. 2. Year ended 31 March 2001. 3. Includes only three months' results of Saatchi & Saatchi. 4. Media Planning Group figures not fully consolidated until 2001.

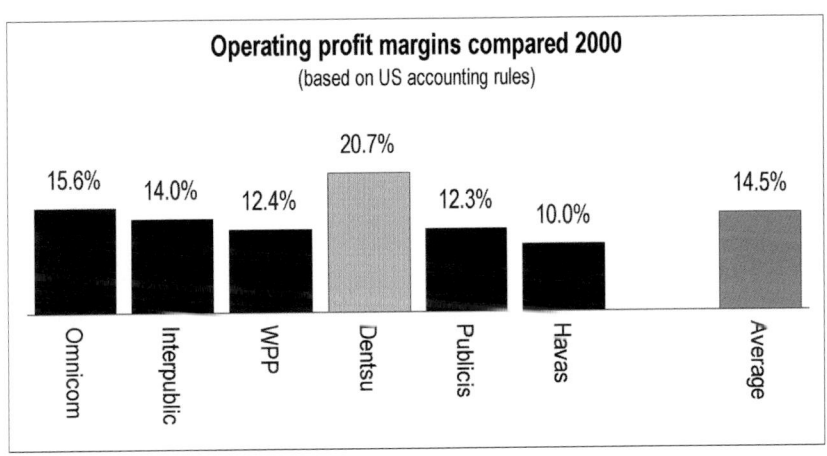

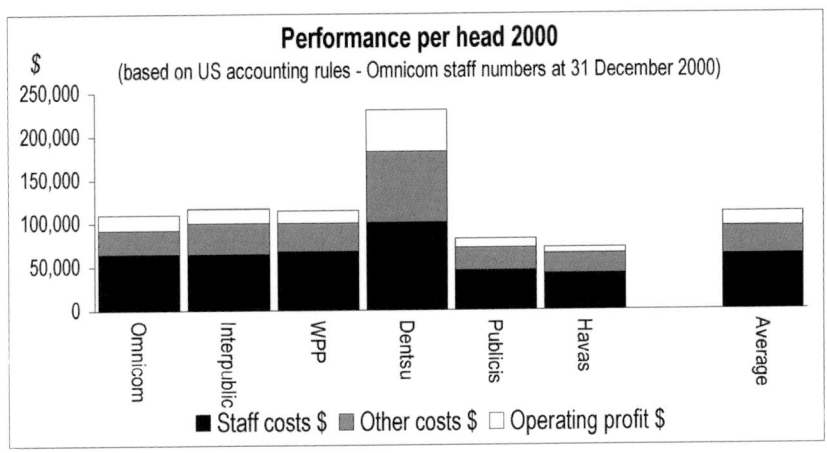

rather than growing organically. But buying big requires more cash than even Dentsu's healthy balance sheet would allow. The company needs to be able to offer marketable shares in addition. Hence the end-November flotation of its shares on the Tokyo Stock Exchange at a price of 420,000 yen per share.

And who will be the eventual target of Dentsu's extra financial muscle-power? Almost certainly the company has ambitions to increase its stake in B|Com3 Group where it already has a 21.8% shareholding.

The background to Dentsu's flotation makes fascinating reading.

The agency was founded exactly 100 years ago by Hoshiro Mitsunaga and almost from the start formed part of a wider Japanese media-owning group. However, in 1936 the Japanese Government insisted that the media-owning activities should be divested. In doing so, Dentsu accepted major shareholdings from the divested media owners — known today as Kyodo News and Jiji Press. Between them, these two companies will still own over 32% of Dentsu after its flotation (see table overleaf). So in practice the agency has retained very close links with the media owners ever since.

Whether this close relationship alone explains Dentsu's high operating margins is unclear. What we do know is that, unlike the UK, TV companies in Japan pay a higher rate of commission than the press. We also know that output per employee — in terms of revenue handled — is double that achieved by the top US and European groups (see table). The ratio of staff costs to revenue is also far better than in the West — at 44.2% compared with between 55.5% and 59.1% elsewhere, despite the average staff cost per employee being much higher. On the face of it, Japanese profit margins benefit from harder working Japanese employees as well as from bigger media commissions.

But the explanation of healthy domestic profits does not end there. Unlike the western model, Dentsu provides its services predominantly through one vertical business entity (albeit subdivided into regional subsidiaries), rather than building up a massive family of discreet companies. That may improve efficiency in Japan, but it has not necessarily proved the best model elsewhere. For example, Omnicom Group fosters discreet business units and enjoys

Dentsu's strong balance sheet
at 31 March 2001

	$m
Fixed assets	
Property, plant and equipment	1,913
Investments and long-term advances	1,550
	3,463
Deferred taxes and other assets	368
Net current assets	1,448
Less:	
Long-term liabilities	-1,804
Net assets	3,475
Shareholders' funds:	
Share capital and reserves	3,277
Minority interests	198
	3,475

some of the best operating profit margins attained in the western world.

Nevertheless, to date Dentsu has been content to keep its structure as uncomplicated as possible when building a worldwide delivery system for its domestic clients.

Not that its overseas excursions have been without their problems. It paid a high price for CDP in the UK and acquired little more than some very heavy debts in return. Its original tie-up with WPP's Young & Rubicam to create links with Europe and the US was unsuccessful although the 51%-owned joint venture Dentsu Young & Rubicam continues to provide coverage in parts of Asia and handles media buying for foreign clients in Japan — a useful revenue earner that has probably helped to protect the Japanese media market from a more direct media buying invasion from abroad.

As the 20th century was drawing to a close, Dentsu clearly decided that its international plans needed a rethink. Reacting to the group's vulnerability to a global challenge from US and European based multinational groups, Dentsu adopted an interesting and pragmatic strategy — it would retain direct control of its

Asian network, but would surrender control of Europe, the Americas and Oceania to B|Com3 in return for its shareholding in that group (see chart). The deal was concluded in March 2000 and since then the partners have been actively working to integrate their respective business interests.

Thus the Dentsu-B|Com3 alliance should provide its partner with a better network for their global clients. In particular, it will offer Japanese advertisers a better worldwide delivery vehicle and provide some consolation if Dentsu loses foreign clients to competitors.

Until recently, the only significant foreign agency involved directly in Japan was Interpublic's McCann-Erickson network which set up a jointly-owned company with Hakuhodo in 1960, providing access to Japanese media for its own clients. This company is now a subsidiary of McCann-Erickson Worldwide.

Among the most threatening of new competitors is Omnicom, which acquired 49% of the seventh largest Japanese agency I&S/ BBDO in 1999. Even before that, WPP had bought a 20% stake in what is now Asatsu-DK and ranks third in Japan.

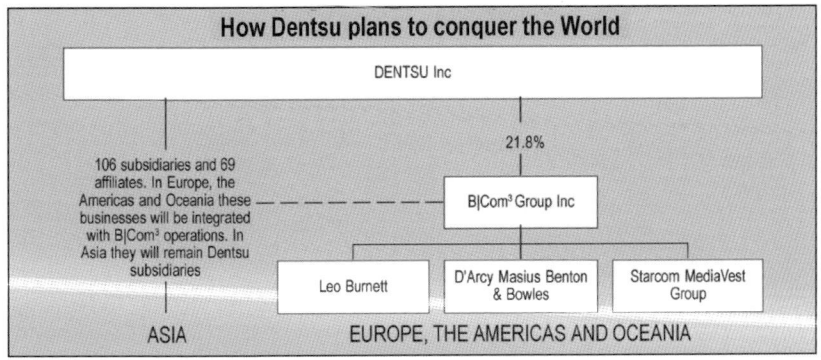

How Dentsu plans to conquer the World

DENTSU Inc

106 subsidiaries and 69 affiliates. In Europe, the Americas and Oceania these businesses will be integrated with B|Com³ operations. In Asia they will remain Dentsu subsidiaries

21.8%

B|Com³ Group Inc

Leo Burnett

D'Arcy Masius Benton & Bowles

Starcom MediaVest Group

ASIA

EUROPE, THE AMERICAS AND OCEANIA

More recently, Interpublic acquired 18.4% of Daiko — Japan's fifth largest agency.

However, the aggregate revenues of these three competitors was little more than one third of Dentsu's revenue last year (see chart). And if that agency can generate over $2.5 billion from (principally) the Japan market alone, while Omnicom could earn revenues of no more than $6.2 billion from the whole world, it deserves a healthy respect.

So what will happen next? Will B|Com3 be prepared to sell control? Does Dentsu want complete control? In an ideal scenario, Dentsu would probably like to see how its new partnership beds down before investing more. But time may not be on its side.

Under its agreement with B|Com3, Dentsu has the right of first refusal to acquire control of that company in priority to any other bidder with effect from 14 March 2002 (and can veto any bid prior to that date), provided B|Com3 has not made a public offering of its shares by then. From 14 March 2003, irrespective of whether B|Com3 has offered its shares to the public, Dentsu will be entitled to increase its holding substantially.

Given the uncertain future ownership of B|Com3, Dentsu cannot afford to be caught out in the face of an alternative bidder. Its public share issue should ensure it is equipped to pre-empt any such offer if it wishes. If it doesn't exercise that right, there will be few other independent multinational networks left to acquire — unless Dentsu fancied Grey Global Group, Publicis or Havas Advertising. After the traumas associated with some of Dentsu's previous international adventures, natural caution is likely to weigh against such a move.

Of course, not everything is rosy at B|Com3. Its margins have been poor and it has just lost the Mars business. Nevertheless, its Starcom MediaVest subsidiary shows promise and, if size alone counts for anything, the combined revenues of Dentsu and B|Com3 last year exceeded $4.3 billion — putting a merged group well up among the biggest in the world.

An alternative scenario would be a bid for Dentsu itself. But unless Japan's media-owning shareholders

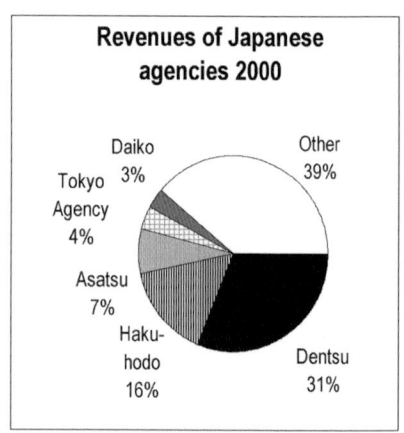

Dentsu shareholders after flotation

Jiji Press 14.3%
Kyodo News 17.8%
Other existing holders 19.8%
New holders 48.1%

Revenues of Japanese agencies 2000

Daiko 3%
Tokyo Agency 4%
Asatsu 7%
Hakuhodo 16%
Other 39%
Dentsu 31%

want an exit and all Japanese nation-
alistic tendencies melt away, it is hard
to imagine control being wrested
away by a group like WPP.

A successful global business will
depend not only on Dentsu's global
partner being strong and profitable
but also on successfully countering
pressure on its domestic margins and
plugging global client leakage from its
core business in Japan. With profits
in the current year expected to show a
decline, the future remains uncertain
to say the least.

How this French marketing group's ambition to become the world leader resulted in over-priced acquisitions, aided by liberal accounting rules.

7

Publicis Push for Power

Publicis was founded as an advertising agency in Paris in 1926 by Marcel Bleustein–Blanchet who also invented radio advertising in France and helped create the first French opinion polls. In 1935, he purchased Radio LL from the radio manufacturer Lucien Lévy and renamed it Radio Cité, from where he introduced France's first news broadcasts as well as its first radio jingles.

The history of advertising agencies as we now know them dates back to the 19th century. Around that time, Charles–Louis Havas extended the services of his French news agency to include advertisement brokerage. That was long before Publicis was founded. The emergence of creative agencies that could be employed to design the advertisements did not gain momentum until the start of the 20th century when media owners awoke to the vast amount of additional revenue it might produce. Even before the Publicis advertising agency had emerged from a French radio station, the Japanese agency Dentsu had been founded by several newspaper owners there (see chapter 6).

Maurice Lévy joined Publicis in 1971 as the director of IT and very quickly moved into the heart of the agency's advertising and marketing business. He took personal responsibility for the international development of the group that today services clients in 108 countries with a complete range of integrated communication, advertising marketing and media services.

Maurice Lévy: chairman and former chief executive of Publicis Groupe

Lévy succeeded Marcel Bleustein-Blanchet as chief executive of the group in 1987. His thirst for growth — mainly by acquisitions — and his hardly concealed ambition to become the biggest player in the industry caused me to describe him as a "buccaneer" whereas his rival Omnicom Group's chief executive John Wren was more of a "beancounter", having previously worked as a consultant with accountants Arthur Andersen and managed the finance function of an Omnicom subsidiary.

Lévy's ambition to acquire became very clear when in September 2000 he announced the purchase of Saatchi & Saatchi — one of the highest profile agency brands at the time — for about £1.3 billion ($1.8 billion). By this time Saatchi & Saatchi was little more than an advertising network, having been divested from the rest of the original group that was rebranded Cordiant Communications and later sold to WPP. The Saatchi image had been tarnished by disappointing results and the departure of Maurice Saatchi whose exit was followed by many of the management team[1].

In 1999 Saatchi & Saatchi had generated group revenue of £401 million on billings of almost £2 billion. That resulted in a post-tax profit of £25 million, almost unchanged from 1998 (although 1998 had benefitted from a £6 millon gain from business disposals). On the face of it, Saatchi was worth nowhere near

_____

1. See chapter 13.

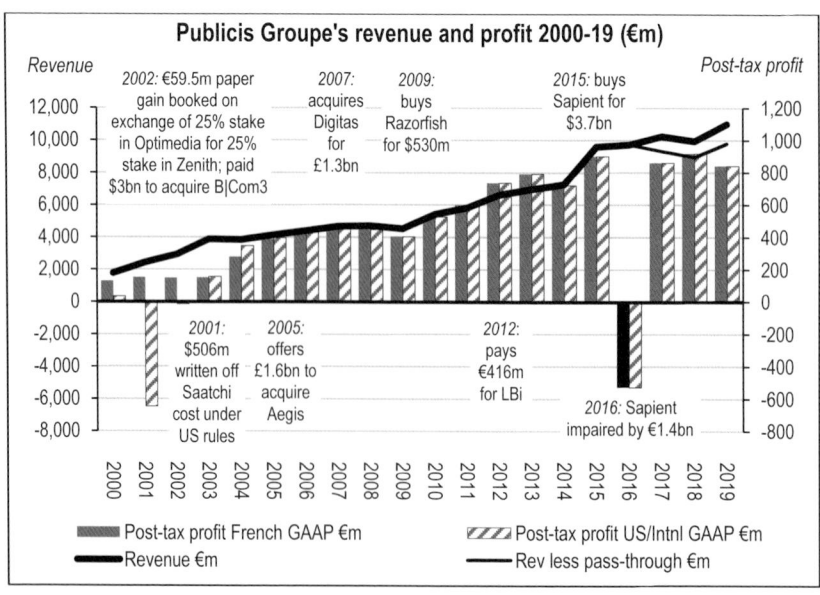

what Publicis was prepared to pay. So it hardly came as a surprise to learn that, in 2001, Publicis had written down the cost of its Saatchi investment by £316 million ($506 million), supposedly to conform to US and international accounting rules that were stricter than those applicable in France.

The French accounting rules applied by Publicis had already come under the spotlight for being more liberal than those in the UK and (particularly) in the US. *Marketing Services Financial Intelligence* noted in 2001 that profits reported by both French groups Publicis and Havas for 2000 would have been slashed by more than two-thirds if they had complied with US accounting rules. It calculated that Publicis' profit would have been 73% lower and that of Havas would have been 67% lower. The report continued:

> By adopting the currently more generous domestic accounting rules, non-US companies have been able to account for acquisitions on a less costly basis and report comparatively higher earnings per share. For example, the liberal French rules applied to the acquisition of Snyder Communications helped Havas to report higher profits in France than permitted in the US. Similarly, the treatment of the Saatchi & Saatchi acquisition last year was one of the main reasons why Publicis reported profits that were four times those calculated under US rules.

Under the US regime, the likely cost of underwriting some of the fall in the price of Publicis shares issued to former Saatchi shareholders

---

How accounting practices differed between US and France in 2002

- France allows acquisitions to be booked at the nominal value, rather than the full (market) value, of new shares issued as consideration.

- Under US rules, if any deferred purchase price is tied to continuing employment, it may have to be treated as an employment cost and charged against profits. In France and the UK the deferred amount is added to the purchase price.

- Where share options are granted at an exercise price below the market price at the date of grant, US rules require the discount to be charged against profits over the vesting period. No such charge is required in France.

- France allows some post-merger reorganisation costs to be accrued as cost of acquisition.

- In France "contingent value rights", which compensate for any fall in the acquirer's shares after they have been used as purchase consideration, are added to the purchase price, but in the US the cost is charged against profits.

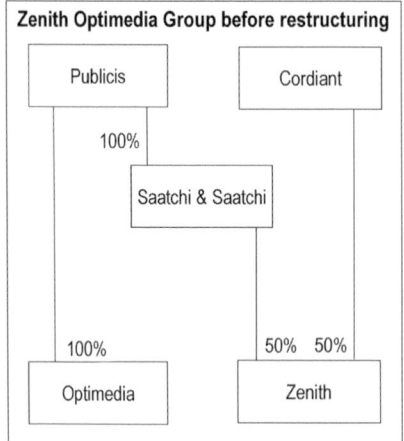

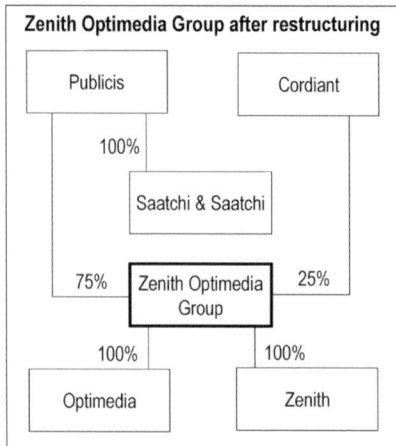

would have been charged against profits whereas this was not required in France. Also, French rules allowed the Saatchi acquisition to be recorded without recognising $2 billion of the cost involved. "As of 31 December 2000 the purchase accounting as determined in accordance with US GAAP was not yet finalised", Publicis confessed in documents filed with the US Securities and Exchange Commission.

The outcome was that Publicis reported a massive loss of $552 million for 2001 under US and international rules, having already reported a $131 post-tax profit under French accounting rules. Accounting adjustments that year included the reversal of a gain recognised on setting up Zenith Optimedia Group as well as writing off the compensation paid to former Saatchi shareholders for the fall in value of the Publicis shares received in exchange.

How was Publicis able to book a $52 million gain on restructuring its media buying businesses?

Until 2001 Saatchi & Saatchi and Cordiant Communications Group had jointly owned Zenith Media, while Publicis owned Optimedia Group. After acquiring Saatchi & Saatchi, Publicis found itself owning 50% of Zenith and 100% of Optimedia. Cordiant was persuaded to sell half of its 50% stake in Zenith in return for acquiring a 25% stake in the enlarged Optimedia group. The two units would be combined under a new holding company Zenith Optimedia Group in which Cordiant would retain its residual 25% minority stake.

French accounting rules allowed Publicis to treat the exchange of shares as a "disposal" of part of its Optimedia stake, giving rise to the paper gain of $52 million that it was able to treat as a realised profit, despite the fact that the consideration was simply another shareholding — namely half of Cordiant's stake in Zenith — and not cash. However, that treatment was not acceptable under international or US rules — hence the adjustment described above.

Lévy's most ambitious initiative was his attempt to persuade the US based Omnicom Group to merge with Publicis. The plan, announced in July 2013, would have created a mammoth global marketing group, outstripping all its competitors with annualised revenue of almost $23 billion and a predicted stock market value of $35.1 billion, after cutting costs by $0.5 billion.

The aggregate of the two group's post-tax profit in 2012 was almost $2 billion whereas the then market leader **WPP** had reported a $1.3 billion profit on revenues of $16.5 billion. The deal was seen to reflect Lévy's entrepreneurial flair and his buccaneering ambition to create the biggest marketing group in the world before he was due to retire about three years later.

Under the proposals Lévy would share the role of chief executive of the merged group with Omnicom's John Wren for the first few years before becoming non-executive chairman. Omnicom's Bruce Crawford would chair the merged group for the first year, handing over to Publicis chair Elisabeth Badinter for the second year.

Although Omnicom was the bigger partner at the time, the deal would have resulted in its shareholders receiving only 50% of the new group's shares, supplemented by a special dividend payment to compensate for their dilution. Publicis shareholders would also have received a dividend supplement, but of a smaller amount.

The special dividend payments could have cost up to $1 billion, but provided the deal was implemented smoothly the new group should not have been saddled with an excessive debt burden relative to its shareholders' funds. Nevertheless healthy profits would still have been needed to service the interest cost of any new borrowings required, as well as to pay for the inevitable bedding in and rationalisation costs that come with any merger.

Despite having more revenue than Publicis, Omnicom's profit was only a whisker ahead of Publicis in 2012 as operating margins remained subdued and finance costs took their toll. So, while Omnicom had struggled to make much progress during the preceding three years, Publicis had been making bigger acquisitions and its profits had almost caught up with those of Omnicom.

However, not all of the Publicis profit growth had arisen from solid earnings. Included in the profit for 2012 was an unrealised paper gain of €62 million ($81 million) reflecting the growth in value of its 49% shareholding in BBH Communications between the date it was first acquired and the acquisition of the rest of the shares on 2012. The situation looked slightly better for Omnicom in the first six months of 2013 when Publicis reported a profit of $417 million and Omnicom reported $494 million.

In the recent past Publicis had made ambitious investments in the digital sector with generally positive results, most recently evidenced by the tie up with AOL, while Omnicom had struggled to recover from its early forays into the digital sector some of which left the group nursing painful losses (see chapter 8).

The geographical spread of the two groups was remarkably similar, both having a substantial presence in North America. This may have offered more opportunities for cost savings from consolidation than opportunities for in-filling gaps in each other's regional coverage. At the time Omnicom and Publicis claimed they could lop $500 million off their combined cost base.

But the merger was not to be. In May 2014 the parties announced that the plan had been abandoned, ostensibly because of an inability to complete it within an acceptable timeframe. Both parties released each other from any financial penalties. Perhaps significantly, the Omnicom board was first to pass a resolution to terminate the talks.

Faced with a revenue standstill, Lévy's acquisition addiction soon re-emerged. In 2015 he added to his string of digital acquisitions by buying the US digital technology consultancy Sapient Corporation for a breath-taking price of $3.7 billion, all in cash. The evidence suggests that Lévy was driven by a strategic determination to acquire as many digital assets as possible to give the group market clout, and to deal with the inevitable rationalisation later. Already the group owned Digitas, LBi, Rosetta and Razorfish, and most recently it had taken a minority stake in the Israeli business Matomy Media Group.

Sapient had made a profit before interest and tax of $120 million in 2013 and looked set to improve on that performance in 2014. Even assuming that Publicis could achieve anticipated synergistic cost savings of €50 million ($63 million), the purchase price represented a very generous multiple of 20 times that enhanced 2013 profit. However, Sapient had also been sitting on a massive cash pile of $280 million the previous June and, assuming this had not been spent since, it would have reduced the effective multiple to

What Publicis Groupe's main digital assets had cost by 2015

Year	Company		€m
2007	Digitas[1]	Technological and marketing applications for e-commerce companies	1,000
2009	Razorfish	Full service global creative digital agency	357
2011	Rosetta Marketing[2]	US digital marketing agency	406
2011	Big Fuel[3]	Social media agency	21
2012	VivaKi	Development and exploitation of Publicis Groupe digital assets	n/a
2012	Pixelpark	German digital marketing agency	30
2013	Poke London	London digital marketing agency	4
2013	Lbi International	Full service global creative digital agency	416
2014	Matomy Media (20%)	Digital advertising sales agency	51
2014	Nurun	Canadian digital design and technology agency	88
2015	Sapient[1]	Digital and e-commerce technology consultancy	2,955
Total cost to date			**5,327**

1. Acquisition price before deducting net cash acquired. 2. Before extra pergormance based payments to employees. 3. Estimated

19 times the enhanced profit.

It took less than two years to discover just how generous some of Lévy's digital deals had been.

In February 2017 Publicis revealed that the internal merger of Sapient with Razorfish had turned sour and had prompted a €1.4 billion ($1.5 billion) impairment charge in its 2016 accounts. As a result Publicis reported a loss of €527 million ($565 million). To add to the gloom, it was predicted that the results for the first half of 2017 would be impacted by some account losses and ongoing difficulties at Razorfish.

Among events influencing the decision to merge Razorfish with Sapient had been:

- A reorganisation of Razorfish in the UK that had contributed to a revenue fall in 2015.
- The departure of Michael Karg, chief executive officer of Razorfish International, to join Ebiquity.
- Dentsu's purchase of the residual 19.4% shareholding in Dentsu Razorfish that had been retained by Publicis following the unravelling of its relationship with the Japanese group in 2012.

The whiff of circumspection about past years' accounting practices still lingered around Publicis, such that the company was driven to issue a very strong rebuttal in 2017 when *Reuters Gouvernance* published an allegation by a French shareholder action group called *Gouvernance en Action* that it had accounted inappropriately for compensation received from a German software publisher following delays in installing its business management software. The group alleged that the compensation of €150 million (£118 million) was included in the Publicis Groupe's financial results for 2014 and that €130 million of the compensation was paid in cash.

SAP is a public company based in Walldorf that described itself as the market leader in computer software developed specifically to support and automate business processes. It reported a profit of €3.6 million (£3 million) for 2016.

Publicis acknowledged that it had been in dispute with an unnamed software and IT services supplier and that the dispute was settled by arbitration. The settlement, which was subject to a confidentiality agreement, provided for Publicis "to be compensated for the costs of the delays and difficulties it sustained". Protected by the confidentiality agreement, Publicis had declined to confirm the identity of the software publisher or the amount of compensation involved.

But Publicis did explain the accounting treatment that it had applied, saying that the compensation was allocated in Publicis Groupe's accounts "in part to the reduction of the book value of the balance sheet assets corresponding to the project, in part to the neutralisation in the 2014 income statement of the extra costs incurred as a result of the delays, and in part to cover forecasted extra costs in the coming years as a result of the delays known by the group".

According to Publicis, the accounting treatment was "validated" by the group's auditors, who confirmed that it was not necessary to mention this information in the notes to the financial statements relating to the 2014 accounts or in the annual report. Publicis reported a post-tax profit of €720 million for 2014, down by 9% from the previous year, despite the SAL compensation receipt. The decline was attributed in part to goodwill write-downs relating to the acquisition of BBH and MSL, and to further costs of the aborted Omnicom merger.

The abortive Omnicom merger was not the first attempt by Lévy to make a bold bid for a US based group. Back in 2002 Publicis had successfully acquired the Bcom3 Group — comprising Leo Burnett (which also held a minority stake in Bartle Bogle Hegarty), D'Arcy Masius Benton & Bowles, and the media buying agency Starcom Mediavest — for about $3 billion.

Prior to the deal, the Japanese Dentsu group had held a 21% stake in Bcom3 (see chapter 6) and so the acquisition enabled Publicis to establish an ongoing strategic partnership with Dentsu as the account below explains. However, as time went by, Dentsu appeared to be gaining very few benefits from the arrangement and in 2012 it was unravelled. Dentsu sold all but 2% of its shareholding back to Publicis for €644 million (£535 million) recording a £17 million profit on the sale.

The acquisition of Bcom3 Group may catapult Publicis Groupe into the premier league of global marketing services groups, but a big question mark remains over whether chief executive officer Maurice Lévy will be able to produce the financial results that justify the scale of investment.

The cost of buying Bcom3 will exceed $3 billion - half as much again as Publicis paid for Saatchi & Saatchi in September 2000. However, annual post-tax profits of Publicis have increased by only $66 million since the company spent $2.3 billion on Saatchi and other smaller acquisitions in the year 2000. That represents a return of just 3% on the amount invested. And the situation would look very much worse if a one-time profit of $52 million derived from reorganising the media operations into Zenith Optimedia Group were to be excluded or if Publicis applied the much stricter US accounting rules in reporting profits and acquisitions (see charts below). Instead Publicis understated the real cost of Saatchi by some $1.8 billion in its group accounts.

So what are the detailed terms of the Bcom3 deal, what is Bcom3 really worth, and what impact is the deal likely to have on Publicis Groupe's future profits?

Apart from the 21% stake acquired by Dentsu at $115.38 per share, Bcom3 is owned by its employees and the shares are held on their behalf by a voting trust. Under the terms of the complicated $3 billion offer, each Bcom3 employee will exchange his current holding for a combination of cash, loan notes and Publicis shares. Some of that cash will come from Dentsu as a result of a share capital reorganisation immediately prior to the main Publicis deal, which will also give Dentsu nearly 15% of the Publicis shares after completion.

As the table[1] shows, each Bcom3 employee share (called an "A" share) will be swapped for cash of $70.92, loan notes to the value of $38.31 and Publicis shares to the value of $48.05 on the offer date. Each loan note will be subject to compulsory exchange for 18 Publicis shares - one on the 1 September each year for a period of 18 years commencing in 2005. If the Publicis share price goes down, so will the value of the deal. Conversely, the deal will be worth more if the share price goes up, and that becomes rather important bearing in mind that the loan notes carry interest of just 0.82% per annum, potentially increasing to 110% of the average annual dividends paid by Publicis over each three-year period from 1 September 2004.

As well as benefiting from the zero risk and low interest costs

1 *See page 83*

How the top multinationals compare

(2001 results based on domestic accounting rules)

Company [1]	Revenue (gross income)	Op profit before amort'n	Operat'g profit margin	Post-tax attrib. profit
	$m	$m	%	$m
Omnicom	6,889	1,064	15.5	503
Interpublic	6,727	-35	-0.5	-505
WPP [2]	5,381	739	13.7	385
Dentsu [3]	2,537	612	24.1	348
Publicis [4]	2,104	254	12.1	131
Havas	1,941	n/a	n/a	-50
B|com3	1,917	212	11.0	26
Average of the above:	**3,928**			**120**

1. Translated at Euro = $0.87, £1 = $1.42, Yen100 = $0.84. 2. Includes full year of Young & Rubicam, 3. Year ended 31 March 2001. 4. Includes full year of Saatchi but op profit reduced by $41m reorganisation. costs.

attaching to the loan notes, Publicis may also be able to treat the notes as "equity" capital rather than debt because their eventual conversion into Publicis shares is compulsory under the scheme. Yet the loan

notes have no voting rights, so in the meantime there can be no threat of former B\|com3 shareholders and Dentsu ganging up on the powerful French shareholders led by Madame Elisabeth Badinter.

The deal contrasts with the structure of the earlier Saatchi & Saatchi acquisition, where Publicis agreed to underwrite part of any post-deal decline in the price of Publicis shares offered to former Saatchi shareholders. It cost Publicis £122 million (or about $175 million), but even that was not enough to compensate for the entire fall in the Publicis share price over the 18-month period.

Although the total cost of B\|com3 is stated as $3 billion, it will certainly be more than that. First, there will be the advisers' costs and then the reorganisation costs. On top of that will be the cost to B\|com3 of buying out existing share options where the market value of shares exceeds the

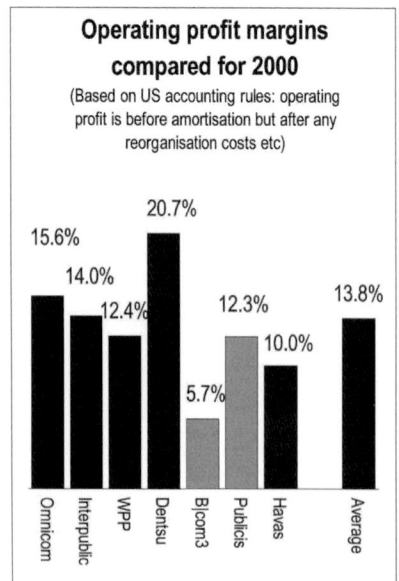

Operating profit margins compared for 2000

(Based on US accounting rules: operating profit is before amortisation but after any reorganisation costs etc)

15.6% 14.0% 20.7% 12.4% 5.7% 12.3% 10.0% 13.8%

Omnicom Interpublic WPP Dentsu B\|com3 Publicis Havas Average

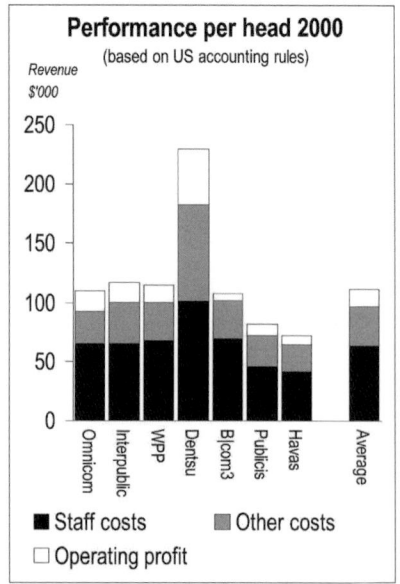

Performance per head 2000

(based on US accounting rules)

Revenue $'000

250 200 150 100 50 0

Omnicom Interpublic WPP Dentsu B\|com3 Publicis Havas Average

■ Staff costs ▨ Other costs ☐ Operating profit

exercise price.

What is Publicis really getting for its $3 billion-plus investment? Most obviously, it is acquiring a revenue stream of $1.9 million and paying a multiple of 1.56 to acquire it. If the group could earn a profit margin of 15% on that revenue, it would contribute a profit before tax and interest of $287 million compared to $212 million achieved in 2001. However, to obtain even a 10% post-tax return on the $3 billion-plus price being offered by Publicis, the enlarged group would need to enhance post-tax profits by $300 million, or by $450 million to earn 15%. That's a high hurdle to jump, bearing in mind that B|com3 contributed just $26 million in 2001 (albeit after $78 million of goodwill amortisation) and the two merging parties together reported post-tax profits of only $157 million.

But the challenge does not stop there. Publicis has not yet reported

What Publicis will pay

Form of consideration	Per B|com3 share[1] $		Total cost
	Staff	Dentsu	$m
Dentsu cash adj't	32.61	-116.39	-
Cash from bonds	38.31	38.31	750
549 euro loan notes redeemable for 18 Publicis shares	38.31	38.31	750
Publicis shares	48.05	178.52	1,500
Proceeds from Publicis:	124.67	255.13	3,000
Effective deal value of a B|com3 share	**157.28**	**138.74**	**3,000**
Post-tax profits of B|com3 in 2001			26
Multiple of post-tax profits			115

Notes: 1. Staff shares were classified as A shares in B|com3, and Dentsu shares were classified as B shares. 2. Net cost excludes cost of buying out share options at excess of market value over exercise price.

its 2001 results under US accounting rules, and says it will not do so until June — just when the merger is intended to be completed. As already indicated, French accounting rules have painted a far more favourable

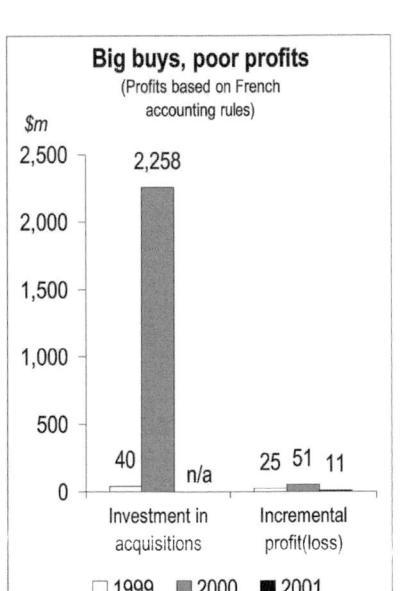

Big buys, poor profits
(Profits based on French accounting rules)

$m

2,258 · 40 · n/a · 25 · 51 · 11

Investment in acquisitions · Incremental profit(loss)

☐ 1999 ■ 2000 ■ 2001

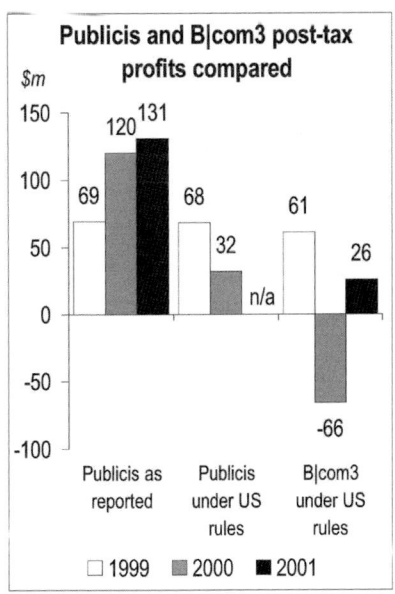

Publicis and B|com3 post-tax profits compared

$m

120 · 131 · 69 · 68 · 32 · n/a · 61 · 26 · -66

Publicis as reported · Publicis under US rules · B|com3 under US rules

☐ 1999 ■ 2000 ■ 2001

picture of how Publicis performed in 2001 than is likely under the US regime. That is why *Marketing Services Financial Intelligence* has already deducted reorganisation costs of $41 million from the $291 million operating profit reported in France. After taking into account items like reorganisation costs, B|com3 and Publicis have at least two features in common under US accounting rules — poor operating profit margins and poor profitability per head.

As the charts on previous pages show, if all the major global groups had adopted the same US accounting rules in the year 2000, Publicis and B|com3 would have been among the poorest performers. And in 2001, margins were among the poorest even under domestic rules.

It would be convenient to argue that the merger will offer opportunities for "economies of scale" or improved efficiency. Experience shows that this is not always the case. Why should two global

businesses that have tolerated under-performance in the past suddenly change behaviour in the future?

Maybe that was what persuaded Dentsu to opt out of going fully global itself and instead to be content with protecting and expanding its high margin domestic income, with the help of a strategic stake in the merged Publicis group on the terms summarised below. Nevertheless $500 million seems a lot to pay for those benefits.

But is the real cost to Dentsu the $500 million claimed? Seemingly not. Under other aspects of the deal Dentsu appears to be due for about $164 million in cash from the sale of bonds. And most of its aggregate continuing investment of almost $1 billion will be held in publicly tradeable Publicis shares.

But what does the future hold for Publicis and Maurice Lévy?

He will need to build top quality business units, managed by top quality personnel, serving top quality

From "Marketing Services Financial Intelligence": March 2002

What's in it for Dentsu?

In return for agreeing not to increase its stake in Publicis beyond 15% of the votes before 2012, Dentsu will enter into a 20-year "Strategic Alliance Agreement" with Publicis before the B|com3 merger is completed. Under the alliance, which will be overseen by a four-person executive including Maurice Levy and Roger Haupt...

■ All existing trading arrangements between Zenith, Saatchi & Saatchi or Publicis and any existing Japanese partners will be terminated within 18 months.

■ Publicis will cancel any plans to acquire advertising agencies in Japan.

■ Publicis will deal exclusively with

Dentsu in Japan.

■ When requested, and subject to client conflict limitations, Publicis companies will represent Dentsu in territories outside Japan, Asia and Africa.

■ Where it suits the parties, Dentsu will consolidate its existing business in Europe and the Americas with the Publicis group.

■ Although Dentsu reserves the right to invest in businesses in Europe, America and Australia, it will consult with Publicis before doing so.

■ Neither Dentsu nor Publicis will partner with WPP, IPG, Omnicom or Havas. In addition Publicis will not partner with Hakuhodo.

■ Dentsu will not expand its Asian

Yutaka Narita: President of Dentsu to join Publicis supervisory board

partnership with WPP and DYR.

■ A global media alliance will be created.

■ Publicis will facilitate the continuation of new business programmes and client relationships which have been jointly developed by Leo Burnett and Dentsu.

clients and making top quality profits. None of that is guaranteed, and the jury remains out on whether this expansionist group can achieve the improvement in business performance that will be required.

How this US group detached its loss-making internet ventures from its reported results while keeping an option to reacquire them,

8
Omnicom's Internet Ingenuity

The marketing industry's initial embrace with digital technology was one of mixed emotions. Young entrepreneurs explored enthusiastically the marketing opportunities presented by social media. Traditional advertising agencies were often sceptical about the true benefits to be obtained. It would be some years before they adjusted fully to the changing media landscape and the need to integrate digital marketing into the mainstream armoury of traditional agencies. In the meantime it became clear that digital marketing was here to stay and so the traditional groups began to invest in some of the entrepreneurial, fast-growing, start-ups.

Omnicom Group – at the time the world's biggest marketing business – dipped several toes into this new pond. But it quickly got cold feet. This chapter recounts an ingenious ploy devised by

437 Madison Avenue, New York: Home to Omnicom and Seneca

the group that had the welcome attraction of keeping the very substantial early losses incurred by its digital agencies out of its annual results. In effect they were putting those businesses into hibernation until, hopefully, they started to make a profit – thanks to a vehicle created by a US buyout specialist called Craig Cogut. That vehicle was called Seneca Investments.

Arguably the ploy was in the best interests of Omnicom shareholders and yet the company volunteered very little information about the arrangement, or the reasons for it, until after the event.

Was Omnicom nervous about having to admit to the early losses incurred? Was the relationship with Seneca entirely at arm's length (Seneca and Omnicom shared the same office building at 437 Madison Avenue, New York)? Was Omnicom too preoccupied with sustaining its share price and keeping its shareholders happy?

I had already become interested in Omnicom's investments in the digital sector during a perusal of its annual report to the US Securities & Exchange Commission for 2000. I read that an investment in Razorfish had contributed a pre-tax gain of $110 million when Omnicom sold part of its holding during that year. Some $64 million of that gain was included in the group's profit for the year. But of greater interest was this little note:

> During the fourth quarter of 1999, the company's ownership interest in Razorfish was diluted below 20%. Given that the company no longer exercised significant influence and as a result of the dilution of its ownership below 20%, the company discontinued accounting for its investment under the equity method.

As we shall see, there was a significant advantage in not having to account for Razorfish using the equity method, namely that Omnicom did not have to include its share of Razorfish's fast growing losses.

My curiosity was aroused still further when Omnicom filed its report to the Securities & Exchange Commission for 2001:

> In May 2001, the company received a non-voting non-participating preferred stock interest in a newly formed company, Seneca Investments LLC, in exchange for its contribution of Communicade, the company's subsidiary that conducted its e-services industry investment activities. The common shareholder of Seneca, who owns all the common stock, is an established private equity investment firm. Upon formation, no debt was assumed by Seneca and no distributions were made to shareholders. The

company has no commitment obligating it to advance funds or provide other capital to Seneca. The preferred stock is non-voting (except on certain extraordinary events) and is entitled to preferential dividends at a rate of 8.5% compounded semi-annually and is redeemable on the 10th anniversary of issuance or earlier upon the occurrence of certain extraordinary events.

The transaction was accounted for in accordance with SFAS 140 *Accounting for Transfers and Servicing Financial Assets and Extinguishments of Liabilities*, and resulted in no gain or loss being recognized by the company on Seneca's formation. Management believes that the carrying value of its preferred

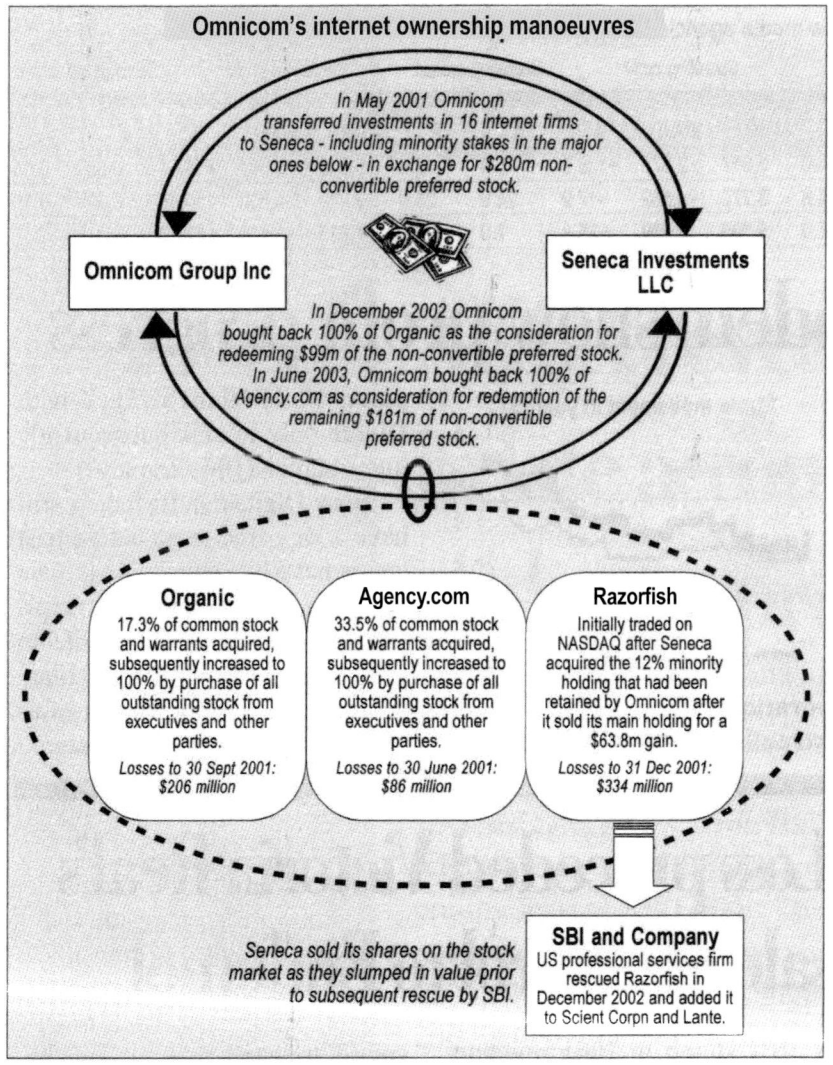

Omnicom's internet ownership manoeuvres

In May 2001 Omnicom transferred investments in 16 internet firms to Seneca - including minority stakes in the major ones below - in exchange for $280m non-convertible preferred stock.

Omnicom Group Inc

Seneca Investments LLC

In December 2002 Omnicom bought back 100% of Organic as the consideration for redeeming $99m of the non-convertible preferred stock. In June 2003, Omnicom bought back 100% of Agency.com as consideration for redemption of the remaining $181m of non-convertible preferred stock.

Organic
17.3% of common stock and warrants acquired, subsequently increased to 100% by purchase of all outstanding stock from executives and other parties.
Losses to 30 Sept 2001: $206 million

Agency.com
33.5% of common stock and warrants acquired, subsequently increased to 100% by purchase of all outstanding stock from executives and other parties.
Losses to 30 June 2001: $86 million

Razorfish
Initially traded on NASDAQ after Seneca acquired the 12% minority holding that had been retained by Omnicom after it sold its main holding for a $63.8m gain.
Losses to 31 Dec 2001: $334 million

Seneca sold its shares on the stock market as they slumped in value prior to subsequent rescue by SBI.

SBI and Company
US professional services firm rescued Razorfish in December 2002 and added it to Scient Corpn and Lante.

investment in Seneca of $280 million at 31 December 2001 approximated its fair value.

What was Omnicom's relationship with Seneca and what were its future intentions?

After I had carried out more detailed research, a full account of Omnicom's arrangement with Seneca was first published in *New Media Agencies Financial Intelligence* in May 2002 and is reproduced below. Little did I know that the story would be picked up by the *Wall Street Journal* which had been pursuing its own, broader, line of enquiry. "Omnicom's Shares Drop Sharply On Concerns Over Accounting" the headline roared from its front page in June 2002.

Among six separate allegations, the paper asserted that Omnicom had failed to disclose adequately the nature and financial implications of the Seneca deal whereby it offloaded its loss-making internet investments. According to the *Wall Street Journal*, Omnicom's chief executive John Wren claimed there were inaccuracies in its article, but the company declined to elaborate. Each of those six allegations is examined in more detail towards the end of this chapter.

Did Seneca make any money out of the companies offloaded to it by Omnicom? It seems unlikely, although my enquiries focussed on only three (albeit probably the biggest) of the 16 companies involved.

Razorfish was one of the first agencies that Seneca shed over the ensuing years and it looks as if Seneca suffered an $8 million loss in doing so, a loss that Omnicom was fortunate to avoid.

Shares in Razorfish were traded on the NASDAQ public stock market and were quoted at $1.21 when Seneca acquired its holding in May 2001. The share price quickly plummeted and disposals began within months, culminating in a final exit in November 2002 when Razorfish was bought by a privately-owned professional services business called SBI & Company at a price equivalent to just over 5 cents per share after adjusting for an interim share consolidation.

Today Razorfish belongs to Publicis Groupe, having been sold on to aQuantive and then to Microsoft in the meantime.

With Razorfish disposed of, Seneca was left holding shares in the two remaining publicly listed digital agencies — Agency. com and Organic — alongside shares in various privately owned businesses. In 2003 Omnicom reacquired both Agency.com and

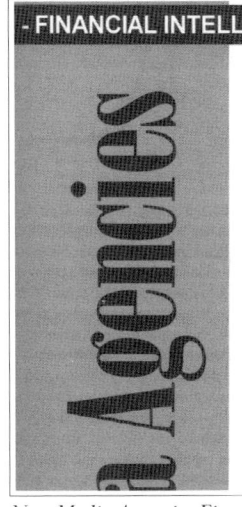

- FINANCIAL INTELLIGENCE - FINANCIAL INTELLIGENCE - FINANCIAL

How Omnicom detached its internet ventures but still kept its options open

On 24 April last year the mighty **Omnicom Group** announced its results for the first quarter. Profits were continuing their upward path despite the depressed market conditions and the devastation of the dotcom industry. But was Omnicom immune to the dotcom fiasco? It had significant minority shareholdings in

New Media Agencies Financial Intelligence (above) was first to reveal Omnicom's controversial plan, followed up as part of the front page story in the Wall Street Journal on 12 June 2002 (below).

| 23676 | S&P 500 F 2787.00 | Stoxx 600 331.80 | U.S. 10 Yr 0/32 Yield | Crude Oil 23.19 | Euro 1.0946 |

THE WALL STREET JOURNAL.

Robert Willott

English Edition ▾ | April 10, 2020 | Print Edition | Video

Home   World   U.S.   Politics   Economy   Business   Tech   Markets   Opinion   Life & Arts   Real Estate   WSJ Magazine   Search Q

WSJ CFO Journal Newsletter
The daily dynamics and strategies in corporate finance, from accounting to regulations.
Sponsored by: **Deloitte.**   READ NOW

Nimble Financing Helped Fuel Growth of an Advertising Giant

But Omnicom's Internet Stakes Spark Boardroom Controversy

By Vanessa O'Connell and Jesse Eisinger Staff Reporters of The Wall Street Journal

NEW YORK -- At the annual meeting of advertising giant Omnicom Group Inc. last month, Chief Executive John Wren boasted about lucrative new assignments to promote such products as Dell personal computers, Saturn sedans and Michelob Light beer. He showed off snappy commercials for Diet Pepsi and Federal Express. And he vowed that despite the worst advertising slowdown in 50 years, the world's largest ad-holding company would continue to deliver double-digit growth in revenue and profit.

One factor behind that impressive success has nothing to do with great ads: Omnicom's long list of acquisitions -- 73 in 2000 and 2001 alone -- and the way it accounts for them. Now a financial issue is starting to stir some controversy inside Omnicom. Last month, the head of the audit committee of its board of directors resigned amid questions about how the company handled a series of soured Internet investments.

Organic, and in doing so revealed at last how the Seneca accounting manoeuvre had enabled it to off-load shares in loss-making internet agencies and to reacquire controlling stakes later without any material impact on its annual profits. The cost of reacquisition was booked at $280 million — exactly the same amount as the value placed on the preferred stock Omnicom received for selling minority interests in the 16 internet investments to Seneca in May 2001. The transactions involved virtually no net cash outlay.

As with Razorfish, by off-loading its other internet investments to Seneca, Omnicom did not have to consider whether there had been any diminution in their value and was also able to avoid inclusion of its share of the trading losses incurred by Agency.com in which it had held a 33% stake.

Here's the Seneca story in full...

On 24 April 2001 the mighty Omnicom Group announced its results for the first quarter. Profits were continuing their upward path despite the depressed market conditions and the devastation of the dotcom industry. But was Omnicom immune to the dotcom fiasco?

It had significant minority share-holdings in three publicly quoted internet consultancies - Agency.com, Organic and Razorfish. All three were incurring losses that would accumulate to over $700 million by the year end. And Organic's principal shareholder was trying to persuade Omnicom to buy him out.

If nothing was done, Omnicom might have faced the prospect of having to accept sizeable write-offs in the value of its investments and, in the case of Agency.com, it would have had to deduct its share of the increasing losses from the profit that Omnicom would hope to report for 2001.

However, a timely deal with buyout financier Craig Cogut and the institutions that fund his investments in distressed companies through Pegasus Partners removed all those potential worries - for the time being at least. Omnicom had put about 16 of its internet investments, including the three public companies, into a holding vehicle Communicade which was sold on to Cogut's new investment company Seneca Invest-

ments on 2 May 2001 in exchange for a special type of non-convertible preferred stock. Omnicom also reduced the number of its nominee directors at each company, thereby avoiding any suggestion that they remained under its influence. By the end of 2001 Omnicom was able to conclude that its ongoing investment in Seneca was sufficiently robust to avoid the need to make any provision for permanent diminution in value.

So what was the financial state of each of the three public companies that were divested by Omnicom? And how was the Seneca deal structured?

Looking first at Razorfish, its financial position was the most vulnerable of the three. By the end of 2001, the company had closed all its overseas subsidiaries, cut its workforce from 1,994 to 270, and incurred a cumulative $334 million loss that had consumed all its capital. Its share price was at rock bottom[1].

A further public share offering was launched which succeeded in raising over $5 million by April 2002. It is possibly too early to be confident about a recovery, but the slimmed down company did manage to report a small profit of $2.5 million in the first quarter of 2002.

At the time of divestment in May 2001, Omnicom had reduced its shareholding in Razorfish from 32% on its flotation to 12%. Being below

1. See chart on page 94

the benchmark of 20%, at which level a significant influence is assumed to be exercised over the investment, it did not have to recognise its share of Razorfish losses in its own financial results. However, if the Seneca deal had not been clinched and Razorfish had verged on collapse by the year end, Omnicom's profits would have suffered a charge for any permanent fall in value of its residual holding.

On the brighter side, Omnicom's profits for the previous year had already included a $63.8 million gain from selling a bigger slice of its original Razorfish shareholding.

If the situation at Razorfish was on a knife-edge, things were not a lot better at Organic. This company too had exhausted virtually all capital by September 2001 after running up cumulative losses of $206 million.

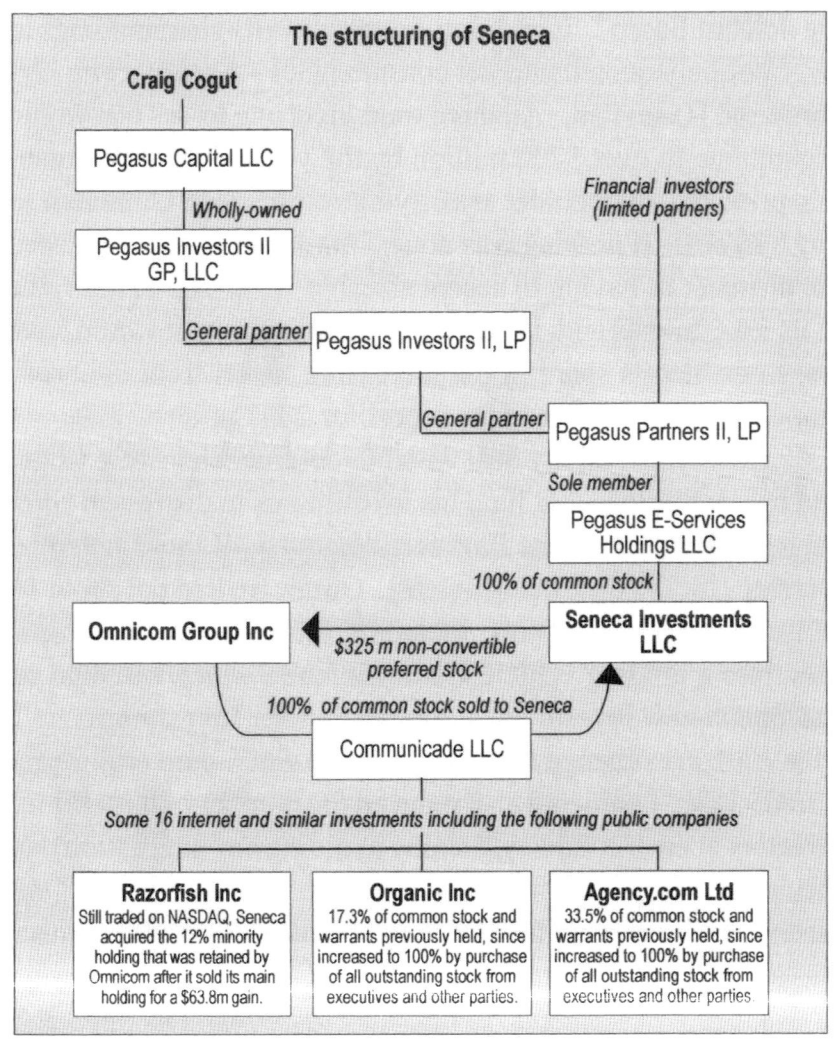

The structuring of Seneca

Craig Cogut

Pegasus Capital LLC

Wholly-owned

Pegasus Investors II GP, LLC

General partner — Pegasus Investors II, LP

Financial investors (limited partners)

General partner — Pegasus Partners II, LP

Sole member

Pegasus E-Services Holdings LLC

100% of common stock

Omnicom Group Inc ◄ — $325 m non-convertible preferred stock — Seneca Investments LLC

100% of common stock sold to Seneca

Communicade LLC

Some 16 internet and similar investments including the following public companies

Razorfish Inc
Still traded on NASDAQ, Seneca acquired the 12% minority holding that was retained by Omnicom after it sold its main holding for a $63.8m gain.

Organic Inc
17.3% of common stock and warrants previously held, since increased to 100% by purchase of all outstanding stock from executives and other parties.

Agency.com Ltd
33.5% of common stock and warrants previously held, since increased to 100% by purchase of all outstanding stock from executives and other parties.

And the implications for Omnicom were more significant than those at Razorfish. At the time of divestment in May 2001, Omnicom owned 17.3% of Organic, though the company was still under the overall control of its chairman Jonathan Nelson. Faced with the rapidly deteriorating financial situation, Nelson had started talks with Omnicom to see whether he could sell his shareholding to that company.

His timing was not ideal as Omnicom would face the prospect of having to include the increased share of Organic's losses in its own results. But another possibility was under consideration.

Seneca was contemplating taking Organic "private" following the proposed acquisition of Omnicom's stake, by buying out the other shareholders and thereby offering an exit for the unfortunate Nelson. And if Seneca was committed to supporting Organic in the future, there would be no need for Omnicom to worry about making any provision for a permanent diminution in the value of Organic shares.

But Omnicom's disengagement from Organic was not quite as clean as it appeared. Alongside its deal with Seneca, Omnicom obtained an option to reacquire some 39 million Organic shares at $0,254

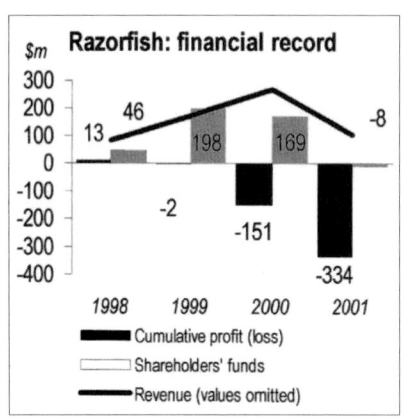

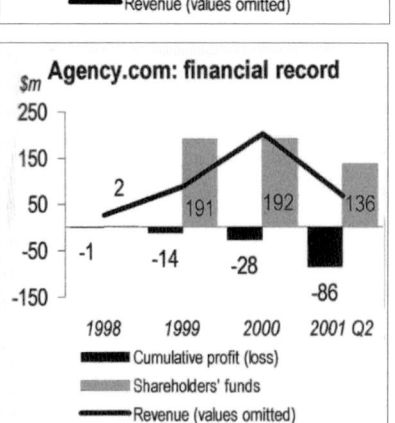

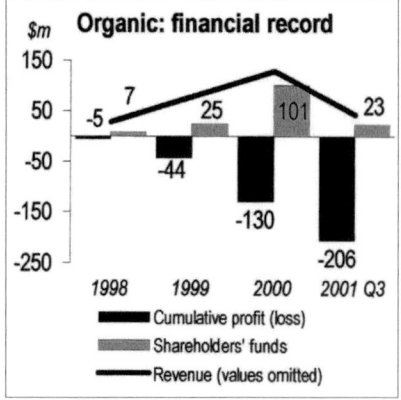

in the future. The option may be exercised either by a cash payment or by converting an outstanding $10 million loan. This would give Omnicom about 30% of the enlarged capital. So, with the help of this side arrangement, Omnicom had not only avoided any dent in its profits arising from Organic's ongoing losses but also secured an opportunity to reinvest when prospects improve.

The third of Omnicom's major investments — Agency.com — also posed a threat to Omnicom's future profit performance. Like the other internet companies, Agency.com had run up losses, but of lesser amounts, and at June 2001 its shareholders' funds still stood at $136 million. Even so, the increasing scale of losses threatened its future viability. Furthermore, Omnicom's 33.5% shareholding in Agency. com was far bigger than in the other two companies and, with a board presence as well, it would have been normal practice to include a share of Agency.com's trading losses within Omnicom's 2001 results.

However, by selling its interest in Agency.com to Seneca and distancing itself from the management, Omnicom would be able to avoid accounting for a share of the losses.

So the deal with Seneca was done. Omnicom exchanged its shareholdings for a special class of share in Seneca. The characteristics of those shares are not known, but they appear not to provide any equity participation in profits or losses and cannot be converted into shares that do. Certainly Omnicom has publicly disclaimed any ongoing shareholder

interest in the three companies examined here, despite the share options described earlier. Could it be that those options are Omnicom's only continuing access to the profit potential of its former internet portfolio?

If Seneca wants to redeem Omnicom's special shares in the future, the price for doing so appears to be $325 million. Whether this will yield a healthy profit for Omnicom

What the mark-up should be on fee-earners

A typical cost structure for a professional services business is illustrated below. Sometimes the operating profit margin will be nearer 20% than 15%, depending on staff utilisation rates, for example. But overhead staff costs should not be more than half the cost of fee-earners.

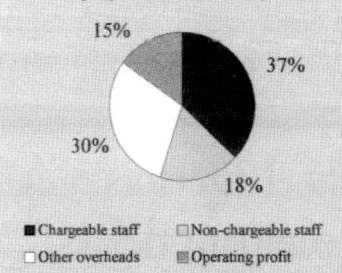

How revenue should be spent in a professional services firm

15%
37%
30%
18%

■ Chargeable staff   □ Non-chargeable staff
□ Other overheads   ▨ Operating profit

At the internet consultancies acquired by Seneca, the chargeable staff costs were far too high, as this table shows:

As % of revenue	1998	1999	2000	2001
Agency.com	60%	52%	49%	66%
Organic	61%	70%	67%	74%
Razorfish	53%	48%	55%	66%
Benchmark assuming 10% idle time	37%	37%	37%	37%

is unclear. All we know is that the companies were transferred to Seneca for neither gain nor loss.

Is Omnicom still exposed to any financial risk? Apart from any outstanding indebtedness from the divested companies and assuming no other side deals with Seneca and/or its backers, it seems that any future risk will be limited to the continuing viability of Seneca itself.

Meanwhile Seneca has a lot of work to do. None of the companies was earning revenue anywhere near the level necessaiy to support the fee—earning staff engaged[1]. Either the staff were seriously under-utilised or their work was seriously under-priced, or both. It is common practice for professional service businesses to charge out fee-earning staff at three times their direct cost.

If maximum productivity can be achieved, that leaves two-thirds of income available to pay for admin staff and other overheads. And ideally total staff costs should absorb 50% and at worst 55% of revenue.

If Craig Cogut's interest in resuscitating distressed companies proves

1 See chart on page 93

successful in this case — and Seneca has been swift to make management changes — he may add substantially to his financial fortune.

But the story did not end there. What may have been initiated as a very shrewd and well-intentioned attempt to achieve the best result for Omnicom shareholders backfired in a massive way when the _Wall Street Journal_ published a critical report on the group's accounting in June 2002.

Instead of winning shareholders' congratulations, confidence in the company was badly undermined, the share price plummeted and lawsuits began. Was it just a sad, but simple, case of poor communication? Or had Omnicom been deliberately massaging its figures?

The accusations made by the _Wall Street Journal_ — summarised below — were based primarily on a mixture of academic opinion and unanswered questions about some complex financial transactions. At the very least the charges deserve serious examination. But it also needs to be remembered that the report was written against a backcloth of investor insecurity following the controversial collapse

---

ALLEGATIONS MADE BY "THE WALL STREET JOURNAL"

1 _That the company selected a method of reporting "organic" revenue growth that was more favourable than that used by its competitors._	**2** _That the company failed to disclose adequately the nature and financial implications of the deal whereby it offloaded its loss-making internet investments._	**3** _That the company does not disclose the total amount of revenue or profit derived from acquisitions in any year._

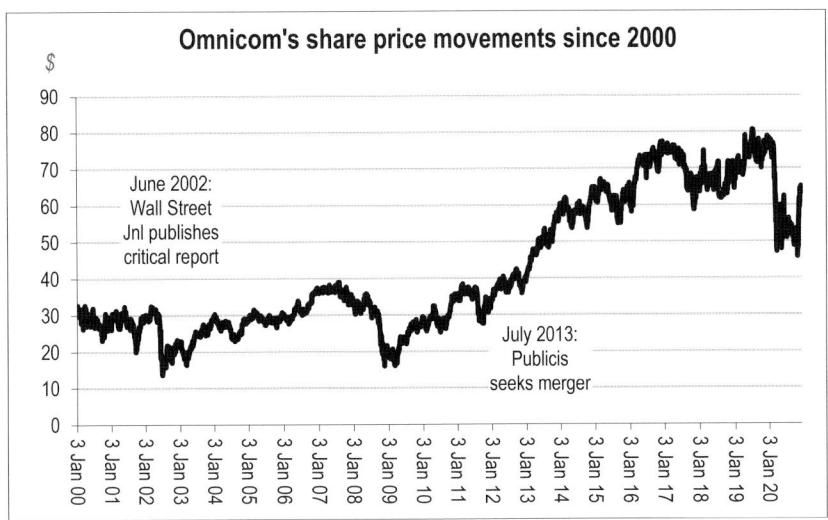

Omnicom Group's share price dropped by 30% over two days after the Wall Street Journal published a critical report on the group's accounting, in June 2002.

of the Enron utilities business and an inevitable desire among journalists to discover another similar scandal.

The first allegation is simple enough, although it has nothing to do with the reporting of financial results in audited financial statements and therefore cannot fairly be described as an accounting flaw.

Acquisitive businesses are expected to demonstrate that at least some of their growth in revenue and profit is derived from the development of existing businesses. It would be a worrying situation if new acquisitions were simply replacing revenues leaking from what the group already owned.

So major companies in the sector — like Omnicom, The Interpublic Group of Companies and WPP Group — all publish statistics purporting to show how much growth has been achieved from existing busi-

---

ALLEGATIONS MADE BY "THE WALL STREET JOURNAL"

4 *That the company's annual operating cash flow declined between 1999 and 2001, and was negative after deducting the cost of acquisitions.*

5 *That the company has "sharply increased" its average net borrowings recently from $172 million in 1998 to $2.1 billion in 2001.*

6 *That the company makes no provision for earn-out liabilities and that arguably they should be treated as remuneration rather than an acquisition cost.*

nesses ("organic" growth) and how much is attributable to newly acquired businesses. There are various ways of calculating organic growth.

One method is to exclude revenue and profits from the latest year's figures if they relate to businesses that were not owned for the whole of the preceding year.

Another possible way is to compare the full amount of revenue and profit reported for the latest year with what would have been achieved if all recently acquired businesses had been owned for the whole of the preceding year, and apparently that is the method adopted by Omnicom. As chief executive officer John Wren admitted: "The one thing we can do is to make sure everyone in the world understands how we do it."

A third variation is to exclude from the latest year just the revenue and profit derived from businesses Omnicom acquired during that year — in other words all revenue and profit is included for businesses owned at the start of the year even if they were acquired towards the end of the preceding year. Clearly this last approach gives the least meaningful comparison.

Perhaps Omnicom should endeavour to agree a method that is acceptable to, and adopted by, its peer group. If by not doing so it stands accused of overstating its rate of organic growth, it cannot hope to retain respect as a leader of the industry.

However, the offence — if proven — is probably far less serious than the massaging of claimed billings practised by many advertising

agencies eager to improve their showing in league tables.

The second allegation is possibly the most substantial and revolves around the decision to transfer Omnicom's investments in 16 internet related businesses to a new company called Seneca Investments set up by venture capitalist Craig Cogut who specialises in distress recovery situations.

The transaction and its implications were described in detail earlier in this chapter. The accounting consequences of the deal were that:
• Omnicom no longer had to account for its share of losses at Agency.com;
• Having replaced the loss-making internet investments in its balance sheet by a single investment in Seneca, no provision was required for any diminution in value of the internet investments.

After concluding the deal and filing vast amounts of legal paperwork at the US Securities & Exchange Commission, Omnicom gave a brief, vague and virtually identical explanation in each of its next two quarterly financial returns:

"In May 2001, the company contributed to a new holding company investments in several companies, primarily in the e-services industry, and cash. Upon contribution, the investments were reclassified from long-term investments and investments in affiliates to cost basis investments and included in other assets in the accompanying balance sheet. No gain or loss was recognized on the transaction".

According to press reports Wren claims that the Seneca deal had been "more fully disclosed than anything else in Omnicom's history". Yet Omnicom failed even to identify the name of the transferee, or to say that the divested businesses had been losing vast amounts of money, or that its balance sheet still valued its stake in the divested businesses via Seneca at $280 million, or that it had retained an option to buy back about 30% of one of its former investments, Organic, at a later date.

Despite several requests for the information, the $280 million valuation was only disclosed in Omnicom's recently filed annual report, almost a year after the divestment took place.

Omnicom CEO John Wren: "Inaccuracies in WSJ story", but greater transparency would ensue.

As Omnicom is now contemplating reacquiring some of the businesses, it is hardly surprising that questions are being asked about whether the divestment was entirely at arm's length. In essence the deal seems to have benefited shareholders, but the price for Omnicom's initial coyness in telling the whole story has been very high indeed.

Allegation number three was that Omnicom failed to disclose the total revenue and profit attributable to acquisitions each year. That's true. It is also true that there is no US accounting obligation to do so and that Omnicom's US competitors are no more forthcoming. By comparison, UK and international accounting standards are far more demanding and helpful.

The next two allegations were linked — that cash flow is on the decline and that net borrowings are on the increase. From the chart overleaf[1] it is clear that those asser-

tions are over-simplistic. For example, operating cash flow has always been negative in the first quarter.

Secondly, the net cash inflow in 1999 (aggregating the first quarter with the remaining three quarters shown in the chart) was unusually high — almost three times net profit for the year — and could not be expected to continue at such a level. In general terms there has been a healthy and steadily improving trend over the four year period.

As for net borrowings, it would be surprising if a growing company did not experience some increase in debt as acquisitions are rarely funded entirely by operating cash flow. But that increase should be matched by an improvement in the amount invested by shareholders. It is this ratio of debt to shareholders' funds ("equity") that matters.

And here the critics have a point. Year end net debt had risen by 540%

---

1. See page 108

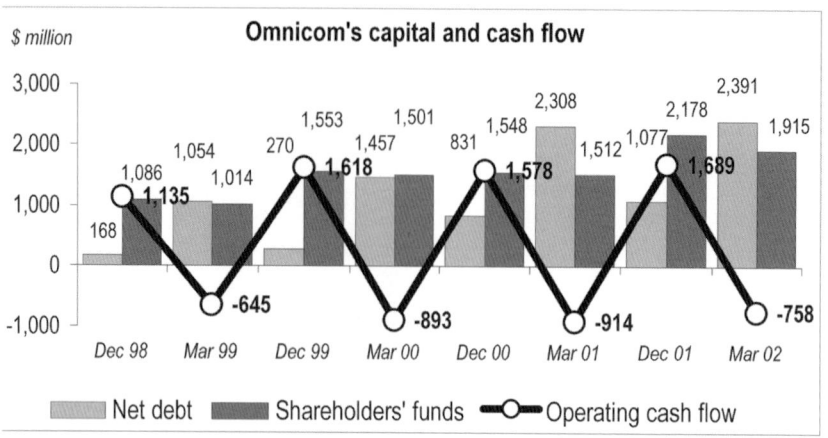

Omnicom's capital and cash flow

Net debt　Shareholders' funds　Operating cash flow

since 1998 whereas shareholders' equity had merely doubled.

The group has become far more dependent on borrowings and the position needs to be watched, particularly as it always deteriorates in the first quarter. The year end debt/equity ratio of 1:2 would be regarded as fairly safe by most financial institutions, but warning bells are usually sounded when the ratio exceeds 1:1 as was the case at 31 March after $369 million was spent on share buy-backs. Curiously, commentators have been slower to question the nature of the borrowings and the treatment of interest thereon.

In 2001 the group raised $850 million in convertible debt carrying no interest coupon. The attraction lay in being able to convert the debt into shares at a later debt when the share price has risen substantially. But as there is no certainty that the conditions for conversion will be met, it is unlikely that the group is required to allocate the "premium" on conversion over the intervening years as a financing cost.

Questions put to Omnicom

by *Marketing Services Financial Intelligence* on this matter have been consistently ignored, feeding suspicions that today's profits are benefiting at the expense of future shareholder dilution.

The final allegation concerns the absence of any provision in the accounts for earn-out commitments arising under acquisition agreements. Such obligations are dependent on the achievement of predetermined profit targets and cannot be calculated precisely until the earnout period has expired.

UK accounting rules now require such obligations to be estimated at each year end and provided for as a liability (unless capable of settlement by the issue of shares in which case the amount may be shown as unissued shares).

But in the US there is no such accounting requirement. Omnicom's chief financial officer Randall Weisenburger recently estimated the liability to be in the range of $250-$350 million. By comparison, Interpublic estimated last December that it could owe as much as $550 million. So Omnicom is in good company and certainly less exposed.

The trouble is that Omnicom has always been less forthcoming than some competitors. For a communications group it has a lot to learn about communications. And it has paid a heavy price.

After Saatchi & Saatchi was demerged, Cordiant aggressively sought new acquisitions. The result? A mountain of debt and the head of its chief executive.

9
Crunch Time for Cordiant

When Saatchi & Saatchi was demerged, Cordiant Communications Group faced a major strategic challenge to become a serious worldwide player without it. Pursuing acquisitions at almost any price, quality remained its Achilles' heel.

The architect of the plan to revitalise the rump of the Cordiant business was Michael Bungey, its chief executive. The son of a lorry driver, Bungey was a graduate of the London School of Economics who had cut his teeth in a marketing environment at Crosse & Blackwell after it had been taken over by Nestlé. From there he joined the Crawfords advertising agency and then moved on to Bensons before setting up his own agency Michael Bungey & Partners.

Later his agency was reported to have been rescued from financial difficulties by joining up with the US agency Dancer Fitzgerald Sample (DFS) in 1984, only to be acquired by Saatchi & Saatchi in 1986. DFS was then merged with another Saatchi owned agency Dorland Advertising. The enlarged Dorland DFS agency was merged with the US based Bates network and Bungey became chairman and chief executive officer of Bates Dorland and Bates Europe in 1988. In 1993, he was appointed president and

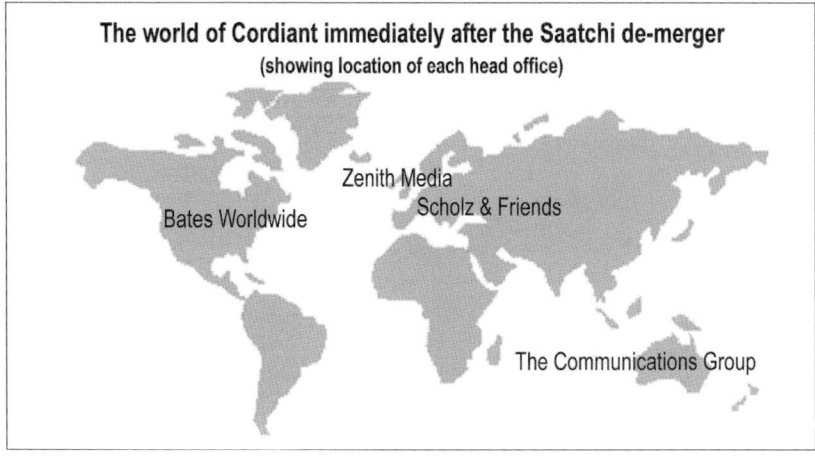

The world of Cordiant immediately after the Saatchi de-merger
(showing location of each head office)

Zenith Media

Scholz & Friends

Bates Worldwide

The Communications Group

chief operating officer of Bates Worldwide, progressing to chief executive officer in April 1994 and chairman in December 1994. He joined the Cordiant board in January 1995.

I met Bungey only once and that was in response to an invitation from a partner of mine to join them for lunch. He came across as an extremely pleasant man, with many of the qualities one would expect to find in an experienced advertising account executive tasked with keeping clients happy and interpreting their wishes to creative teams.

Sadly his period at the helm of Cordiant ended under a cloud, but not before he had made several bold moves to enhance the business.

As we shall see, perhaps the most memorable deal was the £315 million acquisition of a group of companies called the Lighthouse Global Network in September 2000. Lighthouse was set up by two astute businessmen from Chicago — Terence Graunke and Paul Yovovich — who later became associated with a private equity outfit Lake Capital whose acquisition of Engine Group in 2014 saw the departure of its founder Peter Scott shortly afterwards.

Over a two year period the duo acquired a collection of British and other marketing services companies – including public relations agency Financial Dynamics and the Fitch design consultancy – and promptly wrapped them up as an attractive parcel which they sold on to Cordiant at an enormous profit. Lighthouse was reported to have made an adjusted annualised post-tax profit of £8.2 million in 1999 and a post-tax profit of £11.3 million in 2000. implying that Cordiant paid a generous price equating to a multiple of around 32 times the average annual post-tax profit for those two years.

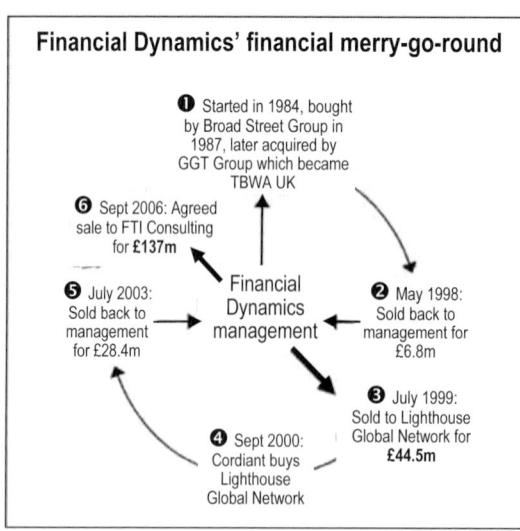

Financial Dynamics' financial merry-go-round

❶ Started in 1984, bought by Broad Street Group in 1987, later acquired by GGT Group which became TBWA UK

❻ Sept 2006: Agreed sale to FTI Consulting for **£137m**

Financial Dynamics management

❺ July 2003: Sold back to management for £28.4m

❷ May 1998: Sold back to management for £6.8m

❸ July 1999: Sold to Lighthouse Global Network for **£44.5m**

❹ Sept 2000: Cordiant buys Lighthouse Global Network

Based on calculations that I made at the time, it seemed that Lighthouse had bought its largest constituent companies at far more modest profit multiples of around 10.

Within a year Cordiant announced that the value of Lighthouse was worth £225 million less than it had cost. Cordiant itself reported a post-tax loss of £278 million loss for that year as well as tough bank constraints on its future spending.

But it's an ill wind that blows nobody any good. Not for the first time would one of the Lighthouse companies – Financial Dynamics – be sold back to its management, headed by Charles Watson.

The first occasion when Financial Dynamics managers had made a handsome profit from buying back their business and selling it on again later was in May 1998 when they had bought the company from the ailing GGT Group (now TBWA UK) for £6.8 million and sold it on within one year to Lighthouse for £44.5 million. That is entirely lawful, of course.

Now, after Cordiant had acquired Lighthouse, the company was sold back to its managers again for £28.4 million with a little financial help from Advent International. Three years after that, in September 2006, Financial Dynamics would be sold again — this time to the US management consultancy firm FTI Consulting for £137 million. Between them, Watson and his colleague Declan Kelly pocketed an estimated £12.8 million.

The account below tells of Cordiant's unsuccessful attempt to survive without the Saatchi agencies. It first appeared in *Marketing Services Financial Intelligence* in June 2003. At the close of this chapter we shall read of the scramble to rescue something from the Cordiant ruins. If anyone wanted a lesson on how to do most damage to a disintegrating company, they need look no further than at the protracted financial fight over what was left of the ailing communications group.

On 14 December 1997, the publicly quoted Cordiant Communications Group split itself in half.

Saatchi & Saatchi — the founding agency business that had built for itself a high profile based on a firm belief in the power of persuasion and panache — went on its own way, leaving behind what had always been seen as the less exciting network: Bates Worldwide. Saatchi also left behind a fragile balance sheet and an historically poorly performing business.

But Bates' poor financial performance had a very different cause from the equally poor performance that had dogged Saatchi. While Saatchi charged a lot for its reputation (then only recently sullied by the acrimonious departure of its founding brothers and their close colleagues), it always spent prolifically.

By contrast, Bates was just a tired and loosely controlled network, with a financial culture that matched. To build a global business that could hold its head up high alongside Omnicom Group, WPP Group and The Interpublic Group of Companies, Cordiant needed more creative muscle, more management and more money. It ignored all three.

Look at the balance sheet at 31 December 1997. Shareholders' funds were in deficit by £80 million and, even after adding back to that deficit all the goodwill that had been written off at the time of earlier acquisitions, there would have been only a modest surplus of £34 million (see accompanying table).

And whilst there were no net borrowings — in fact there was a net cash surplus of almost £25 million — the group had substantial obligations under guarantees totalling £72 million, leaving aside obligations under properties leased by subsidiaries.

On the back of this insubstantial financial foundation the group was to embark on a massive acquisition spree, spending £700 million between 1999 and 2001, and doubling its workforce to 9,420. In doing so, chief executive Michael Bungey in effect "bet the business" in an all-or-nothing gamble. That might have paid off, but for one fatal flaw. He paid far too much for what he bought.

The worst example was first reported in *Marketing Services Financial Intelligence* in December 2000, when Cordiant was seduced into buying a parcel of second-hand companies smartly wrapped up and labelled the Lighthouse Global

Cordiant's fragile financial footing

Shareholders' funds (£m):	Dec 97	Dec 02
Share capital and (mainly non-distributable) reserves	23.5	499.6
Minority interests in subsidiaries	6.1	11.4
	29.6	511.0
Less: Accumulated losses to date (net of tax relief)	109.2	430.1
Net shareholders' funds:	**-79.6**	**80.9**
Goodwill written off against reserves at acquisition [1]	113.2	115.5
Adjusted s/holders' funds:	**33.6**	**196.4**
Net debt (£m):		
Debt due within one year	8.5	14.9
Debt due later than one year	28.4	233.2
Less: Cash balances	-61.7	-96.4
Total borrowings:	**-24.8**	**151.7**
Estimated gearing (debt/equity) ratio:	n/a	1.88:1

Note 1: This goodwill was written off ab initio under earlier accounting rules that no longer apply. Under those rules the audited balance sheet at 31 December 1997 showed a deficit of £79.6 million.

Network. The price paid was excessive by any standard — a multiple of 32 times post-tax profits[1].

Before embarking on this expensive excursion, there had been signs that Cordiant's financial performance was beginning to improve. Revenues moved ahead by a modest 9% between 1997 and 1999, while profit margins climbed from the abysmal level of 7.1% to 10% in the same period. Why the group could not achieve the 15% margin earned by its more efficient rivals remains an unanswered question. What is clear from a geographical analysis is that the depressed margins outside the UK improved while the historically

1   See "The Financial Performance of Marketing Services Companies: 2000", Moore Kingston Smith.

better margins in the UK slipped downwards (see tables).

What is also clear is that Bates was not having any significant success in winning market share, implying that the creative offer remained uninspiring. Without a major boost in its fortunes, Bates was going nowhere and the Cordiant board must have come to the same conclusion. But instead of revitalising Bates, they went buying.

By the end of 1999 Cordiant had announced two sizeable acquisitions – Diamond Ad in Korea and Healthworld Corporation in the US. Diamond Ad was the second largest agency in Korea although it had lost £20 million in the preceding two years. The total cost of the 80% stake was £42 million after allowing for estimated earn-out payments of £26 million. On top of that Cordiant assumed net overdrafts of another £7.1 million.

The following year produced a dramatic leap in operating margins in Asia from 7.6% to 18.6% which was "principally due to the full year contribution of Diamond", according

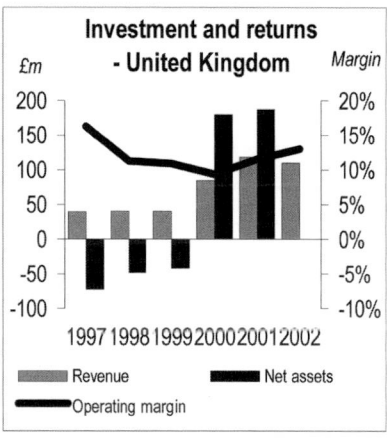

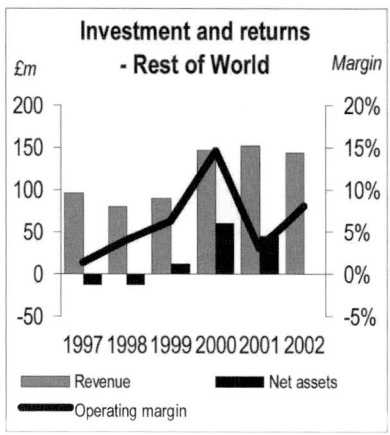

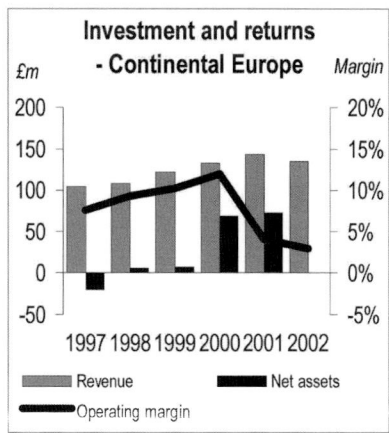

to Art D'Angelo who was Cordiant's finance director at the time. That improvement boosted the margins reported for the region as a whole from 6.3% to 14.7%. Such a recovery seems almost too good to have been true, and was swiftly followed by a collapse to 3.1% a year later.

The Healthworld acquisition was intended to add a considerable specialist healthcare capability to Bates. It was a fashionable area for specialisation and commanded a fashionable price of £162 million. In the year following acquisition Healthworld earned a post-tax profit of £9.6 million, representing a price/ earnings multiple of 16.9. Cordiant had bought at the top of the market and would be unlikely to enjoy the

level of future profits that would justify such a price.

Then came Lighthouse. It coincided with a strategic commit- ment to a multi-disciplined marketing services offering, often described as a "one-stop shop". The group had embraced this notion once before — in the early nineteen eighties when it was still Saatchi & Saatchi — only to discard it.

On paper the Lighthouse parcel of disparate companies would create a multi-disciplined capability overnight. It included several well-known brands such as the Fitch international design consultancy that had once enjoyed the status of a UK public company, but subsequently got into difficulties and parted with

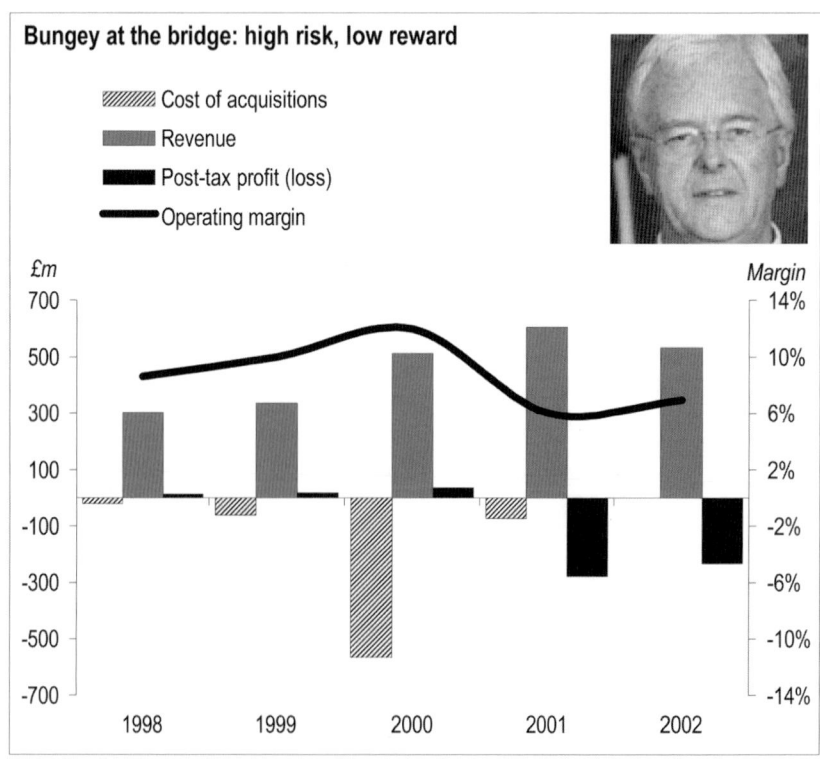

Bungey at the bridge: high risk, low reward

- Cost of acquisitions
- Revenue
- Post-tax profit (loss)
- Operating margin

founder Rodney Fitch. Also in the parcel was Financial Dynamics, a public relations consultancy that had enjoyed more owners than most.

The cost of Lighthouse was £315 million. Far from saving Cordiant from the rocks, it virtually ensured that would be the group's final destination. Cordiant's balance sheet immediately became vulnerable with short-term bank borrowings and other liabilities exceeding current assets by £128 million in December 2000. Goodwill (being the excess of acquisition costs over the tangible net assets acquired) was a whopping £712 million and had only £472 million in long-term shareholders' funds to support it.

The priority at Cordiant changed from expansion to survival. It succeeded in replacing its short term borrowings with $175 million of long term loan notes, but was soon having to face some painful realities. The Lighthouse deal was recognised as being worth far less than it cost and, by the end of 2001, Cordiant had made a £225 million provision for the permanent impairment of this and other acquisitions. Thereby half of Cordiant's shareholders' funds were wiped out.

The deteriorating financial position was alleviated to some extent by a mixed blessing bestowed by the French Publicis Groupe. Having just bought the former Cordiant agency of Saatchi & Saatchi, which shared joint ownership of Zenith Media Holdings with Cordiant, Publicis merged Zenith with its own Optimedia operation and diluted Cordiant's stake in the enlarged business to 25%. This allowed Cordiant to recognise a paper profit of £37 million on the restructuring. It also gave Publicis the right to buy out the remaining 25% soon.

Bates was now suffering from more client defections and lower spends. And several companies acquired by Cordiant wanted to buy themselves out — including George Patterson Bates, Financial Dynamics and Scholtz & Friends.

When Bungey left at the end of 2002, another £171 million was being written off the cost of acquisitions, bringing the cumulative financial result of five years of independence to a loss of £442 million.

For a company that showed so little financial acumen even in good times, it is ironic that the crumbling Cordiant Communications Group's final days of independence should have been subjected to so much meddling by a bunch of financial institutions with very little apparent understanding of — or concern for — the marketing industry, its clients or its employees.

WPP Group may not be the industry's favourite conglomerate, but at least it has plenty of experience and recognises the need for swift and effective action when another company is facing collapse. So what on earth was the inappropriately named Active Value Fund Managers trying to achieve by sinking millions of pounds of other people's money into an attempt to obstruct WPP's rescue plan? And why, with AV's support, did WestLB Panmure put together a thinly capitalised alternative rescue package that, at best, would probably have extended Cord-

Diary of a crumbling Cordiant: February-July 2003

4 February	Cordiant confirms it is in preliminary negotiations for sale of a stake in its Australian operations, including George Patterson Bates.
20 February	Cordiant announces further £155 million write-off re past acquisitions; confirms plans to dispose of Financial Dynamics International, its 77.3% stake in Scholz & Friends and a majority holding in its main Australian business. Banks re-negotiating terms.
25 April	Major client Domecq announces it will terminate contract with Cordiant from October.
29 April	Cordiant confirms tentative approaches which may lead to offer to buy the company.
1 May	Pre-tax loss of £228 million announced for 2002, on top of £271 million loss in previous year; auditors unable to confirm company remains a going concern; negotiations with bankers continue. Confirms intention to sell residual 25% stake in Zenith Optimedia Group to Publicis Groupe in January 2004.
12 May	Cordiant announces that discussions with potential buyers unlikely to produce offer compatible with current share price; also considering possible recapitalisation option; discussions with bankers and other lenders continue.
16 May	Agreement in principle with lenders to maintain support until 15 July 2003.
29 May	Agreement to sell 70% of main Australian business (The Communications Group) reached, subject to shareholder approval.
4 June	Press reports say major Cordiant shareholder Active Value Fund Managers is backing a plan put together with investment bankers WestLB to oust Cordiant's management, inject some new capital and install former Leo Burnett chairman Richard Wheatly with WestLB director Stephen Davidson as finance director.
9 June	Agreement to sell its 77.3% holding in Scholz & Friends reached subject to shareholder approval.
12 June	Cordiant calls shareholders' meeting for 28 June to approve disposal of Australian businesses and Scholz & Friends; trading conditions adversely affected by deteriorating financial position; major clients favour rescue by "industry partner".
13 June	Publicis Groupe rumoured to be working with Cordiant lender - US hedge fund Cerberus Capital Management - on plan to force a pre-packaged receivership that would result in Cordiant being broken up and Publicis acquiring the residual 25% stake in Zenith Optimedia Group for about £3 million instead of £75 million.
16 June	Trading in Cordiant shares suspended by the London Stock Exchange pending "clarification of its financial position".
17 June	WPP secures exclusive negotiating rights with Cordiant for acquisition by scheme of arrangement.
19 June	B&Q reported to have moved its business out of Bates UK to J Walter Thompson.
19 June	Cordiant and WPP announce terms agreed for (a) purchase of all £256 million of outstanding debt due to banks and loan noteholders except £79 million of notes held by Cerberus, and (b) subject to approval by 75% of shareholders, acquisition of all Cordiant's shares at approx 2.4p per share (totalling approx £10 million).
25 June	At request of Active Value, Cordiant convenes shareholders' meeting for 23 July to remove chairman Nigel Stapleton, chief executive David Hearn and finance director Andy Boland, and to replace them by Richard Wheatly and Stephen Davidson (as envisaged in WestLB rescue plan); also to allow Wheatly and Davidson to appoint un-named new chief executive; also to implement recapitalisation per WestLB plan and refrain from disposing of the company in any other way.
25 June	Active Value announces it has increased its shareholding to 25.13%, enabling it to block WPP's scheme of arrangement.
27 June	WPP purchases remaining £79 million of loan notes from Cerberus for £90 million, thereby holding all of Cordiant's outstanding debt
28 June	Shareholders approve sale of 70% of The Communications Group (completion due 30 June) and its 77.3% holding in Scholz & Friends (completed mid-July)
7 July	Agreement reached to sell FD International subject to shareholder approval.
8 July	Mme Nahed Ojjeh belatedly discloses 10.75% holding of Cordiant shares.
10 July	Active Value claims no contact with Mme Ojjeh.
11/12 July	Publicis denies any contact with Mme Ojjeh or further interest in Cordiant apart from a "few specific assets" including Zenith shares; rejects new Active Value proposal.
15 July	Lending facilities expire; shares de-listed to protect value of 25% investment in Zenith Optimedia Group; Wheatly says West LB plan no longer on offer.
23 July	WPP wins 75% shareholder vote. Directors removed. FD Intern'l sale approved.

iant's death throes by another year or so, with the added risk that Richard Wheatly would tarnish the closing years of an otherwise solid career?

The intervention of Publicis Groupe was far more obvious, with the opportunity to acquire the residual 25% shareholding in Zenith Optimedia Group on very favourable terms if Cordiant collapsed into receivership or administration.

Equally, the obstructive stance of the US hedge fund Cerberus Capital Management is understandable, if not particularly endearing. It saw the opportunity to maximise the exit price for its £79 million of loan notes by standing in the way of the FD International sale and holding out for a £90 million pay-off before leaving the stage.

So was Active Value simply

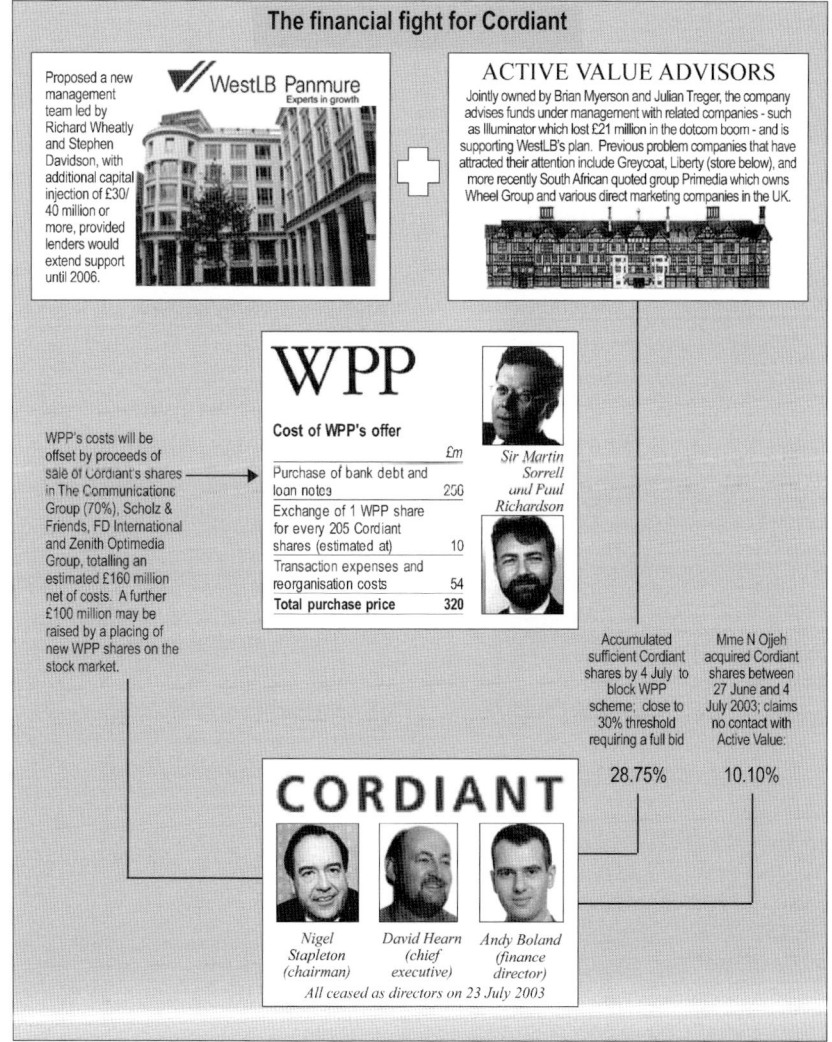

The financial fight for Cordiant

Proposed a new management team led by Richard Wheatly and Stephen Davidson, with additional capital injection of £30/40 million or more, provided lenders would extend support until 2006.

WestLB Panmure
Experts in growth

ACTIVE VALUE ADVISORS
Jointly owned by Brian Myerson and Julian Treger, the company advises funds under management with related companies - such as Illuminator which lost £21 million in the dotcom boom - and is supporting WestLB's plan. Previous problem companies that have attracted their attention include Greycoat, Liberty (store below), and more recently South African quoted group Primedia which owns Wheel Group and various direct marketing companies in the UK.

WPP

WPP's costs will be offset by proceeds of sale of Cordiant's shares in The Communications Group (70%), Scholz & Friends, FD International and Zenith Optimedia Group, totalling an estimated £160 million net of costs. A further £100 million may be raised by a placing of new WPP shares on the stock market.

Cost of WPP's offer

	£m
Purchase of bank debt and loan notes	256
Exchange of 1 WPP share for every 205 Cordiant shares (estimated at)	10
Transaction expenses and reorganisation costs	54
Total purchase price	**320**

Sir Martin Sorrell and Paul Richardson

Accumulated sufficient Cordiant shares by 4 July to block WPP scheme; close to 30% threshold requiring a full bid

Mme N Ojjeh acquired Cordiant shares between 27 June and 4 July 2003; claims no contact with Active Value:

28.75%   10.10%

CORDIANT

Nigel Stapleton (chairman)   David Hearn (chief executive)   Andy Boland (finance director)

All ceased as directors on 23 July 2003

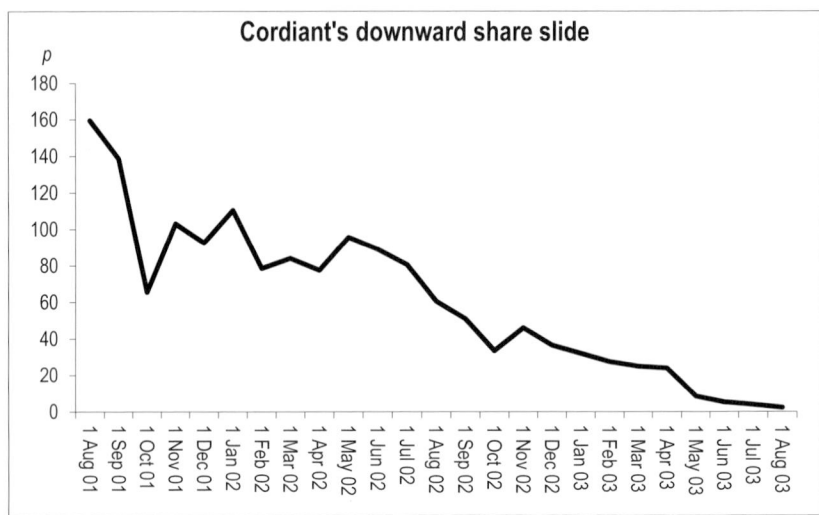

holding a pistol to **WPP**'s head? Or was it seriously hoping to win support for the WestLB plan — later withdrawn — possibly with help from the mysterious Nahed Ojjeh or Publicis? Either way it failed.

Publicis denied wanting anything except the residual stake in Zenith and **WPP** always made clear its intention to put Cordiant into receivership or administration, enabling it to buy back the businesses it wanted, if obstructed in obtaining support from 75% of the shareholders. Fortunately that proved unnecessary. In any event, receivership could not have preceded the de-listing of Cordiant's shares on 15 July without devaluing the price obtainable from selling its Zenith shares to Publicis from £75

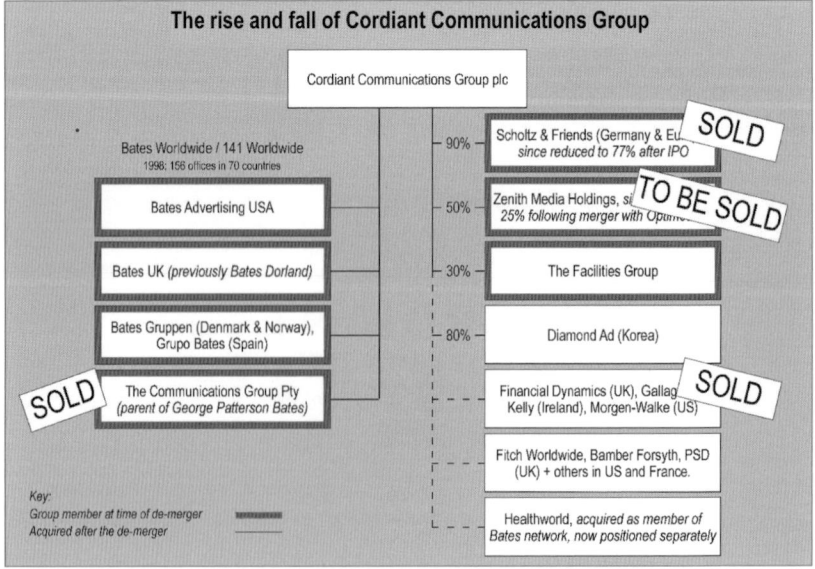

million to £3 million.

Could another party have grabbed Cordiant from a receiver? Unlikely. That would have required a quicker and better offer than the simple transfer of Cordiant's businesses to WPP in settlement of the outstanding £256 million debt.

10

Here Comes Hungry Hakuhodo

My visit to Tokyo in 2003 was memorable in several ways. Most obviously it was memorable for the opportunity to meet with senior executives of both Dentsu and Hakuhodo – at the time the two biggest marketing agencies in Japan. But it was also memorable for the earthquake I experienced while I was there. I had undergone a similar experience when visiting marketing agencies in Los Angeles several years earlier, but maybe that was just coincidence and I should not take it personally.

Like Dentsu, Hakuhodo's business was based almost entirely on Japanese clients many of which competed in global markets for the sale of their cars, TVs, fridges and many, many more consumer and industrial products. It was essential that their Japanese agencies could deliver marketing programmes that resonated with every culture and language throughout the world. To do that would require the agency to have either an international branch network or an association with existing agencies in overseas markets.

United States businesses and their marketing agencies had faced a similar export challenge in the past. But their task had been made rather easier because they were often following in the footsteps of the English speaking British Empire of which some of the US had once been a reluctant part.

We read in chapter 6 how Dentsu had initially addressed this challenge by taking minority shareholdings in indigenous marketing agencies around the world. But for one reason or another that type of arrangement had not really paid off. Maybe the local management's commitment was weakened after sale of a sizeable shareholding. Maybe there were tensions between what was expected in Japan and what was delivered or deemed most appropriate in the UK.

As we shall see, even Dentsu's more ambitious strategic partnership with Bcom3 and its western agencies Leo Burnett, D'Arcy Masius Benton & Bowles and Bartle Bogle Hegarty came unstuck when Publicis pulled the proverbial rug from beneath it.

I was impressed by the time and trouble taken by senior

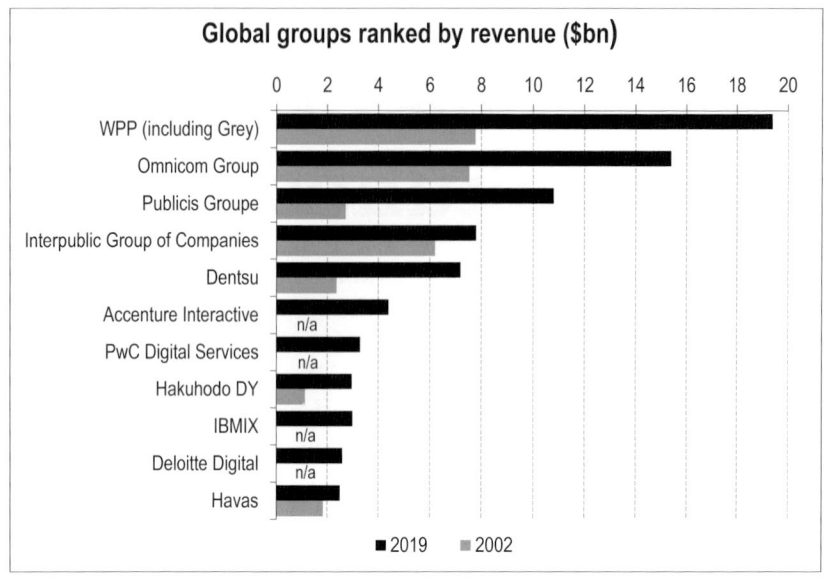

Global groups ranked by revenue ($bn)

executives at Hakuhodo to share with me the company's thinking about is development intentions. Without mentioning their arch rival Dentsu once, they spelt out how Hakuhodo planned to expand its domestic and global footprint. In essence, its plan was to enlarge its market share in Japan by combining with two other agencies and consolidating its domestic media buying power, to expand its footprint in Asia "significantly", and to make minority investments in four US and European locations.

Hakuhodo's expansion into wider Asia included the launch of Hakuhodo & Saigon Advertising Co in Vietnam in 2001. The group had already established a presence in China where its first office was opened in Beijing in 1980. In 2014 the group acquired

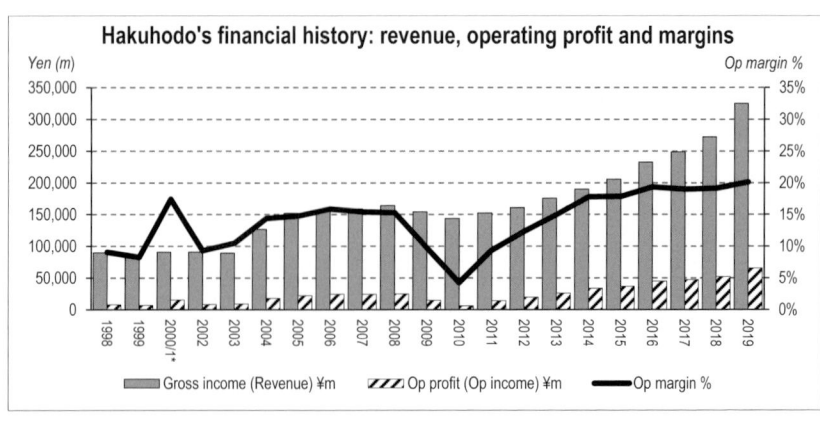

Hakuhodo's financial history: revenue, operating profit and margins

a 60% interest in the Hong Kong based communications agency Grebstad Hicks Communications. Then in 2017 it acquired 100% control of Integrated Communications Group in Singapore with operations in 12 Asia Pacific countries, including Malaysia, Korea, India, Indonesia and Thailand.

Most recently Hakuhodo acquired a majority stake in the publicly listed Taiwanese group Growww Media that owned the advertising agency United Communications Group, event organisers and retail designers Interplan Group and KY-Post, public relations consultancy Pilot Group and the digital agency Medialand.

Hakuhodo's approach to western markets was not dissimilar to that adopted initially by Dentsu. It had eschewed an acquisition of a major western network and so far has appeared to prosper

Hakuhodo's former Tokyo headquarters

without doing so. Like Dentsu, its initial investments in the UK had not been entirely plain sailing. Hakuhodo had acquired minority stakes in two UK domestic agencies, primarily to enable it to service its big Japanese clients that operated on a worldwide basis.

In September 1999 it had acquired a 50% shareholding in the highly profitable agency Group Nexus/H, based in Tunbridge Wells where Suzuki Motor Corporation was a major client The balance of the shares were retained by managing director Ian Norman. Fourteen years later Hakuhodo took total control and changed the name to Southpaw Communications.

In 2002, Hakuhodo had also acquired a 49% stake in the historically very profitable London agency Mustoe Merriman Levy Group Holdings for an estimated £6 million (if the selling shareholders' ongoing interest in the agency's property is excluded, as this remained outside Hakuhodo's ownership). Mustoe's management was able to preserve control of the group for as long as either Nick Mustoe or Andrew Levy remained an employee and shareholder, and provided the agency personnel continued to hold at least 10% of the group's ordinary shares.

However, the agency lost £0.8 million in 2006, attributed to a "loss of revenue from several Japanese clients". In 2007 it was bought by the Tribal Group and merged with Geronimo Communications, allowing Hakuhodo to sever its links. On the face of it, this was not a particularly rewarding investment from Hakuhodo's viewpoint.

Nevertheless, in the context of Hakuhodo's global balance sheet, these excursions into the UK involved relatively small investments that were unlikely to have done much harm if they had turned out to be less than a stunning success. In the event, Southpaw has continued to contribute a healthy return – reporting a post-tax profit of £327,000 in 2018.

Back in 2003, Hakuhodo's investments in the US market were limited to minority shareholdings in the Los Angeles agency Mendelsohn Zien and the New York agency McCaffery Ratner Gottlieb & Lane. After a few years it relinquished its stake in McCaffery, but took control of Mendelsohn Zien in 2009.

In 2015 Hakuhodo made two further investments in North America. One was the outright purchase of the US digital content production agency Digital Kitchen in Seattle, Chicago and Los Angeles. The other was the acquisition of a 100% interest in the Canadian integrated agency Sid Lee International along with a

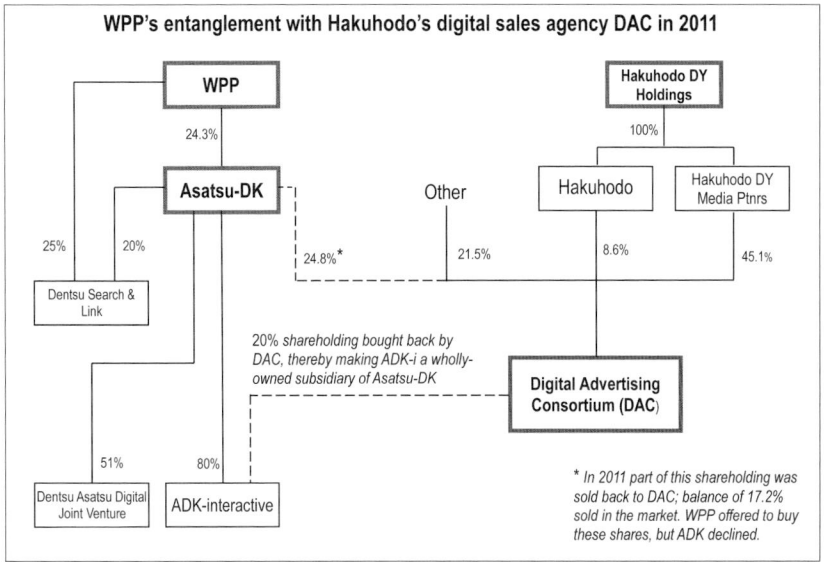

WPP's entanglement with Hakuhodo's digital sales agency DAC in 2011

49% stake in Sid Lee Architecture. It also backed the setting up of production company Stories International to exploit English language versions of Japanese stories in conjunction with Hollywood studios.

Meanwhile, back home in Japan, Hakuhodo's partnership with rival agency Asatsu-DK (ADK) in the Digital Advertising Consortium (DAC) had been unpicked, leaving Hakuhodo as the controlling partner. A few years later, in 2017, this transaction would be called into question by ADK's major shareholder — the British based WPP — leading to a very public falling out.

Faced with a plan by the US private equity investor Bain Capital to take ADK private, WPP sought every possible way to frustrate it. In a war of words, WPP claimed that ADK's disposal of its interest in DAC to Hakuhodo in 2011 had been at a lower price than could have been achieved, as this extract from *Marketing Services Financial Intelligence* revealed:

> Prior to the disposal of its DAC investment, ADK was a minority shareholder alongside Hakuhodo. Then the investing parties decided that they would prefer to pursue their digital ambitions independently. ADK began to look for a buyer for its DAC stake and WPP offered to buy it for a little over ¥4.7 billion.
>
> WPP told *Marketing Services Financial Intelligence* that ADK turned down its offer and instead accepted a lower amount of ¥3.95 billion (comprising a partial buyback by DAC with the

balance of the shares sold on the market). The price difference was the equivalent of £6.4 million. Since then the value of DAC's shares has increased almost eight-fold.

Hakuhodo would have been entitled to choose a buyer offering a lower price than **WPP** claimed to have offered, but in doing so it must be assumed that the company was able to explain why this was in the best interests of Hakuhodo's shareholders.

The success of Hakuhodo's development plan is probably best measured by the group's financial performance in recent years. Between 2002 (just before I met with the company in Tokyo) and 2019, its revenue grew by 163%. Revenues at Dentsu grew by 205% and at Publicis by 298% — both fuelled by major acquisitions. No other global agency did better.

Hakuhodo's post–tax profits have fluctuated over the period, reaching a low point in 2010 as revenue declined. But since then the group has shown a steady improvement in revenue, operating profit and profit margins as the chart at the start of this chapter showed.

By comparison, Dentsu, suffered a major hiccup in 2019 when it reported stagnating revenue, an operating loss of ¥3,358 million ($30.8 million) and a post–tax loss attributable to Dentsu share-holders of ¥80,893 million ($737 million) after bearing substantial Australian asset impairment charges, extensive rationalisation costs and a doubling of finance costs that together amounted to ¥135,500 million ($1.2 billion). Dentsu's links with Publicis have also been unwound since my original report and this may have reduced the inflow of business from the Publicis network.

In the circumstances Hakuhodo may feel reasonably satisfied with its performance over the last 15 years or so, although its thirst for growth may have contributed to a work environment that resulted in the arrest of a former staff member Masaki Nakajima in 2020 on suspicion of working with colleagues to defraud Hakuhodo of ¥700 million (£5 million) over four years by placing fake orders for commercials. So it would be premature to assume that the group has achieved all the goals set out in the business development plan articulated in 2003 and described more fully in the account below that was first published in November 2003.

S tanding in the shadow of Dentsu's dominating 48–storey Tokyo headquarters, Japan's second largest marketing services group is showing signs that it has ambitions to outshine, if not outsell, its bigger rival. It ranks 8th in the world. It's called Hakuhodo and it's tired of being number two. Can it build a bigger and better future?

It is probably no coincidence

Agency rankings in Japan - 2002	Billings Yen (bn)	Share %
1 Dentsu (group)[1]	1,463	31.0
2 Hakuhodo DY (group) [2]	961	20.4
3 Asatsu DK [3]	335	7.1
4 Tokyu Agency	184	3.9
5 I&S/BBDO [4]	97	2.1
6 East Japan Mktg & Communications	87	1.8
7 McCann Erickson [5]	66	1.4
8 Asahi-Kokoku-sha	57	1.2
9 Sogei	50	1.1
10 Delphys	49	1.0

1. Combines Dentsu Inc,Dentsu,Young & Rubicam, Dentsu Kyushi and Dentsu West Japan. 2. Comprises Hakuhodo, Daiko Advtg and Yomiko Advtg. 3 WPP Group has a minoirty shareholding. 4. Omnicom Group has a minority shareholding. 5. Member of The Interpublic Group of Companies.

Agency group world rankings - 2002 [1]	Revenue $ (m)
1 Omnicom Group	7,536
2 WPP Group [2]	6,570
3 The Interpublic Group of Companies	6,204
4 Publicis Groupe [3]	2,712
5 Dentsu (group) [4]	2,360
6 Havas	1,842
7 Grey Global Group	1,200
8 Hakuhodo DY (group) [5]	1,129
9 Asatsu-DK	339
10 TMP Worldwide	335

1. Sources: Advertising Age and companies' accounts. 2 Figures combined with Cordiant Communications Group. 3. Includes Bcom3 Group. 4. Dentsu Inc per March 2003 accounts. 5. Comprises Hakuhodo, Daiko Advtg and Yomiko Advtg.

that Hakuhodo has chosen to locate the head office of its newly enlarged group in a brand new skyscraper right next door to the Dentsu building.

All the signs are that Hakuhodo has decided it cannot stay as it was – lagging a long way behind Japan's market leader – and now intends at the very least to put a lot of clear daylight between it and the many other middle range agency groups that jostle for position below it.

Four recent initiatives are symptomatic of an expansionist strategy:
• In the domestic market, Hakuhodo is combining with two other agencies – Daiko Advertising (in which The Interpublic Group of Companies has an 18.4% share stake) and Yomiko Advertising – under a single holding company, bringing it closer in size to Dentsu and further ahead of Asatsu DK, in which WPP Group has a 20% stake.

• The enlarged group is combining all its media buying power into a single company Hakuhodo DY Media Partners.
• Significant investments have been made in Asia to expand its share of the market in its own "back yard".
• Minority stakes have been acquired in four strategic locations in Europe and the United States as part of a plan to provide an improved delivery network for Asian clients.

On top of these developments the group is known to have been contemplating making an initial public offering ("IPO") of its shares on the Tokyo stock market, possibly towards the end of 2004[1].

This would provide an additional source of acquisition finance – although the holding company's deputy general manager (finance)

1. The company was actually admitted to the Tokyo stock exchange in February 2005

Arata Hayashi is quick to point out that Hakuhodo has over $800 million of cash in its coffers at present.

A public market in Hakuhodo's shares would make it easier to acquire other businesses for shares instead of cash, and for the 10% of employees who hold shares to realise their investment in the future if they so wish. (It might also make Hakuhodo a takeover target.)

Yet, despite all these progressive initiatives, Hakuhodo has quite a hill to climb if it genuinely hopes to outmanoeuvre Dentsu. First, Dentsu has a dominating 31% penetration of the domestic market compared to about 20% achieved by the newly combined Hakuhodo DY group.

Secondly, Dentsu has an almost unbeatable deal with Publicis Groupe which gives it valuable access to inward referred work, as well as ready-made global delivery networks for its domestic clients.

And thirdly, Dentsu has established a stronger presence in "content" (programmes and music) and event marketing which has recently been augmented by a joint venture with Publicis called iSe.

Moreover, Hakuhodo has never achieved profit margins anywhere near as great as those achieved by Dentsu, apart from in 2000 when Hakuhodo underwent a capital restructuring and margins were distorted by a change in accounting date.

Normally operating margins have hovered around 9% to 10% (see chart below – well below the range of 15% to 20% usually achieved by Dentsu and the 13%-15% achieved by leading global groups like WPP and Omnicom Group.

Dentsu attributes its exceptionally high margins in part to added value services like content exploitation, merchandising and event marketing, but its massive share of the Japanese market must also yield media buying benefits – possibly enhanced by its shareholder links with two Japanese media groups.

Hakuhodo's recent financial results have also been hit by $165 million of extra costs accrued for items like employee retirement

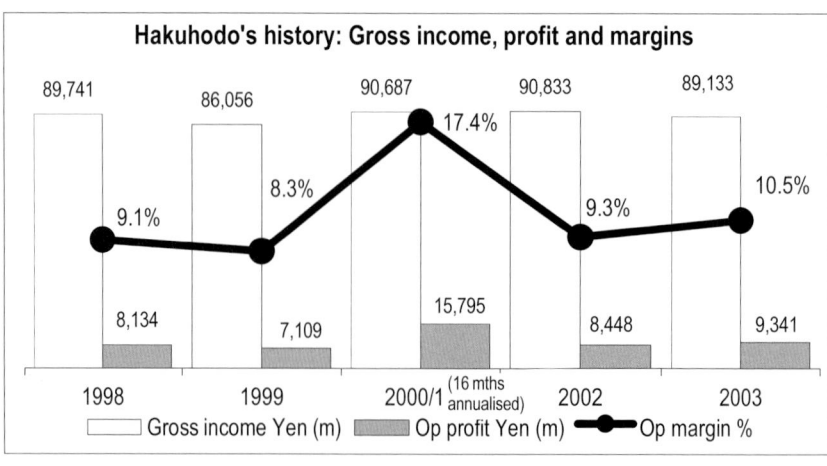

Hakuhodo's history: Gross income, profit and margins

89,741   86,056   90,687   90,833   89,133

17.4%

8.3%

9.1%   9.3%   10.5%

8,134   7,109   15,795   8,448   9,341

1998   1999   2000/1 (16 mths annualised)   2002   2003

☐ Gross income Yen (m)   ▨ Op profit Yen (m)   ●— Op margin %

Tomokazu Jimbo, Hakuhodo's board member responsible for global development.

benefits (some prompted by early retirement) and write-downs of under-performing companies.

Hakuhodo's Arata Hayashi acknowledges that its margins need to improve: "Hakuhodo has established a cost management division which has succeeded in reducing expenses", he says, "We believe the creation of Hakuhodo DY Holdings will provide opportunities to improve the margin in the future as the total amount of media placement becomes larger."

Clearly Hakuhodo's short-term strategy is to strengthen its Asian roots, while establishing a sufficiently viable global delivery capability to satisfy its domestic clients.

Tomokazu Jimbo, Hakuhodo's board member responsible for international developments, sees considerable growth potential in countries like Taiwan, Korea and China, albeit China has yet to yield healthy financial returns. He cites the cosmetic industry as an important growth sector and contrasts it with the more mature industries like cars and technology on which Japan built its post-war economic strength.

But much of the Asian economic growth is fuelled by US expansion into that market, and this may put Japanese agencies at a disadvantage when competing with global marketing groups.

However, Jimbo hints at a potential Japanese counter-weapon: "We have learned to be tolerant of various cultures and to bring out the best of each for the benefit of the whole."

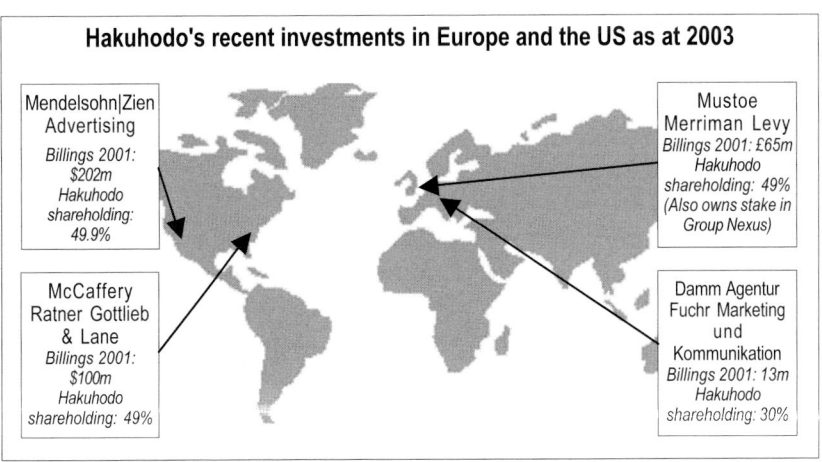

Hakuhodo's recent investments in Europe and the US as at 2003

Mendelsohn|Zien Advertising
Billings 2001: $202m
Hakuhodo shareholding: 49.9%

Mustoe Merriman Levy
Billings 2001: £65m
Hakuhodo shareholding: 49% (Also owns stake in Group Nexus)

McCaffery Ratner Gottlieb & Lane
Billings 2001: $100m
Hakuhodo shareholding: 49%

Damm Agentur Fuchr Marketing und Kommunikation
Billings 2001: 13m
Hakuhodo shareholding: 30%

Reflecting this philosophy, Hakuhodo has been flexible in the way it invests in Asia. In Korea, Malaysia and India it has made a parallel minority investment in a domestic agency alongside a directly controlled subsidiary. "Our international strategy is to put the client first", says Jimbo, implying that business structures must also be driven by market cultures.

Like many other Japanese businesses, Hakuhodo's previous experience of overseas expansion has been quite painful and, as a consequence, it wants to minimise its risk. But there is rarely any gain without some initial financial pain – even Dentsu's tie-up with Publicis cost it a cash outlay of over £300 million net of bond sale proceeds.

By taking minority shareholdings in a limited number of strategically located agencies, Hakuhodo not only reduces its financial exposure but also hopes to avoid the temptation to impose a Japanese advertising culture on alien audiences abroad.

Furthermore, it preserves a strong motivation among the controlling shareholders to continue to build a successful local agency from which all will benefit.

Jimbo claims it has no automatic right to acquire a controlling interest in the future, but it is almost inconceivable that an alternative investor would appear on the horizon when the current management shareholders want to retire.

With satellite agencies in the US, UK and Germany, and a limited presence in France, Hakuhodo is now looking to add Germany, Spain and Italy to its European network. In addition to establishing a delivery network sympathetic to local cultures, Hakuhodo claims to offer a far more integrated approach to client needs than has been available from traditional Western agencies (see chart).

Like Dentsu, it channels all its services through a single integrating account head. It also is far more actively engaged in producing and promoting programme content and

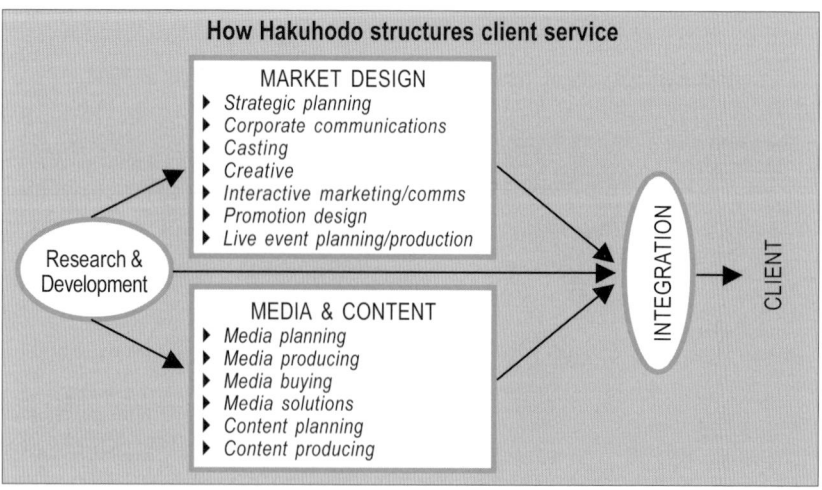

How Hakuhodo structures client service

MARKET DESIGN
▸ Strategic planning
▸ Corporate communications
▸ Casting
▸ Creative
▸ Interactive marketing/comms
▸ Promotion design
▸ Live event planning/production

Research & Development

MEDIA & CONTENT
▸ Media planning
▸ Media producing
▸ Media buying
▸ Media solutions
▸ Content planning
▸ Content producing

INTEGRATION

CLIENT

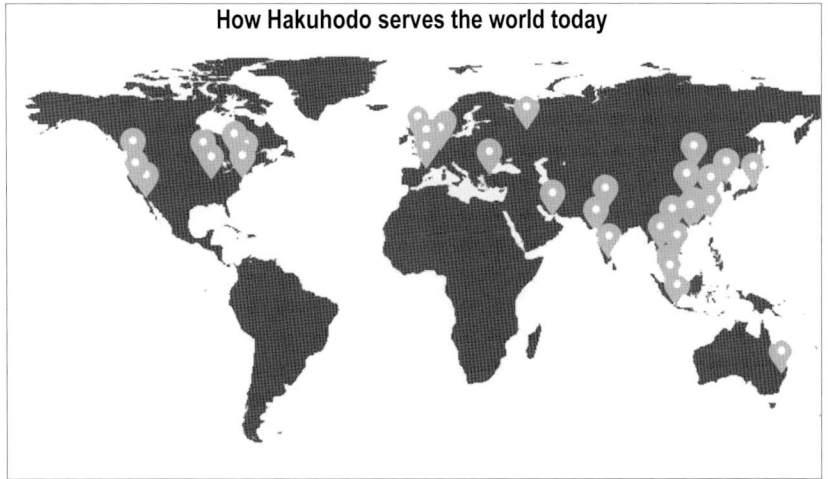

How Hakuhodo serves the world today

live events than its Western equivalents. (Interpublic is still smarting
from its painful foray into motor
sport.) But will all this enough to
propel Hakuhodo upwards in the
international league? Will its closer
affinity with Asian markets, its
backing for local agencies around the
world, and its deep involvement in
all aspects of the marketing mix win
work that might otherwise flow to the
global giants?

Winning profitable business
and international credibility remain
critical to Hakuhodo's future. If its
current strategy fails, it may be driven
into a more substantial relationship
with a Western group.

11

Leagas: Lessons to be Learned

Tim Delaney – a creative talent par excellence – was unwittingly responsible for the launch of my publication *Marketing Services Financial Intelligence* in December 2000.

Delaney was one of the generation of bright young entrepreneurial stars that launched a new wave of advertising agencies in the UK in the nineteen seventies and nineteen eighties. He is said to have started his career in advertising as agency messenger and began copywriting at the age of 19. He clearly had talent as he rose to became creative director at the London office of the US agency BBDO (Batten, Barton, Durstine & Osborn) at age 27 and managing director two years later.

He advised prime minister Jim Callaghan during the 1978-9 election campaign, writing and shooting the 10-minute party political broadcasts while still running the agency. In 1980 he joined forces with Ron Leagas to set up an independent agency, but Leagas departed six years later and set up another agency.

So how did Delaney become the unwitting midwife to *Marketing Services Financial Intelligence?*

One day I received a phone call from Caroline Marshall who at the time was editor of *Campaign,* the advertising industry's weekly magazine. She had been given an exclusive story about the Leagas Delaney agency having been sold to the Canadian Envoy Communications Group for £59 million. She was running a special feature on the deal but was seeking some indication of how profitable the agency had been, knowing that I compiled an

From "Campaign": 6 November 2000

campaign

November 06, 2000

Leagas Delaney sells to Canadians for £59m

By Camilla Palmer

Leagas Delaney, one of the last independent advertising agencies in London, has been bought by Canadian communications group Envoy Communications for £59m.

The deal is heralded by the agency's founder and creative director Tim Delaney as a step towards focusing more on digital and retail design work. Envoy specialises in technology as well as the more conventional disciplines of marketing and design.

Delaney said his clients -- which include Adidas, the BBC and Harrods -- wanted more emphasis put on digital campaigns and retail branding. Envoy's owns

*Tim Delaney: chairman
of Leagas Delaney*

annual survey of UK marketing agencies' performance. My reaction was one of surprise. As far as I could recall, Leagas Delaney had been incurring increasing losses in recent years, but I promised to check on the current position. My research confirmed that recollection.

I kept on asking myself: why would anyone pay £59 million for a loss-making business, even one headed by such a famous creative director as Tim Delaney? Then another question arose. On examining the Envoy offer document it emerged that the acquiring company had not yet secured the funds necessary to complete the purchase. Why would anyone sell their company without ensuring the buyer could pay for it?

And that was not all that I discovered. The purchase price was actually split – as indeed was typical at the time and remains so today – between an initial payment of £25 million and a deferred component geared to performance (an "earnout") that was capped at £34 million. But even if the initial payment was £25 million and not £59 million, why sell to someone who could not guarantee to deliver the cash?

I became increasingly unhappy about the inadequate information being disseminated by an industry whose livelihood should depend on its ability to communicate reliable messages about products, companies and people. Was there a niche for a financially orientated newsletter focussed on the marketing industry?

I put the idea to one of the wisest heads that the marketing industry has produced for many a year. I don't think I told him what had provoked my idea, but he was in favour anyway. So *Marketing Services Financial Intelligence* was launched in December 2000 with a front page headline "Envoy offers over £25m for unprofitable Leagas Delaney Group". This is how the report started:

> Canadian-based Envoy Communications Group has agreed to pay a minimum of £25 million to acquire all of the share capital of Leagas Delaney Group just 30 months after Tim Delaney and his colleagues bought back the company from Abbott Mead

BETWEEN THE BALANCE SHEETS

Vickers for an initial cash outlay of £100,000.

The deal represents quite a coup for its selling shareholders, given that Leagas Delaney Group lost £14,000 in its first trading period after the buy-out and lost another £133,000 in the year ended December 1999.

Clearly Envoy is expecting a better performance in 2000 and beyond.

This chapter tells how the life story of Leagas Delaney unfolded, how it was rescued from financial collapse by Abbott Mead Vickers in 1986, only to be bought back by the management on extended credit terms in 1998, how the much trumpeted sale to Envoy ended in tears, and how the company headed for financial collapse again in 2003, only to be reborn from the wreckage, leaving some creditors behind. The story was first published in *Marketing Services Financial Intelligence* in February 2004.

Since then Leagas Delaney has been run predominantly by Tim Delaney and long-term board colleague and planner Margaret Johnson who between them own all the shares in the parent company. Chris Campkin joined the board in June 2016 as group chief financial officer and left in September 2022. A certified accountant, Campkin's previous career included a six year spell at Bartle Bogle Hegarty.

The reborn Leagas Delaney had established majority-owned subsidiaries in London, Hamburg, Milan, Los Angeles, Cape Town and Shanghai. Until recently, it also had a subsidiary in Prague. But despite this apparently substantial international network, the group's balance sheet showed net assets of a relatively modest £1

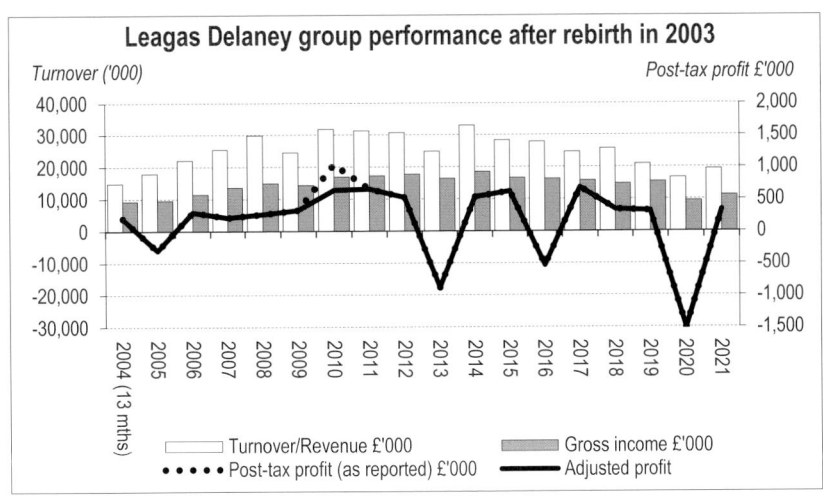

Leagas Delaney group performance after rebirth in 2003

million at 31 December 2021, funded by its shareholders. By that time the group had surrendered control of its Shanghai subsidiary and put its reborn London subsidiary into administration — with a deficiency estimated at £1.4 million in August 2020 — after losing a major client. The rump of that subsidiary was sold to another group company for £128,749.

Throughout this period the group's trading performance had remained chequered, as the chart[1] shows, despite a steadily improving trend in the early years after the agency's rebirth in 2003. The £0.9 million loss in 2013 was explained in these terms:

> 2013 continued to be a year of investment as the group developed its businesses in China and the US. Whilst these constitute the majority of the losses, group income fell as the London business was not able to fully replace all its income following some client losses early on in the year. Fee income outside the UK however continued to grow.

Another reason for that chequered performance was a £401,000 fraud that occurred prior to 2011 and was not discovered until 2013. The accounting rules require the impact of the fraud to be treated as an error in the original accounts for the period(s) in which it occurred, rather than increase the loss reported for 2013 when it was discovered. Thus the cost of the fraud (net of insurance recoveries) was reported as a prior year adjustment at 1 January 2011, indicating that the group's profits had been overstated in one or more periods prior to that date. Seemingly oblivious of this dent in the group's reserves, the group declared dividends of £758,000 in 2011.

In 2016 the group suffered a £0.5 million loss, due in part to a 70% fall in income in China attributed to "changes in the senior management team in the Shanghai office". This time the group decided prudently to cancel a previously declared dividend of £264,000. Along with many other companies, the group was hit by the Covid pandemic in 2020 which contributed towards a loss of £1.5 million for the year. Since then it has returned to profit.

If there are any lessons to be drawn, they are not new. First, creative talent must be translated into maintainable profits to command a healthy financial reward. Secondly, it is unwise to allow global creative ambitions, or the demands of global clients, to outweigh the company's financial resources. Thirdly, don't sell your company to someone without ensuring they have the cash to pay for it. Fourthly, try not to pay yourself regularly more than the

---

1. See page 129.

company earns, even if you think you are worth it.

And finally, make sure your management team includes someone with the nous to recognise these dangers and the strength of character to steer the team away from them.

From its inception The Leagas Delaney Partnership was obsessive about its creative reputation, reflecting Tim Delaney's own personality. But the agency's financial performance has been less impressive.

When at the end of 2003 Tim Delaney and his advisers decided to change the names of Leagas Delaney Group and Leagas Delaney London to the more anonymous TM and TM London, and to form two new companies to succeed them, they may have hoped the move would go unnoticed. If so, they will have been sadly disappointed.

Why would any company go through such a process? What was the financial condition of the London agency and the group at the time? And were creditors at risk?

As more information trickled out, it became known that administrators from Grant Thornton had been appointed at TM London and the group's European holding company Leagas Delaney Europe on 18 December, but not at the group's holding company.

The group described the move as "balance sheet restructuring to streamline our reorganization" now that it no longer had a US operation. But was there more to it than that? Certainly the financial background was less than reassuring.

The group had never made a profit during any year of independent ownership since the original partnership was absorbed into a limited company called The Leagas Delaney Partnership in 1985, although it did a little better under Abbott Mead Vickers' ownership between 1986 and 1998. And the group had never built up sufficient capital to support the type of agency Delaney aspired to own.

For example, when the agency was acquired by a sympathetic Abbott Mead Vickers in July 1986, its fragile balance sheet failed even to meet the credit recognition criteria of media owners. The delicate financial situation also made the company vulnerable to client losses, particularly as the agency had taken on a long-term property commitment in Shaftesbury Avenue.

Within the Abbott Mead stable,

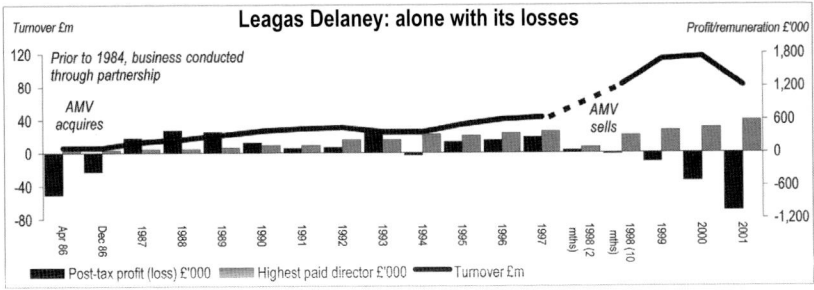

Leagas Delaney: alone with its losses

Turnover £m — Prior to 1984, business conducted through partnership — AMV acquires — AMV sells — Profit/remuneration £'000

Post-tax profit (loss) £'000 — Highest paid director £'000 — Turnover £m

Leagas Delaney London's net assets at 31 December 2001		
Short-term assets and liabilities:		£'000
Short-term liabilities		9,430
Less readily realisable ("current") assets		
Trade debtors	3,142	
Due from other group companies	4,046	
Other (including work in progress)	1,614	8,802
Net short-term (current) liabilities		628
Long-term assets		
Leasehold improvements	2,106	
Office furniture and motors	921	
Investment in internet software company Adgistics	526	
Other	20	3,573
Net assets		2,945

the only obvious strategic benefit of the acquisition was the scope it provided for avoiding client conflicts. Leagas Delaney provided a very modest financial return and none of the profit growth achieved by other top quality agencies in the period.

It therefore came as no great surprise when the management bought back the agency and its US associate for an initial cash payment of £100,000 in April 1998.

But the deal was not as simple as that. Having paid some £3 million to rescue the agency in 1986 and reinvested much of the fairly modest profits earned thereafter, Abbott Mead seemed reluctant to sell it back at a significant loss notwithstanding that it had already written down the original £3 million investment to nil. Instead a price of £4 million was placed on Leagas Delaney.

The difference between this amount and the £100,000 paid in cash was satisfied to the extent of £1.2 million by issuing Abbott Mead with redeemable preference shares in the newly established acquisition vehicle (Leagas Delaney Group — now TM Limited). The remaining £2.7 million of the purchase price was discharged by issuing 5% loan notes secured on Leagas Delaney's assets. In other words, Abbott Mead had sold the business on deferred terms.

The loan and related interest was to be repaid by annual instalments, each payment to be based on 2.5% of gross profit, with any underpayment being settled on 6 April 2008.

But the Leagas Delaney Group was losing money — £1.7 million between the buy-back and December 2001 - so it was excused the repayment due in 2001 and the terms were then amended so that the payments due in April 2002 and April 2003 were delayed until December in each year. Thereafter each annual payment would become due in March up to and including March 2009.

With hindsight it seems incomprehensible that Canadian-based Envoy Communications contemplated buying the loss-making group in 2001 for between £25 million and £60 million. But no-one can blame the shareholders for pursuing what they may have seen as the best prospect for cashing in on the agency's creative reputation.

The principal causes of the post buy-out losses are not too hard to detect. The agency had embarked on an international expansion programme — initially to support its work for Adidas — without an adequate capital base. The expansion therefore had to be funded predominantly by

Terms of the AMV purchase and sale	
What AMV invested	*£'000*
Goodwill at cost	3,075
Other net tangible assets sold back at book value	1,048
Total cost of assets sold back to management	**4,123**
Less: Goodwill written off during AMV's ownership	-3,075
Book value of assets sold	1,048
What AMV received for the sale back to management in 1998	*£'000*
Cash paid by management	100
Preference shares credited to AMV	1,200
5% loan notes due to AMV	2,700
Buy-back price recognised in accounts of AMV and LDG	**4,000**

Diary of Envoy deal failure	
2000 Nov 6	Envoy announces bid - Envoy share price $7.90
Dec	*Marketing Services Financial Intelligence* reveals Leagas' lack of profit record, deal geared to Envoy $8 share price and conditional on Envoy raising cash.
Dec 20	Envoy share price "low" of $3.06.
2001 Feb	Envoy says deal completion, originally planned for January, would be delayed until March.
Mar 6	Envoy says deal will complete in April.
April 6	*Campaign* reports trouble at Leagas' US subsidiary.
May 30	Envoy tells *MSFI*: "Both parties are intent on completing the deal."
June 25	Deal collapses - share price $3.26

prepaid fees from clients. That global development was accompanied by a dabble in the American dotcom bubble and the painful consequences when it burst.

This in turn prompted the disposal of Leagas Delaney San Francisco to its management which now trades as BuderEngel & Friends. But rumours suggest that Leagas Delaney remained financially exposed in the US – possibly in relation to property it had occupied.

The structure of the Leagas Delaney group (see chart)[1] is such that any financial exposure in the US could not affect the European businesses unless there were irrecoverable intra-group debts due to them or they had given cross guarantees to the holding company and/or its now dormant US subsidiary.

All we know at present is that at December 2001 Leagas Delaney London had guaranteed some

obligations of, and was owed over £4 million by, other group companies which may, or may not, have included the US business. Up to that date the London agency on its own was actually making a profit. Indeed it felt sufficiently confident to move into new premises in Alfred Place at a rent of £1.3 million a year, while remaining potentially exposed under the previous lease it had assigned.

Then the agency lost some valuable accounts that included Adidas, Harrods and the BBC. Despite trading profitably, the London agency's balance sheet was not strong (see table opposite). At December 2001 it had short-term ("current") liabilities of £9.4 million, but only £8.8 million of readily realisable ("current") assets — a shortfall in excess of £600,000. And, as already explained, over £4 million of those assets were debts due from other group companies.

Furthermore, most of the longer term assets would be difficult to turn

1 See chart on p.131

into immediate cash, such as the £2.1 million spent on leasehold improvements and an upwardly revalued investment of £526,000 in the internet software business Adgistics.

Given a poor financial performance, some business owners would try to minimise their remuneration packages so as to help build up the capital base. But that was not the case at Leagas Delaney. By 2001 Tim Delaney's remuneration had reached £584,000[1] — doubtless influenced by his own market worth and the need to repay unlawful loans from the company which had grown to £134,000 by the start of that year. Earlier Delaney had run up an entirely lawful loan of £168,000 from Abbott Mead Vickers while it was the parent company.

So with two group companies now in administration where do the London agency's creditors stand? We can only speculate about the financial condition of TM London, as it is now called, until the administrators can provide a statement of affairs.

Promised "within weeks rather than months", the statement will show what the new Leagas Delaney-London has paid to acquire the business and whether that is enough to pay off all the creditors. If

not, the successor business may find goodwill in short supply[2]. And who will provide the capital necessary to secure a stable future for the reborn company?

Some comfort may be gained from the fact that Lloyds-TSB Bank appears to have acquiesced with the restructuring, taking a charge over the assets of the new Leagas Delaney - London. But is that enough to create the required level of confidence in the successor business?

There is little evidence that the transferring of an existing business to a newly formed company — commonly described as a "phoenix" — has been successful with other advertising agencies in the past. Even if the creditors of the London agency are eventually paid in full, their confidence — along with that of clients and staff — will have been shaken.

The Hyundai account — which with Nationwide Building Society comprised the two most important clients — was already under threat when the administrators arrived and has since voted with its feet. Nationwide too may be feeling a little unsure about the future.

1. See chart on p.131.

2. In February 2004, the administrators issued a statement of affairs showing a deficiency of £3.5m as regards creditors after selling the business and paying off the bank

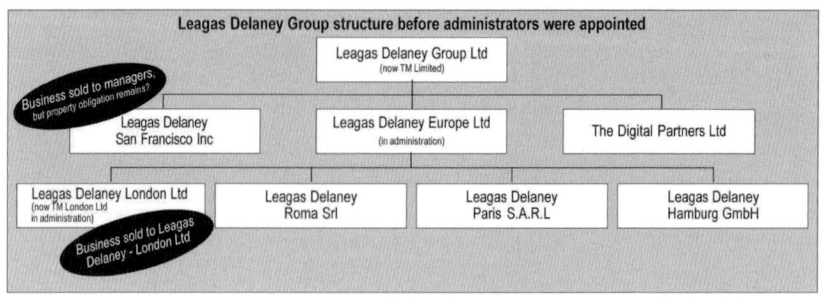

Leagas Delaney Group structure before administrators were appointed

Leagas Delaney Group Ltd
(now TM Limited)

Business sold to managers, but property obligation remains?

Leagas Delaney San Francisco Inc

Leagas Delaney Europe Ltd
(in administration)

The Digital Partners Ltd

Leagas Delaney London Ltd
(now TM London Ltd in administration)

Leagas Delaney Roma Srl

Leagas Delaney Paris S.A.R.L

Leagas Delaney Hamburg GmbH

Business sold to Leagas Delaney - London Ltd

But the measure of a successful advertising agency is not just about finance and profit – or lack of it. We are bound to ask whether personalities have played a part in bringing Leagas Delaney to its present uncertain condition. How will prospective financiers judge the track record of Tim Delaney as a business manager? He has been accused of being a control freak and yet hard to control. Was that why his founding partner Ron Leagas showed immense reluctance to hold less than a controlling interest in the next agency he started?

And why did senior executives like Bruce Haines, Jerry Fielder and Eric McClean also eventually move elsewhere? History shows that, in financial terms, the agency was at its most stable during the period when it was owned by Abbott Mead Vickers (see chart[1]). For some of that time Bruce Haines would have been

1. See page 131

able to call on his former employer Abbott Mead for support when tough decisions were required.

So what does the future hold? No-one doubts Delaney's creative prowess, and his reputation has attracted many young aspiring creative directors to join the agency. But if his restructuring gamble doesn't pay off, his business credibility will be at rock bottom. And he is not getting any younger, although that need not be a handicap to creative achievement.

Maybe the most elegant way forward would be to fold the Leagas Delaney creative spirit into a bigger agency's envelope, where Delaney himself can concentrate on what he does best and allow others to manage the business.

It's a tough situation to face, but there will always be past awards to savour and hopefully a few more to come in the future.

As highly profitable media buying agencies faced up to increasing competition, how strong were their balance sheets and were they still credit worthy?

12

Media Men Under the Microscope

In chapter 5 I recounted how the media buying industry evolved from its traditional home within advertising agencies. I also touched on some of the ways by which media buyers could augment their income, for example by earning undisclosed rebates from media owners. Those concealed rebates had caused considerable embarrassment when they were exposed at Interpublic, as described in chapter 4.

For some years, media owners in the UK had set out a series of criteria that media buying agencies would have to satisfy if they wanted to avoid paying in advance for advertising space they wished to buy. But during that period many of the independent media buying agencies had been swallowed by the global groups and were independent no longer. One consequence was that any media buying agency that failed to meet the solvency tests laid down by media owners might seek to offer a guarantee from its parent company.

In January 2003, *Marketing Services Financial Intelligence* took its first look at the balance sheets of media buying agencies and, where applicable, the holding companies of the larger groups that had absorbed them. It discovered that only five out of 20 major media buying agencies satisfied the prevailing credit worthiness criteria laid down by television companies at December 2001. All of those agencies were privately-owned independents. The table highlights the problems that were facing agencies owned by multi-nationals Omnicom Group, The Interpublic Group of Companies, WPP, Publicis Groupe, Aegis Group, Grey Global Group and Havas, none of which had both positive shareholders' funds and an acceptable debt/equity ratio at 30 June 2002 after deducting intangible assets like goodwill.

Only two of those groups, namely Havas and Publicis, satisfied the other key requirement – to have a surplus of net current assets. A surplus of net current assets is intended to ensure that both the agency and its parent group can pay all their short-term liabilities when they become due. Unlike the parent groups, most

Media buyers' credit status

At 31 December 2001 (or subsequent year end)	Indepen-dent or group?[1]	NCA/ Op exps[2] (weeks)	External Debt/ Equity ratio[3]	Passes net current asset and debt/equity ratio tests? Individually	Group
All Response Media	Havas	25.4	No net debt	☑	☒
BLM Holdings	I	1.1	No net debt	☑	
Brand Connection[4]	IPG	6.9	No net debt	☑	☒
Brilliant Ind Media Specialists	I	Neg NCA	126.2%	☒	
Carat Group UK	Aegis	6.3	No net debt	☑	☒
Initiative Media London	IPG	3.3	No net debt	☑	☒
John Ayling & Associates	I	49.5	No net debt	☑	
Manning Gottlieb OMD	Omn	Neg NCA	No net debt	☒	☒
MediaCom UK	Grey	Neg NCA	No net debt	☒	☒
Mediaedge:cia International	WPP	79.9	No net debt	☑	☒
Mediahead	WPP	6.9	No net debt	☑	☒
Media Planning	Havas	11.4	No net debt	☑	☒
Mediavest (Manchester)	I	2.7	No net debt	☑	
Mindshare Media UK	WPP	5.7	No net debt	☑	☒
OMD UK[5]	Omn	657.6	No net debt	☑	☒
PHD Media	Omn	50.7	No net debt	☑	☒
Starcom Motive	Publicis	12.0	No net debt	☑	☒
TCS Media (Planning & Buying)	I	14.7	No net debt	☑	
Walker Media	I	23.9	90.4%	☑	
Zenith Optimedia Group	Publicis	Neg NCA	No net debt	☒	☒

Notes: 1. Independently owned (I) or subsidiary of multinational group shown. 2. Net current assets expressed in terms of the number of weeks' operating costs they would cover ("Neg NCA" = Negative net current assets). 3. "Debt" = External debt (excluding intra-group debt) net of cash balances; "Equity" = Shareholders' funds net of intangible assets. 4. Year ended 31 December 2000. 5. Figures distorted as staff costs paid by another group company

individual agencies had a surplus and the table shows how many weeks' operating costs could be paid out of that surplus.

Not surprisingly, media owners were starting to look beyond each individual media buying agency to explore the financial health of its parent group. And there were mutterings about demanding prepayment of advertising costs unless better security could be provided. After all, a guarantee from a parent company was only as good as the balance sheet of that company. Some major groups had sought to satisfy media owners by entering into individual arrangements to provide additional security – such as the use of escrow accounts whereby clients' monies are held in a separate bank account on their behalf until the media obligation is discharged. Bank guarantees had also been provided by some groups.

In the circumstances it seemed timely to take another look behind the accounts of media buying agencies in the UK and to explore more fully how they were financed. The resulting report

that accompanies this chapter was published in *Marketing Services Financial Intelligence* in 2004 at which time the credit criteria were:
- Positive net current assets.
- A pre-tax profit for each of the last two years.
- Shareholders' funds greater than £1 million.
- Debt/equity ratio < 1:1

Suspicions about the transparency of media transactions continued to simmer under the surface and were given a further airing in the US by a report from the Association of National Advertisers claiming that "non-transparent practices" were still found to exist across the spectrum of agency media entities in 2016.

It provoked a sharp response from Publicis Groupe: "The ANA has failed its members, advertisers, agencies and the entire industry by releasing a report that relies on allegations about situations involving unnamed companies and individuals to make broad, unsubstantiated and unverifiable assertions", the company said, adding that the document had hidden behind suspicions and anonymity rather than encouraging real accountability, despite "repeated urging by Publicis Groupe and others in the industry to include names and sources in its report".

The report was prepared for the ANA by K2 Intelligence, an investigative, compliance, and cyber defence services firm. Among the scathing accusations of non-transparent business practices employed by US agencies made in the ANA report are these, some of which may or may not have been contract-compliant:
- Cash rebates made by media owners to agencies based on the amount spent on media were not passed on to advertisers and some advertisers were unaware of any rebates returned.
- Rebates were used to provide free media inventory credits.
- Rebates were structured as "service agreements" in which media owners paid agencies for non-media services such as low-value research or consulting initiatives that were often tied to the volume of agency spend and that these services "were being used to obscure what was essentially a rebate".
- Mark-ups on media sold through principal transactions (those where the media was bought by the media agencies as "principal" and then sold on to clients) ranged from approximately 30% to 90% and media buyers were sometimes pressured or incentivised by their agency holding companies to direct client spend to this media, regardless of whether such purchases were in the clients' best interests.

- Dual rate cards were used whereby agencies and holding companies negotiated separate rates with media owners when acting as principals from those when acting as agents.
- Non-transparent business practices were found in the US market where agencies hold equity stakes in media owners/ suppliers. In response to the report, the ANA said it is developing suggested contract language to address media-buying transparency.

In addition, the ANA commissioned Ebiquity and Firm Decisions to develop guidelines and recommendations for ANA members to consider based on K2 Intelligence's findings.

In its statement, Publicis challenged the ANA report's authors to come forward and state their case if they have evidence of wrongdoing by specific agencies: "The unsubstantiated claims are already causing serious damage to the reputation of the industry and endangering the most valuable component of the agency-advertiser relationship: trust", the company said.

One year later, a new ANA survey found that a majority of its members had taken steps to address the transparency issue.

When the media buyers carved out an independent place in the industry some 30 years ago, few envisaged the power and profit they would accumulate. Or that their success would have prompted a growth in media consultancies and auditors.

As highly profitable media buying agencies face up to increasing competition by consolidating their buying power into fewer companies, how strong are their balance sheets

The UK media buying agencies ranked by turnover in 2002

	Year end	Turnover Latest £'000	Growth %	Gross income Latest £'000	Growth %	Pre-tax profit contribution from Trading %	Interest %	Other %	Total £'000	Growth %	Latest margins Gross %	Op profit %	NCA⁵/ Op exps (weeks)	Est debt/ Equity ratio
Aegis Media UK & Ireland	31/12/02	929,475	2.4%	59,372	9.2%	57.2%	42.8%	0.0%	25,887	10.9%	6.4%	24.9%	10.6	No net debt
Zenith Optimedia¹	31/12/02	742,120	9.6%	14,949	-3.3%	76.6%	23.4%	0.0%	4,802	60.8%	2.0%	24.6%	12.9	-1.62
MediaCom UK	30/09/03	601,210	16.0%	27,628	20.4%	65.2%	34.6%	0.2%	7,454	24.3%	4.6%	17.6%	3.2	No net debt
Mindshare Media UK	31/12/02	463,582	5.8%	23,788	3.3%	81.9%	18.1%	0.0%	3,981	62.9%	5.1%	13.7%	24.5	No net debt
Starcom Motive	31/12/02	442,539	14.9%	16,630	3.0%	86.7%	13.3%	0.0%	5,830	6.1%	3.8%	30.4%	17.5	No net debt
OMD UK²	31/12/02	343,157	529.3%	13,942	443.8%	83.1%	16.9%	0.0%	3,318	52.1%	4.1%	19.8%	11.0	No net debt
PHD Media	31/12/02	291,694	2.0%	16,413	-2.9%	72.8%	27.2%	0.0%	6,211	-6.6%	5.6%	27.6%	72.1	No net debt
Initiative Media London	31/12/02	273,211	22.4%	13,730	13.8%	-54.8%	154.8%	0.0%	283	-34.2%	5.0%	-1.1%	7.7	No net debt
Media Planning	31/12/02	205,134	-11.6%	13,845	30.1%	77.7%	22.3%	0.0%	4,002	27.7%	6.7%	22.5%	12.3	No net debt
Manning Gottlieb OMD	31/12/02	198,961	0.7%	10,360	3.0%	84.8%	15.0%	0.2%	3,233	30.3%	5.2%	26.4%	1.1	No net debt
Walker Media	31/12/02	128,199	1.3%	5,044	-1.3%	73.5%	31.7%	-5.2%	1,606	3.3%	3.9%	23.4%	26.3	No net debt
Mediavest (Manchester)³	28/02/03	125,901	7.6%	8,982	15.7%	74.5%	24.1%	1.4%	2,387	22.7%	7.1%	19.8%	3.9	No net debt
Brand Connection	31/12/02	84,634	-2.7%	3,210	-25.3%	121.6%	-21.6%	0.0%	-501	-36.0%	3.8%	-19.0%	Neg NCA	No net debt
Brilliant Independent Media Specialists	31/03/03	75,890	-1.3%	3,847	-1.6%	98.1%	1.9%	0.0%	645	88.4%	5.1%	16.5%	1.5	No net debt
TCS Media (Planning & Buying)	31/05/03	64,014	-17.4%	3,216	-16.1%	-25.8%	104.8%	21.0%	67	-67.6%	5.0%	-0.5%	18.1	No net debt
BLM Holdings	31/05/03	59,765	48.3%	6,601	37.4%	73.3%	26.7%	0.0%	467	-21.8%	11.0%	5.2%	1.6	No net debt
John Ayling & Associates	31/12/02	56,507	-1.0%	2,975	-4.2%	41.0%	59.2%	-0.2%	419	-22.8%	5.3%	5.8%	37.9	No net debt
All Response Media	31/12/02	47,475	46.9%	3,255	46.8%	90.5%	9.5%	0.0%	1,280	87.5%	6.9%	35.6%	28.6	No net debt
Mediahead Communications⁴	31/12/02	45,287	-24.6%	1,767	-27.9%	71.0%	29.0%	0.0%	379	-55.0%	3.9%	15.2%	1.1	No net debt
Mediaedge:cia International Investments	31/12/02	41,425	-42.3%	2,989	-12.4%	-278.0%	378.0%	0.0%	79	102.1%	7.2%	-7.4%	Neg NCA	No net debt
Total		**5,220,182**	**11.9%**	**252,543**	**12.2%**	**68.6%**	**31.4%**	**0.0%**	**71,829**	**25.4%**	**4.8%**	**19.5%**	**13.5**	No net debt

1. Combines Optimedia with Zenith Media in UK. 2. Includes BMP DDB media for first time in 2002. 3. Owned independently, despite name. 4. Lost biggest client in 2003 and ceased trading thereafter. 5. "NCA" = Net current assets, being current assets less current liabilities

BETWEEN THE BALANCE SHEETS

and are they still credit worthy?

If left to themselves, media buying agencies should never be a credit risk. They're profitable (see table), they normally collect cash from clients before paying media owners, and they usually have balance sheets that are prudently managed.

At the end of 2002 (the most recent date for which meaningful figures are available), the cash piling up in the top 20 buying agencies' coffers amounted to a massive £385 million net of any borrowings. Only two agencies owed more than was covered by cash in the bank and the amounts owed to them, so the sector was pretty stable financially. But

there will always be exceptions.

If a media buyer makes an irresponsible judgement – such as committing to a media booking without taking adequate steps to ensure a client can pay – then the agency could easily come unstuck because the gross media cost (and therefore the write-off if the client defaults) would be far greater than the modest commission that would have enhanced its profit and loss account.

So safeguards are necessary, particularly when the buying agency is owned by a global conglomerate that could grab money from the agency's cash pile and whose own balance sheet is less solidly constructed.

How UK media buying agencies met the credit tests in 2003

	Year end	Parent, if not independ-net	Positive net current assets	Pre-tax profit for last 2 years	Share-holders' funds > £1m	Debt/ equity ratio < 1:1	Parent group compl-iance[4]
Aegis Media UK/Ireland	31/12/2002	Aegis Gp	OK	OK	OK	OK	*Fail*
All Response Media	31/12/2002	Havas	OK	OK	OK	OK	*Fail*
BLM Holdings[5]	31/05/2003		OK	Small[5]		OK	n/a
Brand Connection[2]	31/12/2002	Interpublic	*Fail*	*Fail*	*Fail*	OK	*Fail*
Brilliant Ind Media Specialists [5]	31/03/2003		OK	Small[5]		OK	n/a
Initiative Media London	31/12/2002	Interpublic	OK	OK	OK	OK	*Fail*
John Ayling & Associates	31/12/2002		OK	OK	OK	OK	n/a
Manning Gottlieb OMD	31/12/2002	Omnicom	OK	Small[5]		OK	*Fail*
MediaCom UK	30/09/2003	Grey	OK	OK	OK	OK	*Fail*
Mediaedge:cia International Inv	31/12/2002	WPP	*Fail*	*Fail*	*Fail*	OK	*Fail*
Mediahead Comms[3]	31/12/2002	WPP	OK	OK	*Fail*	OK	*Fail*
Media Planning	31/12/2002	Havas	OK	OK	OK	OK	*Fail*
Mediavest (Manchester)[3]	28/02/2003		OK	Small[5]		OK	n/a
Mindshare Media UK	31/12/2002	WPP	OK	OK	OK	OK	*Fail*
OMD UK	31/12/2002	Omnicom	OK	OK	OK	OK	*Fail*
PHD Media	31/12/2002	Omnicom	OK	OK	OK	OK	Fail
Starcom Motive	31/12/2002	Publicis	OK	OK	OK	OK	*Fail*
TCS Media (Planning & Buying)	31/12/2002		OK	Small[5]		OK	n/a
Walker Media	31/12/2002		OK	OK	OK	OK	n/a
Zenith Optimedia[1]	31/12/2002	Publicis	OK	OK	OK	*Fail*	*Fail*
Sample as a whole:			**OK**	**OK**	**OK**	**OK**	

1. Combines Zenith and Optimedia accounts. 2. Brand Connection was formerly known as MBS Media.. 3. Ceased trading subsequently. 4. At 31 December 2003 after deducting intangible assets from shareholders' funds. 5. Small agencies need only £100,000 shareholders' funds and no profit record, but a solvency statement is required instead.

And that's what caused the furore last year. For a long time media owners had accepted guarantees from media agencies' global parents or the use of escrow accounts through which the clients' money travelled en route to the media owner. But media owners began to doubt the value of parent company guarantees, given the balance sheet ratios of some groups.

On top of that they got cold feet about escrow accounts, prompted (it now transpires) by a rather broad-brush and emotive interpretation of a court case outside the industry.

So the terrestrial TV companies demanded stronger parent company balance sheets, bank guarantees or prepayment instead. Those demands were deemed unreasonable, not least because of the substantial cost of bank guarantees.

Agency chiefs retaliated by taking the TV companies to the Office of

How were the media police performing?

While the current focus may be on media buyers and whether they are sufficiently transparent in their accountability, it is also interesting to look at the financial performance of those who offer advertisers various forms of advice and consultancy aimed at providing greater reassurance about the value for money being achieved.

Ironically, most of those companies — apart from the two biggest — are very shy about disclosing anything meaningful about their own financial performance. Some of them are simply very small, and all of them (see list below) are able to hide behind the legal right to file only very abbreviated accounts at Companies House.

The two biggest are both regarded primarily as media "auditors". They are Media Audits Group and BCMG (better known as Billetts). But their financial characteristics are markedly different. BCMG grew faster than Media Audits in 2003, and earned better profit margins while doing so. The "bottom line" post-tax profit of £224,000 reported by BCMG compares with a loss of £37,000 suffered by Media Audits. BCMG was just more efficient.

Media Audits' balance sheet is also much weaker than that of BCMG, presumably because of the funding costs associated with its management buyout. At 30 June last year Media Audits had total borrowings of £5.4 million and a deficiency of shareholders' funds. BCMG had borrowings of a mere £200,000 and a £1.5 million surplus of shareholders' funds.

Media consultants' profitability

	Year ended	Latest turnover (revenue)[1] UK £'000	Foreign £'000	Total £'000	Growth %	Operating profit Latest £'000	Growth %	Operating margin Latest %	Previous %	Post-tax profit Latest £'000	Previous £'000	Number of employees	Per employee Revenue £	Op profit £
Media Audits Group	30/6/03	3,749	6,365	10,114	+11.0	410	-42.3	4.1	7.8	-37	87	133	76,045	3,083
BCMG	30/4/03	5,140	578	5,718	+17.2	390	+176.6	6.8	2.9	224	81	70	81,686	5,571

1. Turnover equates to gross income (or revenue) for these companies as they do not have any bought-in direct costs.

Balance sheet strength of media consultants

	Year ended	Average net debt[2] Short-term £'000	Long-term £'000	S/holders' ave funds £'000	Debt/ equity %	Return on total cap %	Ave debtors Days[1]
Media Audits Group	30/6/03	752	4,512	-427	Deficit	-1.7	74
BCMG	30/4/03	128	31	1,360	13.6	23.8	75

1. After excluding VAT element. 2. Negative amount means net cash instead of debt.

Media consultants not publishing profit and loss accounts

Auditstar
European Media Management
Fairbrother
Michaelides & Bednash
Naked Communications
Yershon Media

Fair Trading, complaining about their alleged abuse of monopolistic powers. Since then tempers seem to have cooled somewhat, partly because the two sides still need to do business together, partly because advertising budgets might have been gently diverted to Sky and other media, and partly because the neurosis that gripped media owners at the depth of the advertising recession is beginning to ease in the wake of some improvement in the economy.

But the fact remains that global groups have balance sheets of variable strength. And two of them – The Interpublic Group of Companies and Havas – have been losing great chunks of money. Ironically, Interpublic's balance sheet looks comparatively strong now after selling off unwanted businesses and refinancing short term borrowings over a longer period.

Whether the improvement in client spending will be enough to save the global groups from any further deterioration in their financial condition remains to be seen, but it now seems more likely that the escrow route will give media owners enough comfort provided the documentation is suitably drafted.

Nevertheless there may be some

Key performance indicators

	Buying agencies	Media auditors
Operating profit margin	19.5%	5.1%
Operating profit + interest/Gross income	28.4%	1.8%
Financial income/Total pre-tax profit	31.4%	n/a
Gross income per head	£94,798	£77,990
Operating profit per head	£18,508	£3,941
Debt/equity ratio	No debt	n/a

other potential financial worries appearing on the media buyers' horizon. As the tables show, while the buying agencies have been highly profitable, nearly one-third of those profits came from the money they made out of cash balances – and that was in a period of lowish interest rates.

As interest rates harden, agencies may be hoping for even better profits from this source. But with competitive pressures growing, media auditors becoming more challenging, and the tentacles of procurement managers penetrating ever further into the affairs of the industry, could the time come when much of this important profit contribution is eroded?

It would be ironic to discover that an industry that thrives on its tough buying abilities had suddenly met its match.

13
Saatchi's Second Coming

In the late nineteen seventies brothers Charles and Maurice Saatchi were the darlings of the stock market as their first advertising agency Saatchi & Saatchi gobbled up rivals around the world Then it went pear-shaped.

In 1989 the group reported its first ever fall in profit after 18 years of growth. Between January and May 1989, it is said that 800 employees (6% of the Saatchi & Saatchi workforce) had been laid off. By the end of 1993 the group had shed some 7,000 staff. Shareholder pressure lead to Maurice being fired as chairman in 1994. He left under a cloud following a long-running rift with finance director Charles Scott over the group's costs.

But every cloud has a silver lining. Brother Charles and many of the senior management team followed Maurice through the exit

Out in the cold: four former Saatchi and Saatchi executives that founded M&C Saatchi – David Kershaw, Maurice Saatchi, Jeremy Sinclair and Bill Muirhead

door. Soon the Saatchis would become born-again ad men as they founded a new agency called M&C Saatchi in January 1995 that would make its headquarters in London's Golden Square[1]

I first met Maurice (now Lord) Saatchi in 1969. As a young man I had been seduced by Haymarket Publishing into becoming the first editor of the weekly magazine *Accountancy Age* when it was launched in December of that year. Although I had been a partner in a small West End firm of accountants for only a matter of months, the opportunity to turn my hand to journalism proved too difficult to resist, and my wife was generous enough to say she would support us if the venture collapsed.

At the time Maurice Saatchi was the business development manager at Haymarket and he had been charged with launching *Accountancy Age*. Rumour has it that the dummy issue of the publication was photographed on the boardroom table so that it could be promoted to the trade by means of an advertisement in another Haymarket magazine *Campaign*.

The centre-spread of the *Accountancy Age* dummy carried a full colour advertisement for Bernie Cornfeld's dubious business Investors Overseas Services – not the ideal example of a blue chip advertiser seeking to endear itself to discerning chartered accountants[2].

In those days Maurice was a mixture of bright energetic ambitious entrepreneur and showman, having recently graduated from the London School of Economics with a first class honours degree in sociology.

The article that follows dates back to July 2004 and reflects on the first nine years of M&C Saatchi's growth, leading up to its arrival on the London stock market. Later we shall learn about an imaginative performance incentive scheme introduced for the group's senior managers.

At the time of writing the Saatchi business was again enmeshed in financial controversy after the company issued a profit warning and then revealed that one or more of its London businesses had been overstating its profits and assets. The news knocked the company's reputation and its share price. The Financial Reporting Council commenced an investigation and the non-executive directors resigned en masse, along with Maurice Saatchi (Charles Saatchi

---

1 For accounts of the rise and fall of Saatchi & Saatchi, see "The Brothers" by Ican Fallon and "Conflicting Accounts" by Kebin Goldmanv

2. See "Do You Sincerely Want To Be Rich?" by Charles Raw, Bruce Page and Godfrey Hodgson

had retired a few years earlier). We shall return to these events in chapter 29. Meanwhile let us explore the early development of M&C Saatchi up to its arrival on the London stock market., as first recounted in July 2004:

On Friday 9 June 2004 the advertising agency M&C Saatchi was expecting to float almost half its shares on the Alternative Investment Market of the London Stock Exchange. Then there was a last-minute hitch.

The hitch was mainly about money, but it was also about bridging the gap between hype and hard-nosed reality. The founders had been encouraging the world's press to believe their business was worth between £70 million and £75 million. When the day of reckoning arrived, the market had the stomach for only £57 million.

Some of the market's caution stemmed from the prevailing conditions which were completely beyond M&C's control. But the fact remained that, although the company was headed up by some experienced heavy-hitters and had built a considerable international presence, in financial terms it could offer nothing more than an undulating and unexciting profit record.

Without a sudden burst of fast and sustainable growth, even the multiple of 12 times post-tax profits eventually adopted for the flotation was a fairly generous valuation.

Inevitably the ques-

tion not far from every prospective investor's lips was: will this newcomer be more reliable than the Saatchi brothers' previous incarnation Saatchi & Saatchi Company?

No-one can fail to admire the success of Saatchi & Saatchi in its heyday. It had captured the imagination of the advertising industry, clients and stock market alike. It became the world's biggest advertising business, offering a bold mixture of panache and genuine creativity as it expanded at a breath-taking pace. It was spectacularly good at self-promo-

THIS DOCUMENT IS IMPORTANT AND REQUIRES YOUR IMMEDIATE ATTENTION. If you are in any doubt about the contents of this document, you should consult a person authorised under the Financial Services and Markets Act 2000 who specialises in advising on the acquisition of shares and other securities.

This document, which is an admission document required by the AIM Rules, does not constitute a prospectus pursuant to the POS Regulations but has been drawn up in accordance with the requirements of the POS Regulations, as required by the AIM Rules. A copy of this document has been delivered to the London Stock Exchange as an admission document in respect of the Ordinary Shares.

The Directors of M&C Saatchi, whose names appear on page 10 of this document, accept responsibility for the information contained in this document. To the best of the knowledge and belief of the Directors, who have taken all reasonable care to ensure that such is the case, the information contained in this document is in accordance with the facts and does not omit anything likely to affect the import of such information.

Application has been made for all of the Ordinary Shares of the Company to be admitted to trading on the Alternative Investment Market of the London Stock Exchange. It is expected that Admission will become effective and dealings for normal settlement in the Ordinary Shares will commence on 14 July 2004. Dealings on AIM before Admission will only be settled if Admission takes place. All dealings in Ordinary Shares prior to the commencement of unconditional dealings will be at the risk of the parties concerned.

AIM is a market designed primarily for emerging or smaller companies to which a higher investment risk tends to be attached than to larger or more established companies. AIM securities are not admitted to the Official List of the UK Listing Authority. A prospective investor should be aware of the risks of investing in such companies and should make the decision to invest only after careful consideration and, if appropriate, consultation with an independent financial adviser. London Stock Exchange plc has not itself examined or approved the contents of this document.

Prospective investors should read the whole text of this document and should be aware that an investment in the Company is speculative and involves a degree of risk. Your attention is drawn to the risk factors set out in Part V of this document.

M&C Saatchi plc

(Incorporated in England and Wales under the Companies Act 1985 with registered number 05114893)

Placing of 28,061,687 Ordinary Shares of 1p each at 125p per share

and

Admission to trading on AIM

Nominated adviser and broker

LEHMAN BROTHERS

Lehman Brothers Europe Limited is acting exclusively as nominated adviser and broker to the Company and Lehman Brothers International (Europe) is acting exclusively as bookrunner in connection with the proposed admission of the Ordinary Shares to trading on AIM. Lehman Brothers Europe Limited and Lehman Brothers International (Europe), which are authorised and regulated in the UK by the Financial Services Authority, will not be responsible to anyone other than the Company for providing the protections afforded to clients of Lehman Brothers Europe Limited or Lehman Brothers International (Europe), as the case may be, or for providing advice in relation to the contents of this document or any other matter. Neither Lehman Brothers Europe Limited nor Lehman Brothers International (Europe) has authorised the contents of any part of this document for the purposes of Regulation 13 (1)(g) of the POS Regulations.

No Ordinary Shares of the Company have been marketed to, nor are any available for purchase in whole or in part by, the public in the UK or elsewhere in connection with the proposed admission of the Ordinary Shares to trading on AIM. This document does not constitute an offer or invitation to any such person to subscribe for or purchase any Ordinary Shares to trading on AIM. The Ordinary Shares have not been and will not be registered under the US Securities Act of 1933, as amended, or under the applicable state securities laws of any state of the US, or under the applicable securities laws of Australia, Canada or Japan. Subject to certain exceptions, the Ordinary Shares may not be offered or sold within the US, Australia, Canada or Japan or to or for the account or benefit of any national, resident or citizen of the US, or any person resident in Australia, Canada or Japan.

What M&C Saatchi was worth

Maintainable profits:	£'000
Pro forma pre-tax profit for 2003 (including ongoing share of subsidiaries' profits)	7,500
Taxation	-2,368
Minority interests	-414
Post-tax profit attributable to ordinary shareholders	4,718
Valuation:	
Share price on flotation	125p
Shares in issue immediately prior to flotation	45,776,827
Market value =	£57,221,034
Multiple of pro forma post-tax profit	12.13
Multiple of profit before interest and tax (EBIT)	9.06

tion, although sometimes it seemed to believe more in its own publicity than in rugged reality. Eventually its ambitions exceeded its abilities, as it contemplated buying what was then the Midland Bank (now HSBC).

At the same time its financial extravagance was beginning to come home to roost, having often paid far more for acquisitions than the subsequent financial return would justify. Not enough attention was paid to the nitty-gritty of financial management and the business eventually slid into a spectacular decline. The founders were shown the door.

So far the Saatchis' second coming has been an undoubted success — operating on a rather more modest scale and probably intentionally so. Its five founders — all from the previous Saatchi business — have many years' experience. The company has a solid base of good clients and delivers some award-winning work. It has shown an enlightened and imaginative approach to motivating the management of

its international offices and other ventures. It has backed some good quality complementary start-ups, the most notable being the media buying agency Walker Media Holdings.

Yet, as the charts below show, M&C Saatchi has not been among the most profitable of businesses and its progress has been somewhat erratic. Indeed absolute profits and profit margins both slipped backwards last year, and that slippage becomes more material if directors' remuneration is adjusted to a consistent annual amount.

The increasing contribution from the 50% stake in Walker Media Holdings also helped mitigate the downward profit trend.

Operating profit margins based on consistent directors' remuneration levels averaged only about 10.8% over the last four years — compared to a benchmark figure of 15% — and dropped to 10.2% last year. Even adopting hypothetical "pro forma" profit and revenue figures based on the structure of the group as it goes forward, rather than on how it was structured in the past, the profit margin in 2003 would only have reached 11.6%. So why didn't the Saatchi founders wait until the profit graph was rising dramatically and the business could command a higher price? Why the rush to take advantage of a brief respite in what had been a very gloomy stock market to pocket some cash now?

Age may have been a factor, as all of the founders apart from 50-year-old David Kershaw are rapidly approaching 60 and are probably ready for a quieter life. Charles Saatchi has already withdrawn from the business and he ceased drawing director's remuneration in 2002.

But even if age was a factor, there are other potential influences too. For example, many of the businesses set up by M&C to deliver international coverage or complementary marketing services (better known as the "Village") had been structured to give the senior management a slice of the particular subsidiary's share ownership.

On the one hand, continuing share ownership encourages the executives to stay with the company and share in (hopefully) ever-increasing rewards. On the other hand, those very same executives would probably like to be able to turn at least some of the increasing value of their shares into cash. The flotation facilitated that process, while giving the parent company a bigger slice of group profits in the future.

However, looking at the figures, it appears that the net additional pre-tax profit to be derived by the group from acquiring many of local executives' shares in subsidiaries will be minimal in the short term and that the main supplement will come from the increase in shareholding from 50% to a controlling 75% in Walker Media Holdings.

The group's Australian business also appears to have created real value.

The building of the international network has probably been one of the main reasons why profit margins have been below standard in the past, notwithstanding the benefit of global income from the British Airways client. The challenge now is to manage the profitability of those businesses and retain the commitment of senior personnel. Success on these two counts alone would distinguish the group from the less impressive performance of its predecessor.

In most cases the deal with subsidiary managers is to defer realisation of roughly half of their shareholdings for another three years or more. That may well help to keep them motivated. Thereafter, the company will have to rely on long-term incentive schemes similar to those applied by larger global groups.

However, the situation at Walker Media looks a little less secure. The management will be able to sell its remaining 25% shareholding after

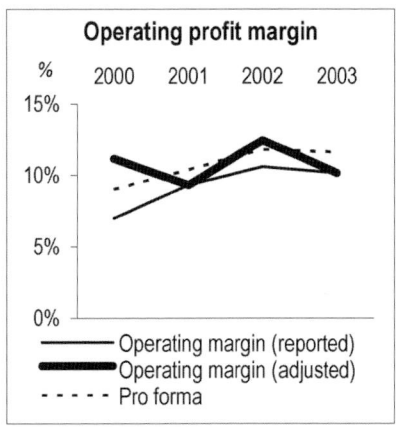

December 2005 (albeit in two annual tranches) on a publicly quoted company valuation basis that results in a multiple of not less than 13 times the most recent post—tax profits. That multiple is higher than M&C Saatchi itself obtained on flotation.

M&C has also conceded some significant rights to Christine Walker and Phil Georgiadis' including:

- Day—to—day operational management to remain in their hands.
- Walker and Georgiadis will be permitted to terminate their employment contracts[1], be released from any restrictive covenants and receive an

1. Christine Walker left the company in 2007, but Phil Georgiadis remained until 2019 after the company had been sold to Publicis .

The fruits of flotation: Who made what in M&C Saatchi

	Operating company if not M&C London		Pre-flotation share capital		Market value on flotation £
			Number	Percent	
David Kershaw			6,250,000	13.7	7,812,500
Lord Maurice Saatchi + trust			6,250,000	13.7	7,812,500
Charles Saatchi			6,250,000	13.7	7,812,500
Muirhead Settlement			6,250,000	13.7	7,812,500
Jeremy Sinclair			6,250,000	13.7	7,812,500
Christine Walker	Walker Media	1	2,177,068	4.8	2,721,335
Moray MacLennan			1,592,629	3.5	1,990,786
Nicholas Hurrell			1,592,629	3.5	1,990,786
Tom Dery	Australia	2	1,502,037	3.3	1,877,546
James Lowther			1,342,870	2.9	1,678,588
Simon Dicketts			1,342,870	2.9	1,678,588
Phil Georgiadis	Walker Media	3	1,004,378	2.2	1,255,473
Timothy Duffy			479,714	1.0	599,643
David Harris			458,444	1.0	573,055
Lisa Thomas			458,444	1.0	573,055
Simon Corah	Australia		398,345	0.9	497,931
Tom McFarlane	Australia		398,345	0.9	497,931
Jonathan Horrocks	Walker Media	4	287,122	0.6	358,903
Alan Jarvie	The Immediate Sales Co	5	202,631	0.4	253,289
Michael Moszynski	The Immediate Sales Co	5	202,631	0.4	253,289
Naseema Sparkes	Australia	6	199,172	0.4	248,965
Michael Daddo	Australia	6	199,172	0.4	248,965
Jason Ross	New Zealand	7	171,304	0.4	214,130
Marie Jackson	New Zealand	7	171,304	0.4	214,130
Janice Chan	Hong Kong		161,557	0.4	201,946
Jonathan Griffith	LA, ex Singapore	8	147,329	0.3	184,161
Katherine Griffith			36,832	0.1	46,040

1. Christine Walker has also retained a 16% shareholding in Walker Media Holdings - currently worth £2.7 million. 2. Tom Dery's shareholding resulted from acquiring his shares in the Australian business and the entire share capital of Tom Dery Financial Pty. 3. Phil Georgiadis has also retained a 7% shareholding in Walker Media Holdings - currently worth £1.3 million. 4. Jonathan Horrocks has also retained a 2% shareholding in Walker Media Holdings - currently worth £0.4 million. 5. Shares derived from a mixture of holdings in M&C Saatchi Worldwide and The Immediate Sales Company. 6. Shares received for surrendering options in M&C Saatchi Australia. 7. Shares received for surrendering options in M&C Saatchi New Zealand. 8. Shares believed to have been derived from Singapore agency.

immediate payment of one year's salary in the event of management interference.

- No management charges to be rendered by M&C Saatchi.
- No competing business to be set up in territories occupied by Walker Media.
- Walker also secured the right to a place on the group's executive committee as well as to chair Walker Media.

While the deal with Walker and Georgiadis was probably the most comprehensive in relation to the ongoing interests of shareholders, the flotation could not have been concluded without also addressing the position of various group employees who held "phantom" shares.

The normal deal for these people was to offer a cash bonus equivalent to the value growth of their phantom shares to date and then to grant options over shares in the newly floated parent company to retain their commitment as the buisness continued into the future.

The new options will not be approved by the Inland Revenue and any future gain may be subject in part to an income tax charge rather than the potentially more favourable capital gains tax treatment. Overseas employees may be subject to different treatment in any event. The cost of the bonuses being paid to former phantom shareholders is likely to hit the group's profit and loss account in the current year — the company says it will pay them "as soon as reasonably practical" after the flotation — unless some very clever financial manoeuvring can be achieved.

One key executive who does not appear among the newly rich shareholders in M&C Saatchi[1] is group finance director Jerry Wales. Having joined the company at the outset, his absence from the list of owners begs a question about whether or not the finance function is being treated more seriously in the Saatchis' second coming than it was treated in the former manifestation.

The answer lies among the phantom shares and bonuses. Why Wales never had any shares remains a mystery, but shortly he will receive a bonus geared to 0.8% of the value of the group on flotation. However, there is a catch. From that potential payout of £454,678 must be deducted the market value of new shares in M&C Saatchi over which he is being granted options. That gobbles up £353,194, leaving a meagre £101,485 as a bonus before tax. That compares with about £3.3 million that each of the founders will receive from the sale of 43% of their shareholdings on flotation. Either we have misunderstood something very important or the finance function in M&C Saatchi has been undervalued.

Fortunately the future looks a little more rosy for Wales. He will earn a basic salary of £200,000, which compares with £250,000 for the continuing founders. And, unlike the four continuing founders, Wales will also participate in the long-term incentive plan ("LTIP").

The LTIP (see panel below) is simpler than those used by many other publicly quoted marketing services groups in the UK, being

1. *See page 150.*

geared to real growth in earnings per share after stripping out any inflation component. Unlike the scheme operated by WPP Group, for example, the M&C scheme does not target total shareholder return (value growth plus dividends added back) and does not depend solely on outperforming other comparable companies.

This may avoid criticism that awards can be earned simply by doing less badly than anyone else, but equally there is no inducement to outperform the others. Arguably the fairest performance target for an LTIP would comprise a requirement to do better than average as well as to exceed company–specific targets. It is also arguable that incentives should not be geared solely to enhancing external shareholder value as this may encourage M&C Saatchi to repeat the mistakes of its predecessor by chasing earnings per share through acquisitions, using overpriced paper, while overlooking the need to maintain or improve internal efficiency measured in terms of profit margins and output per head.

So what can the new public share-holders look forward to? The company's strategy is almost too simple — to retain and attract world-class employees, to create shareholder value, to make further selective office openings, and to have a broad service offering. In no way could this strategy be described as flamboyant or overambitious — and should be easily accommodated within the £10 million of new share capital raised from the flotation.

But the proof will be in the execution. The shareholders from within the company still have over half their share value locked into the company's fortunes and will presumably want to see that value grow. So will participants in the newly-created Share Save scheme for employees.

With 26% of operating profits flowing from Walker Media (and even more when interest income is included), this will be a key component of future success. So too will be the geographical performance which currently depends on Asia Pacific (29%) and the UK (72%) to bail out losses in the US. Performance in the last few years has not produced any organic growth and staff costs

---

Key features in M&C Saatchi's long-term incentive plan ("LTIP")

Eligibility: Any employee or fulltime director unless within six months of retirement (but founders do not intend to participate). Unvested awards will normally lapse on ceasing employment with the company.

Components of Award: 50% in nominal priced option over shares, 50% in cash.

Performance conditions: If, over a five year period (or shorter 3/4 year period if participant elects), real compounded average growth in earnings per share (net of tax, RPI growth and the cost of the LTIP) exceeds 3%, 30% of the award will vest. If such growth reaches 10%, 100% of the award will vest. Where real growth falls between 3% and 10%, the award will vest proportionately.

Individual limit: Subject to discretion of remuneration committee, award in any one year not to exceed 1 x basic salary.

have continued to account for too big a proportion (62%) of revenue. Although the subdued economy has not helped, a strong company should be winning market share in such conditions.

If M&C Saatchi wishes to be truly embraced by the stock market it will have to do better in the future. Past investment in offices must produce much better returns and there will need to be some seriously strong organic growth. Nevertheless, it is encouraging to see a home-grown group join the modest family of companies in the sector that are listed on the stock exchange.

For the stock market this is Saatchis' second coming. Let us hope it stays.

Crossing the Atlantic had proved a costly journey for acquisitive Canadian marketing groups. Would the latest adventurers be more successful?

14
Canadians Craving for Conquests

I have been attracted to Canada and Canadians for as long as I can remember. On one of my business trips, a young Canadian partner in my firm went out of his way to show me the sights, including a visit to Niagara Falls and an evening watching the Toronto Blue Jays in a baseball match.

On another occasion I remember flying across the country from east to west, looking down on the prairies that appeared to have been carefully designed and manicured like a patchwork quilt, alternating between light and shaded squares. I doubt whether it was deliberately cultivated in that way. Nevertheless it conveyed a combination of order and beauty, an experience I shall never forget.

My dealings with people at the Canadian Institute of Chartered Accountants earlier in my career had left me impressed by their approach to accounting, blending a sound foundation of intellectual theory with an element of practical common sense.

Indeed, most Canadians I have met combine warm hospitality with a delightfully disarming desire to do the right thing. There's none of the brashness or arrogance sometimes found among some of their southern neighbours. But there are one or two exceptions as we shall learn later in this book, particularly in chapter 27.

Historically, Canadian businesses had found their biggest export markets close to home, over the border in the US. Net exports to the US exceeded Canadian $42 billion in 2019. But the UK was its second largest trading partner with net trade of almost $12 billion. Yet when Canadian marketing companies have ventured towards the UK, they have rarely been successful, as this chapter illustrates.

The article that follows, published in 2004, sought to provide UK marketing agencies with some helpful information about the three most acquisitive Canadian groups — MDC Partners, Envoy Communications Group and Cossette Communication Group. A lot has happened since.

At the time MDC Partners was run by the eternal optimist Miles Nadal who was always telling us what a successful business

How MDC Partners was funded at 31 December 2019		
	2019	2018
	$m	$m
Net borrowings (excl cash in trust)	780.7	923.7
Deferred acquisition payments	75.2	83.7
Advance billings	171.7	138.5
Total	**1,027.7**	**1,145.9**

MDC's net current liabilities at 31 December 2019		
	2019	2018
	$m	$m
Current assets	623.1	589.9
Current liabilities	-819.6	-742.5
Net current assets (liabilities)	**-196.6**	**-152.7**

he had, notwithstanding the ever-increasing losses being incurred, until time ran out and his questionable practices were exposed. The full story appears in chapter 27.

In March 2019, after a thinly disguised search for a buyer, MDC announced that a private equity fund managed by Stagwell Group had invested $100 million and installed its managing partner Mark Penn as chief executive. Stagwell Group is a Washington–based buy-and-build marketing group headed by Penn who was previously chief executive of the WPP-owned global public relations consultancy Burson Marsteller. In 2017 he had acquired some digital marketing businesses in the UK that were previously owned by the British entrepreneur Neil Hutchinson.

Since arrival Penn appears to have initiated various rationalisation moves after the group had accumulated losses of $470 million by 31 December 2019. Its total borrowings, including advance billings and deferred acquisition obligations, amounted to over $1 billion and its short term liabilities exceeded readily realisable assets by $197 million.

Cossette Communication Group had also been buying businesses in the UK and the US, including Designa (with its subsidiary Identica) and the public relations firm Band & Brown Group. No sooner had the review of Canadian acquirers appeared in *Marketing Services Financial Intelligence* than Cossette was buying advertising agency Miles Calcraft Briginshaw Duffy and its direct marketing subsidiary Elvis Communications. Then, in 2007, Cossette bought Dare Digital.

At the same time, and unbeknown to the acquired companies, Cossette had been the subject of a festering rift between its two founders François Duffar and Claude Lessard. As a result Duffar had left the group in less than joyful circumstances.

In October 2009 the full extent of the rift became public when Duffar launched a takeover bid for the publicly listed group.

Toronto skyline
© Tourism Toronto

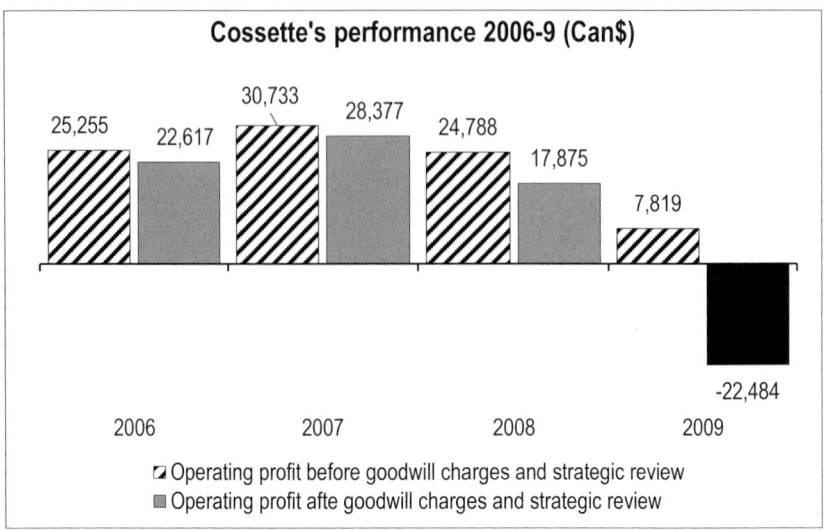

Cossette's performance 2006-9 (Can$)

☑ Operating profit before goodwill charges and strategic review
■ Operating profit afte goodwill charges and strategic review

In response, Lessard and the rest of Cossette's continuing management launched a successful counter-bid, funded by a US private equity fund manager Mill Road Capital.   Once in control, Mill Road proceeded to dismantle Cossette, selling off the UK businesses to whoever would buy them. The rump of the Canadian operations was then sold to the Chinese group Blue Focus.

The third company featured in this chapter is Envoy Communications. It was smaller than MDC or Cossette. Led by Geoffrey Genovese — president, chairman and chief executive officer — it was still intent on expanding its global portfolio after withdrawing from the Leagas Delaney deal described in chapter 11.

Envoy was probably best known for acquiring Toronto retail

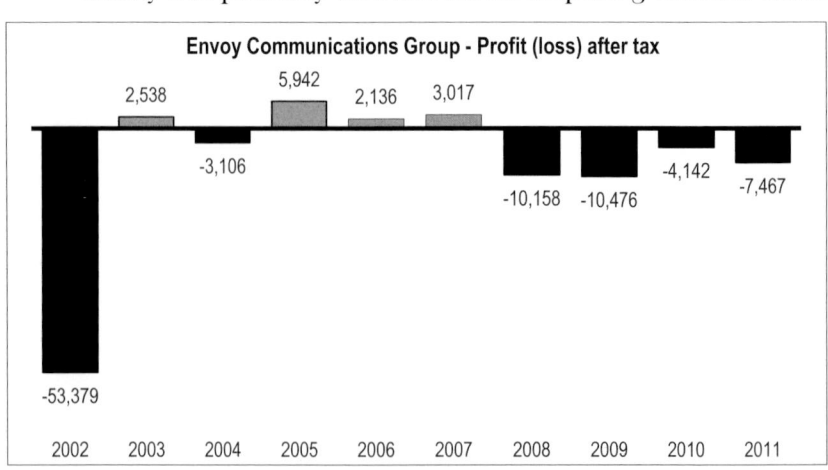

Envoy Communications Group - Profit (loss) after tax

specialist Watt International. It also acquired the Leeds reprographics house Watt Gilchrist and added a controlling stake in the UK branding and design consultancy Parker Williams in 2004. But the relationship did not last long. On September 15, 2006, Envoy sold Watt Gilchrist and Parker Williams Design to Sun Chemical Corporation, reportedly at a profit.

In 2005 Envoy had disposed of its Toronto-based advertising agency John Street to its management at a net gain of about $1.9 million. In 2006 Envoy announced that it had decided to launch a merchant banking organisation called Envoy Capital Group. It would be focused on providing financial services as well as equity and debt capital to small and mid-cap companies.

Five years later, in 2011, Envoy disposed of Watt International, presenting it as "an important step in management's ongoing plan to restructure the business through divestiture of all non-merchant banking assets". Envoy had run up losses of $29 million (see chart) and has since been absorbed by a pharmaceutical company Merus Labs International.

It is impossible to generalise about the causes of the rise and fall of these three marketing groups. However, there is one common theme: each company was driven by an entrepreneur with an ambition to create a major global marketing group, but whose skills were not a match for that ambition. They were people businesses run by the wrong people, and none of those people remain at the helm. It's as simple or as complex as that.

Crossing the Atlantic has proved a costly journey for acquisitive Canadian marketing groups targeting the UK in the past. Will the three Canadian groups currently on the acquisition trail be more successful?

The current interest being shown in UK marketing businesses by Canadian public companies may boost the expectations of entrepreneurs who are ready to sell, but history suggests the need for some caution.

Earlier this year an American creative director was scouting around UK agencies with an offer that seemed hard to refuse. Yet so far no-one here has accepted it. The creative director's name is Chuck Porter and he holds the post of chief strategist at the Toronto-based group MDC Partners. He also chairs the Miami agency Crispin Porter & Bogusky in which MDC bought a 49% stake in 2001.

His message was simple: we want to invest in creative quality and when we make an investment we believe in leaving day-to-day management and majority ownership in the hands of the existing team. In other words, MDC was offering a way for founders to realise some value from their years of hard labour without giving up control of the business. Or so it seemed.

But by the autumn of 2004 MDC was having difficulty securing its group borrowings. Unlike a wholly-owned group, where it is relatively easy to manage cash resources on a group basis and to offer lenders a debenture over all or any of the group's assets, MDC's so-called "partner" agencies are likely to have insisted that their cash remained under local control and that any other assets were not pledged as security without the local shareholders' consent.

To overcome this particular problem, MDC persuaded its partner agencies to pool a lot of their cash resources within a central treasury. It is not known whether those agencies have also agreed to pledge any of their assets as security for group borrowings. What is known is that the partnership deal with Crispin Porter has been amended to enable MDC to consolidate all of that agency's profits into the group, implying that the subtle levers of control have changed hands also.

Confidence in MDC hasn't been

MDC Partners (parent of Maxxcom)

Head office: Toronto

Stock market capitalisation: $283m

Miles Nadal - chairman, president and CEO

Main activities: Security products/ services account for over 20% of revenues; balance is marketing services. Large US interests include **Crispin Porter & Bogusky.**

Acquisitions in UK to date: **Mr Smith Agency** (formerly **Interfocus Network**) - insolvent.

Comment: MDC often acquires large minority shareholdings in companies, so part of its potential profits has leaked out. Lost Can$1.9 million in nine months to 30 Sept 2004. Accounting practices being reviewed by new auditors.

Financial statistics:

Year ended 31 December	2003 Can $m[1]	2002 Can $m[1]
Revenue	448.3	555.9
Operating profit [2]	52.4	78.3
Finance income (costs)	-16.5	-23.2
Post-tax profit	15.8	133.8
Number of employees	3,200	3,200
Op margin on revenue	11.7%	14.1%
Op profit per head	$16,374	$24,468
Debt/equity	1.01:1	1.65:1

1. Translated at Can$ 1.4337 to US$; 2.. Before goodwill amort'n

Envoy Communications Group

Head office: Toronto

Stock market capitalisation: $92m

Geoff Genovese - founder and chief executive officer

Main activities: Mainly **Watts International** design and branding, and **St John's** print/broadcast production and planning. Was forced to dispose of several acqustions when group ran into heavy losses.

Acquisitions in UK to date: **Watts Gilchrist**. Lucky escape from **Leagas Delenay Group** deal.

Comment: Envoy spent big money on acquisitions in the US and Canada in the 1990s only to get overstretched as the recession arrived. Now planning a new expansion phase.

Financial statistics:

Year ended 30 September	2003 Can $m	2002 Can $m
Revenue	42.4	59.1
Operating profit (loss) [1]	2.8	-5.2
Finance income (costs)	-2.7	-1.2
Post-tax profit (loss)	2.5	-53.3
Number of employees	339	339
Op margin on revenue [1]	6.6%	-8.8%
Op profit per head	$8,113	$-15,437
Debt/equity [2]	0.71:1	1.38:1

1.Before goodwill amort'n. 2..Debt since cancelled by share issue.

Cossette Communication Group

Head office: Quebec

Stock market capitalisation: $280m

Claude Lessard - chief executive officer

Main activities: Broad range of below-the-line activities with some advertising and media interests also. Wants international recognition with a presence in many countries. In 2003, 11% of revenue came from US.

Acquisitions in UK to date: **Designa** (and subsidiary **Identica**); **The Band & Brown Group**.

Comment: Strong balance sheet and better track record than competitors. But purchase of Identica raises question of judgement about suitability of acquisitions in UK.

Financial statistics:

Year ended 30 September	2004 Can $m	2003 Can $m
Revenue	181.5	163.7
Operating profit [1]	27.9	25.2
Finance income (costs)	1.2	1.4
Post-tax profit	16.5	16.6
Number of employees	1,350	1,300
Op margin on revenue [1]	15.4	14.8%
Op profit per head	$20,667	$18,538
Debt/equity	No debt	No debt

1. Before amortisation of goodwill/other intangibles.

helped by its uninspiring profit record or the latest rewriting of its financial reports after new auditors questioned past practices and the company had to delay filing its returns with the US Securities and Exchange Commission. Last September the group was still burdened with $43 million of past losses although its debt:equity ratio was a respectable 0.27:1.

Such profits as have been made in recent years arose from the disposal of businesses outside its current focus of marketing services.

To add insult to injury, in November 2004 MDC's marketing holding company Maxxcom decided to call in receivers for the second time to the remaining vestiges of Interfocus Group that it had backed at the time of its UK management buyout from Lowe Group.

Maxxcom had already put receivers into Interfocus Group itself in August 2003 in an attempt to recover some of its £8 million investment, having first transferred the business to Interfocus Network which was later renamed Mr Smith Agency shortly before it collapsed again. Now the Mr Smith Agency is reported to have been acquired by its current management.

To keep matters in perspective, MDC has made a number of partnership investments in the US and the concept on offer will appeal to many agency founders. But while MDC grapples with the challenges of its partnership model, other Canadian groups have been pursuing a more conventional approach to acquisitions.

Based in Quebec, Cossette Communication Group has begun

to spend some of its accumulated reserves on buying companies in the UK. So far it has bought Michael Peter's Designa group – the principal member of which is Identica – and public relations consultancy The Band & Brown Group.

In both cases the cost has been fairly modest and the strategic objective appears to have been to extend the group's existing disciplines onto a larger international playing field. Deal terms have not been disclosed in either case, although the initial outlay on Designa is thought to have been less than £3 million and the initial payments for Band & Brown were less than £5 million. Cossette has a solid track record, earning an operating profit margin of around 15% before charging goodwill amortisation. Net current assets (the resources available to pay current liabilities) amounted to $62 million in September 2004 and its net cash balances were nearly $90 million

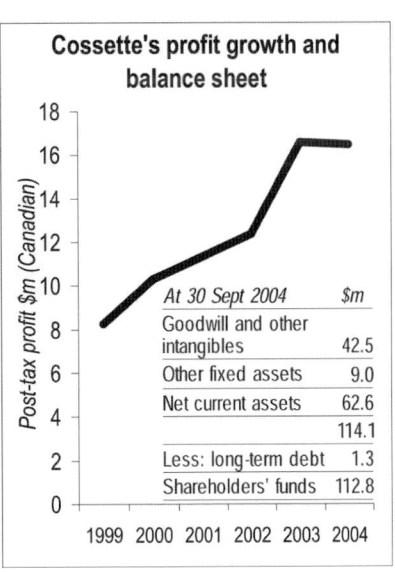

Cossette's profit growth and balance sheet

At 30 Sept 2004	$m
Goodwill and other intangibles	42.5
Other fixed assets	9.0
Net current assets	62.6
	114.1
Less: long-term debt	1.3
Shareholders' funds	112.8

(see chart). Another $14 million was readily available in short-term investments.

"We want to become an internationally recognised communications company with a presence in many countries", the company says. Weighing against these positive signals, the company precipitated a little confidence wobble earlier this month when it parted with its Toronto president Dom Caruso in unexpected circumstances. Leaving that to one side, the test the company now faces is to show that it can select the right acquisitions and manage an international business effectively.

Alongside Cossette's relatively cautious approach to acquisitions and the innovative style adopted by the more heavily borrowed MDC is new-found confidence at Toronto's Envoy Communications Group.

In the UK, Envoy is probably best remembered for its much publicised takeover bid for Leagas Delaney Group in 2000 that was subsequently abandoned. As every reader of *Marketing Services Financial Intelligence* now knows (see chapter 11), this bid showed breath-taking indifference to risk, bearing in mind that its £25 million minimum offer was being made for a company that had never made a profit while under independent ownership.

Equally surprising was the fact that Envoy had not put in place the funds to complete the deal before it was announced.

The Leagas Delaney bid was only one of a series made during the 2000-02 period, most of them nearer to home in Canada and the US but also including Leeds-based design consultancy Gilchrist Brothers. However, the expansion coincided with the market downturn and soon the group was in serious financial difficulties, reporting a loss of $53 million in the year to 30 September 2002 and a bombed out balance sheet where borrowings of $14 million swamped its depleted $10 million shareholders' funds.

Now Envoy has rebuilt its balance sheet by raising $61 million of new share capital and — having disposed of several acquisitions along the way — is talking about future growth involving a "strategic merger and acquisition expansion plan to further enhance its leadership position and expand its business in North America and Europe".

Envoy has forecast a post-tax

Some questions to ask about a Canadian (or any other) suitor

■ How does the buyer's business fit with yours and what value will each bring to the other?

■ Where will the buyer's group be in 5 years' time - size/markets?

■ How involved will the buyer get in your business?

■ How much of the initial price will be cash and is it available?

■ Is the buyer's balance sheet strong enough to be able to pay the earn-out when due?

■ What happens if the buyer is taken over during the earn-out?

■ Have you researched the background of the CEO?

■ How well do you respect and relate to the buyer?

■ Which other UK companies have they bought? Talk to them.

profit of at least $4.7 million for the latest year to 30 September 2004 (despite a modest $2.8 million loss for the first nine months), restoring shareholders' funds to about $80 million of which over $50 million is represented by cash in the bank.

It is interesting to ponder why Canadian groups have not always attracted the best targets or managed to achieve financial success from doing so. Maybe they lack the global clout to attract the best businesses, and sometimes find themselves paying premium prices for mediocre businesses instead. Certainly some have pursued ambitions in excess of their financial or managerial capacity.

One such example was the ill-fated Mosaic Group which collapsed in 2003 owing over $400 million and has been in receivership ever since. Among the UK companies it had swallowed along the way were STH Stretch the Horizon, 2NR (trading as NR Consulting), Field Marketing & Consultancy Group, Zimmer Constantinou Gellett and Europa Merchant Services.

The Mosaic strategy had been to grow its international presence by acquiring "well-run, market-leading firms that have demonstrated a strong track record of earnings and cash flow growth, while offering an increasing 'mosaic' of services to clients". In reality most of its acquisitions did not pass that quality test.

Mosaic's deals were structured with about 50% payable in cash and the balance in shares, not untypical for the sector. But the price included minimal, if any, deferred consideration geared to subsequent performance, leaving most of the risk with the buyer.

With hindsight, the purchase prices often proved to be over-generous even without an earnout element.

Hopefully the current batch of predators will be more successful. More importantly, target companies need to ask the right questions.

Five years of financial surprises costing shareholders roughly $3 billion prompted an investigation by the US Securities & Exchange Commission.

15

Ineptitude at Interpublic

The Interpublic Group of Companies has its origins in New York City where in October 1930 two major US advertising agencies merged. The two agencies — H K McCann Co and Erickson Company — became McCann Erickson, the largest agency in the advertising industry at that time.

Since then the group has striven to become one of the top five global marketing groups alongside WPP, Omnicom, Publicis and Dentsu, acquiring along the way companies like Foote Cone & Belding (FCB), Ammirati Puris AvRutick, Lowe Group, Lintas, Mullen Advertising, Shandwick and many more.

Much of the company's avaricious drive for growth took place in the nineteen eighties and nineties, led by two men - Phil Geier and John Dooner — both of whom were long-serving executives at McCann. Their ambitions prompted a string of acquisitions along with major investments in the newly emerging digital sector (see chapter 4). When I met Geier in his New York office towards the end of that period, there was no hint of the dramas to come, although his enthusiasm for acquisitions appeared to be on the wane.

Nevertheless, between 1997 and 1999 alone, Interpublic had paid out $1.5 billion in cash and shares to acquire well in excess of 140 companies, according to its regulatory filings. During the same

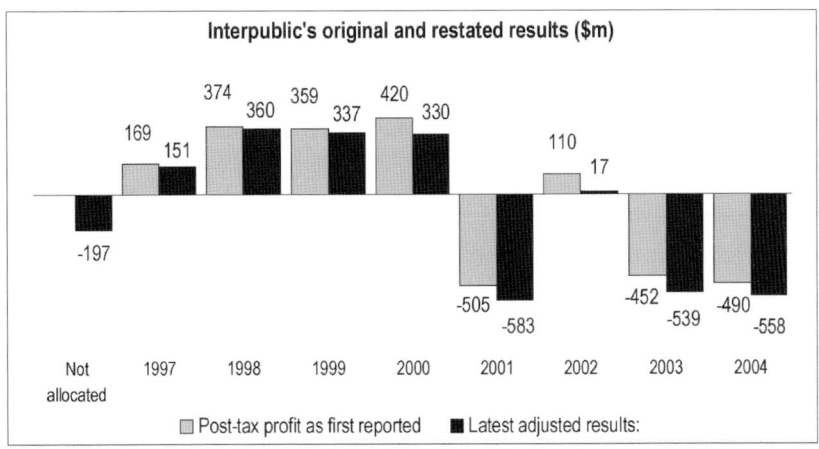

Interpublic's original and restated results ($m)

	Not allocated	1997	1998	1999	2000	2001	2002	2003	2004
Post-tax profit as first reported		169	374	359	420		110		
Latest adjusted results	-197	151	360	337	330	-505 / -583	17	-452 / -539	-490 / -558

■ Post-tax profit as first reported   ■ Latest adjusted results:

period the company also paid out $323 million in cash and shares as deferred consideration for acquisitions made in prior years.

It was not until the turn of the millennium that the true financial consequences of the race for growth began to seep out, as the story that follows in this chapter illustrates all too vividly. Over a period of about 10 years to 2004, Interpublic's profits were overstated by no less than $668 million. Those overstatements not only boosted the prestige of the company and its management, but also enabled it to negotiate acquisitions at favourable prices based on Interpublic's inflated value.

There was also evidence that the accounting rules prevailing at that time made it far too easy to avoid recording the actual value placed on companies that Interpublic acquired, as *Marketing Services Financial Intelligence* reported at the time of the Brands Hatch Leisure acquisition:

> Brands Hatch Leisure was a publicly listed UK group before it was acquired by The Interpublic Group of Companies in December 1999. Post-tax profits for that year were £3.9 million. So why did Interpublic pay $240 million or a multiple of 42 times profits?
>
> The answer may lie in the nature of the deal. The price was satisfied by an exchange of shares and, at that time, US companies were permitted to book the cost at the nominal value of the shares issued (or the book value of net assets acquired, if greater), rather than the market value of the new shares issued. So Interpublic seems to have recorded the cost at about $60 million.
>
> The danger with such an accounting policy – which was also applied to the acquisition of True North – is that managements may risk buying businesses for which the future earnings prospects are less solid than would justify the true cost of acquisition.
>
> At Brands Hatch Leisure, post-tax profits in 2000 showed a slight improvement, reaching £4.7 million with the help of "Daytona" karting centres which were expanded into Hong Kong – a return of just 3% on the true cost of the investment. And that was after including income from the subsequent acquisition of the Silverstone Circuits business as well as TOCA which promotes the British Touring Car Championships.

Interpublic's ambitions were to take a heavy toll both on the company's profits and on the careers of some of its executives. By 2005 Dooner had been displaced and the group was under investigation by the Securities and Exchange Commission in the United States, as well as being subjected to an extensive internal review.

Non-executive director Michael Roth took over the group's

management and made an impressive effort to restore its credibility and financial fortunes. Roth had trained as an accountant and progressed to the position of a partner in PricewaterhouseCoopers at the age of 30. From there he moved into commerce as chief financial officer at Mony Group, one of the oldest and largest mutual life insurance companies in the United States. Nothing could have been farther from marketing.

At Interpublic, one of Roth's first tasks as chief executive was to uncover damning evidence not only of imprudently structured deals and overstated income, but also of loose controls over the businesses acquired. This chapter – first published in 2005 – was my attempt to explain what had gone wrong.

When The Interpublic Group of Companies announced post-tax profits of $359 million for 2000 everything was looking good.

John Dooner had just taken over at the helm after the retirement of chairman and chief executive officer Phil Geier, a merger with True North Communications was in the pipeline, and as a consequence the company was about to become the world's largest marketing services group.

But that was to be the last time Interpublic had anything to celebrate.

In 2001 the company lost $505 million after incurring exceptional costs of more than $1 billion. This and a stream of further exceptional costs and accounting errors have piled up total losses since Geier's retirement of a staggering $1.7 billion.

The regular recurrence of "non-recurring" exceptional items has become something of an industry joke - they have totalled almost $3 billion since 1999.

And, as if that was not enough, a series of accounting errors, culminating in last month's admission that profits had been overstated materially

for many years, lopped $668 million off the originally reported results. How could a company like Interpublic make so many serious mistakes?

Ambition to be number one lay behind a large portion of the massive exceptional costs. The rush to buy more and more companies stored up a host of problems for the future of the group.

Sometimes Interpublic paid over the market rate for acquisitions. Sometimes it paid a market price for a business that did not deserve it. Sometimes it simply failed to manage the acquired business effectively.

The result was that the group had to write down the cost of acquisitions and minority shareholdings in trade investments as it became clear that their book value had been permanently impaired. There were also massive restructuring costs as staff were shed and excess accommodation offloaded (see chart).

Like most acquisitive companies, Interpublic suffered its share of costly disasters towards the end of the dotcom boom. The group invested in several infant internet

Interpublic's tragedy of errors

Post-tax profit (loss):	Earlier	1997	1998	1999	2000	2001	2002	2003	2004	Total
	$m	$m	$m	$m	$m	$m	$m	$m	$m	$m
As originally reported		168.7[1]	374.2[1]	359.4[1]	420.3[1]	-505.3	110.2[2]	-451.7	-490.2[2]	-14.4
Errors subsequently disclosed:										
Adjusted in 2002	-31.6	-16.7	-12.4	-19.2	-23.2	-22.1	-10.7			-135.9
Adjusted in 2003		-1.0	-1.8	-3.6	-4.3	-7.1				-17.8
Adjusted in 2005	-165.0[3]				-62.5	-48.6	-82.8	-87.4	-68.0	-514.3
Total cumulative errors to date	**-196.6**	**-17.7**	**-14.2**	**-22.8**	**-90.0**	**-77.8**	**-93.5**	**-87.4**	**-68.0**	**-668.0**
Restated results	-196.6	151.0	360.0	336.6	330.3	-583.1	16.7	-539.1	-558.2	**-682.4**

1. Restated to reflect merger of True North accounted for using the "pooling of interests" method. 2. Published result grossed up by errors disclosed in earlier quarterly statements. 3. Earlier than 2000 but not allocated to any particular years

businesses, not least MarchFIRST and the Swedish listed consultancy IconMedialab International that proved unrewarding to say the least. So in 2001 provision was made for a $160 million reduction in the value of those investments — but not until after the True North merger deal had been signed[1].

Not only did Interpublic invest in risky new ventures, it also spent vast sums on established businesses that were well past their peak. The True North deal and the earlier acquisition of International Public Relations (formerly Shandwick International) in 1998 were classic examples.

The $2 billion offer for True North was astonishingly high for a poorly performing group and must surely have been driven by the prospect of leapfrogging into the number one position in the industry. Prior to the deal, True North had been obliged to down-size after losing the DaimlerChrysler business. It had also suffered costs arising from the Bozell acquisition and a write-down of its investment in Modem Media. Even without those costs, the acquisition value represented a multiple of

nearly 22 times post-tax profits. After charging those exceptional costs, the multiple jumped to 34.

Such multiples could only be justified by a swift recovery in True North's performance and that was never fully realised. Fortunately the final deal value fell to a still generous $1.6 million as Interpublic's share price dropped sharply by 18%.

After the deal, the group incurred a very expensive round of rationalisation costs, absorbing over $900 million in the course of three years (including a $303 million goodwill impairment provision). In fairness, that figure may have been exacerbated by the impact of a global downturn in demand.

There were plenty of other examples of the group having to write off quite a lot of what it paid to buy

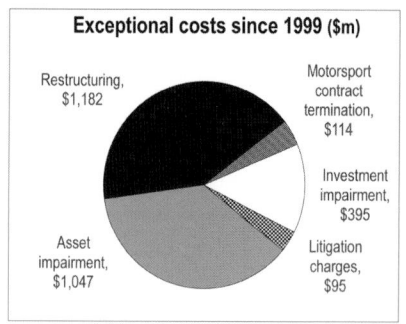

Exceptional costs since 1999 ($m)

Restructuring, $1,182
Motorsport contract termination, $114
Investment impairment, $395
Asset impairment, $1,047
Litigation charges, $95

---

1   See chapter 4

MANAGEMENT'S ASSESSMENT OF INTERNAL CONTROL
Extract from 2004 10-K filing with SEC

1. The Company did not maintain an effective control environment. Specifically, controls were not designed and in place to ensure compliance with the Company's policies and procedures, including those contained in the Company's Code of Conduct. Further, the Company did not maintain a sufficient complement of personnel with an appropriate level of accounting knowledge, experience and training in the application of accounting principles generally accepted in the United States (GAAP) commensurate with the Company's financial reporting requirements. The Company also failed to implement processes to ensure periodic monitoring of its existing internal control activities over financial reporting. By placing, heavy reliance on manual procedures without quality control review and other monitoring controls in place to adequately identify and assess significant risks that may impact financial statements and related disclosures (*sic*). This deficiency resulted in a control environment that allowed instances of falsified books and records, violations of laws, regulations and the Company's policies, misappropriation of assets and improper customer charges and dealings with vendors resulting in the restatement and audit adjustments described below. This deficiency has had a pervasive impact on the Company's control environment and has contributed to the material weaknesses described below.

Control Activities

2. The Company did not maintain effective controls over the accounting for purchase business combinations. Specifically, the Company did not have controls designed and in place to ensure the completeness, accuracy and valuation of revenue and expenses of acquired companies related to periods after the closing date of the transactions. In addition, the Company did not maintain effective controls to ensure the completeness, accuracy and valuation of assets and liabilities recorded for compensatory earn-out and put arrangements or derivatives embedded within acquisition transactions. This deficiency resulted in a restatement of 2004 (first three interim periods) and 2003 interim consolidated financial statements, the 2003 and 2002 annual consolidated financial statements and audit adjustments to the 2004 annual consolidated financial statements and certain interim periods, which primarily impacted revenue, salaries and related expenses, office and general expenses, long lived assets and other charges, goodwill, accrued liabilities, deferred compensation and employee benefits, other non-current liabilities and accumulated deficit.

3. The Company did not maintain effective controls over the accuracy and presentation and disclosure of recording of revenue. Specifically, controls

were not designed and in place to ensure that customer contracts were authorized, that customer contracts were analyzed to select the appropriate method of revenue recognition, and billable job costs were compared to client cost estimates to ensure that no amounts were owed to clients. In addition, controls were not designed and in place to ensure that revenue transactions were analyzed for appropriate presentation and disclosure of billable client pass-through expenses or for recognition of revenue on a gross or net basis. This deficiency resulted in a restatement of 2004 (first three interim periods) and 2003 interim consolidated financial statements, the 2003 and 2002 annual consolidated financial statements and audit adjustments to the 2004 annual consolidated financial statements and certain interim periods, which impacted revenue, office and general expenses, accounts receivable, net, expenditures billable to clients, accounts payable, accrued liabilities and accumulated deficit.

4. The Company did not maintain effective controls to ensure that certain financial statement transactions were appropriately initiated, authorized, processed, documented and accurately recorded. This was primarily evident in the following specific areas:

i.   client contracts, incentives and rebates;
ii.   write-offs of aged accounts receivable, expenditures billable to clients and amounts billable to clients;
iii.   fixed assets purchases, disposals, and leases;
iv.   accounts payable and accrued liabilities;
v.   payments made for employee compensation;
vi.   cash and cash equivalents, wire transfers, and foreign currency transactions;
vii.   arrangements with derivative instruments;
viii. intercompany transactions;
ix.   purchase of equity of investments in unconsolidated entities; and
x.   purchase, disposal or write-off of intangible assets.

This deficiency resulted in a restatement of 2004 (first three interim periods) and 2003 interim consolidated financial statements, the 2003 and 2002 annual consolidated financial statements and audit adjustments to the 2004 annual consolidated financial statements and certain interim periods, which impacted substantially all accounts in the consolidated financial statements.

5. The Company did not maintain effective controls over the complete and accurate recording of leases in accordance with GAAP. Specifically, the Company did not completely evaluate and accurately account for leases with rent holidays, rent escalation clauses, leasehold improvements or asset retirement obligations associated with real estate leases where leasehold

improvements are made. This deficiency resulted in a restatement of 2004 (first three interim periods) and 2003 interim consolidated financial statements, the 2003 and 2002 annual consolidated financial statements and audit adjustments to the 2004 annual consolidated financial statements and certain interim periods, which primarily impacted office and general expenses, restructuring charges, land, buildings and equipment, net, accounts payable, accrued liabilities, other non-current liabilities, and accumulated deficit.

6. The Company did not maintain effective controls over the accounting for income taxes in operations outside of the United States to ensure amounts are accurately accounted for in accordance with GAAP. Specifically, the Company did not have controls designed and in place to ensure that accounting personnel performed the following: recorded income tax provision between current and deferred tax accounts in the balance sheet; reconciled prior years' income tax returns to the appropriate period income tax provision computations; timely identified income tax exposures and contingencies, including interest and penalties; and reconciled tax accounts to tax filings. This deficiency resulted in a restatement of 2004 (first three interim periods) and 2003 interim consolidated financial statements, the 2003 and 2002 annual consolidated financial statements and audit adjustments to the 2004 annual consolidated financial statements and certain interim periods, which impacted accrued liabilities, deferred income taxes, other non-current liabilities and the provision for income taxes.

7. The Company did not maintain effective controls over reporting local income tax in the local statutory accounts or local income tax returns in operations outside of the United States. Specifically, the Company did not have controls designed and in place to ensure that accounting personnel adhere to policy and procedures regarding compliance with local laws and regulations, and reconcile its accounts between GAAP and local income tax reporting. This resulted in the violation of local tax regulations and incomplete and inaccurate recording of income taxes in the Company's consolidated financial statements. This deficiency resulted in a restatement of 2004 (first three interim periods) and 2003 interim consolidated financial statements, the 2003 and 2002 annual consolidated financial statements and audit adjustments to the 2004 annual consolidated financial statements and certain interim periods, which impacted accrued liabilities, deferred income taxes, other non-current liabilities and the provision for income taxes.

8. The Company did not maintain effective controls relating to the completeness and accuracy of local payroll and compensation–related liabilities in certain operations outside of the United States. Specifically the Company did not have controls designed and in place to identify instances where local reporting regulations and payroll tax withholding requirements were not

met. A number of compensation practices were identified which were either not supportable under local law or were not fully in accordance with the Company's policies and procedures. This resulted in improperly omitting, and in certain instances purposefully omitting, certain liabilities in the consolidated financial statements. This deficiency resulted in a restatement of 2004 (first three interim periods) and 2003 interim consolidated financial statements, the 2003 and 2002 annual consolidated financial statements and audit adjustments to the 2004 annual consolidated financial statements and certain interim periods, which impacted salaries and other related expense and accrued expenses.

9. The Company did not maintain effective controls over the accuracy and completeness of the processing and monitoring of intercompany transactions, including appropriate authorization for intercompany charges. Specifically, controls were not designed and in place to ensure that intercompany balances were accurately classified and completely reported in the Company's consolidated financial statements, and intercompany confirmations were not completed timely or accurately between the Company's agencies to ensure proper elimination as part of the consolidation process. This control deficiency resulted in immaterial adjustments to the consolidated financial statements.

10. The Company did not maintain effective controls over the reconciliation of certain financial statement accounts. Specifically, controls were not designed and in place to ensure that the Company's accounts were accurate and agreed to detailed support. This deficiency resulted in a restatement of 2004 (first three interim periods) and 2003 interim consolidated financial statements, the 2003 and 2002 annual consolidated financial statements and audit adjustments to the 2004 annual consolidated financial statements and certain interim periods, which impacted substantially all accounts in the Company's consolidated financial statements.

11. The Company did not maintain effective control over the monitoring of financial statement accounts to value and record them in a timely, accurate and complete manner. Specifically, controls were not designed and in place to:
i.   compare revenue recorded to amounts billed to clients;
ii.   identify contracts with potential client rebates;
iii. analyze collectibility of aged accounts receivable or expenditures billable to clients;
iv.   compare billable job costs to client cost estimates;
v.   review fixed asset records for under utilized, missing or fully depreciated assets;
vi.   ensure that the underlying records support liabilities related to employee compensation, including an inventory of foreign employee pension plans,

census data to calculate pension liabilities and changes made to benefit plans which impact the Company's compliance with certain employment and tax regulations;

vii. review intercompany balances for appropriate classification;

viii. review foreign currency translation adjustments;

ix. analyze accrued expenses and underlying equity of investments in unconsolidated entities;

x. test intangible assets for impairments; or

xi. review equity accounts for appropriate roll-forward.

This deficiency resulted in a restatement of 2004 (first three interim periods) and 2003 interim consolidated financial statements, the 2003 and 2002 annual consolidated financial statements and audit adjustments to the 2004 annual consolidated financial statements and certain interim periods, which impacted substantially all accounts in the Company's consolidated financial statements.

12. The Company did not maintain effective controls over the period end financial reporting process. Specifically, controls were not designed and in place to ensure that (i) journal entries, both recurring and non-recurring, were reviewed and approved, (ii) timely and complete reviews of the financial statements were performed by personnel with knowledge sufficient to reach appropriate accounting conclusions, and (iii) a reconciliation of its legal entity financial results to the financial results recorded in the consolidated financial statements was performed. This deficiency resulted in a restatement of 2004 (first three interim periods) and 2003 interim consolidated financial statements, the 2003 and 2002 annual consolidated financial statements and audit adjustments to the 2004 annual consolidated financial statements and certain interim periods, which impacted substantially all accounts in the Company's consolidated financial statements.

13. The Company did not maintain effective controls over the safeguarding of assets. Specifically, at certain of the Company's international locations, controls were not designed and in place to segregate responsibility and authority between initiating, processing and recording of transactions which impacted many accounts in the Company's consolidated financial statements. This deficiency resulted in certain improper transactions being entered into and those transactions being recorded or not recorded in the Company's financial statements. This deficiency resulted in a restatement of 2004 (first three interim periods) and 2003 interim consolidated financial statements, the 2003 and 2002 annual consolidated financial statements and audit adjustments to the 2004 annual consolidated financial statements and certain interim periods, which impacted substantially all accounts in the Company's consolidated financial statements.

14. The Company did not maintain effective controls over independent

service providers. Specifically, the Company was unable to document, test, and evaluate controls at third party vendors to which the Company outsources its employee benefit enrolment process and certain payroll processing services in North America. This control deficiency did not result in an adjustment to the consolidated financial statements.

15. The Company did not maintain effective controls over access to the Company's financial applications and data. Specifically, controls were not designed and in place to ensure that access to certain financial applications and data at certain locations were adequately restricted. In addition, the Company did not adequately monitor the access to financial applications and data. This control deficiency has had a pervasive impact on the Company's information technology control environment.

16. The Company did not maintain effective controls over spreadsheets used in the Company's financial reporting process. Specifically, controls were not designed and in place to ensure that access was restricted to appropriate personnel, and that unauthorized modification of the data or formulas within spreadsheets was prevented. This control deficiency did not result in material adjustments to the consolidated financial statements.

Information and Communication

17. The Company did not maintain effective controls over the communication of policies and procedures. Specifically, controls were not designed and in place to ensure corporate communications, including the Company's code of conduct, were received by personnel across the Company. This deficiency has had a pervasive impact on the Company's control environment and has contributed to the material weaknesses described above.

Monitoring

18. The Company did not maintain effective controls over monitoring the performance of proper application of the Company's internal controls over financial reporting and related policies and procedures. Specifically, controls were not designed and in place to ensure that the Company identifies and remediates control deficiencies timely. This deficiency has had a pervasive impact on the Company's control environment and has contributed to the many material weaknesses described above.

businesses, or incurring great expenditure rationalising what it had bought.

After buying the Brands Hatch Leisure motor sport businesses in the UK in 1999, the post-acquisition losses and liabilities were so great that Interpublic finally had to extract itself from its contract commitment at a cost of $114 million in 2004. And that was after writing down Interpublic's investment by a total of $190 million during 2002 and 2003. Few now question that the Brands Hatch deal should never have taken place.

The Lowe Group also cost a lot of money over the years after it was merged with Ammirati Puris Lintas and steps were taken to extend its global network. In 2004, a major part of the $294 million impairment provision related to the Lowe business.

The outcome of the Shandwick public relations acquisition underlines how important it is not only to avoid paying above the market rate but also to ensure that the target company is worth the amount actually paid. Shandwick was acquired for about $124 million in exchange for Interpublic shares after earning post-tax profits of about $11 million. That purchase price represented a multiple of 11.3 times the 1997 post-tax profit or nearly 8.3 times the pre-tax profit — on the face of it not excessive when compared with other transactions during that period.

But Shandwick's profit record was erratic, it had just undergone a number of management changes, and it had net liabilities of $50 million (within which was about $70 million owed to its bankers). So its future growth prospects seemed somewhat constrained. By 2001 Shandwick was being merged with another Interpublic consultancy Weber Public Relations to form Weber Shandwick Worldwide. This umbrella.

Ironically Chadlington later hired Phil Geier's right-hand man — retired finance chief Eugene Beard — as a non-executive director.

Interpublic's potential defence that it paid no more than the market rate for the businesses it acquired does not necessarily mean that those prices were realistic. Subsequent experience has shown that acquisition prices often implied over-optimistic assumptions about future growth, as the True North and Brands Hatch deals illustrate all too well.

Any such over-optimistic valuations were fuelled by the knowledge that many of the deals — including those with True North and Brands Hatch — would be accounted for

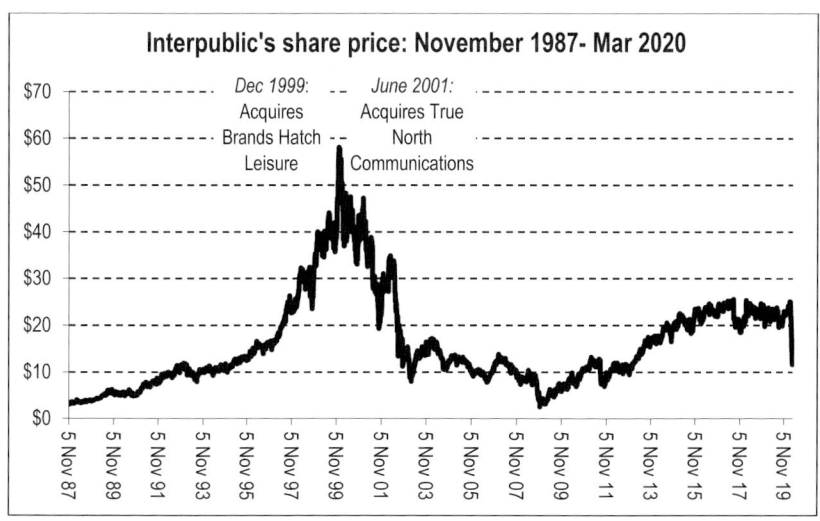

Interpublic's share price: November 1987- Mar 2020

Dec 1999:
Acquires
Brands Hatch
Leisure

June 2001:
Acquires True
North
Communications

"Phil genuinely loved putting together a good deal. He had that passion and talent dating back to his college days when he was the eager campus entrepreneur known as 'Deals Geier'. John Dooner (right) pays tribute on Geier's retirement.

using a method that avoided the need to recognise the full cost.

The method was called "pooling of interests" and has since been outlawed. It allowed the acquirer to show the cost at the greater of the book value of net assets acquired and the nominal value of the shares it issued to make the acquisition, instead of the market price of those shares at the time. At True North, that allowed the purchase value of $1.6 billion to be recorded at a mere $400 million. However, such accounting quirks could not hide the poor earnings that would accrue later to Interpublic shareholders.

No company can be expected to get every deal right, but Interpublic's track record has proved far more expensive than many. Perhaps instead of the college nick-name "Deals Geier", Interpublic's former chairman will come to be known as "Deals Dear".

Irrespective of whether Interpublic allowed over-ambition to cloud its acquisition judgements, the current management team headed by chairman and chief executive officer Michael Roth argues that its predecessors displayed serious shortcomings in the integration of the companies acquired. Indeed the admission of 18 major control weaknesses and consequent accounting errors is a damning indictment of past financial management throughout the organisation[1].

1 *See pages 169-174.*

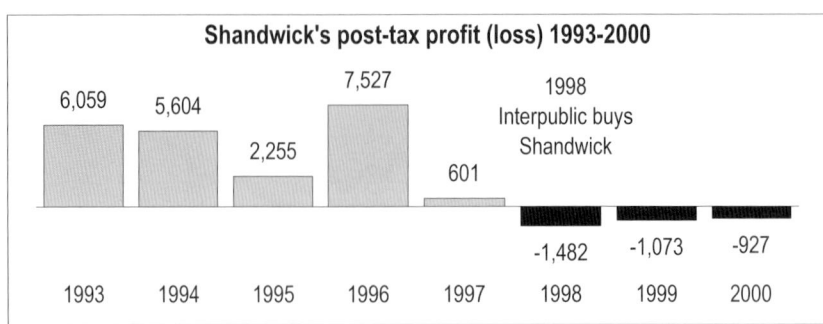

Shandwick's post-tax profit (loss) 1993-2000

6,059 5,604 2,255 7,527 601

1998
Interpublic buys
Shandwick

-1,482 -1,073 -927

1993 1994 1995 1996 1997 1998 1999 2000

The first batch of accounting errors, admitted in 2002, knocked $135.9 million off previously reported post-tax profits.

The errors arose primarily from a failure to recover amounts recharged between McCann Erickson offices for client work. The group rewrote it accounts for the six years to 2002 to reflect this. The UK subsidiary McCann Erickson Advertising alone wrote off £21.4 million in 2002, of which £14.6 million arose from "a worldwide write-off of certain inter-company trading balances believed in previous years by the directors to be recoverable". The group restatement prompted an inquiry by the US Securities & Exchange Commission that is still in progress.

Another, far more modest, downward adjustment of $17.8 million was made in 2003 and then, last autumn, came news of a possible further rewrite — this time with potentiality bigger ramifications, mainly outside the US.

The finally agreed restatement, announced last month, reduced accumulated profits by another $514 million plus $36 million of foreign currency translation adjustments.

Of the $514 million, $185 million was attributed to questionable media buying practices.

Over a period of years the group had included in its profits various volume discounts and other credits received from media owners whereas Interpublic now believes these were contractually due to clients. The group expects to pay out about $250 million over the next two years in settlement of obligations arising from these and other accounting errors.

In making the media adjustments Michael Roth will doubtless have weighed up the need for full compliance with the new Sarbanes-Oxley[1] corporate governance regime against the can of worms the disclosures may have opened for the media buying industry as a whole.

Secondly, the group said it had recognised revenues of $257 million prematurely by using the date of billing instead of the date of contractual entitlement. A large component of this error arose during 2004 under the new management, leaving open the question of whether current practices are now beyond reproach. It may also help to explain why there

1. An Act to protect investors by improving the accuracy and reliability of corporate disclosures

Interpublic's main businesses

McCann WorldGroup *Advertising*	The FCB Group *Advertising*	The Lowe Group *Advertising*	Initiative *Media buying/ planning*
GolinHarris International *Public relations*	Jack Morton Worldwide *Event organisation*	MAGNA Global *Global media buying*	Octogon *Sports sponsorship*
Weber Shandwick *Public relations*	FutureBrand *Design and branding*	Draft Worldwide *Direct marketing*	Universal McCann *Media buying/ planning*

has been yet another recent change in the top financial management, with the appointment of Frank Mergenthaler as chief financial officer in August — the fourth since the Geier-Beard era.

Other errors contributing to the latest accounts restatement included $105 million from the incorrect treatment of certain earn-out payments which are required to be charged as remuneration under US accounting rules, and the inclusion of pre-acquisition profits as part of Interpublic's own results.

Employee misconduct led to another $56 million reduction, 80% of which was attributable to just eight people. The use of personal service companies to remunerate executives in certain countries prompted a further $33 million adjustment, presumably related to potential tax charges. Other errors accounted for $24 million.

Although the net impact of the latest errors added up to $514 million, they had already been mitigated by a credit of $145 million arising from an incorrect impairment provision made as recently as September 2004 — raising again questions about the competence of financial management in the recent past. Even Roth concedes that half the latest errors arose since 2002.

The catalogue of financial weaknesses described in the management report filed with the SEC and reproduced in this chapter[1] confirms that the malaise had infected virtually every part of the group and had undoubtedly been doing so for many

"We have been addressing the consequences of an aggressive growth strategy in the 1990s... The company had under-invested in talent and suffered from poor integration of acquired agencies"
- Interpublic's current chairman Michael Roth, commenting in 2005

years.

To give some added reassurance that the latest figures would be more reliable than might otherwise be assumed, Roth and Mergenthaler significantly expanded the year-end closing procedures, expanded the review of customer contracts and agreements to address revenue recognition issues, and increased the review procedures for lease accounting, expenditure billable to clients, debtors and inter-company transactions.

The cost of this exercise has been enormous. Professional fees in 2004 alone were up by nearly $94 million compared with 2003, and staff costs were up by 17%. "We have extensive work remaining to remedy the material weaknesses", the company admitted, blaming some of the diffi-

1. *See pages 169-174.*

culties on the decentralised structure and the number of disparate accounting systems of "varying quality and sophistication".

But in an effort to restore some confidence, the company says it is developing a "comprehensive remediation plan to address our deficiencies" that will extend into 2006.

Given that further work has yet to be carried out by the company, auditors PricewaterhouseCoopers have been unable to express an opinion on the effectiveness of the company's internal controls over financial reporting.

Nevertheless, the 2004 financial statements themselves were given a clean audit opinion.

What conclusions can be drawn from this sorry tale?

First, growth ambitions must not cloud judgements about the quality of acquisition targets and the earnings potential they bring.

Secondly, no company should embark on a growth strategy without proven financial information and control procedures already in place.

Thirdly, a cultural environment that focuses excessively on revenue and profit growth will almost invariably lead to dubious, corrupt and even fraudulent practices.

Where will Interpublic go from here? The immediate priority is to sort out the weaknesses at Lowe and the media buying units. Core disposals are likely to be resisted in the short term as the group has already worked hard to plug the gaping holes that have appeared in its balance sheet, both by selling the research operation NFO WorldGroup for $419 million in 2003 and refinancing its residual borrowings with a mixture of new share capital and longer term debt.

So there should be sufficient funds to settle direct obligations arising from the accounting errors. But this won't deter more litigation from investors, or the ongoing probe by the Securities & Exchange Commission.

Inevitably recent events will have damaged confidence among investors, clients and staff. Keeping all or any of those constituencies on side will be a daunting challenge. Failure to do so will almost certainly hasten the company's decline.

For someone to sell the same business three times might be indicative either of above-average financial acumen or of simple absentmindedness.

16
Buyout Bonanza at Bray Leino

The village of Filleigh lies just off the main road from Tiverton to Barnstaple in Devon, on the southern edge of Exmoor. The village is dominated by a Grade 1 listed Palladian mansion called Castle Hill, built by Lord Fortesque whose descendants still own much of the land in the area.

Filleigh is also home to a full-service creative agency called Bray Leino. The agency was founded in 1974 as a partnership between David Morgan and Shaun Ryan based in the north Devon coastal town of Lynton. It had one client, Kimberly-Clark. Four years later the partnership was converted into a limited company. Christopher Lawrence joined and Shaun Ryan left a little later.

This chapter tells how David Morgan created an advertising agency in the west of England, sold it, bought it back, sold it again, bought it back again and finally sold it to The Mission Marketing Group when its shares were floated on the London Stock Exchange in 2006. The report that follows first appeared in May 2006 and, looking back, Morgan rightly emphasises that neither buy-back was sought by him. On each occasion it was the changing circumstances of the acquirer that prompted the negotiations.

David Morgan; co-founder of Bray Leino

The story illustrates how one man's commitment to his business, its clients and those who work in it, survived those unexpected consequences. It is a salutary reminder that an attractive-looking buyer can change its spots, unlike the leopard, even if the seller has been as diligent in examining the buyer as the buyer will have been in examining the seller. We have already seen in chapter 11 how Leagas Delaney's

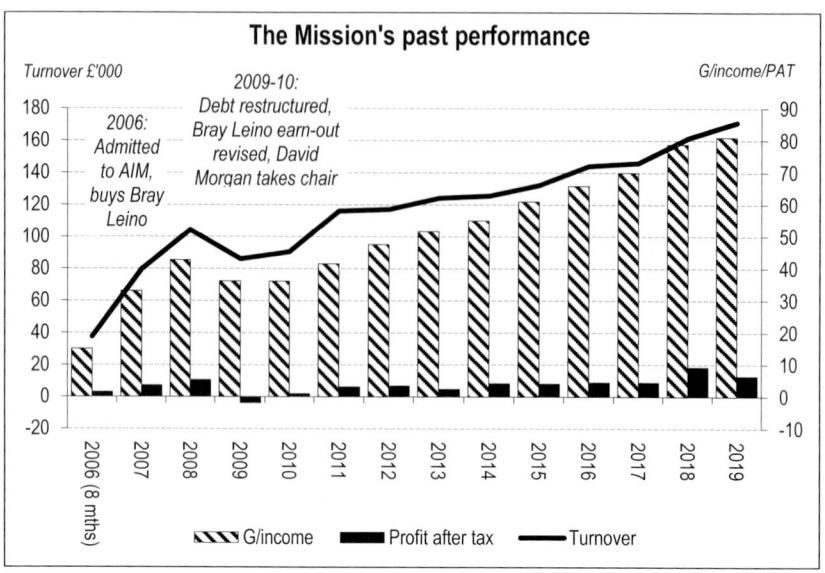

buyer Envoy Communications had not raised the cash needed to complete the purchase and, in chapter 14, how companies acquired by Cossette Communication Group were unaware of a festering rift between that company's founders.

Bray Leino's story did not end with its arrival on the Stock Exchange. Mission could not afford to pay the amount due to Bray Leino's former shareholders under the earn-out arrangement when it became due in 2009, at which point Morgan had planned to retire (He would have been 62 years old then and is now in his early seventies.[1])

Mission had been too ambitious — not only in the acquisitions it had sought under the management of its recently departed founder Martin Banbury but also in the overheads it took upon itself. As *Marketing Services Financial Intelligence* reported at the time:

> Mission's main problem stemmed from its obligations to settle acquisition debts of about £3 million within one year at a time when additional bank funding would be required. Bank borrowings had already reached more than £20 million and finance costs alone were running at about £1.8 million per annum. The banks have agreed to restructure their debt to remove any repayment obligations until 2011.

Mission's bankers had invited Morgan to become chairman of the parent company. His terms included the removal of the existing board (chaired by Francis Maude with Iain Ferguson as chief

---

1. *David Morgan eventually announced his retirement while this book was going to press in 2021.*

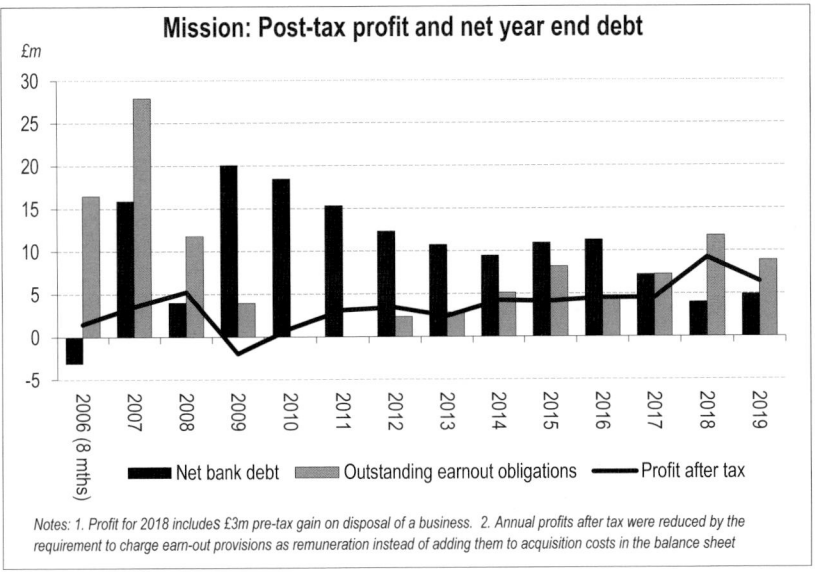

Mission: Post-tax profit and net year end debt

Legend: ■ Net bank debt   ▨ Outstanding earnout obligations   — Profit after tax

Notes: 1. Profit for 2018 includes £3m pre-tax gain on disposal of a business. 2. Annual profits after tax were reduced by the requirement to charge earn-out provisions as remuneration instead of adding them to acquisition costs in the balance sheet

executive) and the appointment to the board of the chief executive officers of five of the six agencies that the group had bought.

"I did that to get them to buy into a Mission strategy, bearing in mind the ill feeling that had built up towards Mission by then", Morgan explained.

Only after he had agreed to take on the chairmanship were the bankers prepared to offer the refinancing package. In return the banks were given the right to subscribe for roughly 3% of the company's share capital at a nominal price of 10p per share with effect from December 2012. Thus, when the group announced the refinancing of its bank debt and the conversion of its immediate earn-out obligations

Mission's changing balance sheets

| | 31 December | |
	2019	2009
Long-term assets	£'000	£'000
Tangible fixed assets	11,537	2,031
Intangible assets	95,859	68,214
	107,396	70,245
Net non-cash current assets:		
Readily realisable assets (excl cash)	42,089	17,483
Short-term liabilities (excl debt)	-36,757	-14,124
	5,332	3,359
Bank debt and deferred acquisition obligations:		
Net bank borrowings	-4,899	-20,076
Deferred acquisition obligations	-8,882	-3,935
	-13,781	-24,011
Other long-term liabilities (mainly lease payments due beyond one year)[1]	-6,646	-174
Net assets	**92,301**	**49,419**

1. *Future lease commitments were not required to be shown as liabilities in 2009.*

from loan notes into shares in April 2010, it also announced that Morgan would become executive chairman. Chief executive Iain Ferguson departed and a new group finance director, Peter Fitzwilliam, was appointed.

Since that time Mission has traded profitably each year and its income has grown steadily. Equally important to Morgan, net borrowings (including earn-out commitments) have fallen from £24 million in 2009 to £13.8 million at the end of 2019 (see chart).

Today's Mission board includes seven people who hold or have held senior executive roles in the group's subsidiary companies. This contrasts with the recent trend among public companies of limiting executive seats on the parent board to the group chief executive and group finance director, with the rest of the positions filled by non-executives.

Doubtless the coronavirus pandemic will have had an adverse impact on the group's performance and cash flow in 2020. In talking about that, Morgan unwittingly displays one of the likely reasons for his success as a manager. In the wake of the coronavirus scare, he has spent a lot of time counselling and reassuring the staff about their job security, and it is clear that he cares. It is also clear that he recognises that confidence is an important component of a successful team.

But why start up in a remote corner of Devon? "I couldn't take commuting on the District Line any longer" is Morgan's simple answer. At the time he worked at the Dorland advertising agency in London's West End (now part of the mighty WPP) and hankered

The Mission Marketing Group share price (p)

after a lifestyle closer to what he remembered from his childhood days, having been born close to Exmoor. If an advertising agency had already existed in the area he says he would have joined that. But there wasn't.

The new agency grew quickly and soon needed bigger offices. By chance he came across the site of an old rectory on the outskirts of Filleigh that had been transformed into a caravan park. Next morning he saw a newspaper advertisement offering the same site for sale. So he bought it.

There are obvious attractions in such a location, but also there can be disadvantages such as the job applications from people who are attracted more by the opportunity for water-skiing than by hard work. Those applications go straight into the bin.

Having chosen a rural location, Bray Leino had to work hard to attract the best people from traditional advertising backgrounds. So the company also invested heavily in graduate recruitment, sometimes taking on as many as 20 in a year. Bray Leino's current chief executive officer Kate Cox started that way.

Asked what qualities it needs to run a successful business like Bray Leino, Morgan responds: "Perspiration and desperation." It's really hard work, he says, and even more so when you're in Devon and your clients are elsewhere. And the "desperation" is all about being driven by fear of what might go wrong next week. "Whatever may happen, standards must not drop", he says.

Would Morgan have done anything differently if he was starting the business again today? "I would have done things a lot quicker", he says. He claims to be naturally risk averse. He hates debt. And he hates uncertainty. Perhaps he would be a little bolder if he was starting again.

For someone to sell the same business twice would be indicative either of above-average financial acumen or of simple absentmindedness. To sell the same business no less than three times seems pretty remarkable. But that is exactly what 59-year-old west country advertising agency entrepreneur David Morgan has done.

David Morgan co-founded Bray Leino in its present form with Christopher Lawrence in 1978.

Since then he has sold it to Delaney Fletcher Delaney (which had a series of subsequent owners and is now part of Creston trading as Delaney Lund Knox Warren & Partners), to DVC Holdings UK (part of the US-based DVC Worldwide marketing group that, for a brief period, was owned by Lake Capital[1]), and most recently to

---

1. *Lake Capital also assembled Lighthouse Global Network and sold it to Cordiant Communications Group – see chapter 9.*

AIM listed The Mission Marketing Group. On each occasion Morgan has banked a useful sum of cash, accumulating gains to date of an estimated £9 million. It is a story of seized opportunities and fortunate timing.

The first deal with Delaney Fletcher Delaney was not entirely a coincidence. Morgan's previous advertising job had been in an agency where Winston Fletcher was a director at the time he resigned to set up shop in Devon.

Like many of London's first generation advertising agency owners at that time, Fletcher had ambitions to build a marcoms group and to float

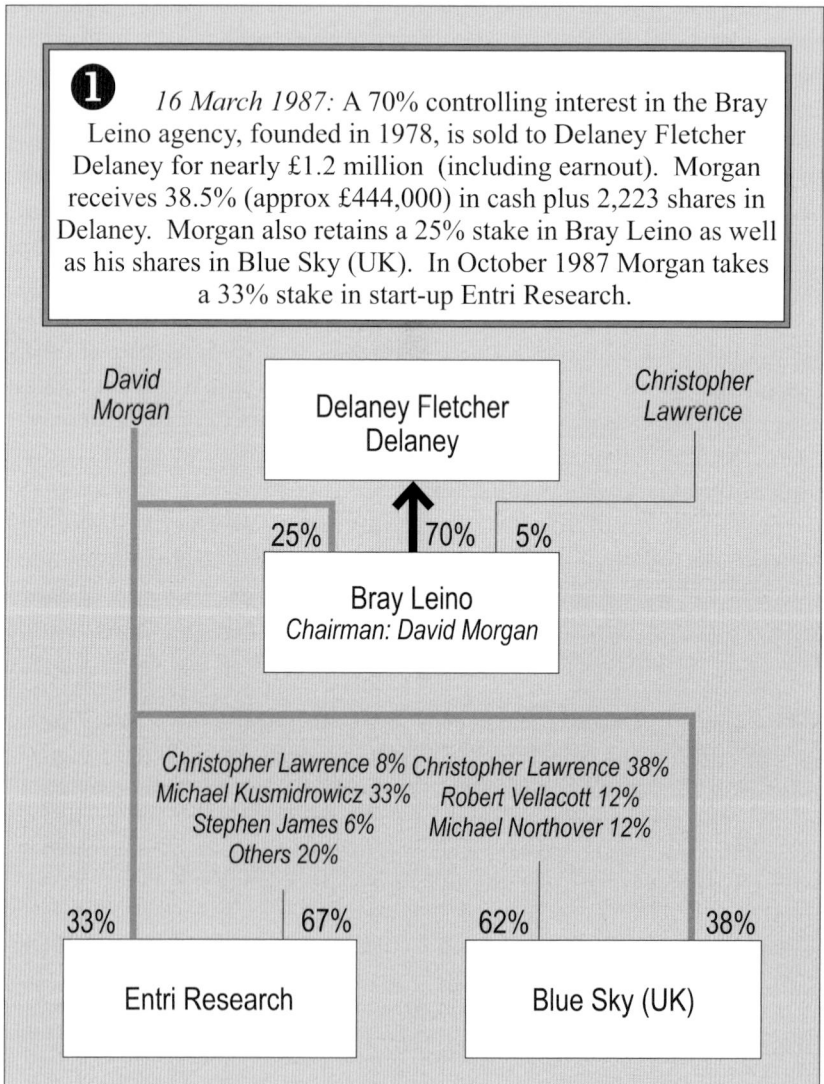

❶ *16 March 1987:* A 70% controlling interest in the Bray Leino agency, founded in 1978, is sold to Delaney Fletcher Delaney for nearly £1.2 million (including earnout). Morgan receives 38.5% (approx £444,000) in cash plus 2,223 shares in Delaney. Morgan also retains a 25% stake in Bray Leino as well as his shares in Blue Sky (UK). In October 1987 Morgan takes a 33% stake in start-up Entri Research.

David Morgan

Christopher Lawrence

Delaney Fletcher Delaney

25% 70% 5%

Bray Leino
Chairman: David Morgan

Christopher Lawrence 8% Christopher Lawrence 38%
Michael Kusmidrowicz 33% Robert Vellacott 12%
Stephen James 6% Michael Northover 12%
Others 20%

33% 67% 62% 38%

Entri Research

Blue Sky (UK)

it on the stock market in due course. Morgan's early success at Bray Leino made him a natural target for Fletcher's attention. The proposition was that Delaney Fletcher Delaney would buy out 70% of Bray Leino's shares, while Morgan would retain 25% (half of his original holding) and Christopher Lawrence would retain 5%.

The deal was agreed in March 1987 and Morgan received £444,000 for the shares he sold, including a substantial earn-out element. In addition, he received 2,223 shares in the Delaney Fletcher Delaney agency and a seat on its board.

Lawrence received around £710,000 for the larger parcel of

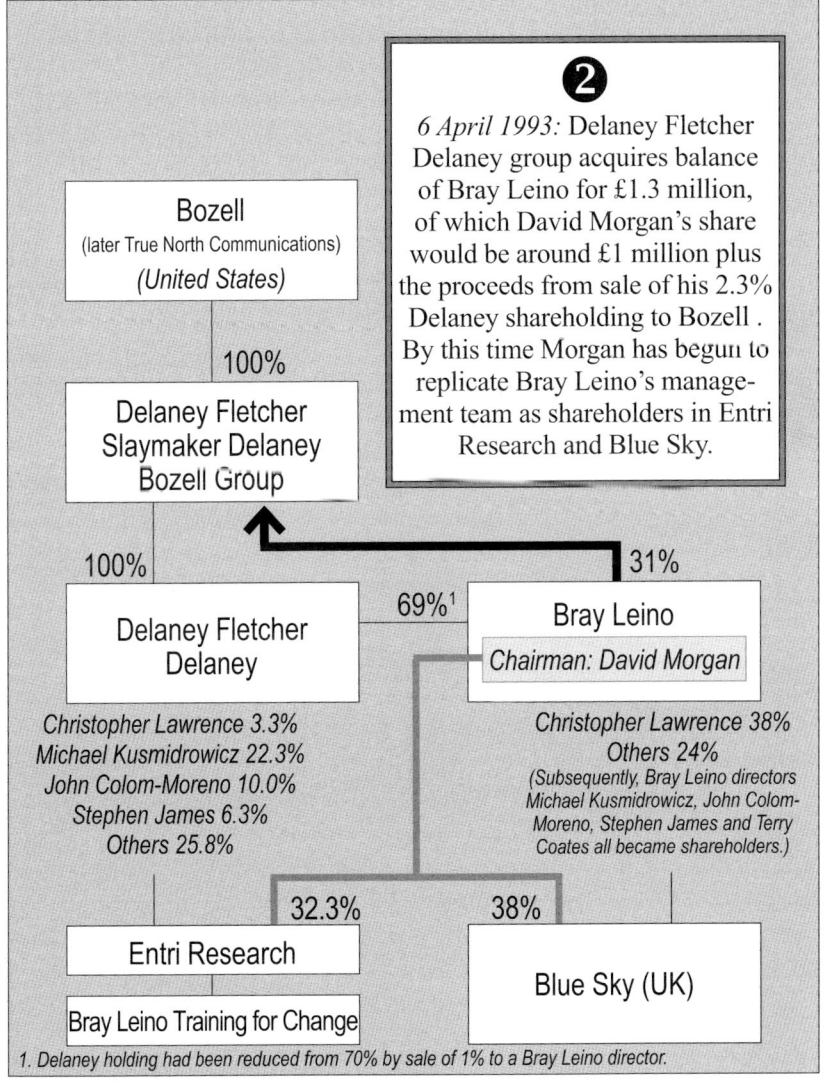

Bozell
(later True North Communications)
(United States)

6 April 1993: Delaney Fletcher Delaney group acquires balance of Bray Leino for £1.3 million, of which David Morgan's share would be around £1 million plus the proceeds from sale of his 2.3% Delaney shareholding to Bozell. By this time Morgan has begun to replicate Bray Leino's management team as shareholders in Entri Research and Blue Sky.

100%

Delaney Fletcher Slaymaker Delaney Bozell Group

100%

69%[1]

31%

Delaney Fletcher Delaney

Christopher Lawrence 3.3%
Michael Kusmidrowicz 22.3%
John Colom-Moreno 10.0%
Stephen James 6.3%
Others 25.8%

Bray Leino
Chairman: David Morgan

Christopher Lawrence 38%
Others 24%
(Subsequently, Bray Leino directors Michael Kusmidrowicz, John Colom-Moreno, Stephen James and Terry Coates all became shareholders.)

32.3%

38%

Entri Research

Bray Leino Training for Change

Blue Sky (UK)

1. Delaney holding had been reduced from 70% by sale of 1% to a Bray Leino director.

shares he sold and his remaining 5% stake was transferred later to another colleague Stephen James.

The value that Delaney Fletcher Delaney placed on Bray Leino in 1987 would seem quite lean by today's standards. The total cash price for 70% of the company, including all the earn-out payments on steadily rising profits, amounted to just eight times the attributable portion of the £202,000 post-tax profit earned for the year to 30 April 1987. So Morgan remained heavily reliant on maximising the value of his residual 25% holding and the newly acquired stake in Delaney to get the scale of reward that might be

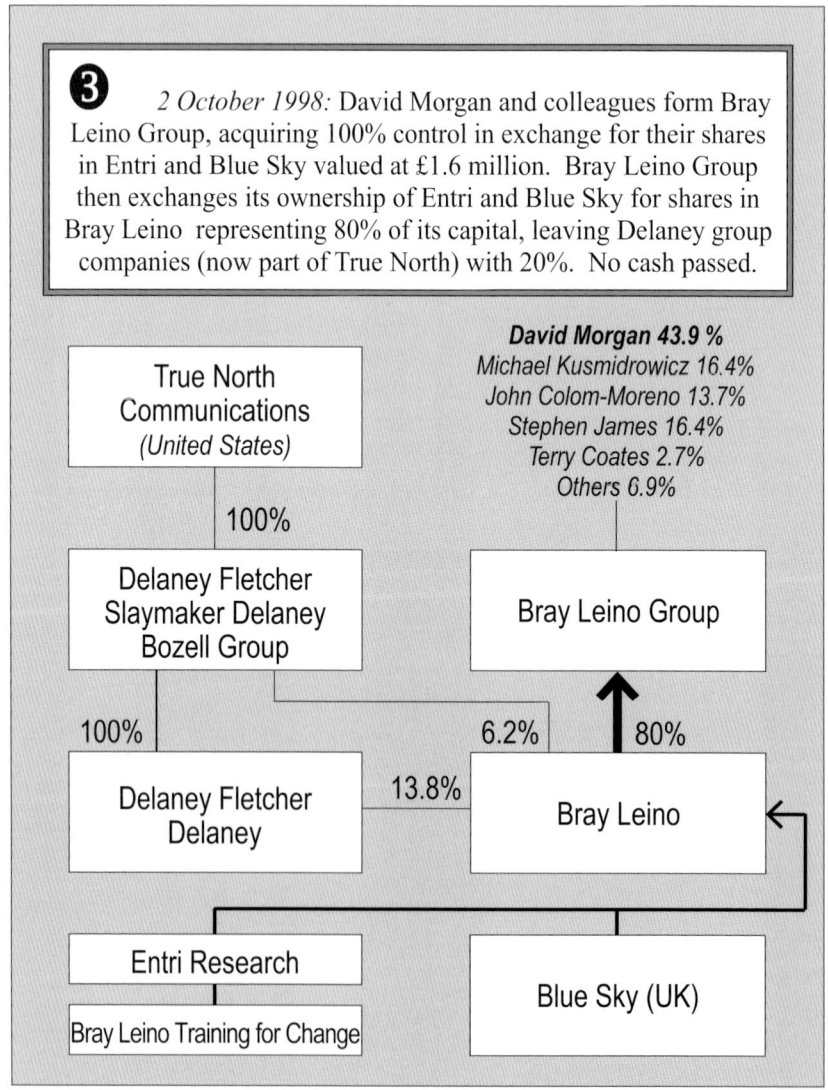

3 *2 October 1998:* David Morgan and colleagues form Bray Leino Group, acquiring 100% control in exchange for their shares in Entri and Blue Sky valued at £1.6 million. Bray Leino Group then exchanges its ownership of Entri and Blue Sky for shares in Bray Leino representing 80% of its capital, leaving Delaney group companies (now part of True North) with 20%. No cash passed.

David Morgan 43.9 %
Michael Kusmidrowicz 16.4%
John Colom-Moreno 13.7%
Stephen James 16.4%
Terry Coates 2.7%
Others 6.9%

True North Communications *(United States)*

100%

Delaney Fletcher Slaymaker Delaney Bozell Group

Bray Leino Group

100%

6.2%

80%

Delaney Fletcher Delaney

13.8%

Bray Leino

Entri Research

Bray Leino Training for Change

Blue Sky (UK)

expected now.

Unusually by present day stand-ards, the deal with Delaney Fletcher Delaney did not prevent Morgan and his management team from investing in related businesses. Alongside Bray Leino they set up three other com-panies — Entri Research, Blue Sky (UK) and Designamo — all of which traded with Bray Leino. Morgan, Lawrence and their wives also owned the premises at Filleigh in Devon that were rented to Bray Leino and its related companies.

Presumably Delaney Fletcher Delaney regarded Morgan's residual 25% share stake in Bray Leino and the terms of the earn-out deal as a

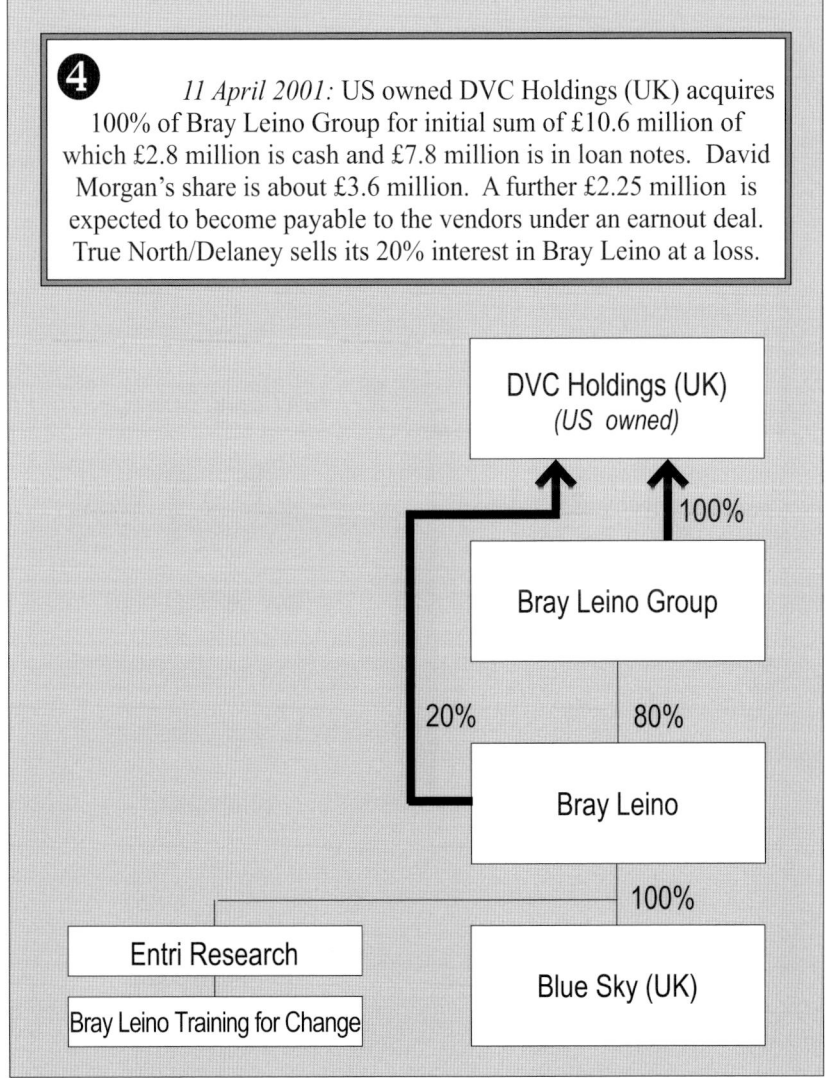

④ *11 April 2001:* US owned DVC Holdings (UK) acquires 100% of Bray Leino Group for initial sum of £10.6 million of which £2.8 million is cash and £7.8 million is in loan notes. David Morgan's share is about £3.6 million. A further £2.25 million is expected to become payable to the vendors under an earnout deal. True North/Delaney sells its 20% interest in Bray Leino at a loss.

sufficient deterrent against devoting too much time to the other companies he and his colleagues still owned. Certainly Bray Leino continued to prosper. But the cost of its acquisition was beginning to make a heavy dent in Delaney Fletcher Delaney's under-capitalised balance sheet and threatening to put its ITV credit recognition at risk. That may have been one of the reasons why Delaney merged with Slaymaker Cowley White Bozell in 1989 and became part of the US-based Bozell network.

In 1993, Morgan and his colleagues exercised an option requiring the Bozell group to buy the rest of their shares in Bray Leino.

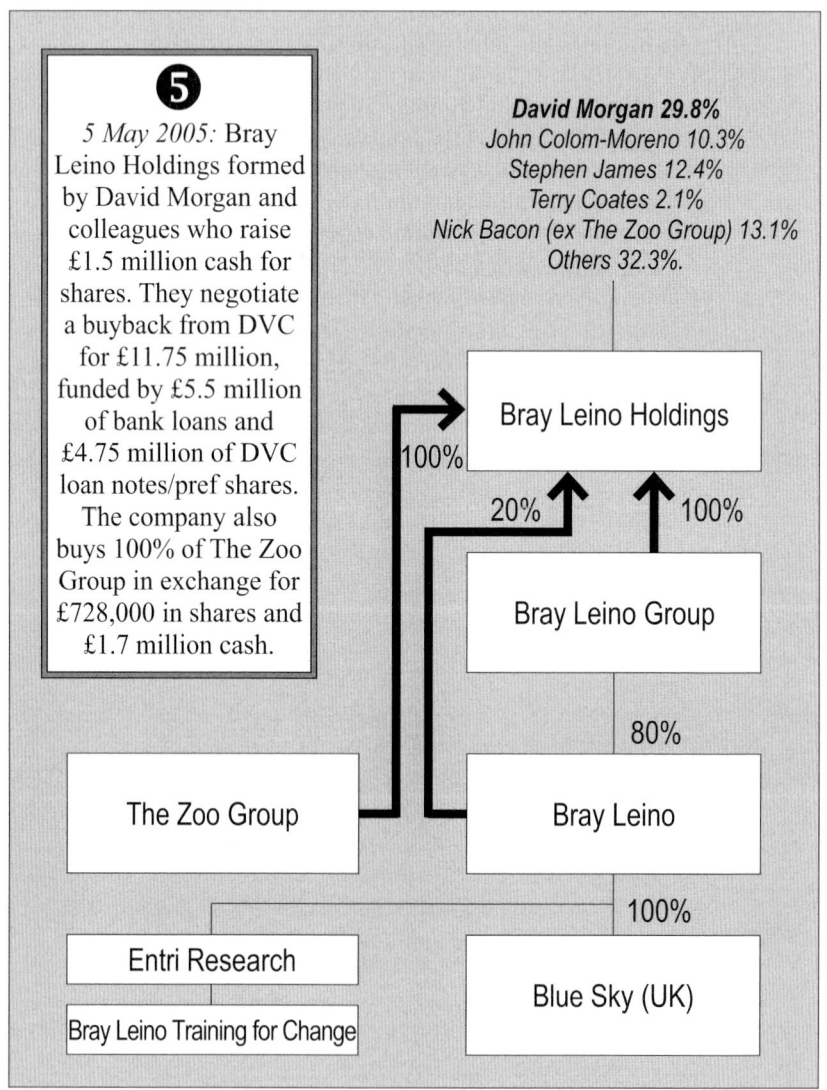

5

5 May 2005: Bray Leino Holdings formed by David Morgan and colleagues who raise £1.5 million cash for shares. They negotiate a buyback from DVC for £11.75 million, funded by £5.5 million of bank loans and £4.75 million of DVC loan notes/pref shares. The company also buys 100% of The Zoo Group in exchange for £728,000 in shares and £1.7 million cash.

David Morgan 29.8%
John Colom-Moreno 10.3%
Stephen James 12.4%
Terry Coates 2.1%
Nick Bacon (ex The Zoo Group) 13.1%
Others 32.3%.

Bray Leino Holdings

100%

20% 100%

Bray Leino Group

80%

The Zoo Group

Bray Leino

100%

Entri Research

Blue Sky (UK)

Bray Leino Training for Change

According to Bozell's accounts, the cost was over £1.3 million of which a little more than £1.1 million flowed out in cash in that particular financial year. By any measure it was a far more lucrative deal than the previous one and Morgan's family slice is likely to have been close to £1 million. Assuming a total purchase price of £1.3 million, the company valuation represented a multiple of over 15 times the post–tax profit for 1993 – a profit that was not to be repeated in the next five years.

Morgan also sold the shares in Delaney that he had received as part of the earlier deal, now representing a modest 2.3% of the Delaney share capital. There is no public record of the consideration paid. Nevertheless, Morgan had so far made around £1.4 million from selling the business he had built up so successfully – and was still managing along with the other business interests he had established outside the Bozell group.

Yet within five years he was buying Bray Leino back again.

This initiative coincided with the takeover of Bozell by True North

Communications in December 1997, a development that resulted in True North reporting a loss of $50 million and may have left Morgan feeling that his Devonshire venture was getting increasingly remote from the centre of an ever-expanding global empire[1]. The combination of a dip in Bray Leino's trading performance and the growing success of Morgan's other companies outside Bray Leino created an ideal opportunity for a deal.

In essence, Morgan reacquired an 80% stake in Bray Leino in exchange for giving True North a 20% share in most of the other companies he part-owned.

Financially he was the clear winner. The deal was completed in October 1998 and involved the formation of a new holding company – Bray Leino Group – which issued its shares to Morgan and his colleagues in exchange for all the shares they held in Blue Sky (UK) and Entri

1. Morgan recently described the circumstances like this: "As Bozell had no strategic need of Bray Leino the relationship became pointless and at about the same time as they were flirting with True North it seemed sensible all round for us to exit. All very decent and amicable."

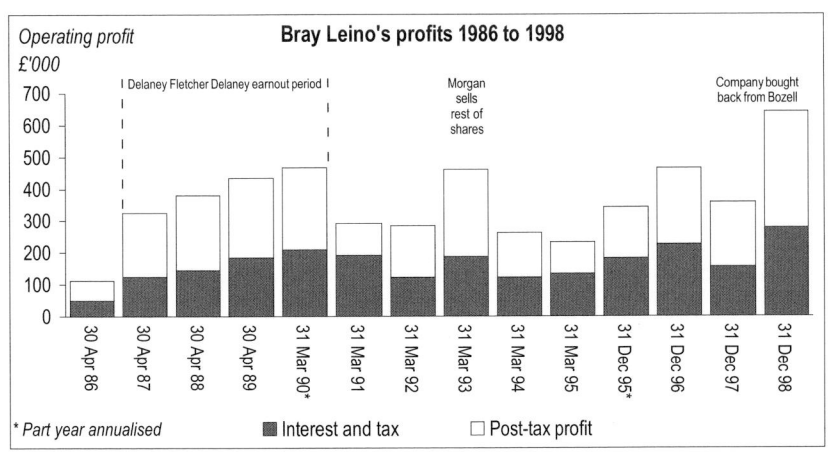

Bray Leino's profits 1986 to 1998
Operating profit £'000

30 Apr 86 · 30 Apr 87 · 30 Apr 88 · 30 Apr 89 · 31 Mar 90* · 31 Mar 91 · 31 Mar 92 · 31 Mar 93 · 31 Mar 94 · 31 Mar 95 · 31 Dec 95* · 31 Dec 96 · 31 Dec 97 · 31 Dec 98

I Delaney Fletcher Delaney earnout period I — Morgan sells rest of shares — Company bought back from Bozell

* Part year annualised   ■ Interest and tax   □ Post-tax profit

Research. This restructuring placed a value of £1.6 million on the companies acquired by the new "group" of which Morgan and his team became the owners without any material cash outlay.

The next element of the deal was for Bray Leino Group to sell on to Bray Leino itself the companies it had just acquired — this time in exchange for new shares in Bray Leino valued also at £1.6 million. This transaction had the effect of diluting the Bozell stake in Bray Leino from 100% to 20%, leaving the dominant 80% holding with Morgan's Bray Leino Group.

Almost as soon as the ink was dry, Bray Leino was reporting a much improved profit of £414,000 after tax. Within two and a half years another buyer was showing interest in the business — this time the US group called DVC Worldwide that was owned by Lake Capital.

In April 2001 DVC offered an initial price of £10.6 million for the group that had cost Morgan virtually nothing to buy back from Bozell, although £2.1 million of the £10.6 million proceeds went to buy out Bozell's residual 20% stake at a substantial loss. At first DVC anticipated paying a further £2.25 million as an earn-out but eventually this was revised down to nil.

Of the initial £10.6 million, it appears that Morgan received around £3.6 million — mainly in loan notes which probably helped mitigate any tax liability — bringing the cumulative reward for his entrepreneurial flair to about £5million over 23 years.

The relationship with DVC lasted until 2005 by the end of which it had disposed of its two UK acquisitions[1].

Morgan and his finance director Terry

1. David Morgan recalls that Lake decided to get rid of its two UK based DVC businesses after the 9/11 tragedy in New York: "They put us both up for sale. They sold Aspen Field Marketing, as it was then called, to private equity but had no sensible offers for Bray Leino. So they came up with another decent and amicable offer for us to buy back. It was their initiative, not mine."

Coates were now well experienced in deal-making and put together a new management buyout package the cost of which was financed to a large extent by DVC itself. Fortuitously, Bray Leino's profits had suffered another dip immediately prior to this deal.

So Morgan's new acquisition vehicle Bray Leino Holdings bought back the businesses for a second time in May 2005 at a price of £11.75 million. Of this, £4.75 million was deferred by DVC in the form of loan notes and preference shares. The remaining £7 million was provided in part by a new share issue that raised about £1.5 million cash and the balance was funded by bank borrowings. Morgan contributed some £440,000 of the new share capital.

Coinciding with the buyback, the group acquired The Zoo Group along with its major shareholder Nicholas Bacon who took on the role of group chief operating officer. The cost was £2.6 million in cash and shares.

By early 2006 Morgan and his team were in serious talks with The Mission Marketing Group about selling on the business again - this time as part of an IPO plan. Morgan's team arranged extra banking facilities, persuaded DVC to surrender the £4 million loan notes for about £2.8 million and also redeemed DVC's preference shares.

That cut the cost of the buy-back from £11.75 million to just over £10.6 million before expenses - virtually the same price as DVC had paid to buy the business three years earlier. Of that reduced cost, the shareholders had contributed about £1.5 million.

On Mission's AIM debut, the Bray Leino shares were acquired for an initial £14.9 million, yielding a handsome profit that added a further £4 million to Morgan's previous £5 million personal gain.

A spate of billion dollar digital deals reflected a renewed urgency among the acquirers to secure a strong position in a constantly evolving market.

17
Digital Deals to Dominate

In chapters 8 and 15 we read about the growth and - in 2001 - the bursting of the "dotcom bubble", and its adverse impact on Omnicom and Interpublic. Despite those dramas, no-one doubted that the internet had brought with it an important new medium for marketing communications.

By 2007 the traditional groups in the industry had developed a more mature attitude towards digital opportunities. They realised that digital expertise had to be an integral part of their overall offer, otherwise independent digital agencies and various management consultancies would carve out an ever-increasing slice of their clients' marketing budgets.

Driven by this threat, while at the same time eager to exploit the additional opportunities presented by digital media, many major marketing companies set off on the acquisition trail again – and were offering juicy prices to achieve their ambitions. But those companies were not the only predators. They were joined by companies that had already established a presence in the digital market and who were eager to deprive their rivals from gaining any competitive strength. It was a perfect environment for digital agencies who wanted to sell.

Bill Gates: founder of Microsoft which bought aQuantive in 2007

Were the buyers paying too much? Would those traditional advertising agency groups be able to adjust to accommodate the digital dimension? And what would be the commercial implications for their clients?

I decided to carry out a review of some of the bigger transactions initiated by major companies. The outcome, reproduced in this chapter, was first published in May 2007 in *New*

Media Agencies Financial Intelligence (later combined with its sister title *Marketing Services Financial Intelligence*, reflecting the convergence of the two business segments).

The chapter focusses on the acquisition of four digital marketing and/or technology companies – Digitas, DoubleClick, 24/7 Real Media and aQuantive. All of those companies were based in the United States, although two of the buyers came from elsewhere. Digitas was acquired by the French group Publicis and 24/7 Media was acquired by the UK's WPP.

Alongside revisiting the original analysis of these deals, it is instructive to consider here whether, with the passage of time, the apparently high prices paid for the acquisitions were justified by subsequent events.

Interestingly, the buyers from the marketing sector paid a significantly lower multiple of the target's profits to secure their deals than the other buyers, with the caveat that some aspects of the Google deal remain shrouded in mystery. But even the smaller multiples paid by those marketing groups were sufficiently generous to suggest that fast growth was expected. Alternatively, everyone simply paid too much in the rush to gain more muscle in the digital market.

The first of the big digital deals took place in January 2007 when Publicis paid $3.3 billion to acquire the US-based digital technology consultancy Digitas which also owned the digital marketing agency Modem Media.

It may prove to have been one of the best deals in terms of value for money. It also proved to be of considerable strategic importance in propelling Publicis from a modest player in the digital market to a strong competitor for the well-established businesses owned by Omnicom Group and for specialist independent digital companies like aQuantive (which, as we shall see, was bought by Microsoft a few months later) and AKQA (bought by WPP in 2012). As noted in chapter 7, the Digitas

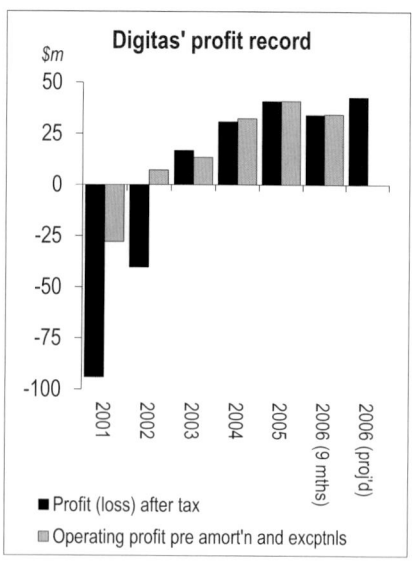

Digitas' profit record

■ Profit (loss) after tax
▨ Operating profit pre amort'n and excptnls

acquisition marked the start of a string of further digital deals that cost Publicis almost $6 billion (€5.3 billion) in the space of eight years.

Digitas had been created in 1999 from a merger of a 20-year-old direct marketing business with a youthful internet consultancy, but the bursting of the dotcom bubble threw the group's finances into melt-down as staff and property costs could not be cut back quickly enough. Losses of $198 million resulted, but the group had sufficient share capital to survive. By the time Publicis took an interest in acquiring the company, it was back in the doldrums again, having been hit by a series of client losses and budget cutbacks. As a result profits had remained static and this was reflected in the Digitas share price.

Doubtless this was one of the factors that enabled Publicis to pay a multiple of "only" 27.2 times the historic post-tax profit to acquire the business. Nevertheless, I calculated that Digitas would have to grow by at least 25% per annum for 10 years to justify the price Publicis was paying, assuming annual synergistic benefits of, say, $10 million and taking into account the fact that Digitas would lose the substantial benefit of a negligible tax charge after it had absorbed past losses in about three years' time.

A 25% growth rate would result in the purchase price equating to a still-generous multiple of 15 times average post-tax profits after discounting those profits back to their present day value. Such

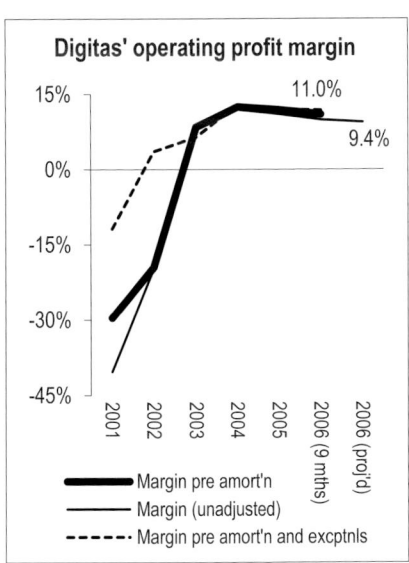

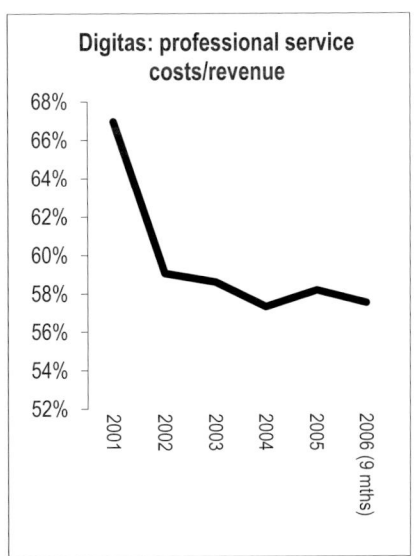

was the irrational optimism in the advertising industry that recurring annual growth of 25% was regarded as modest. But, in Digitas, Publicis was almost certainly acquiring more than just a profit stream. It brought serious clout to its digital armoury, both in technological know-how and marketing expertise. And arguably that was worth paying for, even if the full reward took a while to arrive.

Apart from the anticipated synergistic gains, Publicis may have hoped to improve the profit margin earned on Digitas services. On the face of it there was plenty of scope for improvement, but in practice it may have proved more difficult.

At the time professional services staff alone absorbed 58% of Digitas revenues and, after allowing for administrative staff costs and other operating expenses, the group's operating profit margin had fallen to around 11% before making any charge for goodwill amortisation. And while that margin would have exceeded 12% in two of the three years preceding its acquisition if restructuring costs were also to be ignored, even this would have been well below the 15.3% margin that Publicis had recently achieved from its existing businesses.

Early in the negotiations Publicis tried to persuade Digitas shareholders to accept a mixture of cash and shares, without success, so the entire acquisition price had to be funded from its existing bank facilities.

Hard on the heels of the Digitas acquisition came Microsoft's bid in May 2007 for its Seattle near neighbour aQuantive with a $6 billion cash payment representing a multiple of 111 times the previous year's post-tax profits. With the information now available it is clear that Microsoft paid far too much for this digital advertising and search marketing business.

At the time it seemed likely that Microsoft's primary interest would have been in aQuantive's search and ad-serving businesses, rather than in its Razorfish digital advertising agency. Our analysis concluded: "In the circumstances Microsoft will almost certainly be open to offers for the purchase of Avenue A|Razorfish."

aQuantive had acquired Razorfish in 2004 and merged it with another subsidiary Avenue A. As recounted in chapter 8, Razorfish had had a chequered history — accumulating losses of $334 million by 2001 when Omnicom offloaded its minority stake into the controversial home for sick dotcom victims called Seneca Investments. Ownership of Razorfish was then handed on from one company to another until it was acquired by aQuantive.

In 2009 — two years after its acquisition by Microsoft as part of the aQuantive deal — Razorfish was sold on to Publicis Groupe for an even more astonishing $530 million. After deducting those proceeds, the net cost of the aQuantive deal still amounted to a chunky $5.5 billion. In the circumstances it may not have come as a big surprise when Microsoft made the following announcement on 2 July 2012:

> Microsoft Corp. today announced that it will take a non-cash, non-tax deductible income statement charge for the fourth quarter of fiscal year 2012 for the impairment of goodwill in its Online Services Division segment, mostly related to its 2007 aQuantive acquisition...Microsoft has determined that a write-down of its Online Services Division goodwill of approximately $6.2 billion is required.
>
> Microsoft completed its acquisition of aQuantive, Inc. on August 13, 2007, in an all-cash transaction valued at just over $6.3 billion. While the aQuantive acquisition continues to provide tools for Microsoft's online advertising efforts, the acquisition did not accelerate growth to the degree anticipated contributing to the write down.

Google also appears to have acquired DoubleClick for an unimaginably high price when it bought the business for $3.1 billion in cash from private equity backers Hellman & Friedman and JMI Equity in March 2008. To be more precise, Google paid nearer $3.2 billion but disposed of the Performics search marketing business shortly afterwards for $53 million. Some £2.4 billion of the $3.1 billion cost was allocated to goodwill and $629 million was allocated to customer relationships – assets that would normally be reviewed annually to see whether their value had been impaired.

Hellman & Friedman and JMI had taken the company private in 2005 in a deal reported to have been valued at $1.1 billion. Prior to that deal DoubleClick had accumulated losses of $612 million. But, on the plus side, the company had recently broken into a healthy profit and was sitting on a

Google - its founders Larry Page and Sergey Brin shown here - bought DoubleClick.

big pile of cash and investments totalling $390 million at the end of 2004.

The price paid by the private equity backers in 2005 would have represented a multiple of 28.6 times the post-tax profit for 2004 or 37.9 times the profit before interest, tax, goodwill amortisation and impairment and restructuring charges, were it not for DoubleClick's cash pile and investments. If, as private equity investors tend to do, the cash and investments were stripped out of the company, the multiple becomes 18.9 times the post-tax profit or 25.1 times the profit before interest, tax, goodwill amortisation and impairment and restructuring charges – generous, but not overly so.

Very little information had been published about Double-Click's profitability after it was taken back into private ownership. Indeed, the only clue to DoubleClick's profitability around the time of the Google acquisition appeared later as a note in Google's 2008 annual return to the Securities & Exchange Commission.

The note stated that Google's post-tax profit would have been $4,007 million in 2007 and $4,204 million in 2008 if Double-Click had been owned throughout those two periods. But without DoubleClick for most of those two years, Google reported bigger post-tax profits of $4,203 million and $4,226 million respectively. In other words, the implication is that DoubleClick was actually *losing* money in those two years – $196 million in 2007 and an estimated $119 million in 2008 (after adjusting for the fact that the acquisition took place on 11 March 2008). Back in 2004 Double-Click had reported a post-tax profit of $37.5 million, but that was achieved with the help of $10 million financial income and a $10 million gain from asset disposals.

If these figures can be relied upon, Google paid a massive amount of money for a loss-making business presumably because it would give it technological and competitive advantages – not least in access to commercially valuable data – along with an equally valuable client base. At the time of the acquisition, Google acknowledged that the deal would give it access to DoubleClick's advertisement software and its relationships with web publishers, advertisers and advertising agencies, and would enable it to offer "superior tools for targeting, serving and analysing online ads of all types, significantly benefiting customers and consumers".

Advertisers and agencies would be provided with an easy and efficient way to manage both search and display ads in one place, and to optimise their ad spending across different online media using a common set of metrics. But no-one mentioned that DoubleClick was losing money. No wonder Google refused to comment on my interpretation.

The fourth and final deal examined in this chapter was the purchase of 24/7 Real Media by WPP Group in May 2007. WPP bought the New York based digital agency for $649 million in cash (after offsetting 24/7 Real Media's net cash balances). The company had experienced an erratic trading performance in the years leading up to its sale (see chart), incurring losses in both 2004 and 2006.

The purchase price equated to a very full multiple of 42.7 times the preceding year's profit before interest, tax, amortisation and stock-based remuneration, a multiple that implied rapid growth and/or reflected WPP's pressing need to make more a substantial inroad into the digital market.

WPP acknowledged this, explaining that 24/7 Real Media's technological capabilities and skills, combined with the group's understanding of client demands and media, would play an increasingly important role in providing the best solutions for its clients. WPP also expected to achieve future cost savings of $5 million.

Compared with the major digital acquisitions by Publicis and Microsoft in 2007, 24/7 Real Media was relatively small, but it added further evidence that traditional marketing groups were having to move outside their comfort zone and embrace digital technology with energy and cash. Five years later WPP made another big investment, this time in AKQA, a digital marketing agency that

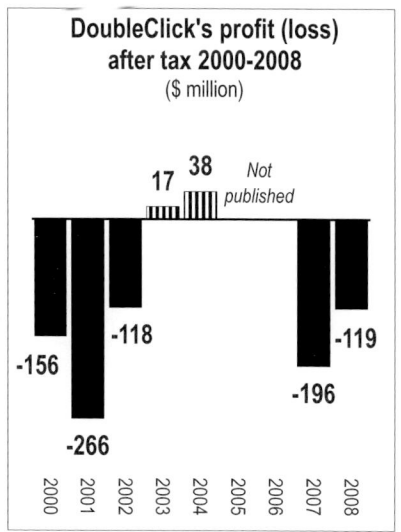

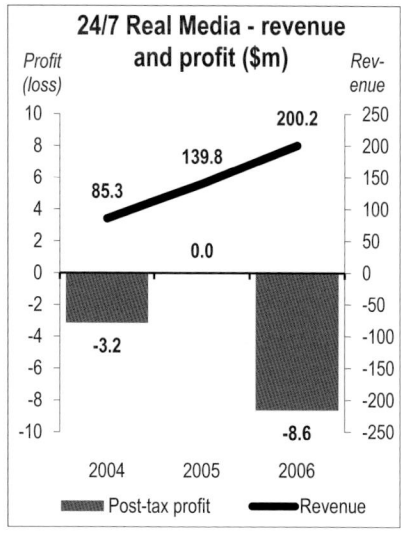

had been born in Britain, but relocated to the United States. WPP placed an enterprise value on AKQA of $540 million.

The recent spate of billion dollar digital deals in the US started last December with the $1.3 billion bid to acquire Digitas by the French Publicis Groupe. The reasoning seemed fairly simple and straight-forward: traditional Publicis advertising agency networks had neither the technological know-how nor the marketing application skills to satisfy their clients' growing need for an effective use of the ever-expanding number of digital marketing corridors. Digitas, with its Modem Media network, could hopefully fill both gaps. And $1.3 billion was a necessary — if expensive — price to pay to gain a more credible foothold in that strategically essential area of business.

But few industry observers would have expected three more big deals to follow so quickly. Since the turn of the year Google has offered $3.1 billion for DoubleClick, WPP Group has offered $649 million for loss-making 24/7 Real Media and, to cap them all, Microsoft has offered $6 billion to acquire aQuantive.

The deals are different but the motive seems the same: to succeed in the digital arena, it is essential to have a big stake both in the technology and in the businesses that use it. And to maximise the profit potential, market domination is very important.

But do these strategic imperatives justify the astonishingly high prices that have been paid for targeted companies? And is it healthy for client facing marketing agencies to share ownership with internet publishers and the companies that own and

exploit search and server technologies? How will clients know they are getting the best value for their money when already they are having to run at breakneck speed to capture any understanding of how the digital market really works? If ever there was a strong justification for an impartial and knowledgeable adviser, this is it.

Looking first at the high prices paid in the recent big deals, they can only be justified either on defensive strategic grounds and/or if resultant market dominance (or something near it) will fuel meteoric profit growth. Both Publicis and WPP may have inclined towards the defensive view that, without a far bigger foray into digital expertise, much of their business would soon be no more than a pale shadow of its glorious past.

The challenge will be to inject this new-found expertise into every part of the traditional agency networks and their clients, and that may not be quite as easy as it sounds.

In one scenario — feared but yet to be proven — internet publishers like Google will have such a detailed knowledge of who responds to their clients' ads that the role of an intermediary agency in price negotiation will become almost superfluous. The real effort will then focus on generating the most effective digital ads. In this scenario the role of the specialist creative digital agency may become all-important and the traditional networks might have to fight hard to win or keep that type of business.

Against such a backcloth it is

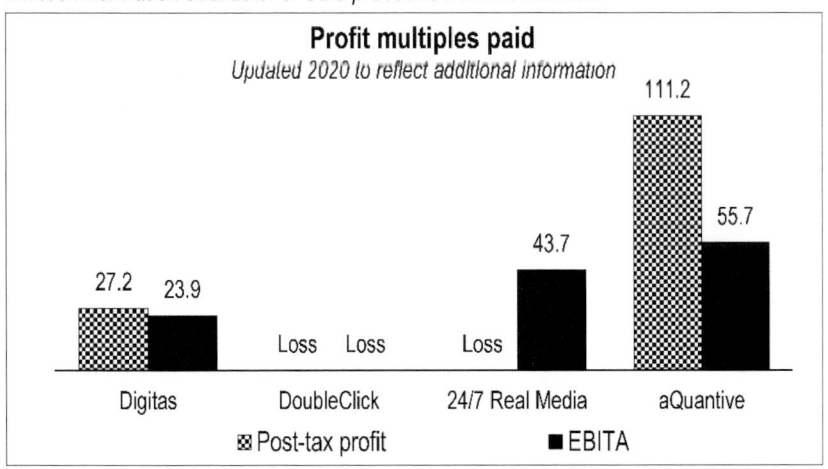

Digitas	DoubleClick	24/7 Real Media	aQuantive
$1.3 bn	$3.1 bn	$0.7 bn	$6.0 bn
Bought by **Publicis Groupe**	Bought by **Google**	Bought by **WPP Group**	Bought by **Microsoft Corp**
Price paid to shareholders: $1,295,000,000	Price paid to shareholders: $3,200,000,000	Price paid to shareholders: $686,000,000	Price paid to shareholders: $6,000,000,000
Expenses: $1,000,000[1]	Expenses: $70,400,000	Expenses: Not disclosed	Expenses: Not disclosed
Less cash acquired: $129,000,000	Less cash acquired: $53,000,000 [2,3]	Less cash acquired: $37,000,000	Less cash acquired: $50,000,000 [1]

1. Estimated. 2. Acquired from private equity consortium led by Hellman & Friedman – limited information available. 3. Sale proceeds from Performics.

Profit multiples paid

Updated 2020 to reflect additional information

	Digitas	DoubleClick	24/7 Real Media	aQuantive
Post-tax profit	27.2	Loss	Loss	111.2
EBITA	23.9	Loss	43.7	55.7

⊠ Post-tax profit   ■ EBITA

The profit multiples above show the price paid by the acquiring company expressed as a multiple of (a) last year's post-tax profit as reported by the target company (a loss at 24/7 Real Media) and (b) last year's profit before interest, tax, share incentive scheme charges, goodwill amortisation/impairment provisions and non-recurring restructuring charges (EBITA).

important to note that, while the companies being acquired by agency network owners Publicis and WPP are both engaged entirely in the digital sector, their activities are markedly different. The Digitas/ Modem Media operation is first and foremost a consultancy that advises clients on the development of their digital marketing capabilities and then executes digital marketing programmes by drawing on its technical know-how and creative skills. Its origins are in direct marketing.

By contrast, 24/7 Real Media's focus is on getting the best out of search marketing and on providing efficient and profitable ad-serving programmes. It competes directly with companies like DoubleClick and aQuantive's Atlas division. It doesn't design websites and it doesn't create advertisements. So, unlike the Publicis-Digitas tie-up, this deal gives WPP a sizeable foothold in the digital technology sector with an offer that will complement, rather than replace, the services provided by its traditional marketing agencies.

But two questions remain unanswered. The first is whether 24/7 Real Media has the scale to compete effectively with the bigger Double-Click and Atlas operations. The second is whether WPP's core marketing services networks have adequate digital expertise to retain credibility with, and maintain revenues from, existing clients.

As the charts show, Digitas has a far more stable and substantial financial track record than 24/7 RealMediia. But maybe WPP was prepared to pay an even higher multiple of profits for 24/7 Real Media than the generous price Publicis paid for Digitas because WPP would thereby acquire a higher margin technology business that would hopefully generate more upside potential. Or

How digital businesses differ[1]

Service	Digitas	DoubleClick	24/7 Real Media	aQuantive
Web and marketing strategy planning	☑			☑
Website design and build (including intranets and extranets)	☑			☑
E-commerce applications	☑			☑
Online advertising and promotion	☑		☑	☑
Email marketing	☑			☑
Direct response TV	☑			
TV and broadband advertising			☑	☑
Wireless/mobile communications	☑		☑	☑
Direct mail	☑			
Events and promotions	☑			
Press advertising	☑			
Internet advertising optimisation	☑		☑	☑
Customer relationship/database management	☑			☑
Adserving		☑	☑	☑
Search management	☑	☑	☑	☑
Online advertisement sales agency		☑	☑	☑
Affiliate marketing technologies		☑		

1. This table is compiled from information published by various companies. It may not be complete or up to date.

did the price simply reflect the rapidly declining pool of acquisition targets?

On the face of it WPP is paying nearly eight times the historic gross income earned by loss-making 24/7Real Media whereas in traditional deals the multiple is normally between one and two, depending on growth potential.

According to WPP's own calculations the purchase price represents a more modest multiple of the current year's income, but it still appears very generous. As a multiple of historic operating profit before tax, interest, and charges for goodwill amortisation, share-based incentive schemes and restructuring costs (in effect the internal cash return before financing costs), WPP is paying an astonishing multiple of 44 whereas more typical deals value the target in single figure multiples.

The purchase price would look far more realistic if the 53% per annum rate of revenue growth achieved over

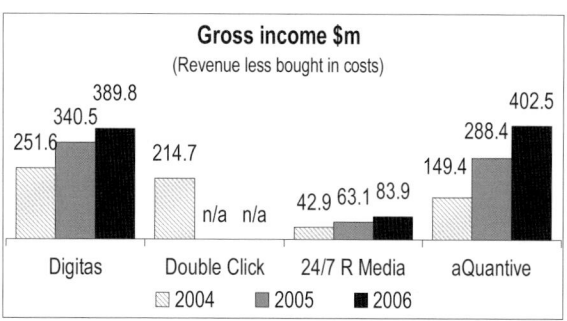

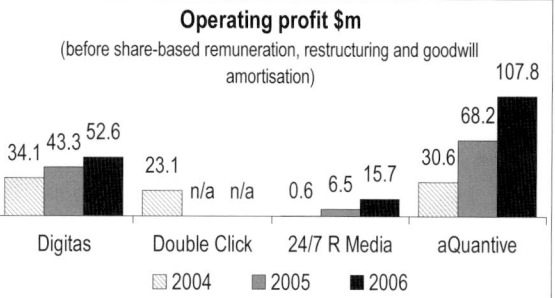

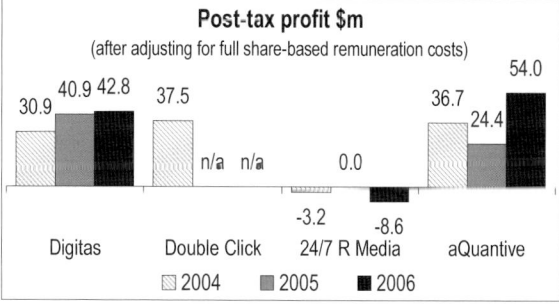

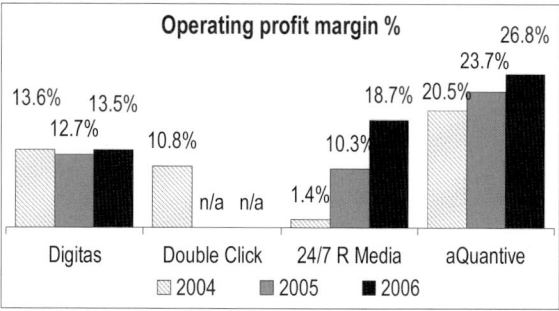

Due to differing US accounting practices and disclosure rules, amounts shown above as "gross income" and "operating profit margin" may not necessarily correspond to the equivalent amounts under UK accounting rules. Nevertheless, amounts shown for "operating profit" and "post-tax profit" are broadly consistent with those arrived at under UK practices.

the last two years could be translated into profit growth and maintained into the future, thereby producing an average annual post-tax return on the investment of somewhere near 10% or a very healthy 30% internal return based on the adjusted operating profit. But even in the digital market such a long-term growth rate sounds too rich to be true.

Whatever the reasoning behind the Digitas and 24/7 Real Media acquisitions, the much bigger Double-Click and aQuantive deals seem to have been predicated on the opportunity to dominate and exploit a huge segment of the digital market by combining their acquirers' existing internet publishing operations with the technology-based revenue opportunities enjoyed by the target companies. There is nothing defensive about that.

Profit margins earned from internet technology exploitation are clearly better than in traditional marketing services, as the chart opposite shows. And the incidental acquisition of aQuantive's digital marketing agency AvenueA|Razorfish by Microsoft is already being seen by some observers as superfluous to its main goal.

Put simply, all of the deals apart from the Publicis-Digitas one are about technology exploitation rather than digital marketing applications. And in the scheme of things the WPP-24/7 Real Media transaction is a relative minnow.

Microsoft is not paying an astronomical multiple of 111 times historic post-tax profits to acquire aQuantive just for a steady earnings stream. There has to be a much bigger prize

to be won from capturing control of the technologies that manage search and other advertising flows, and thereby gain knowledge and influence that will help boost revenues from its digital media. Presumably that was also the appeal of DoubleClick to Google.

Small wonder that Microsoft's chief executive officer Steve Ballmer trumpeted the deal with the words: "Microsoft is intensely committed to creating a thriving advertising business and to partnering closely with all key constituencies...to help maximise the digital advertising opportunity for all." Well, for Microsoft anyway.

The aQuantive deal price of $66.50 per share makes no sense in isolation. When the deal was announced on 18 May, its shares were cruising along comfortably at a price of $36 — a generous enough multiple of 56 times historic profits. At the offer price, aQuantive's historic price/earnings multiple leapt to well over 100 while that of Microsoft remained around 22 — itself a bullish multiple even for the digital sector.

The differential between the multiples commanded by each company was slightly less extreme when based on prospective post-tax profits for the current year. Yet although the acquisition of aQuantive represents a relative modest outlay for a company as big as Microsoft, it is hard to see how the deal terms will avoid a diluting effect on the value of Microsoft's shares for the foreseeable future.

In the circumstances Microsoft will almost certainly be open to offers for the purchase of Avenue A|Razorfish — not so much because it is likely to bring down the price multiple applicable to the more juicy businesses it retains, but in order to choke off some of the conflict criticisms it will inevitably attract.

How has DoubleClick been performing during the last two years under ownership of a private equity syndicate? No figures have been published, but it seems unlikely that the purchase price of $3.1 billion was anything other than a high one in relation to historic profits, not least because Microsoft had already been sniffing around with its bulging wallet.

And it was not alone. Without doubt some of the prices paid to acquire marketing technology businesses will prove to have been excessive. But the strategic shift in emphasis that triggered those premium prices is here to stay.

As the events of the last few months demonstrate, the centre of gravity of the marketing services industry has shifted irrevocably away from traditional creative agencies into the more complicated world of technology. And that shift is not only about the type of advertising that is now required, but also about the way in which it is transmitted to its audience. Advertisers and internet publishers are now able to measure the effectiveness of each advertising transmission with great precision.

So the businesses that supply and manage those technological tools of measurement are becoming most highly valued by clients and online publishers alike. And, as publishers like Google and Microsoft acquire technology suppliers like Double-Click and Atlas, the new risk is that clients will be held to ransom as the information gatherers take advantage of the technology they have acquired.

Meanwhile the money that used to flow into traditional advertising agencies by the bucket load to fund what was sometimes little more than a speculative indulgence by a creative team is now flowing out with no prospect of return. Creative awards are giving way to technological rewards in the minds of discerning clients. The world has changed. The way that the marketing services industry will earn its keep has changed. Forever.

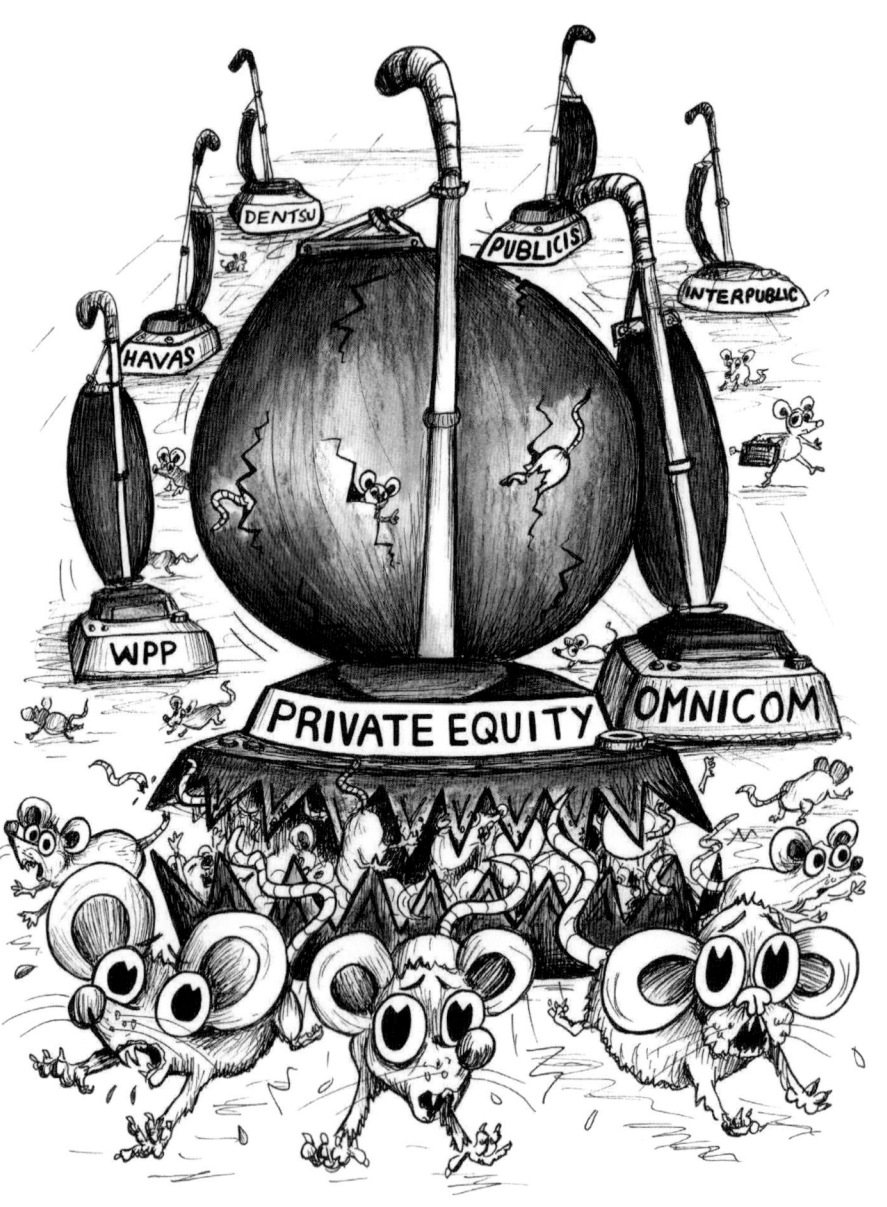

Little has been written about the growing interest of private equity investment houses in the marketing services sector. Is it good or bad for the industry?

18

Who profits from Private Equity?

One of my earliest experiences of private equity finance and its role in management buyouts took place in 1982. I had recently returned to public practice as a partner in the sizeable UK accountancy firm of Spicer and Pegler which had an excellent reputation for its work in the City of London, especially in relation to partnership tax matters. The firm has since been absorbed into Deloitte. More to the point, by the time I joined the firm it had already been engaged to advise on a number of management buyouts.

One day I received a phone call from Paul Buckley, a former board colleague at Haymarket Publishing who had headed up my division and been highly supportive during my time there. He had a friend called John Hegarty (now Sir John Hegarty) who was the creative director at the London office of a Paris-based advertising agency network called TBWA. Hegarty and two of his colleagues, who had been the driving force in making the agency's London office a resounding success from start-up, were contemplating a management buyout. Would I be able to help? I agreed to meet them early that evening with one of my partners who had more experience of that type of transaction.

That was how I met John Bartle, Nigel Bogle and the aforementioned John Hegarty who were to become the founders of Bartle Bogle Hegarty. Three characteristics emerged very swiftly. They were bright. They had integrity. And they were generous, evidenced by the tabling of a splendid bottle of white wine to assist us in our evening deliberations in what I remember was a rather small, almost drab office in St Mary Axe.

The conversation turned from a consideration of how they might pursue their aspirations to how a management buyout might be financed. We explored sources of capital ranging from clearing banks to financial institutions that might be willing to make a longer term investment if the capital requirement proved substantial. That sort of institutional funding used to be called venture capital but today it is more often called private equity – "equity" referring to the desire for a shareholding in the venture and "private" meaning funds provided by a range of financial institutions and other investors as distinct from a public stock market.

This chance introduction was undoubtedly instrumental in my career development at Spicer and Pegler, as the trio were to introduce a number of other clients to the firm and we were able to bathe in their reflected glory as Bartle Bogle Hegarty was launched successfully and grew into one of the most highly regarded names in the industry. The occasion also marked the start of a long, happy and fruitful professional relationship with Richard Smerdon, a partner in solicitors Osborne Clarke. I owe them all a great debt.

As events evolved, the plan for a management buyout transitioned into a breakaway – more of a rarity today than in the nineteen eighties. So the new agency was able to be launched with bank finance alone and institutional funding was unnecessary.

Today, private equity funding has a number of uses. As well as facilitating a management buyout, it can provide the finance required to enable one of a team of founding partners to retire without selling the entire business. Private equity investors can also bring experience and additional expertise to the investee. But, as we shall see, once private equity funding takes place, there will be an almost inevitable expectation that the business will be sold on within a few years. Private equity finance is not designed for the long term, so it is hard to envisage building a business that can remain independent for a generation or more.

This chapter tells how private equity funds had been investing their money in the marketing sector up to 2007. It includes interviews with several of the fund managers and addresses a number of questions that were being raised about this form of finance at the time. Not that there isn't a valuable role that private equity can play. But it has not filled what used to be called the "equity gap" that has long been identified as a financial wasteland lying between relatively short-term clearing bank lending and long-term risk capital raised on the public stock markets.

The table of private equity transactions included in this chapter has been updated from that first published in 2007, showing outcomes that could not have been known at that time. From a private equity investor's viewpoint, the table shows that 17 of the 30 investments had been profitable (before including interest and management fees received), seven had incurred a loss and six were unrealised. However, private equity funds tend to measure the return on their investments simply by comparing the total cash invested (in all forms – debt and equity) with the cash received in return (not only on eventual sale, but also including any interest, dividends and management fees received during the entire investment period). The result expresses the cash return as a multiple of the cash invested - referred to as "money on money" or "cash on cash". For example, a private equity investor may talk about a "3 x cash" return. It is left to the investor to calculate the rate of return after allowing for the time value of money.

One of the worst examples in the table was Billington Cartmell where Hutton Collins invested £24.2 million to facilitate management succession in 2007 and cannot have anticipated that it would lose all that money and wind the company up 12 years later. Vitruvian Partners must also be nursing its wounds after arranging a £41.5 million investment in College Hill that was bailed out by Lloyds Development Capital in 2019 at a loss of £26.7 million.[1]

So private equity investment is risky. To reduce the risk, investors need to be well qualified to understand the market and to assess the management's abilities. Even then, risks will remain and the rewards from success will be offset by losses from failures.

The table confirms that few of the investments were intended to finance buyouts or succession plans on a long-term basis, reflecting the ongoing gap in the funding framework for privately–owned businesses that may only be remedied by a mixture of actions such as:
* reform of the manner in which taxation obstructs the transition of ownership from one management generation to another,
* much longer-term investment financing structures with a more appropriate relationship between income and capital gains, and
* in some cases, a willingness among existing owners not to seek "top dollar" prices for shares being passed from one generation to another.

At present, most companies are created to be sold. Private equity funds trade in such companies, buying and selling with the legitimate aim of profit. That is their prerogative, but it fans the flames of short-termism that can weaken the nation's economic backbone.

A related emerging trend has been for private equity funds to acquire publicly listed companies at a substantial cost and take them private again. This trend raises two important questions. First, do private equity funds have the appropriate skills to enhance the maintainable value of such investments within the typical five-year

_____

1. Vitruvian was asked to confirm that these figures - extracted from published accounts - had been interpreted correctly, but no response was received.

time horizon available, without destroying the creative culture on which those businesses depend? And secondly, will the private equity investors be able to find future buyers with sufficient funds available to provide a healthy return on their multi-million pound investments? Or will they be driven back to the stock market?

In researching this chapter, I was reminded of the lengths that owners of private companies will go in order to conceal their identities and financial involvement. One example arose at Mike Colling & Company, a media planning and buying agency that received an investment from Key Capital Partners via an innocuous new holding company called WHCO3. In its statutory annual return to the Registrar of Companies for 2018 WHCO3 listed the various classes of share but declined to identify their owners, instead referring readers to the share register. *Marketing Services Financial Intelligence* asked the Registrar of Companies whether such a practice was compliant with the law. "I have checked the form as requested and can tell you that the form is not acceptable", an official said. "The form needs to state the names of the shareholder and not refer to the register.[1]" No further action had been taken by the Registrar or the Department for Business until I raised the matter again with the Registrar in May 2021 after WHCO3 had filed another statement in breach of the statutory disclosure requirements. The Registrar contacted the company which filed a further return on 4 June, this time listing all the shareholders as required.

What is the point of granting company owners the protection of limited liability if those same people are allowed to unlawfully conceal their identity and share interests? The distinction between a "private" and a "public" company has nothing to do with whether ownership can be concealed. Since 1855 business owners in Britain have been given the privilege of limiting their personal financial liability by incorporating their businesses. In exchange, the law required more transparency so that people doing business could gain a view about the credentials of those with whom they were dealing. It was as simple as that and the law remains unchanged. Attempts to create more secrecy have been advanced under the bogus banner of easing the burdens on small business. There is a price to pay for limited liability.

The role of private equity investment houses in relation to large retail and manufacturing companies has become the focus of increasing press and political attention. But little has been written about the growing interest such organisations

[1] See s.853F, *Companies Act 2006.*

are taking in the marketing services sector. What do they do? And what has been their impact on the marketing services sector to date?

Critics claim that the mushrooming private equity industry attracted investors who are only interested in making a fast buck, who pay little attention to building businesses for the longer term, and who make far too much money from their adventures.

Even the UK's House of Commons Treasury Committee has been interrogating some of the biggest players in the industry and has raised some challenging issues to which it will be returning this autumn.

So what are the facts? *Marketing Services Financial Intelligence* has examined 17 private equity investments made since 1990 (see table[31]) and at first sight the figures that emerged do indeed suggest the critics may have a point.

Typically the private equity investors succeeded in at least doubling their money within an average of about three years before disappearing into the night, weighed down by the heavy burden of their swag bags. However, the fact that the investors — which generally include some of the senior managers — have made a lot of money is not necessarily a sin in itself. The only question of real importance is whether the investee companies are better placed to succeed in the longer term than they would have been without the investment.

"Management's objective is to grow the business", argues ECI Partners' Sean Whelan. "That's what it's all about." He sees part of the role

of a private equity investor as ensuring the board is composed of people who will help develop the business.

Beringea's Trevor Hope acknowledges that short-termism can stunt development of new service lines or investment in technology. Nevertheless he believes private equity investment can provide owner-managers with a framework within which to discuss and implement succession planning — "to build a real business that has the ability to function without them".

The investee company will only have a good value if it is a sustainable and growing business, says ECI's Whelan: "There has to be something left behind."

But the fact remains that private equity investment is generally for the short term. So it should be used only where it fits within the investee company's own strategic objectives. For example, private equity can provide interim finance to enable a company to grow to the scale that would be suited to a flotation of its shares on the stock market (commonly called an initial public offering or "IPO").

And in recent years private equity has come to the assistance of business executives who are seeking

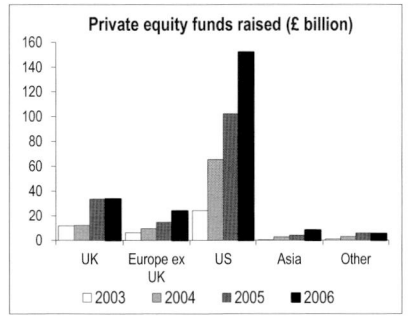

to negotiate a buyout of their business unit from its existing owners. Gone are the days when it was fairly easy for a management team to simply walk out and take clients with them.

Private equity can also facilitate a partial capital realisation by founders who would intend selling the company in the future but wish to enjoy some of the fruits of their labours in the meantime.

In each of these scenarios the notion that the business might remain under independent ownership for the longer term is rarely accommodated. Evidence given by the Treasury to the House Commons Treasury Committee confirmed the picture shown in our table below when it stated that private equity firms invest in companies for three years on average. Other parties suggested the typical length ranged between three and six years. Either way, signing up for a private equity investment is tantamount to agreeing to sell control of the company at a later date.

Private equity houses emphasise that they attach great importance to being able to align their objectives with those of the management, imply-ing that they would not wish to invest where the management is uncom-fortable with whatever exit strategy is being contemplated. "We can and must be flexible according to the needs of the business and the share-holders", says ISIS EP's Neil Bennett. "In some instances we would make an investment in full knowledge that we will be building the business over a longer period of time — for example, we invested in RLA in 2002 and are still invested today."

If the company is really averse to a future sale or IPO, Sean Whelan says he will sit down with the management and revisit the alternatives. "If one founder wants an exit, it may be possible to sell on his shares and ours to another private equity investor while achieving the same value as a trade sale or IPO."

Even where objectives can be successfully aligned the evidence still suggests it would be unusual for that alignment to embrace a long-term investment horizon. In reality the management is far more likely to be seduced by the prospect of sharing in the mouth-watering capital gains that private equity houses have already been able to achieve so swiftly in the marketing industry where companies are commonly built and sold within a decade, leaving buyers with the problem of maintaining a sustainable business thereafter.

Leaving aside the debate about short-termism, there is another issue that arouses concern among critics. They question whether there can ever be a true alignment of interests between an investor who is exclusively focused on creating the maximum return on investment in the shortest possible time and an entrepreneurial management team that will often regard the financial reward as only one component of the company's reason d'être?

Beringea's Trevor Hope sees few grounds for conflict: "In reality the pursuit of financial objectives usually focuses the management on where their real value actually is — they realise that the employees produce the value and that they need to

How private equity houses have invested in the marketing services industry[21]

Year invested	Company	Nature of business	Private equity investor	Amount invested (£m)				Equity votes	Realisation (£m)			Notes
				Ord shares	Pref shares	Loans	Total		Year	Proceeds[1]	Gain[1]	
1990	Blenheim Exhibitions	Exhibitions	Electra Partners	-	-	19.0	19.0	7.76%	1996	45.7	26.7	
1992	RSA Advertising	Cinema advertising	Permira	0.5	8.6	-	9.1	93.85%	1996	58.3	49.2	
1993	Aegis Media	Media buying	Electra Partners	-	15.0	0.0	15.0	n/a	1998	n/a	n/a	2
1994	Reading Room	Digital	Eclipse VCT	0.5	-	0.5	1.0	24.83%		1.4	0.4	
1997	WAA	DM	Foresight Venture Partners (former name Advent VCT)	1.2	-	-	1.2	29.35%		0.1	-1.1	
1997	Lorica Group	Design	3i	0.2	-	1.5	1.7	38.30%	2007	2.5	0.8	3
1998	Poulter Group	Marketing services	Murray Johnstone VCTs; Sth Yorkshire Pension Authority	0.5	0.0	1.1	1.5	49.75%	2004	1.6	0.1	
2001	Xtreme Information Services	Advertising monitoring	Veronis Suhler Stevenson (VSS)	26.0	-	4.0	30.0	27.7%	2010/14	34.0	4.0	15
2003	Financial Dynamics	Public relations	Advent Partners; Global Private Equity	2.3	16.3	4.5	23.0	66.61%	2006	47.7	24.7	4
2004	Bounty Group	Baby products marketing	ECI Ventures	0.8	3.9	4.3	9.0	76.50%	2007	46.6	37.7	
2004	MORI	Market research	ISIS EP; Caledonian Investments	1.0	0.0	20.0	21.0	53.60%	2005	41.4	20.5	
2005	ILG Digital	Digital media planning and buying	Beringea Proven VCTs and Chrysalis VCTs	2.4	0.0	0.0	2.4	17.99%	2008	9.1	6.7	5
2005	RLA Group	Marketing services	ISIS (Baronsmead VCTs)	1.7	2.1	0.0	3.8	48.97%	2008	5.8	2.0	
2005	Green Issues Communications	Public affairs agency	ISIS EP (Baronsmead VCTs, FIS Nominee)	0.2	0.0	1.8	2.0	48.16%	2009	0	-2.0	6
2005	Gyro International	Direct marketing and promotions	Beringea, Electra, Matrix, & Eclipse (Proven VCT)	0.9	1.1	1.1	3.0	31.73%	2008	21.0	12.0	7
2005	Loewy Group	Design	Risk Capital Partners	-	-	1.0	1.0	23.10%	2006	2.5	1.5	12
2007	AKQA (US)	Digital marketing agency	General Atlantic Partners	n/a	n/a	n/a	112.5	[80%]	2012	274.4	161.9	8
2007	Loewy Group	Design	Veronis Suhler Stevenson (VSS Mezzanine Partners)	5.0	1.4	16.1	22.5	19.00%	2011	1.0	-21.5	9
2007	Latitude Group	Digital	Vitruvian Partners	0.5	-	22.4	22.9	89.60%	2014	0.0	-22.9	10
2007	Engine Group, The	Marketing services	Loudwater Trust	8.0	-	-	8.0	12.03%	2010	3.6	-4.4	11
2007	Billington Cartmell	Integrated communications	Hutton Collins	0.0	-	24.2	24.2	40.0%	2019	0	-24.2	17
2008	ILG Digital	Digital media planning and buying	ECI Partners	0.6	-	17.9	18.5	60.77%	2010	0.0	-18.5	13
2010	Engine Group, The	Marketing services	HIG Capital	-	-	32.5	32.5	n/a	2010	41.9	9.4	11
2011	College Hill (now Instinctif Partners)	Financial/consumer public relations	Vitruvian Partners	0.4	-	41.1	41.5	66.58%	2019	14.8	-26.7	16
2014	MSQ Partners Group	Marketing services	NVM Private Equity	1.0	-	6.8	7.8	40.0%	2019	10.2	2.4	18
2015	Chime Communications	Sports marketing and comms	Providence Equity Partners	265.2	-	358.2	623.4	100.00%	Investment retained			20
2016	Creston	Marketing services	DBAY Advisers	40.0	-	35.0	75.0	100.00%	Investment retained			20
2017	Mike Colling & Company	Media Buying	Key Capital Partners	2.8	-	3.8	6.6	52.5%	Investment retained			14
2019	MSQ Partners Group	Marketing services	Lloyds Development Capital	0.2	-	25.6	25.8	49.90%	Investment retained			19
2019	Ensco 1327 (prev. Instinctif Partners)	Financial/consumer public relations	Lloyds Development Capital	0.3	-	20.1	20.4	n/a	Investment retained			
2020	Huntsworth	Healthcare and public relations	Clayton Dubilier & Rice	69.7	-	330.0	399.7	100.00%	Investment retained			20

1. This table attempts to show the gain or loss on the capital invested, but the true return is normally measured by reference to the total cash return on the cash outlay – i.e. the total return would include interest, dividends and management fees received, but it is not possible to ascertain these figures. Sometimes estimates have been made in which case this has been noted. 2. Sold on to FAT Media in 2018 for £1 Media. 3. Loan already repaid during ownership period. 4. Proceeds approximate. 5. Bought by ECI Partners – see below. 6. In administration – assets sold to Instinctif for £5. 7. Some figures based on earlier analysis by "Marketing Services Financial Intelligence". 8. Cost and equity percentage based on press reports, sale based on WPP figure of $343m for enterprise value. 9. Sold to Writtle in exchange for £2m and merged with Callcredit Information Systems. 10. Insolvent – bought back from administrator for £2m and merged with Callcredit Information Systems. 11. Sold to HIG which later sold to Lake Capital in US. 12. Equity subsequently diluted to approx.18% by shares issued as consideration for acquisitions. 13. Went into administration – unable to confirm some figures. 14. Founder Mike Colling still owned 35%. 15. VSS investment exchanged for shares in Ebiquity at 50% loss but later sold on market for £34m. 16. Sold on to LDC – see below. 17. Wound up by Hutton Collins. 18. Refinanced by Lloyds Development Capital – see below. 19. Lloyds Development Capital owns 67% of the equity, but a minority of votes. 20. Lloyds Development Capital owns 87% of the equity stake – proceeds allocated pro rata to equity stake for purposes of this table. 21. Original 2007 table updated to 31 December 2020.

protect that value by providing strong remuneration packages, opportunities to do good and challenging work and a positive working environment. In a service industry, the inability to provide outstanding creative and ultimately competitive services will be uncovered pretty quickly."

Bennett also argues against the risk of conflicts emerging over the investee company's own investment plans: "Our aim is to increase shareholder value for the benefit of all shareholders", he says. "The value of a business is what someone will pay for it. Since a purchaser will not pay a premium for a business that is seeing its foundations undermined, any investor would clearly avoid pursuing such a strategy."

Bennett believes that potential acquirers will quickly detect any under-investment — whether in

people or systems — and so it is in the private equity shareholders' interests to invest for the future. Nevertheless Sean Whelan accepts there can be differing views about, for example, whether to make an acquisition shortly before the private equity investor would be hoping for an exit.

It would be unrealistic to assume that every private equity investment is an outstanding example of aligned objectives and mutual profit. When some of Murray Johnstone's venture capital trusts first invested in the Leeds-based agency Poulter Group, they probably hoped for something more than a stream of trading losses and a lucky escape with their initial investment broadly intact.

Investment in private companies can be risky and critics of private equity investors occasionally need to be reminded of that. But at Poulter

---

Tax incentives for private equity investments in September 2007

The history

Raising long-term capital for medium-sized private companies has never been easy although a century or so ago merchant banks were more ready to do so in support of British trade. Since the Second World War successive governments have tried to create incentives for equity investment in what is always seen as a fairly high risk segment of business. Only a handful of institutions - notably 3i and Charterhouse - attempted to fill this equity gap on a medium to long-term basis and their enthusiasm waned as bigger and better returns were identified among large management buyouts and in transactions with companies already - or shortly to be - listed on the stock market. So the growth in the private equity phenomenon has clearly filled an important gap, encouraged by a very benevolent tax regime designed to prompt individuals to reinvest some of their wealth in privately-owned ventures.

The tax regime

If an individual invests in a qualifying "venture capital trust" (VCT) which in turn invests those funds in a portfolio of private businesses, the investor may obtain income tax relief at 30% on the cost of the investment and be exempt from capital gains tax on disposal of the shares, provided they have been held for at least five years. If an individual invests directly into a qualifying company there are equally favourable tax incentives. They may qualify under the Enterprise Investment Scheme (EIS) and gain income tax relief at 20%[1] on the cost of the investment and also be exempt from tax on any gain on disposal after three years. Non-EIS investors may qualify for "business taper relief" whereby the gain will be taxed at only 10% if the shares are held for at least two years[2].

Private equity managers

Most private equity establishments allow or encourage their investment managers to share in a proportion of any gain derived from their investments. Some even lend the capital to the managers to invest. These managers enjoy the full taper relief[2] benefits that are available to individual investors although it is argued that they do not share equally in the downside risks[3].

1. Since increased to 30% 2. Business taper relief is no longer available . The taxation of private equity fund managers and their "carried interest" is a very complex area and professional advice should be sought

---

the private equity investors did manage to exit unscathed and to pass the funding baton on to the Bank of Scotland. The bank must have heaved a massive sigh of relief when the company was later bought by Bezier Acquisitions after accumulating losses of over £1 million and exhausting all of its shareholders' funds.

Another company where the alignment of interests between investor and investee seemed to go astray was Loewy Group. Having pursued an acquisition programme backed by Risk Capital Partners, the relationship was unwound in December 2006 after just two years and replaced more recently by a much bigger investment from the US-based VSS Mezzanine Partners.

Apparently the scale of Loewy's ambitions extended beyond RCP's appetite in a sector which is not its primary focus. Nevertheless RCP made a healthy £1.5 million profit on the investment and everyone parted friends. Loewy Group's finance director Bryan Wilsher offers four tips to prospective investee companies: "Get independent advisers to find and negotiate the private equity deal, make sure there's a competition, short-list only candidates that understand people businesses in the marketing sector, and check they have experience of the 'buy and build' model."

Both Wilsher and Bounty Group's Simon Williamson declare themselves well pleased with their private equity partners. Whether their junior managers and clients will be as pleased when ownership passes on remains to be seen.

"Changes provide opportunities", says Trevor Hope. "The ultimate sale will potentially see owner managers move away and thereby provide an opportunity for others to step up."

Looked at dispassionately, private equity can play a valuable role in the development of the marketing services sector, but that role would be much more valuable if it was not strongly influenced by factors that fuel a short term perspective. The single most appealing feature of remaining independent and private is the ability of the management to be in control of its own destiny — something that neither a trade sale nor an IPO can offer.

Yet by setting short-term exit horizons that almost invariably deliver ownership to someone else, private equity investors also deny owners the control over their destiny that many would value. They do indeed want too much too soon.

In fairness ECI's Whelan points out that many funds have a fixed 10 year life, so investments have to be realised within that time horizon (or sold on to another fund). And the tax regime too encourages a short term view — requiring shares in a VCT to be held for only five years to avoid the up-front tax benefits having to be repaid, and for employees and private investors to hold shares directly for no longer than two years to qualify for a 10% capital gains tax rate.

Perhaps a regime that allowed individuals to enjoy only half of the potential tax benefits if shares were held for four years and for the full benefits to be earned only after eight years would help to calm the rush to realise.

19

TNS: Researching the Researcher

Over the years as an adviser to various market research companies, I developed the view that they tended to be considerably less profitable than most other branches of marketing services. I wondered whether this was because researchers were too keen on their job — particularly in qualitative market research where objective interpretation would be an important part of the role.

I sensed that clients tended to get so interested in the initial research findings that they would ask questions — not unreasonably. And the researchers were equally intrigued by the questions and the issues they raised. So they would happily rise to the intellectual challenge by revisiting their work and devoting a lot of time thinking about the issues — perhaps even doing even more research — before going back to the client. This could be very helpful to the client and very expensive for the research company, particularly if the fee initially quoted had assumed a specific number of hours would be spent on the job. The situation was made worse by those researchers who had difficulty either in resisting the temptation to do more work than had been allowed for or in asking for an increased fee for the extra work.

Profitability may also have been hampered because many research assignments were of a relatively short-term nature and did not provide the security of a regular flow of income in the form of a retainer. And the demand for short-term research projects could oscillate between feast and famine.

Such were the limited profit margins in research that most consultancies watched their pennies with great care. I recall a client whom I had advised from start-up. I will call him Henry. With start-ups, I would try to keep in close touch in the early stages, as many did not have a great deal of first-hand experience in financial management.

Henry was a highly professional and well regarded researcher who ran his business on his own. He would send me quarterly financial figures, but seemed loathe to meet up. Hoping this reluctance might have more to do with fees than with any personal dislike towards me, I devised a means of meeting without any cost. Claridges Hotel was just round the corner from our Mayfair offices and it served a very good breakfast at a surprisingly modest price. So I suggested a quarterly breakfast meeting at my expense. Henry took the bait and would arrive by bicycle which he carefully pad-locked to Claridges' railings. That saved him the cost of a parking meter as well as the bus fare.

When WPP decided in 2008 that it would like to compete with Germany's largest market research institute GfK in an attempt to acquire the UK public company Taylor Nelson Sofres, I was just a little sceptical about the merits of doing so, not least because The Interpublic Group had incurred a $300 million write off when it sold its US research company NFO WorldGroup to Taylor Nelson only a few years earlier.

NFO had traded profitably during the three years leading up to sale, but its operating profit margin had ranged between a lowly 4.7% and a more respectable 11.2%. The average margin for the three years was 8.2%, fuelling my scepticism. The operating margin enjoyed by healthy advertising and other marketing agencies tends to be closer to 15%. Apart from its low profit margins, NFO was also heavily in debt – debt that Taylor Nelson would add to its own. Indeed Taylor Nelson was reported to have had the most vulnerable balance sheet among listed marketing companies in 2004.

Taylor Nelson must have believed that the debt burden was a risk worth taking to get to third place among global market infor-mation groups. The price paid for NFO – representing a multiple

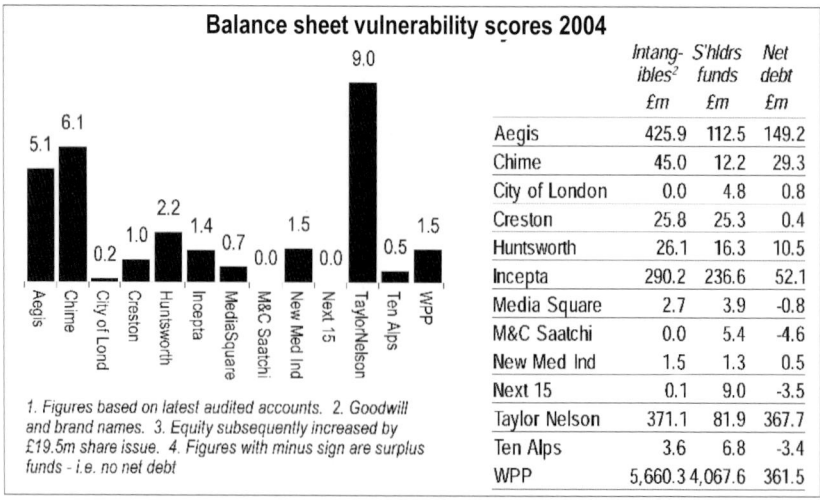

Balance sheet vulnerability scores 2004

	Intang-ibles[2] £m	S'hldrs funds £m	Net debt £m
Aegis	425.9	112.5	149.2
Chime	45.0	12.2	29.3
City of London	0.0	4.8	0.8
Creston	25.8	25.3	0.4
Huntsworth	26.1	16.3	10.5
Incepta	290.2	236.6	52.1
Media Square	2.7	3.9	-0.8
M&C Saatchi	0.0	5.4	-4.6
New Med Ind	1.5	1.3	0.5
Next 15	0.1	9.0	-3.5
Taylor Nelson	371.1	81.9	367.7
Ten Alps	3.6	6.8	-3.4
WPP	5,660.3	4,067.6	361.5

1. Figures based on latest audited accounts. 2. Goodwill and brand names. 3. Equity subsequently increased by £19.5m share issue. 4. Figures with minus sign are surplus funds - i.e. no net debt

of 13 times post-tax profits – was more modest than witnessed in some other deals around that time and probably reflected Interpublic's urgent need to raise some cash. It also recognised that NFO had shown minimal revenue growth in recent years, squeezing profits out of improved margins.

Taylor Nelson's suitor GfK was founded in 1934 by an association of German university teachers, among them Ludwig Erhard. In April 2005 it acquired NOP World (owner of the National Opinion Poll), based mostly in the United Kingdom, the United States and Italy. And in 2011 it acquired Knowledge Networks, based in California. The account that follows, written during the bid battle in July 2008, explored how GfK fought with WPP's Kantar research division to acquire TNS and ponders why WPP seemed determined to win.

The GfK merger proposal never appeared to garner a great deal of support – either from its own shareholders or those of WPP. As soon as the formal bid terms were announced in June 2008, their share prices began to lose ground. Even the TNS shareholders soon lost some of their initial enthusiasm (see chart).

The merger looked like a defensive consolidation ploy, prompted by a recognition that the operating profit margins achieved by both parties had lagged behind those in other segments of the marketing services sector. A declared aim of a margin in excess of 15% in the "medium term" met with scepticism from industry observers who were quick to point out that other research businesses had difficulty achieving margins at that level. We were

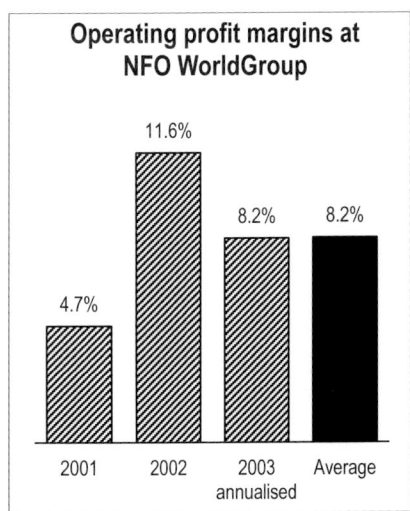

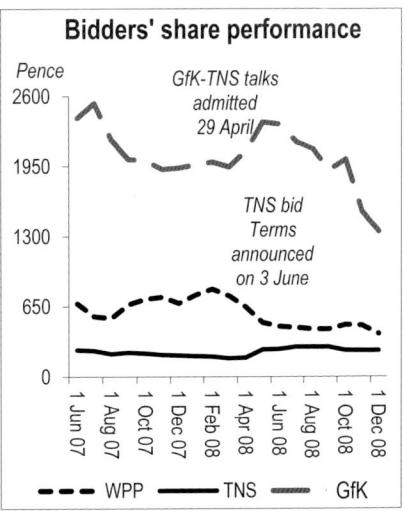

told that the merged businesses would be seeking annual cost savings of €97 million (£76 million) by the end of the third year, but this would necessitate a one-off rationalisation charge of €120 million (£94 million).

Having had its initial approach rebuffed by TNS, WPP was still expected to re-enter the fray with a hostile bid and this duly occurred. WPP offered a £1 billion mixture of cash and shares that was large enough to send GfK limping away from the battle.

But WPP's love affair with research, fostered by the division's chief executive Eric Salama ever since he had joined the group from The Henley Centre as Sir Martin's Sorrell's director of strategy in 1994, was soon to end.

In October 2018, beleaguered by recent client losses since the departure of Sorrell as its chief executive, WPP at last conceded that it should dispose of a controlling interest in its research operations which by then traded under the Kantar brand. The newly appointed chief executive Mark Read said the board had approved a formal process to review the strategic options that would maximise shareholders' value. At the time WPP's shares had sunk to their lowest point in five years.

"We believe in the potential for Kantar but given our many priorities, we need to make tough choices and we believe that the best way to unlock this potential is with a strategic or financial partner", Read explained. "It is envisaged that WPP will remain a share owner with strategic links to ensure that the benefits to clients are realised. Preparations are underway, involving Kantar management, and unsolicited expressions of interest have been received."

Kantar had under-performed consistently over many years, often producing the lowest profit margins and revenue growth of any of the group's business segments. The return on some of the group's investments in this sector had also been disappointing, most recently in the US business comScore that had previously absorbed some of Kantar's operations. The research division had continued its decline in the third quarter of 2018, although WPP was eager to point out that the rate of decline had slowed. Revenue less pass-through costs from the division had fallen by 7.8% in the latest nine months (or by 1.8% on a like-for-like basis). North America remained difficult and the United Kingdom had also slipped back recently, with Kantar Insights and Kantar Media coming "under pressure". The group had also written down the value of its investment in its Irish subsidiary Media Watch by £31 million.

Among WPP's research businesses, Added Value had run up losses of £22.8 million by the end of 2018 and was subsequently selected to become the main UK research company under the new name of Kantar Consulting, presumably in the hope that there would be some future profits that could take advantage of Added Value's historic tax loss. The business of Kantar Retail UK was also taken under Added Value's wing after running up accumulated losses of £9.3 million. Elsewhere a company called The Kantar Group had accumulated losses of £84.5 million arising from the "stewardship element of the inter-company service fee charges" – principally under-recovered staff costs.

Buyers for Kantar seemed in short supply as the months passed although WPP claimed there was "strong interest" in March 2019 – just as the group revealed a 41.5% fall in overall post-tax profit and a 2.6% fall in net revenue (revenue less pass-through costs) in 2018.

In December 2019 WPP announced that it had sold 60% of Kantar to Bain Capital Private Equity. Perhaps potential trade buyers had been rather less enthusiastic than initially anticipated. Following the final completion of the sale, the aggregate net proceeds were expected to be approximately £2.4 billion.

After years of indulgence in the research sector, often producing disappointing results, WPP wrote off £210 million on its 60% disposal. Fortunately, the group was able to offset the loss by a credit of £284 million attributed to "exchange adjustments recycled to the income statement". Even so, the outcome was a sad return on the group's near £3 billion investment in market research businesses.

Within three months chief executive Eric Salama had left. His replacement Alexis Nasard lasted only until April 2021 when the newly created and heavily borrowed Luxembourg based acquisition vehicle Kantar Global Holdings reported a group loss of £326 million – dragged down by reorganisation costs of £200 million, amortisation charges of $170 million on intangible assets like customer relationships, and finance costs of $191 million.

I f ever there was a case for a researcher to be researched, Taylor Nelson Sofres must be the one. But its desire to merge with German research firm GfK rather than fall into the hands of WPP Group's Kantar research division has put both those potential partners under the spotlight also.

The decision facing investors in Taylor Nelson Sofres ("TNS") in the wake of proposals from GfK and WPP Group is quite simple: would they prefer to realise the majority of their shareholding in cash now or would they prefer to retain the prospect of significantly enhanced earnings from their shareholding in the future?

WPP has now made a firm offer to give TNS shareholders an immediate cash payment of 173p – worth 70% of the 248p market value of TNS shares at the time – and to supplement that with another 87.6p in WPP shares. So the total value of the WPP offer is 260.6p per TNS share and one third of that value is dependant on the future performance of both companies – a future that seems less than exciting in the current climate. Looking at the synergistic savings of £52 million that WPP hopes to achieve in due course by merging TNS with its Kantar group, as well as the financing costs of the deal, it would appear that the ongoing annual benefit would be less than one penny per TNS share or less than 1% of the current value of a WPP share.

By contrast the prospect of a merger with GfK offers TNS shareholders nothing today but potentially a lot more in the future. Calculations by *Marketing Services Financial Intelligence* suggest that earnings per TNS share could be boosted by as much as 50% from three different sources.

First, each TNS share could benefit from promised synergistic gains – TNS claims these will be worth £76 million per annum within three years. Secondly, the financing cost of the all-share merger is much less than that of a WPP takeover. And thirdly, GfK shareholders will be receiving roughly the same number of shares in TNS as existing TNS shareholders whereas GfK's profit record when translated at current exchange rates is materially better.

Why is it possible for TNS to purchase GfK shares at what looks like a discount?

The most likely explanation is GfK's unusual share structure whereby at present 56% of the company is owned by a mutual association of research customers called GfK-Nürnberg. That share stake protects the company from any hostile bid or from any merger that does not satisfy the shareholders' aspirations. So at present the market price of a GfK share reflects this major restriction on free market-ability. It is this right of veto that WPP sought to exploit as a risk that could jeopardise the merger, thereby making its own offer more appealing

Hajo Riesenbeck : chairman of GfK's supervisory board

TNS chief executive David Lowden: Profits improving.

WPP Group chief executive Sir Martin Sorrell: likes a fight

How TNS and GfK's past performance compares

Profit for year ended 31 December 2007	GfK[1] £m	TNS £m	Total £m
Sales revenue[3]	**914.6**	**1,067.7**	**1,982.3**
Operating profit before goodwill and exceptional charges	122.9	117.3	240.2
Goodwill and exceptional items	-15.5	-14.6	-30.1
Adjusted operating profit	107.4	102.7	210.1
Other income	2.4	0.4	2.8
Finance costs	-17.6	-19.9	-37.5
Taxation	-20.2	-24.7	-44.9
Minority interests	6.4	2.2	8.6
Profit after tax[2]	**65.5**	**56.3**	**121.8**
Operating profit margin on sales:			
Before goodwill and exceptionals	13.4%	11.0%	12.1%
After goodwill and exceptionals	11.7%	9.6%	10.6%

Balance sheet items at 31 December 2007:

Intangible assets (goodwill) [4]	738.5	604.0	1,342.5
Working capital (net current assets)	-94.9	4.2	-90.7
Shareholders' funds [4,5]	401.1	259.8	660.9
Net borrowings ("Debt")	345.5	351.3	798.1
Debt/equity ratio[5]:	0.86:1	1.35:1	0.61:1[5]

1. Translated at rate on 12 June 2008 of €1.27052 to £1 to reflect approx current UK value of GfK earnings. 2. Profit attributable to parent company shareholders only. 3. Reported "gross income" of the two companies varied substantially but has been adjusted in the merger prospectus to achieve greater comparability. However, no such measure is available for Kantar and so we have used the profit margin on revenues as the appropriate measure for comparison purposes. This is lower than the margin on gross income. 4. TNS intangibles and shareholders' funds increased by £144.7m goodwill previously written off against reserves. 5. After the merger, shareholders' funds will be boosted further by approximately £600 million - being the excess of the market value of TNS shares issued to former GfK shareholders over the existing value of GfK shareholders' funds.

to TNS shareholders.

However, the administrative board of the GfK-Nürnberg consortium voted in favour of the merger on 4 July after which its managing director Dr Raimund Wildner said that he was confident that the vote of the members "will also be positive".

Even so, the fact that the GfK merger offers TNS investors more likelihood of enhanced earnings per share does not guarantee its success in the face of the WPP alternative. One potential obstacle would be the inherent pressure on fund managers to maximise their own performance,

not least because of the performance related bonuses they can earn.

A deal with WPP at a premium price would boost a fund's investment portfolio, despite the partial dependence on future performance, whereas a merger with GfK would offer no immediate investment gain. Indeed the TNS share price may decline a little initially, particularly as it had climbed to within 5% of the WPP offer value by the time it was obliged by the Takeover Panel to firm up its proposal or withdraw.

And no-one should anticipate any further immediate improvement in share price in anticipation of synergistic gains, even though they have been reviewed by an independent firm of accountants and a bank. Fund managers are unlikely to be persuaded to retain their TNS shares and to reject the WPP offer unless they can be convinced about the ability of the GfK and TNS managements to deliver a far better return than they would obtain from reinvesting the proceeds from a sale to WPP.

So the spotlight falls primarily on the TNS track record. As the tables and chart show, that record has not always been one of constant improvement, although the recent appointment of David Lowden as chief executive has been accompanied by upward growth in profits and margins.

Its previously erratic progress was not helped when in 2003 the group acquired NFO WorldGroup from The Interpublic Group of Companies as the luckless

US owner faced serious financial pressures. The deal may have alleviated Interpublic's indebtedness and boosted TNS's US presence, but it placed the TNS balance sheet under considerable strain from which

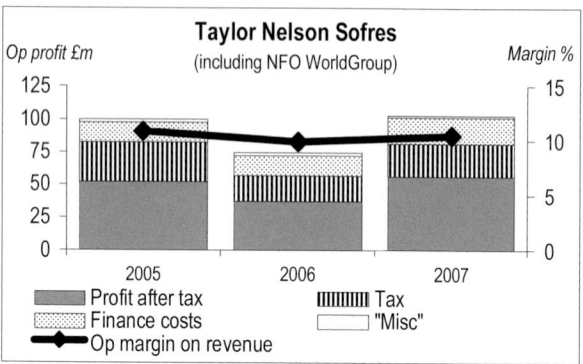

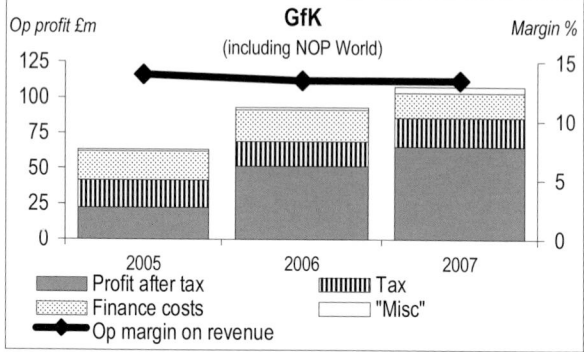

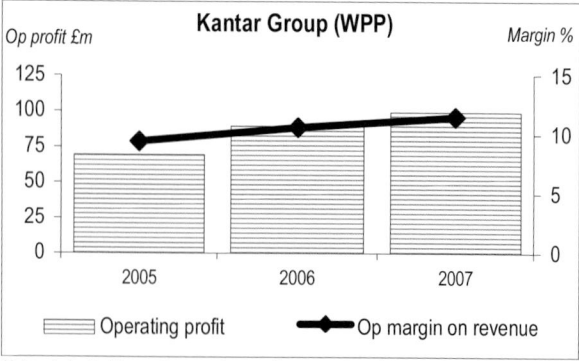

Notes: 1. Audited figures for gross income, finance costs and taxation have not been provided in respect of the Kantar group. 2 Operating profits are taken from audited accounts without adjustment. 3. Operating margins are based on operating profits adjusted to exclude items like goodwill impairment and restructuring costs.

it is still trying to recover.

By last December TNS still owed much more to its bankers and other financiers than the total amount provided by its shareholders. And the position seems to have got worse since then as the group continued to acquire more companies — notably the US digital intelligence business of Compete which cost an initial $75 million in cash.

In 2006 TNS suffered a serious profit slippage after its US operations lost a major client and suffered from margin pressures. But the situation appears to have improved since. However, operating profit margins remain below expectations — even allowing for the fact that the research sector always seems to struggle to achieve the benchmark margin on gross income that other marketing services companies seem able to achieve.

A comparison of profit margins is not helped by the diversity of approach used in defining the component terms. All the players in this particular saga have cited figures for operating profit that have not been measured in accordance with standard accounting requirements and instead have opted to exclude various costs that would drag down results.

The main exclusions are amounts written off past acquisition costs and amounts spent on restructuring activities. While such costs may not occur every year and may not always have an immediate cash impact, their exclusion allows companies to give an exaggerated impression of the profit actually earned per share in past

periods and thereby raise expectations of even better results in the future. In our charts and tables we have adhered to statutory reporting requirements unless otherwise stated.

The definitions adopted for "gross income" are even more diverse than those used for operating profit. Historically GfK appears to have charged all direct costs as well as bought-in costs before arriving at the gross income amount whereas TNS simply charged bought-in costs (mainly interviewers and focus group costs). Kantar has published no gross income information at all.

Indeed WPP seems content to have argued its case until now with the minimum of hard information to back it up. Given all these obstacles to comparability we have chosen to ignore gross income and instead to compare operating margins as a percentage of total revenue. The outcome shows that GfK and Kantar have both outperformed TNS. Even allowing for the lack of hard information about Kantar, it would appear that a merger of TNS with either party should provide a spur to improve its own margins. Otherwise it will dilute the performances being achieved by the others.

Indeed the recent past performance of both GfK and Kantar appears more consistent and impressive than that of TNS. If this is so, and assuming the trend can be maintained, the key questions remaining are:

• Which partner offers the best strategic fit in terms of geography and segment specialisation?
• Which partner offers the better

long-term prospects for business development, profit growth and staff fulfilment?
• Which of the deals offers most to the chosen partner?

TNS, GfK and Kantar are of remarkably similar size, measured by revenues. But Kantar stands out as having more complementary geographical spread, with a bigger North American presence and less dominant European coverage according to WPP. Indeed the geographical coverage of both TNS and GfK is so similar as to beg the question of whether a merger will offer any material opportunities to strengthen a regional presence where penetration is currently under weight.

A similar picture emerges in relation to market specialisation. Both TNS and GfK lay claim to common segments of the research market – consumer and retail, media, business services (including finance), technology, healthcare and stakeholders (like employees).

Given their size perhaps it is not surprising that there is little difference between the market specialisations claimed.

The same may be true of Kantar although it is more difficult to tell. In WPP's last annual report Kantar's chief executive officer Eric Salama made mention of retail, healthcare, employee satisfaction and consumer trends. So if no-one seems to have any particularly unique areas of specialisation, business growth will be more dependant on each company's ability to innovate and respond to changing market circumstances.

All parties have recognised the need to develop cost-effective syndicated services while maximising custom research opportunities that offer healthy profit margins. But a group that is exclusively dedicated to research is likely to be most acutely aware of the need to maintain market leadership in as many specialisations as possible.

The argument against a dedicated and exclusive commitment to research is the lack of opportunities for cross-selling to other group-owned marketing networks, something that WPP could theoretically offer in spades. And while history shows that the cross-selling benefits are frequently over-stated

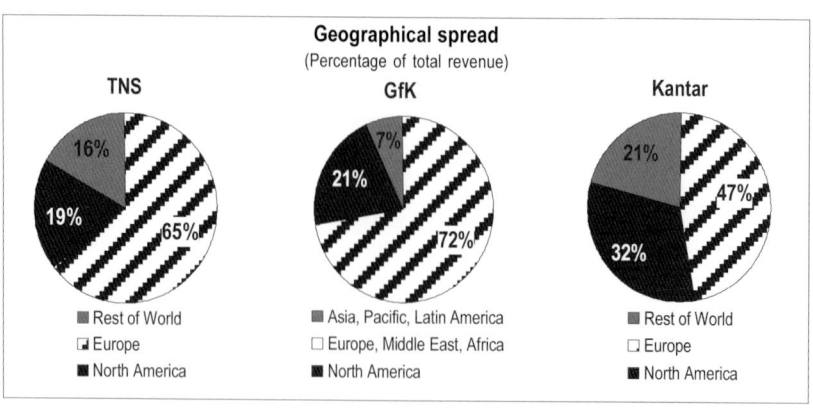

Geographical spread
(Percentage of total revenue)

TNS

- Rest of World
- Europe
- North America

GfK

- Asia, Pacific, Latin America
- Europe, Middle East, Africa
- North America

Kantar

- Rest of World
- Europe
- North America

and under-delivered in global multi-discipline groups, the potential cannot be ignored completely.

Similarly opportunities to establish or acquire additional business units in fast-growing regions may arise more often under the umbrella of a big multi-disciplined global group. So the strategic arguments are finely balanced between the potential benefits of exclusive dedication to a market-leading research capability and the potential opportunities for cross-selling within a more widely based global marketing services group.

In the longer term, WPP may offer more scope for business development but perhaps less opportunity for key staff to gain fulfilment as they become servants of a more remote master. Growth in profits and profit margins seem to be available with either prospective partner although WPP is likely to be a little more ruthless in its execution of such aspirations.

As for the potential benefits to be gained by each prospective partner, the GfK merger offers an excellent opportunity to loosen the restrictions on marketability that have been holding back its share price, while increasing its international clout and retaining a strong influence over the future development of a dedicated research business.

WPP will be looking to enhance the global penetration of a division that would become its second biggest business segment and which it believes offers better growth prospects than some traditional activities.

More subtly, it will offer Sir Martin Sorrell's strategy specialist and protégé Eric Salama the opportunity to achieve a higher profile within the group and increase the prospects of becoming his master's eventual successor. However, such ambitions may have been sullied by Salama's past involvement in the development of the ill-fated Red Cell micro network that has now been transformed into the United group.

Given the uncertain state of worldwide economies this may not be the best time for WPP to be borrowing over £1 billion in pursuit of its growth ambitions. But Sorrell seems committed and is not known for giving up easily.

20

Ricketts' Ruinous Rationale

Garfield Hugh Ashton Ricketts came to Britain from the United States in 2001 and in March of that year set up a company called Round 2 International-UK. It marked the start of his ambition to expand overseas from his Los Angeles based media buying business.

In October 2001 *Campaign* reported that Round 2 planned to open a UK office in Covent Garden imminently, promising clients a "new-wave" approach to media buying. The office would be run by Ken Jamie and Roy Davis, and span broadcast, outdoor, print and online planning and buying. We were told that the agency planned to service clients in the UK and Europe "and the rest of the world" from London.

But, apart from running up a £292,000 loss, that ambition did not translate into anything very noteworthy until March 2010 when Ricketts acquired the Newcastle-based advertising agency

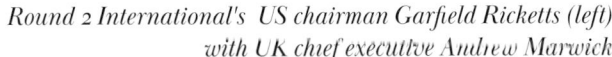

Round 2 International's US chairman Garfield Ricketts (left) with UK chief executive Andrew Marwick

Robson Brown accompanied by talk of using the acquisition "as a platform for growth across the UK and eventually the globe".

My interest was aroused later that year when Ricketts' UK business collapsed into administration. On examination I found that three companies he had acquired were already known to me and I was more than a little surprised to learn that they had each fallen victim to Ricketts' ambition.

I had never heard of Ricketts before then and felt driven to find out more. In the pages that follow you can read what I discovered. It first appeared in *Marketing Services Financial Intelligence* in February 2011 and provides some lessons for every entrepreneur who wishes to sell his or her business. To some extent the lessons are similar to those learned at Leagas Delaney and highlighted in chapter 11, namely to make sure the buyer has the resources with which to pay and not to let the buyer mortgage the assets of your former business until he has paid the purchase consideration in full.

Was Ricketts simply someone who was carried away by his own ambition? Was he, or were the sellers, badly advised? Did he knowingly enter into arrangements that, put at their mildest, would place an intolerable financial burden on the group? Or was it a combination of all three?

It is widely understood that, in business, it is unwise to "borrow short and lend long". Put another way, it is unwise to use short-term borrowings to finance long term investments. This is because insufficient cash may be available to pay all the day-to-day creditors if it has been tied up for a long term. But if Ricketts knew this, he certainly ignored it.

As we shall see, Ricketts introduced very little cash of his own or from banks. Instead quite a lot of his finance was raised on a short-term basis by borrowing against amounts due from customers. It's called invoice discounting, because the lender takes a slice of the invoice value as a reward for making a loan until the invoice is paid.

Here is an example of how things can go terribly wrong.

An element of mystery continues to surround the circumstances in which three previously sound UK advertising agencies were acquired by Garfield Ricketts' Round 2 International-UK in 2010, only to fall into the hands of administrators Zolfo Cooper in November of that year.

How could any company realistically expect to acquire businesses estimated to have been worth the best part of £12 million with hardly any spare cash to start with? And why would any agency succumb to such audicious overtures?

The takeover victims were financially strong and well regarded — Newcastle agency Robson Brown, London-based media buyer Austin West Media and Bath agency Attinger Jack Advertising. Robson Brown has since been rescued by The Mission Marketing Group, while the former owners of Austin West and Attinger Jack each stepped in to find new homes for those businesses.

As we shall see, the rapid depletion of the three companies' assets under Ricketts' rule is astonishing and begs the question of whether at least some of those assets were used by Round2 to help pay for the companies it acquired.

Taken together, the audited net assets of the three acquired agencies totalled £5.3 million according to their last published balance sheets before acquisition. That included cash of £4 million. On the appointment of administrators last November, those net assets were declared to have a negative worth of nearly £10 million – a dramatic decline of over £15 million.

Between 28 February 2009 – the date of its last accounts – and the appointment of administrators, Robson Brown lost net assets of nearly £9 million (see table). The administrators believe that the ordinary creditors of Robson Brown will get back less than 19p for every £1 they are owed.

At Austin West Media net assets of £700,000 plummeted by £3.6 million in just 11 months to a deficiency

of £2.9 million. At Attinger Jack, net assets of £1.3 million were eroded by £3.1 million to a deficiency of £1.6 million in 13 months. Even in the midst of a recession it is hard to believe those resources would have been eroded so quickly by adverse trading conditions alone.

Indeed Robson Brown should have been able to withstand the loss of its Dreams account for some while, having previously had net assets of £3.3 million of which £2 million was net cash (see table) and that's before adding in some additional assets held by its immediate parent company Latefrost.

So where did Garfield Ricketts and his Round 2 company come from? How did Round 2 fund its acquisitions? Why did it choose to

Where did Robson Brown's assets go?

Net assets	28 Feb 09 Audited £'000	29 Nov 10[1] Book value £'000	Realisable £'000
Tangible assets	358	142	60
Investments	207	-	-
Total fixed assets:	**565**	**142**	**60**
Stocks/WIP	592	-	-
Debtors	4,906	4,278	2,846
Cash	3,508	6	6
Bank overdraft	-1,566	-	-
Centric Commercial Finance		-1,590	-1,590
Trade creditors	-2,371	-3,531	-3,531
Due to shareholders and employees		-2,504	-2,504
Other creditors (including tax)	-2,283	-647	-647
Net current assets (liabilities)	**2,786**	**-3,988**	**-5,420**
Long-term liabilities	-20	-	-
Net assets (deficiency) funded by shareholders	**3,331**	**-3,846**	**-5,360**

1. Per administrators' statement of affairs

acquire three separate agencies within the short space of a year instead of treading more cautiously? And where did all their assets go?

Ricketts first set up a media buying business in Los Angeles in 1993 by moving from his role of media director at the sports gear business LA Gear and taking the company's media buying account with him as his first client. By last year he was claiming to have built up media billings of $100 million from offices in Los Angeles, San Francisco and London, although of course only a very small percentage of those billings would have been available to meet the running costs of the media agencies themselves.

Ricketts had established a presence in Britain in 2001 in the name of Round 2 International-UK. By the end of 2009 that company had run up a deficiency of £292,000. Undaunted, the company then embarked on an ambitious acquisition spree, apparently with the aim of eventually creating a global network.

No-one seems to be able to explain why Ricketts chose to acquire companies in three different UK locations, other than because their owners' advancing age and natural curiosity had prompted them to respond to unsolicited mailshots from Ricketts' UK financial advisers Menzies. Before Ricketts started his UK acquisitions, the share capital of Round 2 International-UK had been increased to £500,000 - apparently paid for by Ricketts himself. But much of that would have been absorbed by the past deficiency of £292,000. So very little cash would have been left for use in buying targeted companies that were clearly worth very much more.

Where did the rest of the cash come from? According to the administrators, the acquisitions were "highly leveraged" deals - in other words they relied heavily on borrowed money. Surprisingly, little if any money was borrowed from clearing banks. Instead each of the deals was funded in part at least by loans from a commercial finance business called

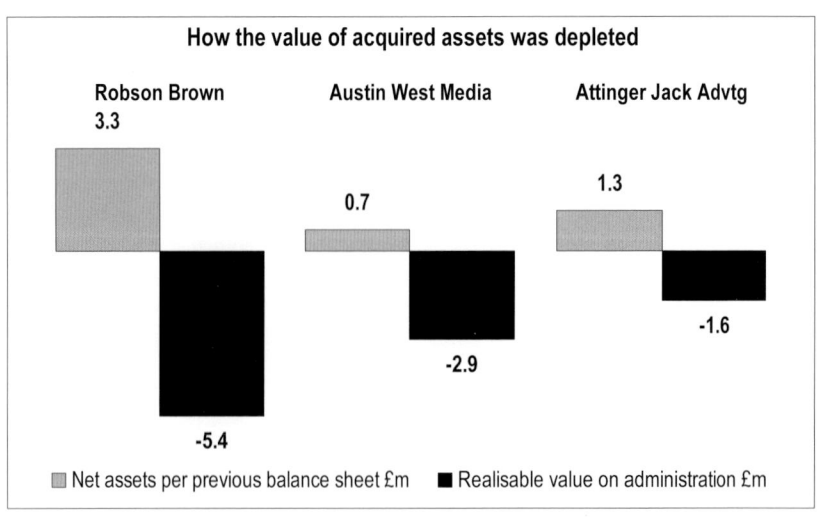

How the value of acquired assets was depleted

Robson Brown 3.3

Austin West Media 0.7

Attinger Jack Advtg 1.3

-5.4

-2.9

-1.6

Net assets per previous balance sheet £m   Realisable value on administration £m

Centric. Centric specialises in lending against assets, often by advancing a percentage of the value of sales invoices until the clients pay, as was the case with Ricketts' companies. Invoice discounting can be an expensive form of financing. What's more, it does not provide the type of reliable long-term capital that is desirable to finance acquisitions.

As security, Centric took a charge over the assets of the UK companies that Ricketts had acquired. It was Centric that subsequently initiated the administration proceedings. Of course it is possible that Garfield Ricketts' US business provided some of its own money to help fund the acquisitions, although the only contribution identified so far is an initial subscription of a miserly £150 for shares that were subsequently transferred to Ricketts.

Any further contribution from the US business in the form of significant loans seems fairly improbable as there is no evidence of any security being taken over the UK assets by the US company. However, in the absence of any accounts since 2009 and the limited information available from the administrators, no firm conclusions could be drawn.

A few weeks before the administrators were appointed, a further £560,000 of long-term share capital was provided by Ricketts in exchange for "monies owed by the company". Perhaps this was a last minute attempt to shore up the balance sheet in the face of media owners' concerns.

If that was the only capital provided by Ricketts and his US company, it seems unlikely that the rest of the acquisition costs could have been funded by invoice discounting alone. So how else might the deals have been financed?

After the Robson Brown deal, an obvious source of funding for further acquisitions would have been any cash remaining in the Robson Brown coffers, leaving the agency much the weaker as a result.

However, it is not beyond the bounds of possibility that the cash pile might already have been drawn upon to help pay for the acquisition of Robson Brown itself. Sometimes surplus profits retained in target companies are distributed to the sellers as part of the deal, but in the case of the Round 2 acquisitions caution would have been necessary to ensure that any stripping out of assets did not jeopardise the credit recognition terms imposed by the media owners' trade bodies.

Alternatively it is possible for an acquirer to make use of the target's surplus assets to fund the purchase indirectly, although there are rules designed to ensure that any such action does not prejudice creditors. Again media owners' credit recognition requirements would have to be satisfied to avoid having to prepay for advertising space.

According to people familiar with the situation, Ricketts and his advisers claimed to understand the media owners' credit recognition requirements in the UK and the consequent need to conserve working capital. However, as events turned out, that understanding now appears to have been less than adequate. Fortunately for Ricketts, not all of the acquisition price of each company had to be paid up front.

Whether by design or otherwise, this clearly eased Round 2's cash outflows. It may also have provided Round 2 with some financial leverage in the event that any claims might become due against the sellers under warranty commitments. In the circumstances it would be surprising if the sellers' advisers had not encouraged the sellers to seek some security in respect of Round 2's deferred obligations, perhaps in the form of bank or similar guarantees.

Whether or not such security was sought, none appears to have been given. If it was resisted, alarm bells should have started to ring loud and clear. Unlike most agency deals, the deferred amount was not linked to the achievement of any predetermined future profit targets (commonly known as an "earn-out").

Diary of a disaster	
1 January 2010:	Ricketts' acquisition vehicle - Round 2 International UK - had a deficiency of shareholders' funds of £292,000.
5 March 2010:	Round 2 International UK passes resolution to increase its authorised capital to a maximum of £500,000 in ordinary shares and £250,000 in redeemable preference shares. At the same time it allotted 249,850 ordinary shares and 250,000 redeemable preference shares to Garfield Ricketts personally, resulting in total issued capital of £500,000.
	Round 2 International UK pledges all its assets and those of certain subsidiaries to Centric SPV1, a corporate finance house that specialises in invoice discounting and asset-based loans.
	Round 2 International UK acquires the Robson Brown parent Latefrost. Group accounts of Latefrost showed it had net assets of £4 million at 28 February 2009 and net current assets of £3.6 million, of which £2 million was in cash (after deducting borrowings). It earned a profit of £190,000 in the year ending on that date.
8 April 2010:	Round 2 International UK further mortgages its assets and those of certain subsidiaries to Centric SPV1.
	Round 2 International UK buys Austin West Communications after it had reported a group profit of £382,000 for 2009. Austin West Communications had net assets of £838,000 and net current assets of £797,000 at the end of that year, including £2 million cash at bank.
21 June 2010:	Round 2 International UK further mortgages its assets and those of certain subsidiaries to Centric SPV1.
August 2010:	Round 2 International UK buys Bath-based Attinger Jack. It had net assets of £1.3 million in October 2009 and net current assets of £646,000. In the year to 31 October 2009 it made only a modest profit of £26,000 before paying a dividend.
29 September 2010:	Round 2 International UK passes a resolution permitting Ricketts to convert into ordinary shares the £250,000 redeemable preference shares attributed to him.
	Round 2 International UK issues 560,872 ordinary shares to Ricketts "in full and final settlement and satisfaction of the sum of £560,872, being monies owed by the company to Garfield Ricketts". This resulted in the total share capital becoming £1,060,872.
29 November 2010	Acquired companies go into administration.

The reason becomes clearer when the rest of the deal terms are examined more carefully.

In a display of mind-boggling naivety Ricketts allowed the former owners to retire from their company directorships as soon as the ink was dry. So none of them would have been in a position to influence the future financial performance of the companies they had sold and it would have been hard to persuade them to link any of the deferred purchase price to results in such circumstances.

Alas, none of the former owners of Robson Brown, Austin West Media and Attinger Jack Advertising received the deferred portion of the purchase price that was owed for their businesses. At Robson Brown alone, former shareholders and employees were owed £2.5 million when the administrators were appointed. None of that £2.5 million was secured and presumably none of it will ever be paid.

It could be argued that the former owners of the three agencies placed too much confidence in the ability of Round 2 to meet its deferred purchase obligations. Perhaps they relied on assurances from Ricketts and his advisers without feeling a need to seek any more solid comfort. Or perhaps the overall terms of the Ricketts offer were simply too seductive to resist. Certainly Ricketts and his advisers are said to have come across as a convincing team.

The most credible explanation of the financial failure to emerge so far is that Round 2 was inadequately capitalised and used every available device to generate the cash required to pay for its acquisitions, including cash that would more appropriately have been retained as working capital.

But even raiding the cash coffers of acquired companies and borrowing against unpaid invoices was not enough. No longer able to satisfy their credit recognition conditions, the media owners started to withdraw credit facilities from the infant group and to demand cash in advance. Soon the group was engulfed by cash flow difficulties. The administrators' report asserts that the situation was made even worse by a reduction in credit insurance cover.

Ricketts and his advisers had translated a collection of individually sound businesses into a highly borrowed group, relying substantially on sales invoice discounting for its working capital, and vulnerable to the economic downturn that was to follow. That working capital was provided by Centric Commercial Finance – the one party to exit with its debts fully repaid after appointing Zolfo Cooper as administrators.

Was the Bank of Scotland prize money intended to provide a £3m gain to senior executives at Iris as well as to fund international growth?

21

Intriguing Investment in Iris

Iris Nation was one of the many digital marketing agencies to emerge in the final stages of the last century. It was founded by Stephen Bell, Claire Humphris, Ian Millner, Sam Noble, Sean Reynolds, Jo Schwarz, Stuart Shanley and Adam Wright. Julian Dodds was also an initial investor but he sold his shares in 2005.

They built a successful business and shared ownership with many of the company's senior personnel. But it has not been an uneventful journey.

For example, the Iris founders and senior managers were able to use £3.3 million of the funds awarded under the Bank of Scotland's *Corporate Entrepreneur Challenge* in 2007 to realise personal gains on some of their shareholdings while the company was losing money and needed to conserve capital to support its declared global expansion ambitions. Was part of the Bank of Scotland prize money really intended to provide an early financial gain to senior executives in addition to funding international growth?

A wider share ownership scheme, introduced in 2009 with the help of funds received as part of the Bank of Scotland award, resulted in a swathe of shareholders owing material amounts of money to the company, a situation that was eventually resolved by an imaginative restructuring of the share capital.

And a bumpy trend in profits and losses, caused in part by the cost of the company's international ambitions, put an occasional strain on the group's finances.

It would seem that the Iris founders faced the same dilemma as many other successful entrepreneurs: how to realise some of the value they had created without giving up control prematurely. So it may be more than a coincidence that several of the major transactions in which the company engaged included — or were followed swiftly by — an arrangement for the disposal of some of the founders' shares, whether or not that may have been the primary motivation.

The story told in the pages that follow was first published in *Marketing Services Financial Intelligence* in August 2011. It records events that took place after Iris had made a regular profit in every one of its first nine years, reaching £1.1 million in 2007. Over the next three years the pursuit of its growth ambitions resulted in losses totalling £7.3 million.

At 31 December 2010 Iris had run up borrowings of £5.4 million and its balance sheet was in a very delicate condition with a £1.6 million deficiency of shareholders' funds, short-term liabilities exceeding readily realisable assets by £5.3 million and net borrowings of £3.8 million. Within readily realisable assets was an amount of £5.8 million due from employees in respect of shares issued to them by the employee benefit trust.

As we shall see, the bank was putting pressure on Iris to pay off its loans. Having already applied the best part of £7 million of the Bank of Scotland award for the benefit of the founders and the employee share trust, the company was running short of capital, so set about a restructuring and turned to outside investors to keep its balance sheet intact.

The restructuring took place late in 2010, involving "the removal of layers of unnecessary management and the closure of offices based in Madrid, Munich and Paris". Matters were not helped by write-offs of £890,000 attributed to a "thorough detailed review of the balance sheet at 31 December 2010" following the changes in senior non-founder management: "As a result of this process, the directors have identified a number of assets that were not recoverable and liabilities that were not provided for", the com-

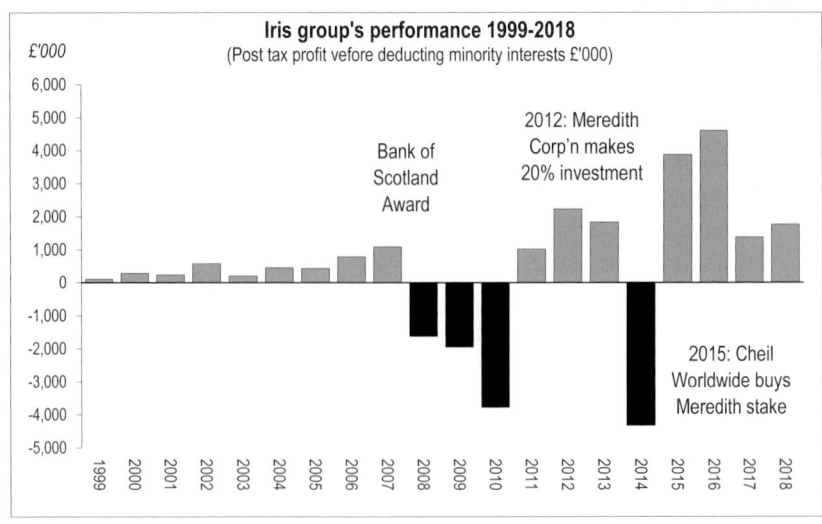

Iris group's performance 1999-2018
(Post tax profit vefore deducting minority interests £'000)

£'000

Bank of Scotland Award

2012: Meredith Corp'n makes 20% investment

2015: Cheil Worldwide buys Meredith stake

pany said. A number of the items involved were considered to have been "incorrectly accounted for" at 31 December 2009. Other initiatives taken by the group included:

- improving commercial governance in the organisation to maximise returns.
- reducing non-client value driving resources.
- switching to a partnership model in markets where there is perceived to be a higher risk.
- integrating agencies more formally to enable the group to work across disciplines around client needs more easily.

The office closures and redundancies highlighted the risks associated with trying to create a global business while being overly dependent on one client. In the two years to December 2009 the group had increased its turnover by 58% after opening offices in the United States, Australia, India, China, Germany and the Netherlands. Much of the expansion was based on business from Sony Ericsson. Other clients included Coca Cola, Shell and Adidas. But turnover growth came to a grinding halt in 2010.

Iris was not the first company to find itself in this position, but its experience reinforces the need for those who have ambitious plans for their company to ensure that their aspirations are built on solid foundations. Those foundations include having a handful of broadly similar sized clients, without undue dependence on any one of them, and ensuring there is adequate long-term capital to withstand any setbacks.

In its search for new capital Iris found a friend in the US media owner and marketing business Meredith Corporation. Meredith bought a 20% stake in Iris for £8 million in October 2011, valuing the whole at £40 million or thereabouts. But Iris had reported losses in the three preceding years and reported a post-tax profit of only £1 million in 2011 – and that was after capitalising nearly £2 million of US start-up costs and inter-company balances due from subsidiaries in Sydney, Singapore and Madrid, despite having closed its Madrid office in 2010.

On the face of it Meredith had been rather generous, but its calculations probably took more notice of the underlying operating profit stripped of the abnormal items. That operating profit would have been £4.2 million in 2011 before allowing for amortisation of intangible assets, costs of reorganisation and the Meredith deal, along with the start-up expenses incurred abroad that had been capitalised.

One half of the shares acquired by Meredith provided Iris

with additional working capital of £4 million, or at least most of it did. A modest amount of £275,000 was used to buy out the $2.75 million investment made by the Bank of Scotland's private equity subsidiary Uberior Equity as part of the original *Corporate Entrepreneur Challenge* Award, leaving Uberior nursing a £2.5 million loss on its holding.

The other half of the $8 million was used to buy shares from founders and senior managers. Many of these shareholders had also participated in the earlier share sale that utilised part of the proceeds of the Bank of Scotland *Corporate Entrepreneur Challenge* Award. None of the other 40 or so smaller shareholders (employees and others) participated in the latest share sale.

Buoyed up by its Meredith capital injection, all may have seemed well at Iris. But there was a snag.

Under the terms of the deal, Meredith had secured an option to require Iris to buy back the entire 20% shareholding for £8 million during 2014. Whether or not the Meredith investment was meant to be that short-term, the mere creation of the option resulted in Iris being obliged to treat the deal for accounting purposes as if the option would definitely be exercised. The immediate accounting effect was to reduce the Iris net assets by the discounted present value of the amount that would be payable in 2014 on exercise of the option.

Bearing in mind that half of Meredith's £8 million investment had already gone straight out into the pockets of Iris managers, the accounting presentation resulted in a worse-looking balance sheet than before the investment was made — showing a deficiency of shareholders' funds of £4.2 million compared with a deficiency of £1.6 million a year earlier.

That created another potential snag. Without eliminating the deficiency in shareholders' funds, Iris would not be able to pay a dividend out of future profits. And that may not have been a very happy position for Meredith to be in, even if the management and employers had been comfortable with it. What's more, the bank may have preferred to be lending to a company in which its shareholders still had some capital left in the business.

Fortunately, the £3.7 million deficiency of shareholders' funds comprised a mixture of items — £10 million in "permanent" share capital, offset by £4.8 million in accumulated losses and £8.9 million of other deficiencies. So Iris was able to seek court permission to convert about £9 million of its permanent share capital into distributable reserves, thereby wiping out the accumulated losses and enabling dividends to be paid in future if desired. In the meantime the total amount of the shareholders' deficiency remained unchanged. Only the composition had been altered.

Having tidied up its balance sheet in this small way, there remained one rather larger outstanding embarrassment. Among its short-term debtors there remained £5.8 million owed to the company's share trust by employee shareholders who had each been issued with shares priced at £359 on the basis that only £1 had to be paid up front. The balance was treated as a loan and would become repayable when the shares were sold. Until then the probability of the employee shareholders being able to repay the loans must have been somewhat limited.

To remove this £5.8 million debt from the Iris balance sheet, a complicated capital reorganisation was embarked upon in 2012. It involved the creation of a new holding company called Iris Worldwide Holdings and this is what happened next:

> When the new company was formed, its shares were issued at a premium over their nominal value and in effect some of that "premium" was applied to cancel the partly paid shares and replace them with the fully paid equivalent. The acquisition of Iris Nation Worldwide by Iris Worldwide Holdings took place at a price of £36 million – a value far in excess of the £8 million book value attributed to the underlying tangible net assets at the end of 2012.
>
> Fortunately, Iris was able to apply a technical procedure called "merger accounting" to avoid recognising the £28 million (or thereabouts) shortfall as goodwill, with the potential risk of a charge against future profits if such an amount could not be supported in the event of an asset impairment review.
>
> Instead the shortfall has been treated as a reduction of shareholders' funds, leaving the newly created group with a £6 million deficiency even after allowing for a modest £1.8 million post-tax profit for 2013.
>
> Asked to confirm whether one of the outcomes of the restructure had been to eliminate the obligations among employee shareholders to pay the outstanding portion of £359 per share due to the employee trust for shares they had acquired in Iris Nation Worldwide, by substituting a similar number of fully paid shares in Iris Worldwide Holdings, joint global chief executive Ian Millner said this was not the main objective, but "a positive by-product".
>
> "We were trying to create a much more effective share scheme for our people", Millner explained. "We obviously spent a considerable amount of time making this change and considered the pros and cons carefully...and consulted at length our

shareholders, Meredith (the US investor), our lawyers, tax advisers, the bank and HMRC."

Meanwhile the 2014 deadline was approaching when Meredith might ask Iris to buy back its shareholding for £8 million. There were tentative signs that this might happen when Meredith extended its exercise deadline by one year and Iris set aside a dedicated reserve to reflect the likely cost (although that piece of accounting did not in itself set aside any cash for the purpose).

Then in November 2014, the Korean marketing group Cheil Worldwide announced that it had bought out Meredith's investment as part of a wider arrangement that would allow it to acquire up to 100% of Iris over the following five years. Cheil is part of the Samsung business empire.

Iris had reported a post-tax profit of £1.8 million in 2013, slightly down on the £2.2 million achieved in 2012. Would that have been sufficient to support a valuation close to the £40 million put on the business by Meredith in 2011? Further investigation showed that Cheil had paid £25.5 million for its 65% stake — precisely equivalent to a £40 million valuation for the entire company.

With the benefit of hindsight, Meredith may have done rather well, even to recover the full amount of its investment. Figures emerged later to show that Iris' operating profit on normal activities had fallen by 66% in 2014 after losing the Sony account. Iris had also incurred costs totalling a massive £5.9 million relating primarily to the Cheil deal, resulting in a post-tax loss for the year of £4.3 million (see table).

Iris Worldwide's final year of independence		
Year ended 31 December	2014	2013
	£'000	£'000
Turnover	92,956	75,554
Cost of sales	-36,979	-23,938
Gross income	55,977	51,616
Non-recurring items:[1]		
Transaction costs[2]	-1,248	-
Meredith licence fee	-1,900	-
Restructuring costs	-715	-158
Staff bonuses	-1,210	-1,340
Share incentive charges	-808	-
Development cost amortisation	-80	-
Amortisation/impairment of goodwill	-72	-416
Other operating costs	-54,141	-46,290
Operating profit (loss)	-4,197	3,412
Finance income (costs)	-701	-446
Taxation	459	-1,146
Minority interests	111	15
Profit after tax	-4,328	1,835
Operating profit margin on revenue	-7.5%	6.6%
Adjusted operating profit [3] £'000	1,836	5,326
Adjusted op profit margin[3]	3.3%	10.3%

1. Non-recurring items are those not expected to recur after the post year end sale of the company to Cheil. 2. These costs relate to the sale of the company to Cheil and are recoverable from selling shareholders, although the amount has been charged against profits rather than presented as a debtor. 3. Adjusted to exclude development costs, amortisation/impairment, and all non-recurring charges.

The founders and senior managers of marketing agency Iris Nation Worldwide were able to use £3.3 million of the funds awarded under the Bank of Scotland's *Corporate Entrepreneur Challenge* to realise a gain on their existing shareholdings while the company was losing money and needed to conserve capital to support its declared global expansion ambitions.

The aim of the Bank of Scotland's Challenge was to find entrepreneurs who showed the greatest potential for growth and success. Iris won the competition in 2007 and the award was formalised in the early part of 2008. It comprised £5 million of interest-free loan capital for the business and an investment of almost £2.8 million in shares by the bank's private equity subsidiary Uberior Equity.

If growth and success were key objectives, the Iris experience raises questions about how well the Bank of Scotland award scheme was conceived and administered, and about whether the bank's funds were used in a manner that was most likely to achieve its stated aims.

No-one can doubt that Iris had growth ambitions. The company spelt them out very clearly in its annual report for 2008: "The performance in 2008 reflects the continued commitment to establishing Iris as one of the world's leading independent integrated advertising networks. The accelerated international growth shown in 2008, resulting in Iris establishing 15 offices globally, has created the platform for further future overseas expansion."

Yet, even as the 2008 financial year was closing, the company was applying £3.3 million of its newly awarded funds, not to pay for international expansion, but to provide a big capital gain to 10 of its senior managers, despite the fact that the group would show a loss of £1.6 million for the year (of which £0.4 million of costs were not discovered until the following year).

The capital gain was achieved as part of a laudable plan to create wider share ownership in the group, although the purchase of the senior managers' shares would not have been essential to the success of such a scheme. The plan was approved on 12 December 2008 when the bank facilities were modified to encompass lending funds to the company's employee benefit trust.

As already explained, £3.3

million of those funds were then used to buy back shares from the senior managers at an average price of £278 per share and a further £3.6 million was used to subscribe for new shares at £359 per share, providing the employee trust with about 24,000 shares for future allocation to employees. It is not clear why more than one price was adopted by the employee trust for these transactions, but a share price of £359 would have valued the loss-making company as a whole at an astonishing £20 million.

Iris joint chief executive officer Ian Millner

The senior managers had originally bought their shares for £1 each and so nearly all of the £3.3 million pay-out was profit. Worthy of less celebration was the fact that the purchase of the senior managers' shares had an adverse impact on the group's balance sheet as a substantial portion of the funds provided by the Bank of Scotland a few months earlier had gone straight out of the company into the hands of the selling shareholders – to some extent replacing permanent shareholders' funds with time limited debt.

Asked to confirm that £3.3 million of the funds provided by Bank of Scotland were used to enable the Iris employee benefit trust to purchase some shares from senior executives in 2008, Iris joint global chief executive Ian Millner said: "It was some time ago now, so you'll have to forgive me for not being able to recall the detail".

Yet Millner had signed all the public documents in December 2008,

including one showing that he personally received £400,000 for the sale of some of his shareholding, something most people would be unlikely to forget. When copies of those documents were presented to Millner he replied: "I'll need to just check this with our CFO, as I'm not clear on exactly what we did... What you are talking about happened quite a while ago and was done by our chairman and commercial director (both of whom are no longer with us)."

When Bank of Scotland's new owner Lloyds Banking Group was asked to explain whether the aim of the award was to provide funds for the further expansion of the business or to provide a capital gain to the senior managers, all the spokesperson would say was: "As part of the entry process, entrants were required to complete a comprehensive application form, which requested a considerable amount of information about the business' financial performance. It also required them to outline how they would utilise the finance facility awarded as part of the competition's prize."

Most of the people involved with administering the Bank of Scotland award are no longer employed within the enlarged organisation and the spokesperson for Lloyds was unable to confirm whether or not the funds awarded to Iris were actually utilised strictly in the manner outlined in the application form. However, he said he would have expected the bank to have monitored how Iris spent its funds and to have ensured they were in accordance with the purposes for which the facility was approved.

Therefore it is conceivable that the Bank of Scotland was content for a large portion of its facility to flow to the Iris senior managers rather than to the business itself, begging a question about how this fitted into the declared aims of the award. We may never know the answer to that question. "Due to customer confidentiality, we cannot discuss a specific company's banking relationship with us", the Lloyds spokesperson said.

The possibility of a future share buyback may have been one of the reasons why Bank of Scotland included a £2.8 million equity component alongside the £5 million loan facility. Even if this was so, it only partially compensated for the reduction in shareholders' funds arising from the purchase of shares from senior managers. It is at least as likely that the equity component was designed to compensate the bank for the risk it was taking and the loss of revenue it would otherwise have earned on its £5 million interest-free loan.

Whether or not the Bank of Scotland's funds were used entirely in the manner originally envisaged, the adverse impact on the Iris balance sheet for 2008 was made worse by its poor trading performance.

By 31 December that year, the group had negative shareholders' funds and its short-term liabilities exceeded readily realisable assets by a whopping £6 million (although, to be fair, the company said that some of those short-term liabilities arose from a "technical" breach of the bank loan agreement that was subsequently remedied).

Shortly afterwards the company's weakened balance sheet was improved by a curious quirk of accounting when the employee benefit trust offered Iris employees the opportunity to buy most of the shares it had acquired with the aid of the Bank of Scotland's finance.

At the offer price of £359 per share, this might have been expected to contribute a useful £6.5 million to the Iris coffers, except for one important constraint: the employees could not reasonably be expected to afford that amount of money and

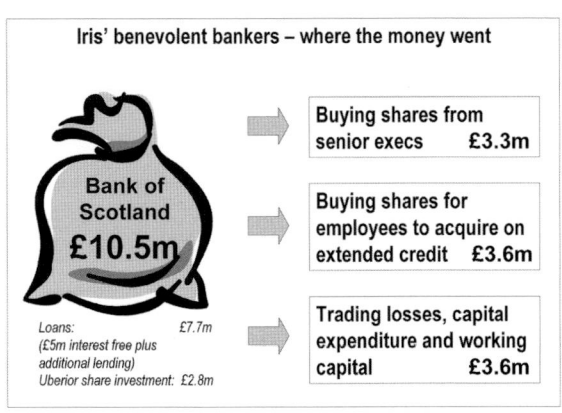

Iris' benevolent bankers – where the money went

Bank of Scotland £10.5m

Loans: £7.7m
(£5m interest free plus additional lending)
Uberior share investment: £2.8m

Buying shares from senior execs £3.3m

Buying shares for employees to acquire on extended credit £3.6m

Trading losses, capital expenditure and working capital £3.6m so they were asked to pay only £1 per share in cash at the time. The balance would only become payable when the shares were sold, presumably even if the shares were to be sold for less than £359.

Meanwhile Iris would have to find a way to meet the repayment terms of the bank funding that was used by the employee trust to buy the shares in the first place. Whether any employee would have been prepared to pay the full £359 up front for a share in a loss-making company being valued at £20 million may never be known.

When Iris came to record this employee share issue in its 2009 accounts, instead of showing just the £18,000 cash received from employees for their shares as an enhancement to its shareholders' funds, it included the full sale value of £6.5 million in accordance with prevailing accounting rules.

That large increase in shareholders' funds may have looked good on paper, but as the share sales hadn't generated anything more than a token pot of cash for Iris, its balance sheet was saddled with a massive £6.5 million of outstanding debts due from the employees. And the ability of those employees to pay for their shares will be influenced by whatever value they can realise when they sell the shares in the future. That in turn will depend on the financial success of the group.

Iris continued to trade at a loss during 2009. By the end of that year the company had spent all its cheap money, not just in establishing employee share schemes or providing a capital gain on the founders' shares, but also in building a business presence in the United States, Singapore, Australia, India, China, Germany and the Netherlands.

By August 2010 cash seemed to be running short. Iris was reported to be closing its German office and cutting back staff in London. It remains

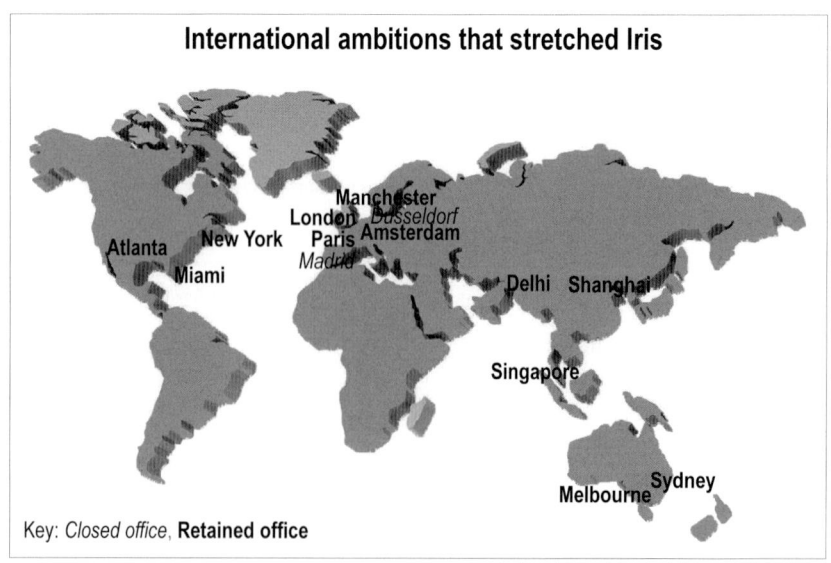

International ambitions that stretched Iris

Manchester
London Düsseldorf
Atlanta New York Paris Amsterdam
Miami Madrid
Delhi Shanghai
Singapore
Melbourne Sydney

Key: *Closed office*, **Retained office**

to be seen whether the group has bucked the recent trend and made a profit in that year as a whole, but the signs are that the company's bankers had begun to get cold feet.

Under the terms of the original loan awarded under the Bank of Scotland's *Entrepreneur Challenge*, the interest-free period would have expired in June this year, after which interest would be payable at 3.25 percentage points above LIBOR.

At the same time, quarterly repayments of the outstanding loan would have commenced with the intention of repaying all of the debt by June 2013. However, the loan terms appear to have been amended early in 2010, removing the interest and repayment holidays with immediate effect.

Thus loans totalling some £5.4 million net of cash would have to be repaid by equal quarterly instalments ending on 24 June 2013 and the interest cost to the group would be rather more than originally assumed. Whether Iris can generate the cash flow to meet quarterly debt repayments in the region of £500,000, including interest, remains to be seen.

Writing on the *Smarta* online entrepreneurs' network, Ian Millner blamed the change in banking terms on the global financial crisis that precipitated the takeover of the company's original bankers by Lloyds Banking Group. He claims that, as a result, the banking relationship changed substantially. Be that as it may, an outsider might argue that the pay-out of £3.3 million to senior managers during a period of expansion also contributed to a weaker capital structure that made the achievement of the founders' global ambitions susceptible to greater risk than would otherwise have been the case. Hopefully the worst is past.

A story of misjudged acquisitions that often cost a lot to finance. Eschewing "earn-out" deals, the company sought out lower priced cash purchases

22

Media Square Laid Bare

Jeremy Middleton is an extremely affable gentleman whose life has been spent in the marketing industry. His first exposure to the industry followed the death of his father in 1981 which left his mother running a Buxton public relations consultancy called Osborne Publicity Services.

Jeremy Middleton: new broom swept old guard from the Media Square board.

When Jeremy joined his mother in the family business it was losing around £5,000 in a year and had a bank overdraft of £15,000. According to press reports, Middleton's first job after school had been as a chef after studying the subject at a catering college near home at Buxton. Then he ran *The George* pub in Buxton for a few years.

Osborne Publicity changed its name to Equanim and, as we shall see, it was making a pre-tax profit of £150,000 by 2000 when it was acquired by a young public company called Media Square. And that is where this chapter's story begins.

In essence it is a story of an entrepreneur with an appetite for growth. In particular it reflects one person's bias against buying companies on an "earn-out" basis, where the total cost is determined by profits made after acquisition. Jeremy Middleton preferred to buy companies outright, but that may have resulted in Media Square buying some less successful businesses whose owners had more modest price expectations.

Competition among prospective buyers of such companies would also have been less, so the purchase price would have been relatively realistic. The challenge was very much about breathing new life into tired companies. That doesn't always work.

Middleton's aversion to earn-outs had some justification. Research I commissioned in 1989 from Dr Roger Hussey of the Bristol Business School concluded, among other things, that earn-outs "can lead to a discrepancy between the desire of vendors to create short term profits, and so maximise their earn–out capability, and the acquirer's wish for the long–term success of the company".[1]

Despite the disappointing outcome of his involvement with Media Square, Jeremy always seemed ready to listen to criticism, explain his view of events and, if necessary, to defend his actions. Even after publication of the report that follows, first published in January 2012, I found him good company, friendly and always eager to chat about any piece of news emerging from the industry. So read on to learn more about how Media Square grew and why eventually it failed.

Towards the end of the story we hear how a new management team — led by ex McKinsey management consultants Roger Parry and Peter Reid — failed to prevent Media Square from falling into administration. But they were able to buy it back from the administrators — what is a called a "phoenix". Something similar happened at Leagas Delaney (see chapter 11). The duo persuaded Media Square's former bankers Lloyds to lend their new company MSQ Partners £11 million for the purchase, notwithstanding that Lloyds had lost a large amount of money when Media Square failed.

Although the shares had become valueless and the banks had lost a lot of money, ordinary creditors of the trading subsidiaries were more fortunate:

> The administrators also confirmed that Lloyds Banking Group will have suffered a substantial loss on its lending that totalled £21.5 million at 31 August, prior to recovering £3.25 million from the sale of a Newmarket property. Most of the group's creditors are due for payment by individual subsidiaries and currently remain outside the scope of the administration that relates solely to the parent company. According to administrators Pricewaterhouse Coopers, "the individual subsidiaries are unaffected and their creditors will be paid as normal". "There are no inter–company balances where subsidiaries owe money to plc", commented PwC partner Zelf Hussain. "There is no risk of me pursuing the subsidiaries for any balances."[2]

But some of Media Square's shareholders would not accept the collapse so readily. The board was accused of breaching its fiduciary duties to its shareholders by Bob Morton whose company Hawk Investment Holdings held a substantial stake in the failed business.

---

1 *"Earn–out Agreements – Their impact on Marketing Services Companies": Research commissioned by Spicer & Oppenheim and conducted by Dr Roger Hussey of the Bristol Business School, December 1989.*

2 *From "Marketing Services Financial Intelligence" 10 December, 2011*

We shall read more about Bob Morton in chapter 25. Morton alleged that Media Square's shareholders were "kept in the dark and not kept informed at any stage". Speaking to *Marketing Services Financial Intelligence* at the time, Morton claimed that all the advisers had colluded with the Media Square board to do a deal for the benefit of the board instead of the shareholders. "I am pursing our possible options", he said. Morton had spent several years agitating the board of Media Square through his Hawk shareholding, but Hawk had reduced its stake to 7.1% in 2010 and there is no evidence that Morton took the matter any further.

It could be argued - with some justification - that the rescue of Media Square by means of a financial reconstruction supported by its bankers preserved many components of the group as going concerns without cost to their ordinary creditors, and that Peter Reid and other shareholding members of the management team deserve any financial rewards they may earn. It is not beyond the bounds of possibility that Lloyds Banking Group will eventually recover some or all of its earlier losses, provided MSQ can build a sufficiently profitable future. ,

Looking back, Roger Parry's earlier claim to have turned Media Square round was somewhat premature, as former shareholders will testify. But at the very least the decision he took with Peter Reid to put the company into adminstration enabled it to shed much of its debt burden and re-boot the rest of the group as a going concern. Many of the employees will have retained their jobs and Reid was able to sift the less promising companies from those with better prospects.

Nevertheless, questions remain about the way in which managements of failed companies are able to reacquire the assets after administration. This is what *Marketing Services Financial Intelligence* had to say after the Media Square affair:

> The question of whether the management team of an insolvent company should be permitted to mount a buyout is as important as it is complex, especially in the case of a publicly owned company. At Media Square, despite their best efforts the incumbent managers had failed to restore the company's fortunes, so why should they have been "rewarded" with a second chance? And who determines whether the price paid for the buyout is the best available, or whether the management should be allowed to buy at a price that may be less than it would have been if the business, or its component parts, had been sold sooner?
>
> A deal of this type is often described as a "phoenix".

That term is commonly applied where creditors as well as share-holders in the failed business lose money only to find that the same management team reappears from the ashes to carry on the same business with an ownership interest cloaked in new corporate clothing.

At Media Square, the initial indications are that the bank and the shareholders have lost serious sums of money, but that the ordinary creditors have been paid or will be paid in the ordinary course of business. Even assuming that proves to be the case, is it reasonable for the bank and the administrators to have done a deal with the former management behind the scenes without first seeking the approval of either creditors or shareholders of the failed business? Clearly Bob Morton, whose company Hawk Investment Holdings had a 7% stake, thinks not.

Insolvency specialists will be the first to point out that time is of the essence in the face of financial failure. Once the clients and staff jump ship, nothing remains to be sold. It might be argued that a deal could have been struck that was contin-gent upon shareholder and/or creditor approval. But what would happen in the meantime? The trade would probably grind to a halt as no-one would extend any further credit while the situation remained in limbo, clients would lose confidence, and good staff would be open to seduction by every head-hunter in town.

So if there is anything unsavoury about a pre-packaged phoenix deal, perhaps it would be better to make it unlawful for a former director of an insolvent company to become a director of or shareholder in any company that acquires a business from that insolvent company or any of its subsidiaries within five years of the insolvency. At least everyone would then know where they stood.

So far the Government has shown no signs of legislating in this way. However, new rules were introduced in 2021 relating to pre-pack sales when made to a connected party within eight weeks of an administrator being appointed. In such circumstances the deal must gain formal creditor ratification or be sanctioned by an "Evaluator" who must demonstrate sufficient relevant knowledge and experience to make the report.

How MSQ Partners was funded
At 28 February 2014

Sources of funds:		£'000
Bank finance:		
Bank loans due within one year	16,929	
Less; Unrestricted cash	-5,730	11,199
Short-term liabilities less readily realisable assets		6,784
Provisions and long-term liabilities		1,143
Total funds available		**19,126**
Absorbed by		
Deficiency of shareholders' funds		3,688
Long-term assets:		
Intangible goodwill	13,869	
Other long-term fixed assets	1,569	15,438
Total funds employed		**19,126**

Another aspect of the **MSQ** phoenix arrangement came to light soon afterwards. Uberior Trading, a company that had become part of the Lloyds Banking Group after Lloyds acquired Halifax Bank of Scotland (HBOS), was identified as a party to the shareholders' agreement governing the conduct of **MSQ** Partners. As previously mentioned, Lloyds Banking Group reportedly lost a large amount of money on the appointment of administrators to Media Square. As a result of these arrangements, senior board members of the defunct Media Square and its bankers have emerged as part owners of the new company whereas the outside ordinary shareholders in Media Square have lost their entire investment without being given any opportunity to acquire shares in the successor business. At present that is entirely lawful.

In July 2014 **MSQ** needed some more long-term capital as losses had been accumulating again. It found a welcome investor in NVM Private Equity, which was prepared to provide £7.8 million. In return for subscribing £1 million of share capital to **MSQ**'s new parent company, NVM was granted 40% of the voting rights, 40% of any dividends declared and an entitlement to share in 99.9% of the first £1 million of funds available to shareholders on liquidation. The balance of the funding package came in the form of a £6.8 million loan.

For anyone reasonably familiar with private equity investments it will come as no surprise that **MSQ** was looking for another new backer to replace NVM in 2019. As explained in chapter 18, private equity investments do not normally extend beyond five years, by which time the investor will hope that a realisation oppor-

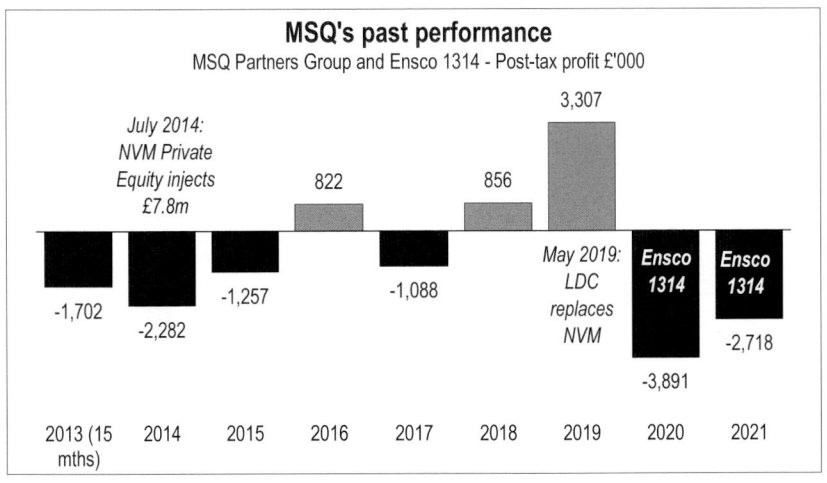

MSQ's past performance
MSQ Partners Group and Ensco 1314 - Post-tax profit £'000

July 2014:
NVM Private
Equity injects
£7.8m

822

856

3,307

May 2019:
LDC
replaces
NVM

Ensco
1314

Ensco
1314

-1,702

-2,282

-1,257

-1,088

-3,891

-2,718

2013 (15
mths)   2014   2015   2016   2017   2018   2019   2020   2021

tunity will have arisen — such as a trade sale of the company or a flotation on the stock market — or that a replacement investor can be found. MSQ had not been sold or floated on the stock market, so a new backer was sought.

As the years passed MSQ had shed a number of unwanted subsidiaries and in 2019 its pre-tax profit rocketed up to £3.3 million, far ahead of anything previously achieved (see chart). If that level of profitability was considered to be maintainable, it would have had a material bearing on the price paid to buy out NVM and some other departing shareholders.

The replacement investor came in the form of a company with the innocuous name of Ensco 1314, but with a shareholder that had a long association with MSQ — Lloyds Banking Group. Lloyds Development Capital (LDC) and HSBC together provided Ensco with £33.4 million to finance the acquisition, of which just £0.2 million was used to buy shares for LDC. The balance was in loans, generating interest charges that would push the group back into a loss in 2020, albeit payment of those interest charges would be deferred until 2026 unless MSQ were to be sold or listed on a stock exchange before then. From those funds Ensco paid £19.8 million in cash and a further £5.8 million in loan notes and shares to acquire MSQ's shares, with about another £1.5 million payable in contingent consideration.

Ensco bought out NVM Private Equity and the rest of the shareholders just before the existing lending arrangements expired. Those shareholders included retiring chairman Roger Parry (who had held 15% of the equity) and two other non-executive directors. As part of the arrangement the continuing management reinvested in Ensco. On conclusion, Lloyds Development Capital owned 67%

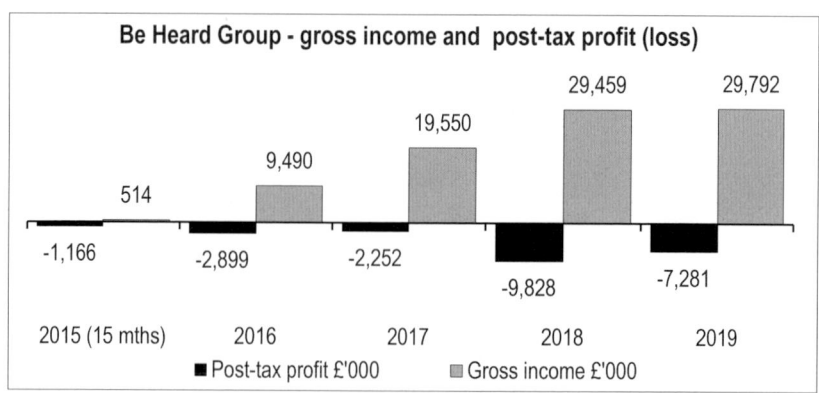

Be Heard Group - gross income and post-tax profit (loss)

	2015 (15 mths)	2016	2017	2018	2019
Post-tax profit £'000	-1,166	-2,899	-2,252	-9,828	-7,281
Gross income £'000	514	9,490	19,550	29,459	29,792

of the Ensco's equity and had 49.9% of the voting power. The management and non-executive directors held the balance. Buoyed with financial support from LDC, MSQ was looking for acquisitions. Into its sights came a little public company called Be Heard Group[1] that had gathered up a number of digital agencies, initially under the leadership of Peter Scott[2] when he set out to establish another marketing business after parting from The Engine Group.

Be Heard Group had run up losses in excess of £22 million by the end of 2019 (see chart) and its short-term liabilities exceeded readily realisable assets by about £5 million. Those liabilities included ongoing earn-out commitments of £6.5 million due to vendors of acquired subsidiaries. By this time Peter Scott had left the group and Simon Pyper had inherited his mantle on an interim basis after joining as chief financial officer a few months earlier.

MSQ offered to buy out the Be Heard Group shareholders for £6.23 million and to provide further financial support alongside HSBC. Under the deal terms each of Be Heard's non-executive directors would leave, along with chief executive Simon Pyper. The deal, combining two loss-making and highly-borrowed companies, was completed on 2 September 2020, contributing to MSQ's interest-laden loss of £2.7 million for the year to February 2021. And, in a small re-writing of history, MSQ's chief executive Peter Reid signed himself off as the company's "founder".

For the full story of how the group was founded, read on...

T he story of Media Square is first and foremost a story of misjudged acquisitions some of which cost a lot to finance and often failed to generate anything like the profits expected of them. Over its 11-year

---

1. *MSQ also bought Maher Bird Holdings in March 2021*
2. *See chapter 23 for an account of Scott's roles in Engine Group, Aegis Group and WCRS*

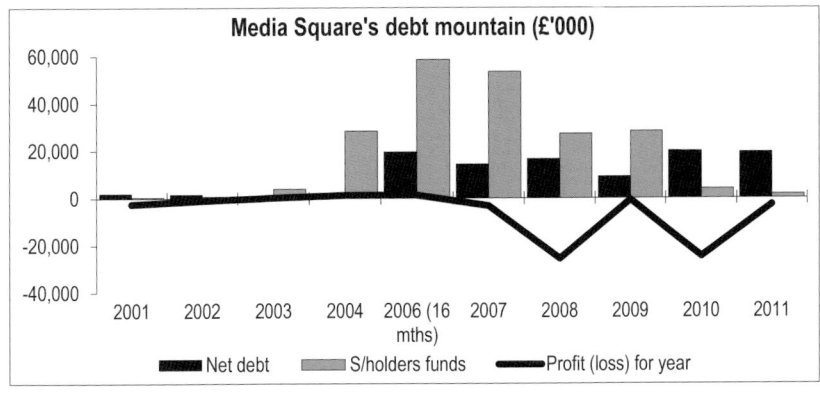

life the company acquired over 70 businesses at a total cost in the region of £105 million.

Much of that was funded by bank borrowings with interest costs that had to be met out of trading profits that rarely materialised. Eventually it proved impossible to meet the interest charges, let alone make regular repayments of the borrowings, without selling some of the acquired companies. Even that was not enough to save the group from financial collapse and the appointment of administrators from Pricewaterhouse Coopers in December 2011.

So many misjudgements and mistakes were made during Media Square's life that it provides an object lesson for anyone else contemplating building a marcoms group. Many of those mistakes can be attributed to business naivety and financial innocence, and even to bad luck, but rarely have so many combined to create such a fatal outcome.

Media Square began life in the Midlands in June 2000 at the peak of the dotcom bubble with the express intention of becoming a public company that would acquire a portfolio of businesses engaged in marketing and e-commerce.

Its three founding directors were well known to each other. One was the former trade minister and computer buff John Butcher who was also a director of employment agency Pertemps Group. Pertemps chairman Timothy Watts took a shareholding in Media Square and looked to Butcher to represent his interest. Pertemps also became a founding customer of Media Square.

The second board member was the entrepreneur Christopher Swan who had built up the Finelist Group, an automotive parts distributor, and sold it for a substantial sum. Butcher had also occupied a non-executive seat on the Finelist board.

The third member of the cosy trio was accountant Russell Stevens who had founded the Hamiltons accountancy firm and been fined £500 in 1999 for professional misconduct. Stevens took the role of chief executive while Butcher and Swan held non-executive positions.

On 14 September 2000, Media Square raised nearly £1 million of new capital when its shares were introduced to the stock market – almost doubling the initial capital that had been subscribed by Butcher, Swan, Stevens and Watts. Between the four of them they continued to control almost 55% of the company.

It was not long before Media Square was making its first acquisition. In February 2001 it bought a modest digital printing and design business called e-plan for £3.1 million, including professional costs and net liabilities assumed. Most of the purchase price was satisfied by the issue of shares in Media Square. As a result the shareholdings of existing Media Square investors were diluted and e-plan's four vendors finished up owning 42% of the company. One of those four was e-plan's managing director Ian Watson.

As part of the deal, Watson took over as chief executive of Media Square and Stevens became finance director. But not for long. By the financial year end of 31 October

2001, it was clear that e-plan had been an expensive mistake. In the 13 months to 31 October, e-plan lost £535,000. Worse still, Media Square had to write down the cost of its investment by £1.9 million. As if that was not enough grief, the group was also found to have "inadequate" cost control and forecasting systems.

So within a year of becoming a public company Media Square had wiped out nearly all of its shareholders' funds by investing in a printing business that was hardly at the leading edge of electronic marketing. It had also become heavily dependent on bank overdrafts, hire purchase debt, finance leases and loans from the former owners of e-plan - not a very auspicious start, but one that would become a recurring feature on the Media Square balance sheet during the rest of its life.

Russell Stevens appears to have taken much of the blame for the initial shortcomings as his contract was terminated on 23 November 2001.

Kevin Steeds: brought into Media Square as chairman

In what now seems a slightly surprising choice, e-plan's finance director Mark Cupitt took over Stevens' role as group finance director.

Before leaving, Stevens had approached another possible acquisition target. It was called Equanim Group and it was run by chief executive Jeremy Middleton and commercial director Graeme Burns.

Equanim was, in essence, a series of small design, advertising, public relations and photography businesses serving mainly regional clients from offices in Buxton, Sheffield, Leeds, Manchester and Macclesfield, with some major national names such as Marks & Spencer, Axa Insurance and Dairy Crest on the client list too. Equanim had been established as a group in 1998, although its origins dated back to 1981 when, on the death of Jeremy Middleton's father, he joined his mother's Buxton-based public relations business.

By any standard Equanim was a fairly small business with sales oscillating between £4 million and £5 million per annum. Like e-plan, the group was hit by the recession and lost £60,000 in 2001 before allowing for finance costs and tax. In the previous year, the group had made a profit of £150,000 before interest and tax. Media Square's first approach was rebuffed, but talks resumed in 2002 and eventually terms were agreed.

In May that year Media Square announced the acquisition of Equanim for £1.2 million payable in Media Square shares and loan notes, although "acquisition" proved to be something of a misnomer. In view of the size of Equanim relative to the

The rise and fall of Media Square

Date (approx)	Event(s)
August 2000	Media Square (MSQ) floated as cash shell with a dot.com strategy, raising approx £1m from high net worth individuals in the West Midlands.
March 2001	Acquires e.plan solutions Ltd, an e-business support services company (printer and web site builder) for up to £4.5 million in cash, shares and loan notes.
August 2001	Acquires Tin Can Design, Worcester, for a few tens of thousands.
June 2002	Acquires Equanim Group for £1.1 million in shares and raises £450k of new money from high net worth individuals.
October 2002	Board restructured. All original directors step down. Kevin Steeds appointed as non-exec chair, John Nixon as non-exec director.
	Tin Can disposed of to management
January 2003	Acquires Fourninety Ltd for £125k cash. Acquires business and assets of FI System Ltd (Manchester-based direct marketing business) and Brand New Media (Leeds-based online marketing business) for £150k cash.
February 2003	Group withdraws financial support from e.plan solutions Ltd. Company subsequently placed into administration.
May 2003	Acquires business and assets of LeFevre Communications (Oxford based PR company) for £100k.
July 2003	Acquires business and assets of BANC (London-based advertising agency) for £50k.
Aug/Sept 2003	First institutional fundraising to pay down debt and restructure balance sheet. £3.1 million raised at 8p per share and £600k raised at 12p per share.
October 2003	Acquires business and assets of preprint Imaging (Leeds-based artwork and reprographics company) for £100k. Business immediately merged with Fourninety Lid.
March 2004	Acquires IAS Marketing and Communications Group (Macclesfield-based integrated advertising and marketing agency) for approx £500k.
April 2004	Second institutional fundraising round – "war chest" of £10.1million raised at 18p per share.
May 2004	Acquires Marketplace Holdings (experiential marketing business based in Abingdon) for approx £500k.
August 2004	Acquires Clark, McKay & Walpole, a leading London-based direct marketing agency, for approx £5.4 million.
October 2004	Acquires Arnold Interactive (London-based online agency) from Havas Group, for up to £600k Acquires Coutts Holdings plc, an AIM listed retail marketing and POP business, for £21 million Third institutional fundraising secures £6 million of new equity at 17.5p per share.
November 2004	Disposes of Coutts East London freehold property for £7.1 million Disposes of Coutts packaging business (Essex Corrugated) for £3.4 million.
August 2005	Acquires Symbian Print Intelligence for up to £1 million.
September 2005	Launches offer to acquire Marketing Services Group (MSG) from Huntsworth plc for £63 million. Successfully raises £30 million of new equity at 25p per share. Secures new banking facilities of approx £50 million.
November 2005	Completes acquisition of MSG from Huntsworth for a total of £55 million.
November 2006	Disposes of Karen Earl Sponsorship Ltd (part of MSG) for £4 million in cash
February 2006	Disposes of Digital Advertising and Marketing Ltd (Tangozebra) – part of the MSG – for £15 million in cash. Disposes of Finex / Silver Bullet – part of MSG – for £500k in cash.
June 2007	Jeremy Middleton resigns as chief executive.
July 2007	Roger Parry appointed executive chairman.
2007-2010	More subsidiaries sold/closed at a loss.
2009-10	Bob Morton and Peter Lunch try to remove Parry.
June 2011	Gate management buyout rebuffed.
August 2011	Balance sheet categorised as "vulnerable" by *Marketing Services Financial Intelligence*.
December 2011	Administrators appointed. Managers buy back group for £11 million.

struggling Media Square, the transaction was classified as a reverse takeover
by Equanim under AIM rules.

Under the deal Media Square
had agreed to offer executive board
positions to Jeremy Middleton and
Graeme Burns and before long the
new brooms were sweeping all of
the old guard out of the boardroom.
What Middleton and Burns discovered was a rapidly deteriorating
financial position as e-plan continued
to lose money and was leaking cash
like a sieve. Instead of developing
Equanim, their first priority was to
sort out the trouble the group was
already in.

"The net result was that we got
rid of the entire board on 15 October
2002 and appointed Kevin Steeds as
our chairman", Middleton recalls.
"Kevin was a great coup for us."

Steeds was a well-respected
finance director who had recently
left another publicly listed marketing
group called Incepta Group.

The period from May to October 2002 had been very turbulent,
culminating in e-plan being put into
administration and Media Square
ending up with just the Equanim
business and £1.6 million of debt.

It is open to question whether
Media Square should have paid £1.2
million, albeit in shares rather than
cash, for a business like Equanim that
made £150,000 before tax and interest in a good year and lost £60,000
in a bad year. But as that valuation
represented a solid multiple of eight
times the profit before tax and interest earned in the good year, it's hardly
surprising that Middleton accepted it.
After the deal was done — which also

included some additional fund-raising
on the stock market — Middleton
owned almost one-third of Media
Square while Graeme Burns had a
much smaller 1% stake.

Now Middleton faced the major
leap from running a modest public
relations business in Buxton to managing a publicly-listed company with
big growth ambitions but little, if any,
financial resources. And the state of
the economy didn't help.

But the new team of Steeds,
Middleton and Burns was optimistic. Writing to shareholders in
March 2003, the company said:
"As previously stated, the group is
committed to the rapid expansion of
its business. The difficult economic
climate means that the capital cost of
future acquisitions will remain low for
the next year or so. We fully intend
to take advantage of this situation
to build a larger and more robust
business that is capable of delivering
substantial and sustainable shareholder value."

The only snag was that Media
Square didn't have much money.

So the deals were small and
almost invariably involved sellers in
distress. Reporting on the year to 31
October 2003 the company said it
had spent just £834,000 in cash on
no less than six acquisitions — e-prin-
cipals, Fourninety, Blakedew 394,
Le Fevre Communications, Bean
Andrews Norways Cramphorn (or
BANC as it was known) and Pre-
Print Imaging.

Of that total cash outlay of
£834,000 a mere £2 was spent on
acquiring three of the companies,
although further costs were incurred

on professional fees and in one case a loan of £125,000 was also taken over by the company. One of those three acquisitions was Fourninety, a company previously owned by Jeremy Middleton who says the acquisition helped to ease Media Square's debt load: "This company brought a chunk of cash with it and annualised sales of £4 million", he says.

In every case, the target companies owed more than was owed to them. So by the time those extra liabilities were taken into account the real cost of the six businesses was much greater – somewhere nearer £1.7 million. However, helped by the earlier re-organisation, the group reported a profit of £255,692 for the year to 31 October 2003.

Equally noteworthy was the fact that those early deals differentiated Media Square from its rivals in a very significant way. Instead of courting fast growing profitable agencies and following the popular trend of gearing the purchase price to profits earned over the next three to five years (the "earn-out"), Media Square had found a niche among low-cost distress situations for which most if not all of the more modest purchase price was paid up front.

This aversion to deferred earn-out obligations remained prevalent throughout the company's life. In Middleton's view earn-outs encouraged vendors to ramp performance as much as possible for three or five years, and then leave the buyer with the problem of declining earnings afterwards: "I could not find any examples where, over a five year period, they were actually value accre-tive for the buyer", he said. "It may be that I did not look hard enough, but at the time there were numerous quoted marcoms groups where badly structured earn-outs were killing them."

Be that as it may, at this stage in Media Square's evolution there were two big unanswered questions. First, would the type of company being acquired by Media Square have the quality, calibre and reputation to generate consistent growth in profits? And secondly, was Media Square cutting itself off from potentially the most valuable acquisition targets that thought they could find more attractive earn-out offers elsewhere?

With a profitable performance behind it, 2004 became a transformational year for Media Square in more ways than one. It was able to raise new capital on the stock market in various tranches totalling £16.5 million net of expenses. It made its first substantial acquisition of a prosperous and successful sales promotion agency Clarke McKay & Walpole. It lost its chairman Kevin Steeds. And it made an audacious £22 million bid for another established public company Coutts Holdings that specialised in retail communications and display fittings.

Suddenly Media Square was making serious sums of money from businesses generating well over twice the turnover reported in 2003. And all of this was achieved without recourse to material borrowings. At 31 October 2004, net debt totalled just £2 million (see chart[1]). Shortly afterwards the group received a further £10 million cash boost from

1. See page 257

selling a freehold property and a packaging business that had both been acquired with Coutts.

If Media Square had taken a year or two to exploit the fruits of its debt-free new acquisitions, its future might have taken a different course. But with confidence bolstered by the group's swiftly enhanced stature and the encouragement of a fee-lusting City, it was ready to contemplate even bigger deals. And one particular company saw this as a heaven-sent opportunity to offload unwanted assets.

In May 2005 Lord Chadlington's global public relations group Huntsworth had acquired Incepta Group with the primary aim of absorbing some of its strong public relations brands that included Citigate. But Incepta also owned a diverse range of other marketing businesses that Huntsworth did not want. Who better to seduce into buying them than the ambitious fast-growing relatively new kid on the block, Media Square?

From Media Square's position, the opportunity was too good to miss. In a single deal the size and reach of the group would be dramatically enlarged, adding 1,000 employees and some well-known marketing businesses that included the Smarts integrated marketing agency, designers Lloyd Northover and Holmes & Marchant, the Dynamo direct marketing business and the Gate Worldwide advertising network with a major presence in the Far East.

By this time the former Coutts chairman Robert Essex had taken the chair at Media Square after Kevin Steeds had resigned to found his own new venture Cello Group (something he had been planning for some time, unbeknown to Media Square). Essex took the view that a price tag of £63 million was excessive for a parcel of businesses that in aggregate was shown to have made a post-tax profit of only £3.7 million in the year to 28 February 2005.

But Middleton points out that it was always intended to reduce the overall cost by disposing of some of the acquired businesses and assets afterwards.

Essex was also unsettled by a sprinkling of vague hints in the draft offer document, such as the reference to some of the businesses having suffered from under-investment and to the uncertainty caused by the merger between Huntsworth and Incepta having had a "negative effect on trading at the start of the current financial year". He therefore declined to support the proposed deal.

According to Middleton, the rest of the Media Square board, doubtless encouraged by its advisers, unanimously supported the deal and Essex resigned just before it was completed in November 2005 — not an ideal predicament for any company. The Huntsworth deal transformed Media Square yet again — but in financial terms not for the better.

From being almost debt-free, the group took on bank borrowings of about £20 million. And the financial period ending on 28 February 2006 was the last in which Media Square made even a small amount of profit. In the words of Robert Essex, the Huntsworth deal was Media Square's

"Stalingrad moment".

Media Square had put its balance sheet into the most vulnerable position since the company was formed. Of the total capital of £78 million provided by banks and shareholders, almost 90% was represented by a single item in the group's balance sheet – intangible goodwill (see chart above). That item reflected the amount by which the price paid for the Huntsworth companies and other previous acquisitions, calculated mainly by reference to the perceived profit-earning capability of those companies, exceeded the value of physical assets acquired.

In other words, the value attributed to nearly 90% of the group's assets was based on a mixture of hope and the immeasurable talents of the people employed. If the profit-earning capabilities of acquired companies fell short of expectations, there would be a big goodwill write-off that would dent both profits and the value of shareholders' funds employed. As sure as night follows day, that in turn would have an adverse impact on the group's ability to meet some of the lending criteria imposed by the banks. And that's what happened.

The focus of Media Square's management was no longer on expansion, but on rationalising the businesses it had acquired, reducing its load of debt and trying to reassure investors. The group sold its Karen Earl Sponsorship subsidiary, its digital agency Tangozebra and one of its direct marketing businesses SBG Finex. The net proceeds were £13.4 million all of which was applied to reduce bank borrowings.

Around this time a bizarre attempt was made to reassure investors by appointing Kelvin Mac-Kenzie, former editor of *The Sun*, as chairman. It backfired. No-one outside Media Square, apart from the advisers who recommended him, could see what relevant expertise MacKenzie would bring. After all, a good communicator is ultimately only as good as the story he has to tell. MacKenzie's term of office lasted only 15 months.

Inevitably the financial pressures led to the occasional board room tension, not least on how best to achieve a turnround in the group's deteriorating financial condition. The view of the executive directors, lead by Middleton, was that a substantial improvement in profitability would not be possible within the timeframes being demanded by investors who had lost confidence in the group's current strategy.

So Middleton put forward what he regarded as a radical plan to revitalise the operating subsidiaries in the group. That plan involved making available up to 25% of the shares in each company to its senior management to be funded by cash payments or by foregoing future bonus entitlements. The group's pile of debt would be allocated as far as practicable to the operating subsidiaries and secured solely on the assets of the borrower if possible. The investing managers would only be permitted to benefit from their investment if there was a future disposal of their company or by dividends after the allocated bank debt had been repaid. Meanwhile Media Square would retain voting control of each subsidiary.

The Middleton plan was met with scepticism by the non-executive directors on the board, namely private equity fund manager Michael George and Pertemps Group finance director Nigel Bacon who by this time had become interim chairman. In response to what was tantamount to a vote of no confidence, Middleton offered to resign. The board agreed to seek a successor and Middleton remained involved in the selection process. Three candidates are thought to have been short-listed: Mike Greenlees, Rupert Howell and Roger Parry. Parry won.

The selection was a curious one, given the appointee was to combine the time-consuming roles of chief executive and chairman. Parry was already a director of YouGov, Johnston Press, the Future publishing house and Mobile Streams, as well as Shakespeare's Globe Trust. He was a former McKinsey management consultant who had also worked at WCRS Group under Peter Scott during the period of its transmog-

rification into Carat and then Aegis Group.

It may be mere coincidence, but the conclusion of Parry's tenure at several of the aforementioned companies coincided with, or was swiftly followed by, a collapse in performance and value. At Future, the massive investment in the United States market over a number of years was subjected to a £17 million impairment charge immediately after Parry's departure in September 2011. That charge, along with restructuring costs, contributed to a loss of over £19 million.

At Johnston Press, the picture was even more depressing. Parry stepped down in March 2009 after eight years in the chair, when the group reported a loss of £365 million that included write-downs of £510 million relating to various publishing titles.

But back in July 2007 Parry was still proud to promote his skills as a turnround specialist. Indeed in his first annual report to Media Square shareholders Parry announced that "the turn-around at Media Square is now entering its final stage and is

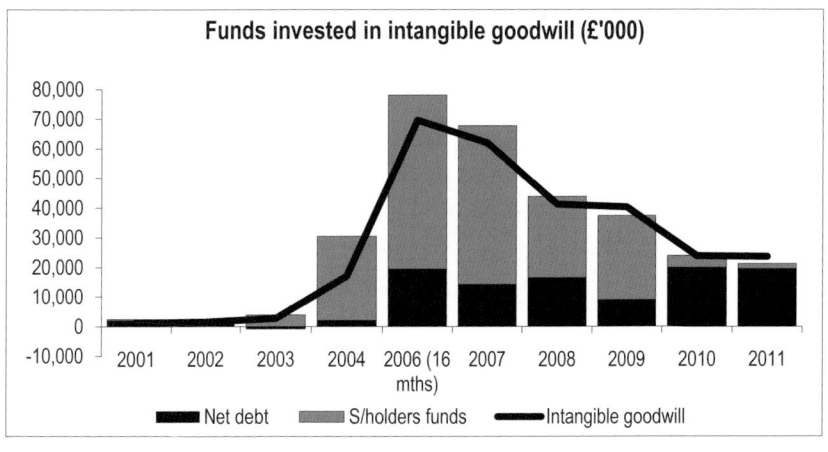

Funds invested in intangible goodwill (£'000)

going very well". Four and half years later under Parry's chairmanship (initially as executive chairman), Media Square was bust.

No-one will ever know whether, if Media Square had sold off its most valuable subsidiaries at an earlier date and closed the rest, the bank and shareholders would have finished up in a better position.

Certainly shareholders who remained loyal to the end would have been much better off if the company had not rejected an offer from investor Promethean Investments in October 2006 that valued the entire group in the region of £45 million. Without any such deals, a "go it alone" road to recovery would have required two key components – cutting borrowings (and related interest) and making the business more profitable. Media Square failed on both counts.

The last balance sheet before Parry took charge showed the group had net borrowings of £14.3 million. On top of that, the amount owed to short-term creditors like trade suppliers exceeded readily realisable assets like debtors and work in progress by £3 million.

In the last balance sheet before going into administration, the group had net borrowings of £19.5 million (excluding £5 million of prepayments by clients for projects in progress). In addition, the company owed its short-term creditors nearly £10 million more than the value of debtors and work in progress combined. In other words the borrowings had increased, rather than reduced, despite a number of asset sales in the mean-

time. So financing costs will have increased too.

Among businesses disposed of during the period were Coutts Retail Communications, three subsidiaries of Illuminas, twentysix New York, Arken and the Hong Kong office of Lloyd Northover. Most were disposed of at a loss and the cash proceeds were relatively modest. As for improved profitability, the group's operating profit margin on revenue in the year to February 2007 was a meagre 3.7%. In the six months to 31 August 2011, the margin was an even more meagre 3.2%.

Many of the businesses that Media Square acquired failed to generate anything like the scale of profits that should have been expected of them. Indeed, cumulative losses grew from £5 million in 2007 to £59 million in 2011 as the costs of past acquisitions were savagely written down, interest charges eroded potential profits and continuing reorganisation costs took their toll.

It's little wonder that Media Square was adjudged to have by far the most vulnerable balance sheet of all publicly listed marketing groups in last year's annual analysis published in *Marketing Services Financial Intelligence* (see opposite).

The perilous plight of the group inevitably attracted the attention of opportunistic buyers. Some — like Bob Morton and Peter Lynch — adopted the Trojan Horse technique of buying shares and agitating for changes in top management from within, but without success. Managers of subsidiaries such as Gate Worldwide contemplated buying back their

Roger Parry: turn-round "going very well"

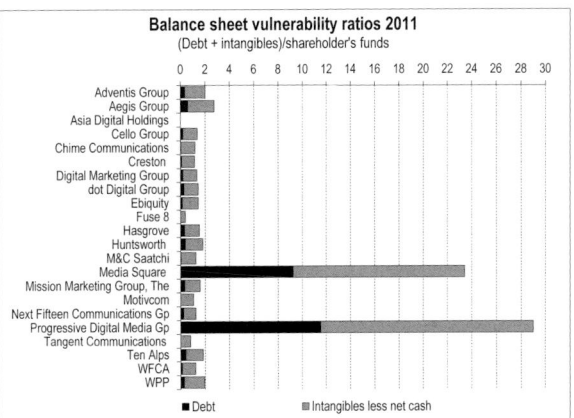

business, but were rebuffed. Through-out this period the group's financial health continued to decline, despite the occasional positive noise from Parry and his fellow McKinsey alum-nus Peter Reid who inherited the role of chief executive in January 2010.

Such was the desire to paint a picture of success that, in May 2010, Parry expressed "great pleasure and, indeed, a considerable sense of relief" that the structural turnround of Media Square had "now been com-pleted". That triumphant language was not reflected in the financial results. The accounts showed that:

- The loss for the year to 28 Feb-ruary had leapt to £24.6 million from £0.7 million in the previous year and even its so-called "head-line" results showed a poorer outcome than in the previous year.
- After including clients' advance receipts, net debt had hardly changed from the amount out-standing before Parry started his structural turnround.
- The group's short-term liabilities exceeded its readily realisable assets by over £5 million — twice

as big a shortfall as reported a year previously.

- Shareholders had a mere £4 million stake in the business com-pared with £6 million provided by clients in advance payments — the bank had vastly more money at risk than either of them.

At the same time Parry announced his impending retirement as chair-man, but then changed his mind and stayed.

When the bank eventually called a halt to this financial soap opera last December ordinary shareholders lost all of their investment and the bank wrote off a large chunk of its lending[1].

The only winners seem to have been the senior management, not least Roger Parry and Peter Reid, who participated in a "phoenix" style buyout of the operating companies with lots of financial support from – you've probably guessed – Media Square's bank and its private equity subsidiary.

---

1. Administrators appointed by the company reported in December 2012 that they had paid out £11 million of the £24 million due to Bank of Scotland (by then part of Lloyds Banking Group) and that "no further monies would be distributed".

23
Anatomy of Aegis

The sale of the UK's only independent publicly-listed media buying group to Dentsu in March 2013 marked the culmination of a strategy designed to break up what had become an under-performing business. But a study of the anatomy of Aegis must start with a company founded by four young advertising wizards in 1979.

That agency was Wight Collins Rutherford Scott (or WCRS) and the partners were Robin Wight, Ron Collins, Andrew Rutherford and Peter Scott. Under Robin Wight's creative direction, it produced well-known advertisements for clients like Orange, BMW and Qualcast mowers.

This chapter is more about Peter Scott and his role in the evolution of WCRS into a media buying and planning agency, and about what happened after that. However, it would be a pity to move on without a few words about Robin Wight. A Cambridge graduate, he is bright, creative, colourful and witty. He is also adventurous, both in his work and in his attitude to life.

I first came across him at a relatively small London agency called Euro Advertising, best known for its work on Audi motor cars before Bartle Bogle Hegarty won the business. Euro was also enlisted by Haymarket Publishing to promote some of its magazine titles, one of which was *Investors Guardian*, a weekly for the City of London investment community that was acquired with what turned out to be a forlorn hope of upgrading it to become a serious competitor to *The Investors Chronicle*[1].

In typically enthusiastic style Robin arrived with his concept drawings to show us his ideas for the required advertisement. We fell about laughing, but the drawings were judged totally unsuitable.

We asked Robin to go away and do something a little more serious (and boring) that might sell a few magazines to serious City gents. To this day I still wonder whether Robin simply wanted to get some appreciation for his witty idea, probably already resigned

---

1. *We hired a brilliant team of young people many of whom were to develop successful careers with national media although sadly Investors Guardian could not defy the economic odds that were set against it.*

to the prospect of it being rejected. One could not help liking him and recognising his natural talent. That enthusiasm and talent has also benefited a number of charities, not least the Duke of Edinburgh's Award where as chairman of the Award's Charter for Business he is reported to have helped raise £50 million.

The last time I met Robin was on the London Underground. I was diving onto the Bakerloo Line at Paddington Station on the way to a meeting. Spotting an empty seat, I headed straight for it. Then, as I sat there poring through *The Financial Times,* I sensed something intriguing about the fellow traveller sitting beside me. He was wearing a purply-violet coloured suit and yellow shirt. I wondered...then raised my eyes slowly...and, yes, it was the same slightly built bespectacled Robin. No-one else could be travelling on the Underground in such bright colours. And it is colour that he has brought to the advertising industry.

This Aegis story, first published in June 2013, is full of lessons — including one about how ambitions to conquer the United States market can prove very risky and financially disastrous. It also highlights the difficult challenges that attend attempts at diversification, especially when that diversification involves the research industry (as we previously noted in chapter 19[1]). And towards the end, it illustrates how the investment community's preoccupation with short-term returns can lead to the disintegration of an under-performing company that might otherwise have been restored to better health over the medium term. Once broken up, it is impossible to judge whether any longer-term benefit to investors had been sacrificed for the sake of a short-term gain. And, flush with that gain, the investors won't care.

Peter Scott: the man behind the creation of Aegis Group

As we shall see, Aegis had sold its WCRS advertising agency to the French group Havas and parted with the group's chief executive Peter Scott long before it was sold to Dentsu. But both were to reappear in December 2004 when Scott, with Robin Wight and other managers, bought back a 75.1% stake in the agency and its related companies. The investment cost £14.25 million and the cash was

1. *See page 219*

provided by a large group of some 30 founding shareholders and Barclays Bank via a newly created holding company subsequently called The Engine Group. Of the £14.25 million purchase price, £11 million was paid on completion and the balance was left outstanding as a loan note.

Most of the shareholders were employees, but alongside them were a few well known names like public relations consultant Matthew Freud. Freud has always shown a penchant for a punt. Back in 2005 he and former *News of the World* editor Piers Morgan had bought the *UK Press Gazette* which owned the rights to the British Press Awards on which its financial viability relied. But sadly it fell into administration in November 2006 after the Awards were boycotted by several newspaper groups that felt the ownership was insufficiently independent of the industry[1].

Freud's public relations company featured in *Marketing Services Financial Intelligence* in 2018 after showing how to delay filing accounts at Companies House by simply shortening the accounting year end by a single day just before the officially registered date arrived. Each time this happened, the company's filing deadline was extended by a further three months. In 2018, Freud exploited

---

1. *See Administrators' Proposals - Companies Court 8838 of 2006 . The UK Press Gazette was bought from the administrators by a company owned by Mike Danson – see page 363*

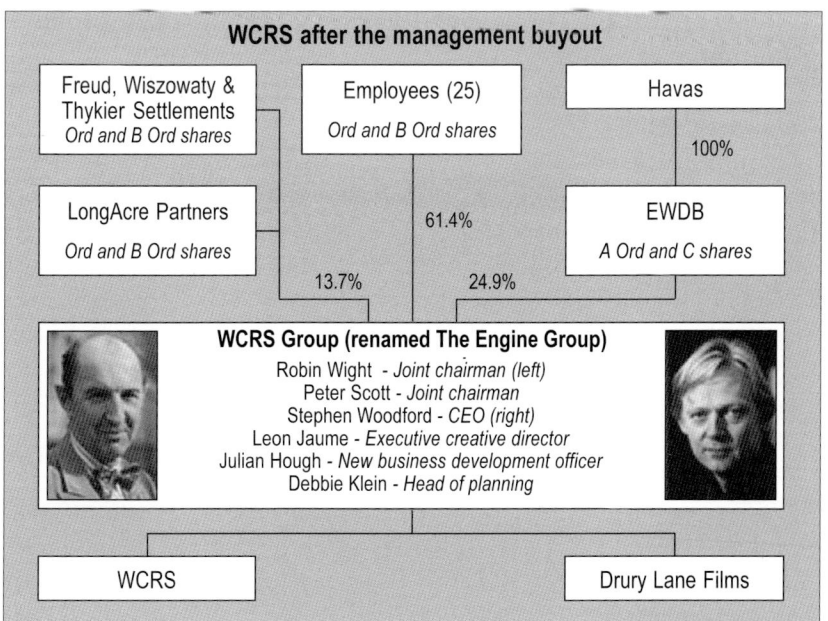

this facility twice in succession, thereby extending the filing date by six months even though the year end had been changed by only two days[1].

With the reacquisition of WCRS, it was as if Peter Scott had been yearning to recreate the days when he had been one of London's advertising supremos. He soon set about assembling a sizeable marketing group with ambitions for a stock market listing or perhaps an eventual sale. Indeed, under the buyout terms, Havas was entitled to require the shareholders to accept a third party offer to buy the company if its shares had not been admitted to the London stock exchange within two years.

The chances of a successful stock exchange listing by the end of 2006 seemed fairly remote when Engine recorded a loss of £67,000 for that year. Its balance sheet was also quite weak with short-term liabilities exceeding readily realisable assets by £7.6 million and bank borrowings of nearly £16 million. Shareholders' funds comprised equity of a meagre £1.9 million plus loan notes of £8.3 million.

Fortunately the prospect of an enforced outright sale had been avoided in October 2005, when Havas agreed to sell its residual shareholding to Aegis and to surrender its loan note for a total of £6 million. That transaction was financed from some of the proceeds of a new share issue and additional bank borrowings.

Set free from Havas, Scott led Engine on a £42.5 million acquisition spree between 2006 and 2008. Of that cost, £28 million was spent in cash, while the balance was satisfied in Engine shares. There was lots of activity that suggested a flotation on the stock exchange was still on the agenda. This would have provided two immediate benefits – a strength-

Engine's balance sheets at 31 December			
	2006	2008	2013
Assets	£'000	£'000	£'000
Intangible assets	28,874	67,166	109,377
Tangible long-term assets:			
Property, plant and equipment	1,250	5,645	5,884
Deferred tax	789	3,678	1,308
Investments	1	1	1
Total long-term assets	30,913	76,490	116,570
Readily realisable assets less short-term liabilities (excl cash)	-7,559	-15,442	-7,887
Long-term liabilities (excl debt)	-5,548	-5,993	-5,729
Net non-cash assets	17,806	55,055	102,954
Financed by:			
Net borrowings	7,558	19,303	23,998
Shareholder loan notes	8,348	21	45,945
Shareholders' funds	1,900	35,730	33,011
Capital employed	**17,806**	**55,055**	**102,954**

1. In 2021 the Government announced plans to curtail this practice.

ening of the group's debt laden balance sheet and an opportunity for employees and others who backed the Havas buyout in 2005 to realise at least some of their investment.

Negotiations with the cash-rich media buying group BLM Holdings got under way as part of a wider plan to seek a stock market flotation. But the talks collapsed in April 2007. Instead Engine raised £8 million in share capital from the Guernsey-based Loudwater Trust. The proceeds were sufficient to pay off the loans due to Engine employees after they had elected to convert about 15% of those loans into Engine shares. But it did little to address the level of bank borrowings which were nudging £20 million by the end of 2008.

So Scott set out on a fund-raising trail again in 2009. In 2010 the company announced a £32.5 million investment by private equity fund manager HIG Capital. However, most of the proceeds went to 120 of Engine's shareholders and only £10 million went towards strengthening Engine's balance sheet. Scott banked £3.1 million, Robin Wight received £2.7 million and Loudwater Trust received £2 million.

By now Engine's appetite for acquisitions had paled. Only £5 million was invested between 2011 and 2013, bringing the total spent on acquisitions since the buyout in 2005 to £74.4 million. Of that, about £51 million had been in the form of cash and expenses. After allowing for interest charges, the aggregate profit earned from

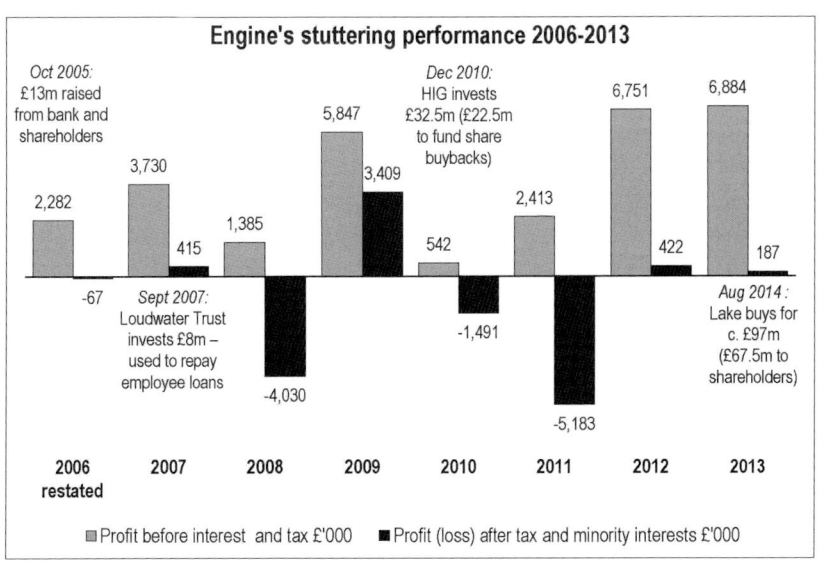

Engine's stuttering performance 2006-2013

Oct 2005:
£13m raised
from bank and
shareholders

Dec 2010:
HIG invests
£32.5m (£22.5m
to fund share
buybacks)

Sept 2007:
Loudwater Trust
invests £8m –
used to repay
employee loans

Aug 2014 :
Lake buys for
c. £97m
(£67.5m to
shareholders)

2006 restated: 2,282, -67
2007: 3,730, 415
2008: 1,385, -4,030
2009: 5,847, 3,409
2010: 542, -1,491
2011: 2,413, -5,183
2012: 6,751, 422
2013: 6,884, 187

■ Profit before interest and tax £'000   ■ Profit (loss) after tax and minority interests £'000

the date of the buyout in 2005 to the end of 2013 was non-existent. Of course, interest charges made up part of the private equity investors' return and cannot be ignored. Nevertheless no-one else had anything much to show for their efforts. Until 2014.

The time would soon be approaching when private equity backer HIG would be seeking an exit, and yet the prospect of a stock exchange listing seemed as far away as ever. In September 2013 *Marketing Services Financial Intelligence* had speculated on what might happen next:

> It is an open secret that chairman and chief executive Peter Scott would like to be able to obtain a stock market listing for the group eventually, but the climate has not been conducive to such an initiative in the recent past. With private equity investors and employee shareholders probably hoping to realise their holdings at a profit before too long, the pressure for a realisation event must be mounting.
>
> Scott denied that Engine had been in any discussions about a merger with another group already listed on the stock market. And, if a stock market listing of its own is not likely in the short term, it seems possible that private equity investors like HIG Capital and Loudwater Trust will soon be contemplating selling their shareholdings on to another private equity group.

On 31 July 2014 it was announced that a US private equity investor Lake Capital would be buying The Engine Group at an "enterprise value" of £96 million[1]. Half of that £96 million would be applied to repaying loan notes due to HIG Capital and various other shareholders. Another £26 million would be used to repay bank borrowings. Just £19.5 million remained available to pay for Engine's shares.

There was an argument about how the share proceeds should be allocated between those who had already left the company and those who had remained, but eventually an equitable outcome was achieved. Scott left shortly afterwards.

Now let us return to the main subject of this chapter – the story of Aegis itself. In 2020 Dentsu decided to drop the "Aegis" name from the international network and to rebrand it Dentsu International. The international business was at a standstill, reporting a 1.9% organic decline and acknowledging that it faced "continued challenges in some key markets". Then, hit by the coronavirus pandemic, the international network suffered a revenue decline of 12.3% in the first half of 2020, within which the second quarter

---

1. *On 2 March 2022 the public company Next Fifteen Communications Group announced that it had conditionally agreed to acquire the UK businesses of Engine Group.*

showed an even faster fall of 20%. This was followed by a decision to hire Wendy Clark from DDB as global chief executive officer of the international network which was brought under the single global brand of Dentsu.

Wendy Clark's tenure was short-lived. Dentsu announced that from January 2023 it would combine its domestic and international operations under a single chief executive Hiroshi Igarashi and structure its business into four regional units - Japan, Americas, EMEA, and APAC. Clark would therefore be leaving and Angela Tangas would move from Australia and New Zealand to become chief executive officer for the UK and Ireland.

As Aegis passed into history, let us recall how it began...

The story of Aegis Group starts in 1988 with a well established marketing company that had expanded boldly into a variety of disciplines and built up a significant international presence. That company was known as **WCRS Group** and its shares were listed on the London Stock Exchange. It is a story of flair and flaws, involving many comings and goings of chief executive. Flair was evidenced by the bold decisions to build a global advertising network and then to bolt on a very big media buying business. The flaws were to do so without sufficient financial means to sustain those businesses, and later to invest in market research businesses that rarely generated the return on investment that investors would have hoped for.

In 1988 the WCRS Group

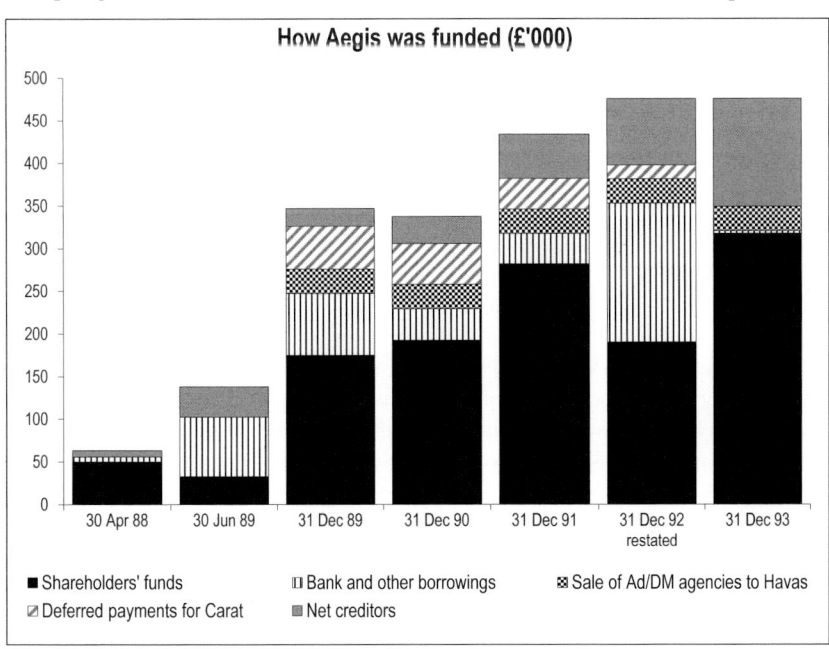

How Aegis was funded (£'000)

- ■ Shareholders' funds
- ▥ Bank and other borrowings
- ▨ Sale of Ad/DM agencies to Havas
- ▨ Deferred payments for Carat
- ■ Net creditors

included agencies like FCO, Della Femina McNamee, Biss Lancaster, Creamer Dickson Basford, Alan Pascoe Associates, Siebert/Head, The Saunders Design Company, Cohn & Wells and The Ball Partnership.

All the signs were that WCRS wanted to emulate the handful of UK marketing groups that had obtained stock market quotations with ambitions to conquer the world – companies like Saatchi & Saatchi, WPP Group, Abbott Mead Vickers, Lowe Howard-Spink, Collett Dickenson Pearce and Boase Massimi Pollitt, to name just a few.

Only a few months previously WCRS had acquired 49% of the French agency Group Belier from Eurocom (now Havas) in exchange for a 20% stake in a number of WCRS advertising and direct marketing agencies around the English speaking world.

At the time the WCRS chief executive Peter Scott (now chief executive of The Engine Group[1]) claimed that the Belier deal was "pioneering" both in concept and structure: "Rather than approach the diverse markets of Europe through outright acquisition, we established a partnership with France's leading advertising group, a group which was already the sixth largest in Europe", he explained.

For the year to 30 April 1988 the group reported a post-tax profit of almost £11 million and a balance sheet that was sound. It had gross assets of £95 million, net borrowings of £5.8 million and shareholders'

funds of £18 million.

But within a year the group's insatiable ambition would set it on a course of further expansion and a radical transformation that eventually would lead to management humiliation and the birth of what we now know as Aegis Group.

The catalyst for transformation was the opportunity to buy the French advertising space buying business Carat, perceived as a cash cow in an industry that had become as obsessed with borrowing money to buy businesses as it had been with winning creative awards. Carat would also bring more media buying power and negotiating leverage to clients of the WCRS agency network – a powerful benefit that all the major marketing groups had begun to recognise as the growth in "media independents" threatened their territory.

Ahead of the Carat deal came the stock market crash of October 1987 that had brought many businesses back to earth, but WCRS seemed unperturbed and made no mention of it in its 1988 annual report.

WCRS acquired an initial 50% stake in Carat for about £85 million in May 1989 and, in doing so, also acquired an indirect minority stake in the UK listed media buying group TMD Advertising Holdings, headed by David Reich. The deal was funded mainly by bank loans, although some £9 million of the price was deferred. As a result WCRS became a serious international player not only in creative advertising but in media buying as well. It also became seriously in debt[2].

---

1. *Peter Scott left The Engine Group in November 2014 after it had been taken over by Lake Capital.*

2. *See chart on page 275*

Less than six months later **WCRS** agreed to buy the remaining 50% shareholding in Carat for a much higher price of about £182 million — around five times the size of the WCRS balance sheet prior to that time. However, the WCRS accounts showed the purchase consideration as £132 million and included a further £50 million due to the vendors as a reduction in the net assets acquired.

Discharging that purchase price may have presented quite a challenge because only £14 million was settled in "cash movements" — an outlay that increased the hyper-acquisitive group's overall net bank borrowings to £72 million[1].

That level of debt would have been even bigger if the group had not raised £43.5 million in cash during December 1989 from selling to Eurocom a further 40% of the group's stake in the WCRS Adver-

1. *See chart on page* 275

tising network along with part of the shareholding in Group Belier that it had acquired only a few months previously — by then known collectively as Eurocom WCRS Della Femina Ball (or "EWDB").

So much for the agreement that had been trumpeted as "both pioneering in concept and in structure", giving **WCRS** a slice of the French advertising market alongside its controlling stake in many other agencies around the world. Now **WCRS** had surrendered control of that advertising agency network seemingly in order to help pay for the rest of the Carat shares because it could not afford to develop both. As Peter Scott put it at the time, the decision followed "an analysis of the financial resources needed to accelerate the international development of the network".

Apart from the £14 million paid in cash for the second tranche of

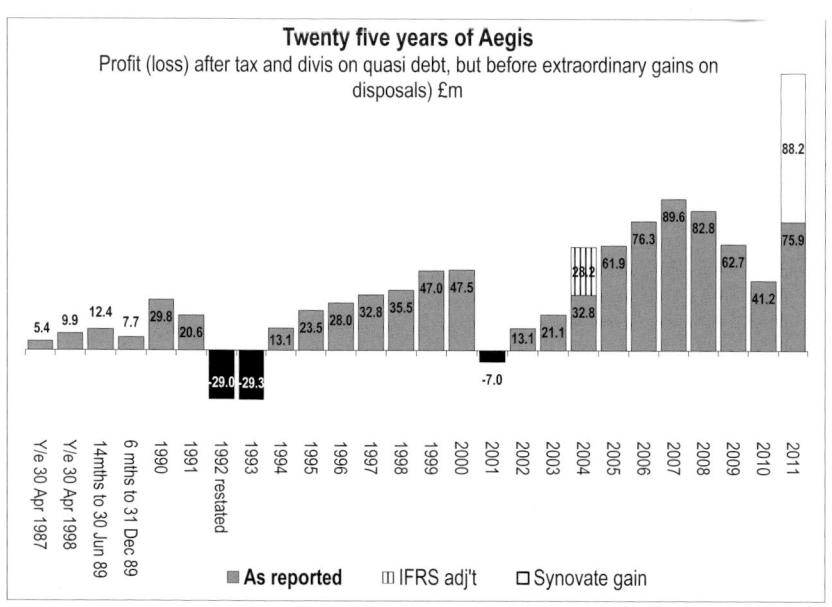

Twenty five years of Aegis
Profit (loss) after tax and divis on quasi debt, but before extraordinary gains on disposals) £m

Carat shares, the rest of the purchase price was settled by the issue of WCRS ordinary shares worth £46 million and the issue of redeemable convertible preference shares in a WCRS subsidiary for £72 million which, as we shall see, were soon to be treated as nothing more than an extra pile of debt. The £50 million of debt due to Carat vendors was deferred for payment over the following four years, and that obligation was eventually discharged with the assistance of a major new fund-raising exercise in 1993 that also enabled the group to refinance its convertible preference shares.

In the meantime borrowings increased further when in May 1991 the group acquired the 70.1% of TMD that it had not inherited with Carat. The cash outlay on TMD, net of cash already residing in TMD's coffers, was somewhere in the region of £15 million. To fund this expenditure and deferred payments relating to earlier acquisitions, the group raised about £27.5 million by means of a new share issue in June 1991. Despite this cash injection, short-term liabilities exceeded readily realisable assets by £37 million at the end of 1991 – a figure that would grow to £62 million by December 1992[1]. The pressure was on to reduce costs and raise more cash. Shareholders had to forego a final dividend and the group embarked on a massive cost-cutting programme.

To reflect its transformation into a media focussed business, WCRS had changed its name to Aegis Group in 1990. In 1992 the group disposed

1 See chart on page 275

of its remaining 40% shareholding in the EWDB advertising agency network to Havas at a thumping loss of £14.1 million, compounded by a £7.5 million loss on disposal of the Alan Pascoe sports sponsorship business.

A year earlier, the group had declined to include the results of its EWDB advertising network in its own financial statements, explaining that "the group is not in a position to exercise significant influence" over the affairs of the 40%-owned company. With hindsight and the revelation of the £14.1 million loss on sale, that reads like a statement of the exceptionally obvious.

By 1993 the group was focussed entirely on the Carat media business. But no sooner had it assimilated the Carat operation than it was struck by two more unexpected nasty surprises. First the accounting rule-makers introduced a requirement for companies like Aegis to treat funds raised in the form of redeemable preference shares – which by their nature were unlikely to provide permanent capital - as if they were loans. At a stroke the Aegis balance sheet was weakened by £72 million, being the amount of redeemable convertible preference shares previously included as share capital and now restated as borrowings. On top of that, some £3.3 million of refinancing cost had to be charged against profits.

The bad news did not end there. Early in 1994, the French competition authority announced it was planning to fine Carat FFr 35 million (£4.2 million) in relation to alleged anti-competitive activities in the nineteen eighties. A provision for this fine was included in the 1993 accounts, although it was recovered a year later following an appeal. New laws (*Loi Sapin*) also demanded more transparency in French media transactions, requiring all discounts paid by media owners to agencies to be remitted to the agencies' clients. Media agencies' profit margins in France would never be the same again.

In the two years to 31 December 1993, Aegis lost over £58 million. It also lost its chairman and chief executive Peter Scott and its finance director Charles Stern, along with David Reich and Alan Pascoe, followed later by chief operating officer Thierry Vial Collet and chief financial officer Michel Lefebvre. Compensation totalling £3.6 million was paid in 1992 to three former directors — believed to be Peter Scott, David Reich and Alan Pascoe.

Non-executive director Frank Law took over as chairman and Carat executive Charles Hochman was appointed chief executive officer, although with hindsight that appears to have been an interim step while the group looked outside for a strong successor to Peter Scott in the shape of Reed Elsevier Group chairman and chief executive Crispin Davis.

Meanwhile Law brought in two heavyweight non-executives – Sir Kit McMahon, former chairman of Midland Bank and a deputy governor of the Bank of England, and Sir Peter Thompson, a former chairman and chief executive of National Freight Corporation. Then, in December 1993, Omnicom's finance chief Fred Meyer joined as another non-executive when the US group injected additional share capital as part of the refinancing rescue package referred to earlier.

Under Crispin Davis' leadership Aegis returned to profitable growth, but shortly before his departure in 1999 he set the company on a new path, adding an embryonic research division to trade alongside the group's media business. It was a decision that may have appeared wise at the time, but it sowed the seeds of the group's eventual destruction as an independent public company.

In 1998 the group had declared that its strategic goal was to "develop and extend our range of services to cover the universe of communication for our clients". On the face of it, a strategy that broadened the business base so as to be less dependent on media buying alone may have sounded entirely credible to investors.

However, those investors may not have anticipated that within six months this strategy would result in a £148 million bid for the US publicly listed market research company Market Facts. And even fewer of those investors would have expected the acquisition to plunge the group back into a post-tax loss of £7 million by 2001. But Market Facts failed to generate even enough profit to cover the amortisation of the excessive acquisition cost, let alone the interest on funds used for the acquisition.

Left to pick up the pieces from this disastrous foray was a new management team of the prominent accountant Lord Sharman as chairman and Doug Flynn as chief executive officer. Both had assumed their new posts on the day after Crispin Davis departed in September 1999, although Flynn — an Australian — had joined the Aegis board a year earlier as a non-executive director while still employed as managing director of News International. For reasons that no longer seem very clear, Flynn adhered to part of his predecessor's strategy, building up a portfolio of market research companies (in due course re-branded "Synovate"), extending the geographical scope of its media buying business and expanding into digital marketing. But he stopped short of re-shaping Aegis into a multi-disciplined global marketing group.

Over the next 11 years Aegis would spend somewhere in the region of £550 million on acquiring research businesses, before taking into account any subsequent write-offs or impairment charges. After allowing for the borrowing costs associated with those acquisitions, it would be hard to argue that they generated anywhere near enough profit to justify the overall investment. But successive manage-ments continued to defend the case for sustaining the research division.

Indeed, for a brief while after the Market Facts débâcle in 2001, there were signs that the new strategy might actually be working. Group profits began to recover, although it would take five years before they reached their 2000 peak again. And, long before then, shareholders' patience had begun to wear rather thin.

Figures published by *Marketing Services Financial Intelligence* showed that in 2003 the return on share-holders' funds invested in market research was starkly lower than that obtained from investment in media buying – the return on market research, before allowing for any amortisation of the goodwill element of the investment, was estimated at 2.5% whereas media activities showed a return of 12.8%.

Those more profitable media activities took a knock when, in November 2003, the joint chief executives of Aegis Media Europe — Bruno Kemoun and Eryck Rebbouh — left to set up a competing business

In: Robert Lerwill   *Out: Doug Flynn*

called **KR Media**.

Then, in May 2004, shareholders voted against Flynn's 2003 remuneration package under which he had drawn £1.2 million in salary and bonus, plus 700,000 share options and over one million shares under the latest performance plan. That looked rather generous when compared with the subdued £21 million post-tax profit that Aegis earned for its shareholders. (Flynn's package would also have yielded him over £2.4 million if his contract were to have been terminated by the company during 2004.)

Also in 2004 Aegis added another string to its bow in the shape of a digital marketing division that became known as "Isobar". Then rumours developed that Flynn might be about to leave and in February 2005 he did just that, taking the job of chief executive at hygiene and security firm Rentokil Initial. Ironically if Flynn had stayed for another year he would have been able to take some credit for rebuilding group profits to exceed for the first time the level last achieved

in 2000. But instead his departure, followed by a decline in the Aegis share price, attracted attention from potential predators.

Sharman moved swiftly to replace Flynn – inviting non-executive director Robert Lerwill to assume the role. Lerwill had made his name in the marketing industry as group finance director at **WPP** until he moved on to Cable & Wireless where he held an executive board position until 2003. In 2000 he had joined the Aegis board as a non-executive director.

With hindsight Lerwill might regard the Aegis chief executive's role to have been something of a poisoned chalice. He was the fourth person to take on the position since the unceremonious departure of Peter Scott in 1992. And the appointment proved to be a challenging one.

No sooner had Lerwill got his feet under the chief executive's desk than onto the stage came French entrepreneur Vincent Bolloré whose company Bolloré Media was in the process of building a 23% stake in a

Out: Lord Sharman

In: John Napier

rival group Havas that would lead to a boardroom coup there.

Then Bolloré started building a shareholding in Aegis, prompting speculation that he had plans to put Havas and Aegis together.

To add to the drama the Havas arch-rival Publicis Groupe made a tentative takeover approach to Aegis, valuing the group at £1.57 billion – less than half of what shareholders would eventually receive after the sale of Synovate to Ipsos and disposal of the rump to Dentsu for £3.2 billion. In City-speak Aegis was "in play" and everyone waited for an outright bid.

From this point onwards, Sharman and Lerwill were forced to concentrate their attention on what was best for Aegis shareholders. There was little appetite for doing a deal with either Bolloré or Publicis at what was regarded as an opportunistically knocked-down price. But the only way to avoid that outcome would be either to find a more generous suitor or to rebuild profits and confidence in the business.

Meanwhile Bolloré persisted in demanding seats on the board and Aegis persisted in rejecting his overtures. Lerwill succeeded in building profits and making selective acquisitions, although the research legacy he had inherited never really earned its keep. By the end of 2007 profits had grown by 47% since he took on the role three years earlier.

In July 2008 Lord Sharman retired as chairman and John Napier was appointed in his place. Napier brought with him a commitment to enhance shareholder value – often achieved by parcelling up businesses for onward sale and/or breaking up businesses that could generate a better selling price if disposed of in parts. Among his former companies were AGB Research, water utility Kelda, grocery wholesaler Booker and recruitment outfit Hays. Most recently he had been chairman of the insurance giant RSA Group.

It was not long before cracks appeared between the strategy being followed by Lerwill and the direction favoured by Napier. By November 2008 Lerwill had cleared his desk, taking with him a £1.4 million termination payment, and thereafter Napier combined the chief executive and chairman roles.

From "Marketing Services Financial Intelligence" 13 January 2009

Napier's game plan for Aegis becomes clearer

So now John Napier's game plan for Aegis is becoming clearer. According to press reports investment bankers Merrill Lynch have been appointed to conduct a strategic review and we may therefore assume that a sale or break-up is high on the agenda, but by no means a certainty

Napier took his axe to the payroll and three non-executive directors resigned. Explaining his actions, Napier claimed to have identified a number of unfortunate trends, namely:

- Following years of continuing growth, there was a tendency to develop capacity in advance of revenue, which, he said, had limited the scope for improving efficiency.
- There was a Keynesian "stickiness" in variable costs – "particularly wage and performance bonus elements". By stickiness, he meant that costs were not being adjusted downwards instantaneously in response to changes in economic conditions.

The outcome was a 5% reduction in headcount, leading to a £39.4 million redundancy bill spread over 2008 and 2009. Napier claimed there would be a future annual cost saving of £20 million although the full benefit would not be achieved until 2011. Conspicuous by its absence was any meaningful development strategy.

For those who may have been in any doubt about Napier's intentions, he was soon showing his hand by appointing Merrill Lynch to conduct a strategic review: "We may therefore assume that a sale or break-up is high on the agenda, but by no means a certainty", observed *Marketing Services Financial Intelligence* at the time, while the Aegis public relations machine used every opportunity to deny any such intention albeit with little credibility.

Acquisitions would continue, including a major expansion in Australasia with the purchase of Mitchell Communications in 2010 and further extensions to the group's digital search marketing capability around the world.

If a break-up was the best way to realise value for Aegis shareholders,

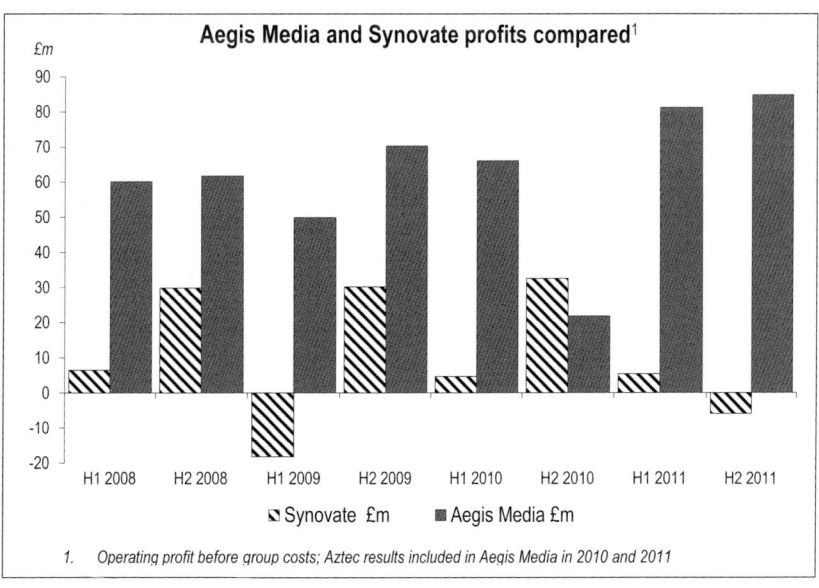

Aegis Media and Synovate profits compared[1]

1. *Operating profit before group costs; Aztec results included in Aegis Media in 2010 and 2011*

the first priority would be to remove the drain on profitability arising from the poor returns being achieved from the Synovate research division. That was undoubtedly depressing investor attitudes towards any future growth in the share price.

Matters were not helped by an economic slowdown that had held back the group's growth in the first half of 2009, especially at Synovate where its ad hoc custom market research business suffered particularly badly and contributed to an operating loss in that unit (see chart).

Synovate avoided a loss in the first half of 2010, but the rest of that year showed little improvement on 2009. The year's profit contribution to the group was £37.3 million before central costs, finance charges and tax, while net assets employed were £516 million.

Roughly speaking the division earned a return of 7% on those assets while the media and digital business produced a return of over 11%.

Nevertheless, in March 2011 the newly installed Aegis group chief executive Jerry Buhlmann – a media agency man through and through – was claiming that a "strong recovery" had been achieved at Synovate during 2010.

Events would soon explain why Buhlmann was so bullish. On 6 June 2011 Aegis admitted it was negotiating the sale of Synovate to the French group Ipsos. In the longer term Buhlmann's confidence might have appeared somewhat misplaced as Synovate failed to make any more profit before its sale in October 2011. In its defence Aegis claimed that the

final quarter of the Synovate year was always more profitable than the other periods.

The outcome of the Ipsos deal was the receipt of about £507 million in cash – enough to reimburse virtually all the cash consumed in acquiring the research businesses in the first place and to record a paper profit on disposal of £88.2 million. However, that paper profit probably arose in part at least from earlier write-downs in the book value of Synovate assets.

Aegis promised to pay out £200 million of the sale proceeds to its shareholders immediately after completion, closing a chapter on its ill-chosen excursion into the world of research. Freed from the drain of Synovate, observers watched in vain for any sign of an Aegis development strategy that would make good use of the rest of the cash realised from the sale to Ipsos.

While the Aegis management had been boasting of a strong recovery at Synovate during 2010 and seeking an exit from that business, its core media division had become the victim of a £37 million bad debt scandal when a Spanish client Nueva Rumasa filed for insolvency. How and why Aegis was exposed to such a large bad debt remains something of a mystery. At the very least it would appear that credit controls were less than adequate, although no detailed explanation or remedial action was mentioned in the annual report.

In 2010 Aegis group profits fell to another low of £41.2 million – less than half the profit reported immediately before John Napier took the chair[1]. But perhaps annual profits were of secondary importance to the disposal of the group's component parts.

Judging by the profit reported for 2011, packaging the rump of Aegis for outright sale must have been high on the agenda. Stripped of the Synovate business and the gain from its sale, the rest of the group made a post-tax profit of £75.9 million – the fourth highest profit in the group's history. But who would want to buy one of the biggest independent global media buying businesses with a useful digital business attached? And who would be able to afford it?

Groups like Omnicom, WPP, Publicis, Havas and Interpublic already had sizeable media buying units. So with hindsight it should have come as no surprise that the bid came from Dentsu in July 2012.

Dentsu offered to pay almost £3.2 billion in cash, or 240p per share, representing a hefty premium of 45% over the average Aegis share price during the preceding three months. The offer price represented a multiple in excess of 26 times the maintainable Aegis profit after interest on net debt and after tax. On the face of it Dentsu was making an expensive and bold move to become a truly global player after its previous smaller excursions into the western world had failed to generate the

footprint or the profit it doubtless desired (see chapter 6).

Faced with the prospect of pocketing a £355 million gain on his company's shareholding, Vincent Bolloré announced himself well satisfied with the labours of Napier and Buhlmann whose appointment he claimed to have welcomed: "Since then, the Bolloré Group has continuously supported the outstanding achievements of this new management team, illustrated by the excellent terms of the disposal of Synovate and the considerable international expansion of Aegis", Bolloré said.

As if in anticipation of such an acquisition, earlier in the year Dentsu had freed itself from its ties with Publicis and banked some cash as a result. Dentsu had also extended its McGarry Bowen creative agency brand from the United States to spearhead its European expansion.

Shareholders voted overwhelmingly in favour of the Dentsu offer, bringing to a satisfactory conclusion Napier's plan to deliver Aegis shareholders better value from their investment. Whether that improvement in value could have been achieved without Napier's favoured break-up will never be known.

What is known is that, in pursuing that course, another big British marketing group fell into foreign hands.

---

1. *See chart on page* 277

How the founder and another top executive were allowed to walk away from a "people business" with a slice of the business.

24
Ringing the Changes at Chime

Tim Bell or, as he later became, Baron Bell of Belgravia was born six months before me and in the same Southgate suburb of London. But we didn't meet until seventy years later, in 2011.

This chapter tells of the final period in Bell's career, a career during which he built Chime Communications into an international group with its shares traded on the London stock exchange, only to leave it in 2012 with colleague Piers Pottinger, taking with them the core public relations consultancy. The story that follows was first published in July 2012 and drew heavily on interviews I carried out at the time with Lord Bell and Chime's chief executive Chris Satterthwaite. It was clear that there had been a divergence of views about the strategic direction in which Chime should travel.

Bell's career started as a post boy at ABC Television, having left Queen Elizabeth's Grammar School in Barnet at the age of 16. After working in several advertising agencies, he helped found Saatchi & Saatchi Company from where he would eventually branch out on his own, albeit under the financial umbrella of another advertising agency Lowe Howard-Spink. As we shall see, Bell, Pottinger and several other senior executives negotiated a management buyout from Lowe in 1989 and Chime became an independent public relations consultancy. Later WPP invested in Chime, providing additional capital to fund its acquisition aspirations.

Clearly Bell liked to run his own show and it is sad to note that

Lord Bell: Happier out of the public company spotlight?

life after Chime may not have been an altogether happy one. Indeed the months that followed his departure with the Bell Pottinger public relations business must have been very painful. In swift succession he had a stroke (another one was to kill him in 2019), was caught up in a South African client scandal, fell out with the Bell Pottinger's chief executive James Henderson and retired from the company.

So what happened to Chime and Bell Pottinger after their divorce?

Chime continued under the leadership of Chris Satterthwaite as a multi-disciplined marketing group with a specific focus on the sports sector. It had retained a 25% shareholding in Bell Pottinger and so was not immune to that company's financial performance. Indeed, even before the divestment, Bell Pottinger was heading for a profit downturn.

In November 2011 Chime had warned that its results for that year would be hit by restructuring costs following the early cessation of a public relations contract with the US Government. Looking further forward the company said that its public relations activities would represent a smaller proportion of total profit contribution as its sports marketing, advertising and research divisions expanded.

However, future profits became somewhat illusive as a series of restructuring and other abnormal expenses hit the company in 2012 and 2013. One such abnormal item was the £3.2 million write-down of the book value of the German public relations subsidiary MMK in 2013.

The commitment to sports marketing was evidenced by some major acquisitions, one of which was Just Marketing — a US consultancy founded by Zak Brown. Brown was 41 years old at the time of the deal and had begun his racing career in 1986 on karting circuits in the United States, winning 22 races in five seasons from 1986 to 1990. In 2009 Brown co-founded the professional sports car racing team United Autosports which was based in the UK and had run up losses of £3.1 million by the end of 2012.

The terms were agreed in 2013. Chime would pay up to £43.6 million for the business, but this was conditional on Just Marketing delivering signed revenue contracts in 2015, 2016 and 2017. Chime was understandably anxious to ensure a continuation of Just Mar-

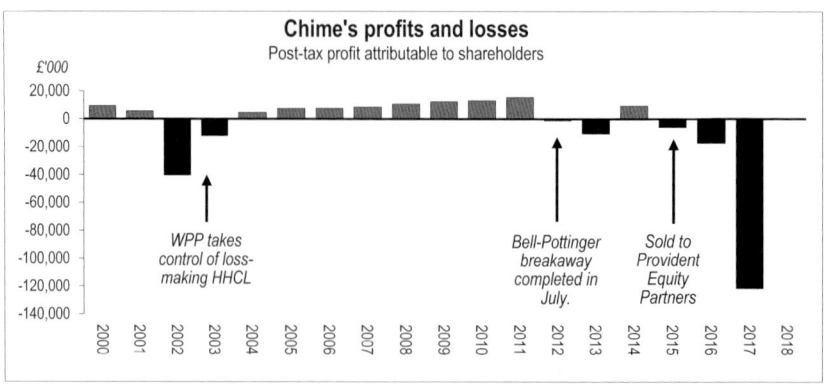

keting's revenue growth, knowing that it had relied to a significant extent on maintaining good relationships with organisations that sanction races, particularly the National Association for Stock Car Auto Racing and Formula 1.

Unfortunately the Just Marketing deal caused a little excitement at **WPP** which not only held shares in Chime but also had a stake of about 20% in Just Marketing's parent company and was thought to have had ambitions to acquire the entire business.

As some of Just Marketing's purchase price was to be settled in Chime shares, **WPP**'s shareholding in Chime might have been diluted. Recognising this, Chime had offered to structure the deal not only to avoid dilution but also to enhance **WPP**'s shareholding in Chime to 24.9%. But **WPP** rejected that offer. It wanted more and threatened to sell its Chime shares unless it could increase its holding to 29.9%, despite the fact that the two **WPP** representatives on the Chime board had voted in favour of the final deal terms. So **WPP** was diluted, although it eventually swallowed its pride and restored its shareholding percentage to the pre-deal level by buying more shares in the market in 2015.

This was not the first occasion on which **WPP** had intervened in Chime's acquisition plans. Back in 2004, Chime had been in talks about merging with Incepta Group, but they are thought to have failed because **WPP** wanted a better deal for its then 19% shareholding in Chime.

By the time the Just Marketing deal had been done, a few clouds were beginning to appear on Chime's horizon. The group reported a loss of £2.7 million in 2013 after incurring a number of abnormal costs including the aforementioned goodwill writedown at **MMK** as well as deferred acquisition payments charged as

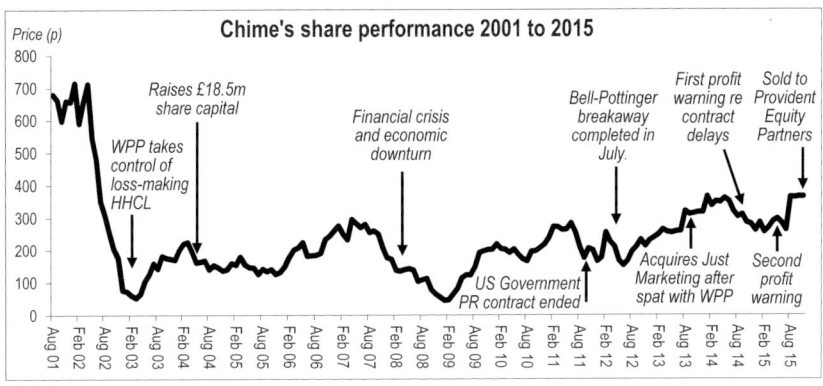

remuneration. Then, in November 2014, it issued a profit warning after experiencing delays in concluding two long-term contracts in its sports and entertainment division. "While this will affect our profit projections for 2014", Satterthwaite acknowledged, "our prospects for 2015 remain very exciting."

In the event, the group achieved a post-tax profit of £9.5 million in 2014, but the outcome for 2015 proved to be less exciting than anticipated. In May of that year Chime issued a further profit warning, saying that trading had started slowly in its sports marketing division as a result of further delays in two major contract negotiations. "Consequently the full year results will be below expectation", the company said.

The succession of profit warnings unsettled investors and prompted Chime's management to start listening more seriously to approaches that had been made by a private equity fund manager called Providence Equity Partners. If a deal could be agreed, the company could be taken away from the glare of the stock market and institutional investors.

On 30 July 2015, Chime announced that it had received a potential cash offer of £370 million which had the support of its minority shareholder WPP. While the offer looked extremely generous for a company that had just reported a post-tax profit of £9.5 million, it became more realistic when related to Chime's potential profit of £26.5 million if financial items, acquisition payments treated as remuneration, minority interests and tax were to be excluded. On that basis the offer price would be nearer 14 times the adjusted profit.

The private equity deal was successfully concluded in July 2015. Predictably, much of the purchase payment was structured as debt which had reached £226 million by the end of 2016, or £255 million if deferred acquisition payments were to be included. Interest would be payable at rates ranging between 4.25% and 4.75% above LIBOR. That debt was matched by shareholders' funds of £278 million – a debt/equity ratio of 0.9:1.

Burdened by increased debt, restructuring and acquisition-related costs, Chime reported a loss of £6.2 million for the five months under new ownership in 2015, a loss of a further £17.4 million in 2016 and a startling loss of £121.6 million in 2017.

Much of the 2017 loss was caused by a £93 million charge for the impairment of past acquisition costs, especially those incurred on businesses in the sports and entertainment division (£70 million).

Further restructuring costs accounted for £16 million. Reflecting on Chime's performance at the time, *Marketing Services Financial Intelligence* commented:

> Looking behind the bare numbers, there is evidence that the underlying business was suffering from creeping staff costs. Stripped of all the exceptional item and amortisation, the group would have made an operating profit of £38.6 million, equivalent to an operating profit margin of 13.8% on gross income and still rather lower than the 15% that is regarded as a benchmark.
>
> However, staff costs ate into 68.1% of gross income, roughly two percentage points more than in the previous year and materially more than the industry benchmark.
>
> That means Chime forfeited about £6 million in the year that would otherwise have improved its operating profit. And think how much more profit might have been generated if staff costs had been nearer 60% of gross income.

Typically a private equity backer like Providence would be seeking to realise its shareholding within five years of acquisition. Initial steps often take the form of random disposals — either because the particular business is a drag on profits with little prospect of improvement or because it can be sold at a premium on a stand-alone basis without having any detrimental impact on the value of the rest of the group. Providence decided to sell Chime's Open Health business in this piecemeal manner in December 2018. The cash proceeds were £78.6 million and the profit was £9.9 million.

Leaving aside such piecemeal sales, Providence would have been expected to be looking for a buyer for the group by 2020. At the time of writing no signs of a bid or flotation had emerged. Given the recent losses, the timing may not be ideal. Indeed, in the midst of a coronavirus pandemic and hints of a recession to come, it was unlikely that there would have been a long queue of potential buyers eager to pay the sort of price that Providence might have hoped for. Nevertheless, Chime was able to report a much improved profit of £17.3 million for 2021, helped by a £13.4 million gain on disposal of its Corporate Citizenship business.

Meanwhile, as we shall see, Bell Pottinger had continued its political lobbying and high-profile public relations activities with a client list that was, to say the least, eyebrow-raising. Its work for the US Department of Defense during the Iraq war was reported to have involved creating fake terrorist videos, fake news articles for Arab news channels and propaganda videos. Other reports referred to the doctoring of *Wikipedia* accounts on behalf of clients.

Then the firm became engulfed in a controversial propaganda campaign in South Africa on behalf of a client called Oakbay Investments that was controlled by the influential Gupta family which in turn had strong ties to the then President Zuma's government. When news got out, Bell Pottinger found itself facing a storm of criticism.

So in September 2017 lawyers Herbert Smith Freehills were instructed to carry out an independent review. The report was highly critical of the project, including observations like this:

> The BP account team was primarily responsible for devising the strategy behind the economic emancipation campaign and for creating and commissioning content for the social media and press aspects of that campaign. Certain material that we have seen that was created for the campaign was negative or targeted towards wealthy white South African individuals or corporates and/or was potentially racially divisive and/or potentially offensive and was created in breach of relevant ethical principles.

The scandal resulted in Bell Pottinger being expelled from its professional body, the Public Relations and Communications Association, for breaching its code of conduct. Bell Pottinger's chief executive and shareholder James Henderson departed, along with the lead partner Victoria Geoghegan, and Chime wrote off the 25% shareholding it had retained at the time of the divestment. Fortunately for Bell he had already sold his Bell Pottinger shares back to the company for almost £1.2 million.

The reputational damage was so great that clients and staff were soon leaving Bell Pottinger. In September 2017 the accountancy firm BDO was asked to help the company with a financial restructuring plan, but it was too late. On 12 September Bell Pottinger went into administration, having been "heavily impacted financially by the well-publicised issue resulting in losses of clients, partners and staff".

Branches in Dubai, Bahrein and Singapore were either sold or closed. Shareholders, preferential and unsecured creditors were not expected to receive anything. The administrators were able to recover only 10% of the £5.2 million debt due to Lloyds Bank.

In terms of lessons to be learned, Bell was undoubtedly a dominant leader whose first love was public relations. Readers may judge for themselves, but arguably he was loathe to share power or purpose, and so eventually this led to division – both in succession planning and in strategic direction. An unhappy experience with the HHCL advertising agency seemed to have reinforced his desire to focus on public relations and so the notion of expanding into sports marketing was probably too hard for him to digest. While happy to be in the spotlight of success (either when advising someone like Lady Thatcher or a Middle Eastern sheik, or celebrating good profits), he never enjoyed being put under the spotlight by inquisitive shareholders as the chairman of a public company.

For someone who spent much of his working life burnishing the reputations of others, it was sad to see his own reputation being severely corroded in an interview with *BBC Newsnight*'s Kirsty Wark in September 2017. Inevitably people are at the heart of businesses in the marketing sector. Choosing the right people, putting them in the right jobs and managing them in the broadest sense is a massive challenge that sometimes exceeds the skills, strength and experience of even the most talented entrepreneur.

When Lord Bell announced to Chime Communications' chief executive Chris Satterthwaite that he would like to buy out most of the Bell Pottinger public relations businesses with his colleague Piers Pottinger, and to give up his chairmanship of the group, it must have come as a bit of a surprise. After all, it's not every day of the week that the chairman and vice chairman of a public company propose to walk away with some of its prize assets.

Satterthwaite's instinctive reaction was that such an initiative should not be encouraged. It would give all the wrong signals about where a senior executive's loyalty should lie. Satterthwaite still holds that view. So does Sir Martin Sorrell, whose company WPP has a 21% shareholding in Chime.

Yet on 30 June Lord Bell and Piers Pottinger left Chime to run their new company BPP Communications, taking seven subsidiaries and several senior staff with them. Why

was it allowed to happen?

The answer lies in a single word: pragmatism. In essence, the divestment resolved a number of emerging issues, not least Lord Bell's growing discomfort at the head of a company that he felt could no longer be run in the best interests of anyone other than the shareholders in response to what he regarded as excessive pressure from the stock market.

To see the divestment in a proper context it is important to understand

Chime's recent share price 2011-12 (p)

a little of what makes Lord Bell tick. He is undoubtedly a very effective and successful communications adviser – evidenced by the long list of powerful personalities that have retained his services, including Lady Thatcher, FW deKlerk (who as president of South Africa brought the apartheid system of racial segregation to an end and negotiated a transition to majority rule), and the US admin-istration for whom he advised the Iraqi government on the "promotion of democracy".

And while some of his assign-ments generated very substantial fees, Lord Bell is swift to point out that the Conservative Party never paid him anything, although doubtless his reputation was enhanced mightily.

What emerges from conversation with Lord Bell is that he likes doing things he believes in and he does them with a passion. He takes legitimate pride in his successes, whether political, commercial or philanthropic, citing for example his involvement with Comic Relief and his work with deKlerk to overcome apartheid. But he is probably driven by the fear of failure – not necessarily failure in the public eye, but failure according to his own standards and aspirations. If he is on your side, you can feel the strength of his emotional support. He says he believes in being true to himself, but probably beats himself up too much in the process. Without doubt he was stung by recent criticism of some aspects of his company's public relations activities in *The Independent*.

So it may come as no surprise to find that Lord Bell seems rarely to

have been happy in his career unless he has been in the driving seat of his businesses. And if in his seventy-first year Bell ceases to enjoy the drive, he would prefer to change direction rather than turn off the engine. As we shall see, that has been a trade-mark of the Bell character ever since the days he joined the embryonic Saatchi and Saatchi in 1970.

Once known as the third brother at Saatchi and Saatchi, it was only when Lord Bell is said to have become increasingly isolated from the decision-makers that he was enticed away by Frank Lowe in 1985 to join his advertising empire and see his name put over the door as Lowe Howard-Spink & Bell.

But the attraction was short lived. Perhaps in some ways the two men were too alike, both having strong personalities, both uninhibited about speaking their mind, both wanting to be leading the charge and both needing to be recognised for what they were doing. As with magnets, too like poles began to repel and matters were made worse when *Campaign* sang Bell's praises in its "Hall of Fame" publication.

Meanwhile Bell had set up Lowe Bell Communications as a consul-tancy that could generate income from, among other sources, the connections he had built up while working for the Conservative Party and helping Lady Thatcher win her general elections. In doing so he was able to apply his advertising expe-rience on a wider communications playing field that included many of the services typically provided under the generic title of "public relations".

Then in 1986 Lowe Howard-Spink & Bell bought the established public relations consultancy Good Relations that was already listed on the stock market. With Good Relations came its chief executive Alan Cornish, its managing director Piers Pottinger and its group finance director Mark Smith.

Despite being engaged in the communications business, people from advertising and public relations backgrounds are often like oil and water – they just don't seem to mix. And this soon became apparent at Lowe. In Bell's view, many advertising professionals view public relations consultants as "spivs who like to go to lunch", while public relations consultants view advertising people as a "bunch of witterers paid vast sums for doing very little".

With relationships between Lowe and Bell less than ideal, and tensions emerging between the advertising and public relations teams in the Lowe group, Alan Cornish and Piers

Pottinger sat down with Bell and suggested they should negotiate a buyout. Lowe agreed. Shortly afterwards a controlling interest in the rest of the Lowe group was bought by The Interpublic Group of Companies. Bell was back in control of his own destiny and in 1994 he floated the business on the London Stock Exchange as Chime Communications. Eighteen years later, he is clearly not enjoying the ride as much as he did.

The Bell Pottinger business has become the subject of several contentious news stories in recent months. Its reputation took a knock when it admitted to editing clients' entries in *Wikipedia* to improve their image. Then there were allegations that the agency had been providing lobbying services to dubious regimes and writing UN speeches for the Sri Lankan president. On top of all that, the US Government terminated its lucrative contract prematurely, making a dent in projected public relations profits for the year. None

Leaving:
Deputy chairman Piers Pottinger

Staying:
Chief executive Chris Satterthwaite

of this helped the Chime share price which had sunk to its lowest point since February 2009.

Against this backcloth it is hardly surprising that Lord Bell began to wonder whether he really wanted to be running a high profile public company when all he received in return for his and his company's efforts was flack from the media and tut-tutting from a stock market that never seemed satisfied with the company's undoubted success. The proposed divestment will allow him to carry on doing what he likes doing most – counselling clients – but out of the public glare. "I'm happiest when dealing with people and their problems, and finding solutions", Bell says.

There can be no doubt that Bell has a different management style from his chief executive Chris Satterthwaite and has not always seen eye to eye with him. But Bell's hope and belief is that the divestment will prove a "brilliant transaction for them and for me". For his part, Satterthwaite also sees real benefits to be gained from the divestment, despite his inherent antipathy towards management teams being allowed to buy out chunks of their business.

So what does the buyout mean in relation to Chime's business as a whole? How important is its public relations activities and how reliant is the group on Bell Pottinger revenues?

Last year, Chime's public relations business was by far the biggest component of the group, contributing 41% of operating income (revenue less bought in direct costs) and 53% of operating profit before deduction

of central corporate costs[1].

But the departing Bell Pottinger agencies were only part of the group's public relations business. The remainder will continue under the Good Relations brand, led by the former Bell Pottinger chairman Kevin Murray.

According to Chime, the divested businesses contributed less than 8% of the group's total operating profit in 2011, or about one-seventh of the operating profit earned from all of the group's public relations activities (not least because Chime benefited from only a 60% stake in the profitable Pelham Bell Pottinger public relations subsidiary at the time[2]).

And the operating profit margin earned by the divested businesses was a depressing 8.4%, compared with 15.3% for the group as a whole[3]. That disappointing performance may be only a temporary hiccup, made worse by the loss of the US Government business, but on the face of it the divestment is not going to do very much harm to Chime's ongoing performance.

Although public relations has been the biggest contributor to group profits for most of Chime's 23 year life, there have been exceptions — not

1. References to operating profit and operating income are to statutory, rather than adjusted "headline", amounts after excluding the proportion attributable to the 40% minority interest held in Pelham Bell Pottinger before disposal to BPP.

2. Figures are stated after excluding 40% of the Pelham Bell Pottinger results attributable to minority interests

3. The operating margin is based on figures for operating profit and operating income shown in the statutory accounts before excluding various items to arrive at so-called "highlighted" operating profit which would have given a more favourable impression.

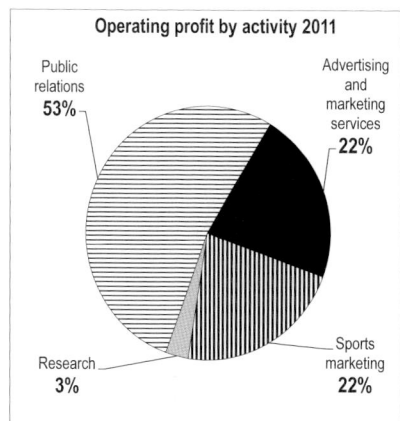

Operating profit by activity 2011

Public relations **53%**

Advertising and marketing services **22%**

Sports marketing **22%**

Research **3%**

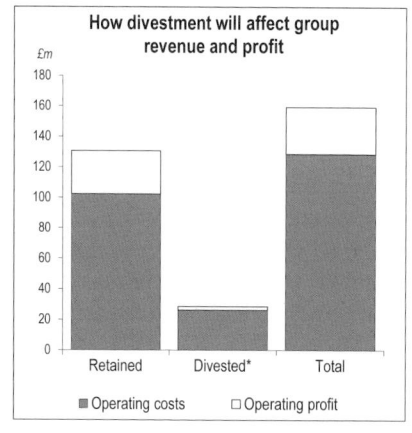

How divestment will affect group revenue and profit

£m

■ Operating costs   □ Operating profit

least when the group first embarked on a diversification course in 1997 by acquiring the advertising agency HHCL & Partners and some related companies.

The impetus for diversification has been attributed to a number of factors, among them the view widely held in the nineteen nineties that clients wanted a wider range of services from a single co-ordinated source. At the same time, Chime's management thought that advertising agencies commanded higher valuations on the stock market and that a multi-disciplined group could benefit from cross-referrals.

According to Bell, HHCL made the first approach. Encouraged by shareholders to be acquisitive and seeing the potential benefits that might be gained, Bell acceded to the suggestion that HHCL's managing partner Rupert Howell should be appointed joint chief executive of Chime alongside Piers Pottinger. But Howell's apparent belief in the superiority of advertising as a communications tool did not go down too well with other parts of Chime, any more than industry rumours that he

was expecting to inherit Lord Bell's mantle in due course.

Matters came to a head when HHCL's profitability took a turn for the worse on the arrival of the new millennium. Revenues started a downward spiral and HHCL's profit slumped by 75% in 2001 alone, as the company lost one third of its business and spent £1.3 million on redundancies.

By September 2002, Howell had departed and Bell was talking to his former Saatchi colleague Sir Martin Sorrell about selling the HHCL agency to WPP.

It was then that Chris Satterthwaite was appointed chief executive of the group. He brought to the task experience as a client at HJ Heinz, as well as having worked in several of the key marketing disciplines. Apart from being one of Howell's partners at the HHCL advertising agency, Satterthwaite had worked for the major sales promotion and direct marketing agency IMP. And he had been appointed chief executive of the Chime public relations subsidiary Bell Pottinger Communications after the HHCL takeover. Satterthwaite readily acknowledges the breadth of experience he gained.

The year 2002 proved to be the nadir in Chime's fortunes. It reported a loss of £37 million after writing down the goodwill attributed to past acquisitions by £29 million and incurring various other restructuring costs. The following year showed some improvement when the loss was reduced to £12 million, much of that loss arising from the sale of an initial 49% stake in HHCL (the balance was sold in 2006).

It would be understandable if the HHCL experience had numbed Chime's enthusiasm for expansion and diversification. But once the Chime balance sheet had been restored by a new share issue in 2004, the appetite for growth returned. In 2005 the group bought another advertising agency VCCP — now one of the top 10 advertising agencies in the UK with clients that include O2, Hiscox, Compare the Market and Coors lite — and added a couple of small public relations businesses. In the same year Bell Pottinger opened a Middle East office in Dubai.

Since then Chime has invested in research businesses, data analytics, design, corporate responsibility consultancy, healthcare communica-

tions, digital search, financial public relations and – most significantly – sports marketing.

Chime's interest in sports marketing began in 2007 when it acquired Fast Track Sales. Last year sports marketing accounted for 22% of group operating profit.

Today Chime's involvement embraces consultancy for sponsors, rights sales for sports federations and rights holders, communications and activation around sponsors' investments, event management, advice to cities bidding for global sports events, branding of major sports events and corporate hospitality. "It's the full service nature of the group with 600 people in 11 cities, half of whom are outside the UK and exposed to growing markets that makes the business exciting", Satterthwaite says.

"Big western brands go east via sport", he adds, emphasising how sport offers global audience penetration for big brands. "Our development strategy focuses on the sports capitals of the world", he says.

Apparently the London Organising Committee of the Olympic Games estimates that the television audience for the event will be 4.3 billion — two thirds of the world's population — and so it's hardly

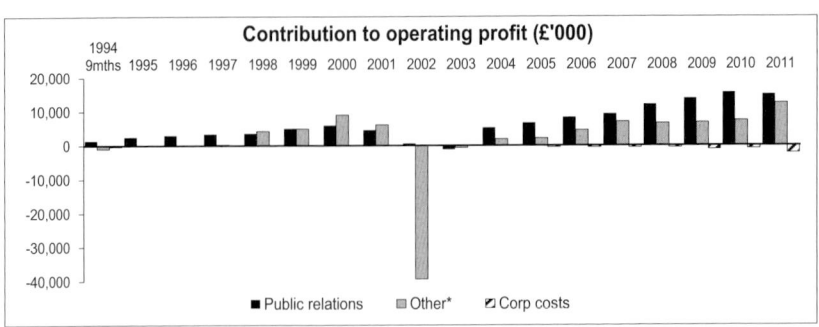

Contribution to operating profit (£'000)

surprising that rights sales continue to grow.

While Satterthwaite asserts his desire for Chime's future to be based on a more balanced portfolio of activities he cannot disguise his enthusiasm for sports marketing which he believes will provide the company with better revenue visibility because of the longer contract periods involved.

In Satterthwaite's view sports marketing could eventually provide 50% of Chime's profits. Asked whether that would represent too dominant a proportion of Chime's business, Satterthwaite skates around the question in true sporting style by pointing out that some shareholders favour a "pure play" business rather than a multi-disciplined one.

Satterthwaite also argues against the view that sports marketing may be here today and gone tomorrow, like the popularity of digital investment in the dotcom era. "IMG has been around for 50 years", he says, referring to the self-styled global leader in sports marketing.

None of this answers the question

What Chime gets for selling Bell Pottinger to BPP Communications

Of the £19.6 million purchase consideration £14.9 million was payable in cash on completion or shortly thereafter, and a further £4.1 million was satisfied by the issue of preference and ordinary shares, together valued at £4.1 million and representing 25% of BPP Communications' share capital.

Subject to compliance with the terms of its financing documents, BPP intends to apply 40% of the BPP group's annual consolidated profits in redemption of the preference shares and, once the preference shares are fully redeemed, in paying dividends on the ordinary shares. Even after redemption of the preference shares, Chime will share in 25% of the future profits and capital appreciation of BPP.

A shareholders' agreement gives Chime the following rights, among others:
- at least one seat on the BPP board for as long as Chime is a shareholder;
- an entitlement to a 50% share of any gain enjoyed by the other shareholders in BPP from the unapproved sale of that company in the second year after divestment or 25% of such gain in the third year after divestment.
- the right on specified future dates to sell its shareholding back to BPP or otherwise to find a buyer for its shares within agreed procedures.
- Prior to 1 July 2014 the shareholders of BPP shall not effect a sale which would result in a single party holding 50% or more of the voting rights in BPP without Chime's consent, unless there is no reasonable prospect of BPP avoiding an insolvent liquidation.
- Upon a sale which would result in a single person holding 60% or more of the voting rights in BPP, customary "drag along" provisions will allow BPP to require Chime to sell its shares alongside any others
- Upon a sale which would result in a single party holding 50% or more of BPP's voting rights, customary "tag along" provisions will allow Chime to insist on its shares being sold alongside the others if it so wishes.

Upon a change of control of Chime, BPP may acquire the Chime shareholding at market value.

How Chime developed over 23 years

1989	Management buyout from **Lowe Howard Spink & Bell plc**.
1994	Floats shares on the London Stock Exchange with initial market capitalisation of £19 million.
1997	Acquires **HHCL Group** with WPP taking 29.9% stake.
1998	Acquires **Opinion Leader Research**.
	Acquires **Pure Media**.
1999	Acquires **Landmark Communications** and **Teamspirit**.
2000	Acquires **Harvard Public Relations** and **Insight Marketing & Communications**.
	Acquisition of **QBO**, now called Bell Pottinger Public Relations.
2001	Acquires **The Smart Company**, a corporate and social responsibility consultancy, now merged into Corporate Citizenship.
	Acquires **MMK Markt & Medien Kommunikation** GmbH, a consumer and corporate public relations business.
2002	Acquires **Ingram Group Promotions**, a sales promotion business, now called Branded Moments of Truth (BMT).
2003	Sells 49% of HHCL to WPP.
	Sets up **Resonate**, a consumer public relations company.
	Acquires 70% of **TTA Public Relations**, a property marketing business.
2004	**Placing and Open Offer** and reduction of debt by £18.5 million to £10.8 million.
	Acquire **Traffic Werbeagentur** GmbH, a German marketing communications consultancy.
2005	Launches **Bell Pottinger Middle East in Dubai**, UAE.
	Acquires **VCCP**, an integrated marketing services agency based in London.
	Acquires **Baxter Hulme**, a public relations company based in Macclesfield.
	Acquire **De Facto Communications**, a healthcare and life science public relations consultancy.
2006	Sells remaining 51% of HHCL to WPP.
	Launches **VCCP Search**, a dedicated search engine marketing agency.
2007	Launches **VCCP Blue**.
	Acquires a 75% stake in **Facts International**, a fieldwork research company.
	Launches **Bell Pottinger Communications USA** in Washington DC.
	Acquires the UK sports marketing agency **Fast Track Sales** and its subsidiaries.
	Opens **Bell Pottinger Middle East in Abu Dhabi**.
	Acquires **The Corporate Citizenship Company**, a global corporate responsibility consultancy.
	Acquires specialist sports public relations company **Stuart Higgins Communications**.
2008	Launches **Brand Democracy**, a consumer and campaign research company.
	Launches **Bell Pottinger Health**, a healthcare public relations company.
	Acquires **MC-Bio Communications**, a corporate healthcare public relations company ro join Bell Pottinger Health.
	Acquires **Bankbrae Holdings**, a sports marketing and PR company trading as The Sports Business, to join Fast Track Group.
	Opens **VCCP's office in Berlin**, Germany.
	VCCP and Fast Track offices open in Doha, Qatar.
	Purchases a 40% stake in **SomeOne**, a design practice.
	Launches **Icon**, an integrated brand communications agency.
	Sets up **Caucus World**, an online research company.
2009	Opens **Bell Pottinger Middle East** in Bahrain.
	Acquires **Ptarmigan** in Leeds, now called Ptarmigan Bell Pottinger.
	Launches **VCCP Health**, an advertising agency specialising in the healthcare sector.
	Opens **The Sports Business** office in London.
	Acquires **Essentially Group**, a sports marketing, media, management and services company.
	Sets up **Bell Pottinger Change & Internal Communications**.
2010	Acquires **Pelham**, a financial PR company, renames as Pelham Bell Pottinger.
	Acquires **Tree**, a data analytics business.
	Opens **VCCP's office in Prague** to service the Czech Republic and Slovakia.
	Opens **Pelham Bell Pottinger's office in Singapore**.
	Acquires **pmplegacy**, a global sports events consultancy.
	Acquires **acefieldwork**, a face-to-face field research company.
	Opens **Fast Track's office in Hong Kong**.
2011	Launches **Open Health**, the first channel and discipline neutral agency in the health communications sector.
	Launches **Chime Ventures** to back entrepreneurs to fuel Chime's organic growth.
	Essentially's hospitality team rebranded as **Full Access Hospitality**.
	Acquires **Icon** engaged in branding implementation for major sporting events.
	Acquires healthcare PR company **Lane, Earl & Cox** for Open Health.
	Acquires **Golden Goal Sports Ventures** in Brazil.
	Acquire **Reynolds-MacKenzie**, a healthcare public relations company.
	Acquires marketing strategy company **Gulliford Consulting** for VCCP.
	Acquires advertising agency **Hooper Galton** for for VCCP.
	Acquires rugby player agency **Essentially France**.
2012	Acquires **Succinct Communications**, a provider of medical communications for prescription medicines, to join Open Health.
	Chime's Insight and Engagement Division (CIE) launches **Watermelon Research**, a new bespoke digital research agency.
	Acquires **McKenzie Clark**, a specialist graphics and branding company.
	Acquires **iLUKA**, an events management and activation company.
	Acquires 40% of **Strat Agile**, a data analytics company based in Singapore, for Tree.
	VCCP acquires **Rough Hill**, a youth marketing agency specialising in digital, social and experiential.

of whether Chime will be hurt by the defection of a part of its public relations division with its high profile leaders. Satterthwaite points out that the Good Relations rump being retained will still be a Top 10 public relations group: "Some of our biggest clients are Good Relations clients, not Bell Pottinger clients", he says.

And the divestment deal leaves Chime with a 25% stake in the departing businesses, as well as various other non-solicitation and non-compete safeguards for a limited period. Chime also has protection in the event that Bell and his colleagues decide they want to sell their newly acquired business (see table).

Bell's new company **BBP Communications** has paid £19.6 million in cash and shares for the businesses it has acquired. According to Chime, this purchase price equates to a not overly generous multiple of eight times the 2011 profit of the businesses being divested, that profit being before interest and tax. If, as anticipated, those businesses suffer a dip in profitability this year, the actual multiple of currently maintainable profits may prove to be a little higher.

There can be no doubt that Bell wants to carry on working, and that his natural comfort zone is in public relations. But his desire for a lower profile may not last. After all, this is the man who enjoyed working with some of the highest profile politicians and businessmen in the world[1].

---

1. *Sadly Lord Bell died on 25 August 2019*

25

Bob Morton's Corporate Gambles

Bob Morton is a chartered ac-countant who has been prepared to risk his money in a range of business enterprises, but not always successfully. As we shall read, much of that money came from his share of the sale proceeds when Euro Exhaust Centres was sold to Kwik Fit in 1979. Since then Morton's reputation has been sullied by a series of censures by the Takeover Panel.

Bob Morton: thrice disciplined by the Takeover Panel

This chapter describes the cir-cumstances prompting one of those censures — relating to an investment in Armour Group and first published in 2015. It also reveals the range of Morton's business investments that have come within the sights of his Jersey based offshore vehicle Hawk Investment Holdings, including in particular two investments in marketing companies. One of those companies — Porta Com-munications — was listed on the London stock exchange, of which more later. Regrettably, the story includes quite a lot of evidence of Morton being "economical with the actualité" — a phrase famously used by the former MP Alan Clark in response to cross-examina-tion in an unconnected court hearing at the Old Bailey in 1992.

The Hearings Committee of the Takeover Panel was far blunter in its criticism of Morton in one of the investigations con-ducted by its Executive — this time into the purchase of shares in Hubco Investments plc:

> In the Committee's judgment Mr Morton's dishonesty in his dealings with the Executive was particularly sustained and serious. It must also have regard to the fact that, by the time this matter was reported to the Executive, Mr Morton had been disci-plined on three previous occasions for breaches of the Code. On one such occasion he had been warned of the importance of taking care to provide correct and complete information to

the Executive and on another he had been publicly censured for attempting to conceal an obligation to make a Rule 9 mandatory offer. Finally, Mr Morton not only misled the Executive himself, he involved Mr Garner in the enterprise, a friend of his son who had reason to be grateful to Mr Morton for his support for his online retail company and who is now facing a heavy price for having been induced to support him in putting forward an untrue, concocted story.

Mr Morton's conduct in systematically lying to the Executive and in inventing an agreement to purchase Hubco's shares on trust for Mr Garner is no less serious because it later transpired that the whole matter could have been sorted out satisfactorily had he acted honestly and reported the facts to the Executive as he was advised to do at the outset[1].

The Panel's Committee concluded that in its opinion Morton was someone "who is not likely to comply with the Code". Furthermore the attempted deception of the Executive in the course of its investigation was so serious and so prolonged as to merit "cold-shouldering" of Messrs Morton and Garner for periods of six years and four years respectively, commencing on 21 December 2016. The effect of a cold-shoulder order is that no entity or professional adviser regulated by the Financial Conduct Authority may act for the individuals concerned on any transactions that are governed by the Takeover Code. "Cold-shouldering" is the most severe form of sanction available to the Panel.

Another example of past non-disclosure occurred while Morton was chairman of Porta Communications, but after my original report had appeared in *Marketing Services Financial Intelligence*. In July 2016 the company revealed belatedly that Morton had been a director of no less than eight companies at the time of, or within 12 months preceding, their liquidation or entering into administrative receivership. Porta listed seven of the companies as RSM Tenon Group, Amilyn, Langley Metal Products, Merritts Industrial Services, QBF Group, Tangent Techniques Group and Baron Corporation. At Baron Corporation there was a shortfall in its ability to pay creditors that was estimated at £1,045,917 when put into creditors' voluntary liquidation in 2001. Such a shortfall pales into insignificance when compared with the £84 million deficiency faced by creditors of RSM Tenon.

Earlier in 2016 Porta Communications had announced that Morton had been involved with an eighth company called Cryptic

---

1 *Arthur Leonard Robert Morton and John Benjamin Garner - Ruling of the Takeover Panel Hearings Committee: 10 January 2017.*

Software that went into liquidation owing creditors £1.8 million two months after he resigned as a director.

Meanwhile Morton's company Hawk Investment Holdings poured more cash into Porta Communications, bringing the total amount loaned to £3.45 million. But no matter how much money was lent to the company, it still reported losses (see chart). In May 2016, it was announced that companies associated with Morton had taken additional security for the loans they had advanced.

By August 2016, Porta's share price had fallen so low that the company was unable to complete the purchase of a further 15% of its Redleaf Polhill subsidiary without a capital reorganisation. Under a put and call option agreement, the vendors of Redleaf had been entitled to require Porta to buy a further 15% of the company's shares for £805,427 of which 50% would be settled in cash. The balance was to be satisfied by the issue of Porta shares at their mid-market price. Unfortunately the Porta share price had been languishing at around one half of its 10p nominal value which posed a problem as company law prohibits the issue of shares at less than their nominal value. This necessitated splitting each existing 10p share into 10 shares of 1p.

On 11 October 2016, as the group faced its biggest loss to date, Morton stood down as chairman (citing health reasons) and the group's founder and chief executive officer David Wright took his place. Steffan Williams was appointed chief executive officer. Morton's companies agreed to defer the deadline for repaying a £5 million loan that otherwise would have been due for repayment by the end of that year. It seemed as though the payback on this particular investment gamble might be slow to pay off.

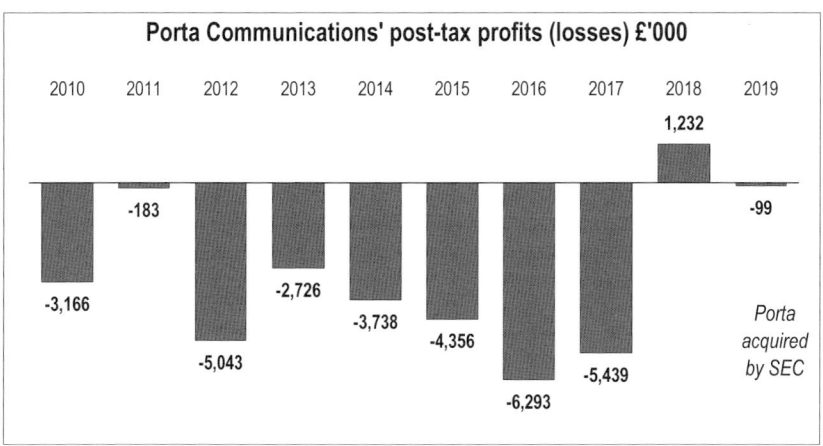

Porta Communications' post-tax profits (losses) £'000

2010	2011	2012	2013	2014	2015	2016	2017	2018	2019
-3,166	-183	-5,043	-2,726	-3,738	-4,356	-6,293	-5,439	1,232	-99

Porta acquired by SEC

Porta's poor performance continued into 2017. But soon help would be on the way from Italy. SEC, an Italian public relations group with subsidiary businesses in Spain, Brussels and Germany, agreed to inject almost £3 million as additional share capital, giving it a 19.3% stake. SEC also negotiated a commercial collaboration agreement. The capital injection reduced Porta's high ratio of borrowings to share capital (debt:equity) that had been a factor in its balance sheet being judged one of the most vulnerable in the annual survey conducted among UK listed marketing groups by *Marketing Service Financial Intelligence.*

At the same time, Porta renegotiated loans provided by companies associated with Morton. Debts of £311,375 and £417,779 due to Hawk Investment Holdings and Retro Grand respectively were replaced by shares. A Hawk discounted bond and a Retro Grand convertible loan were both replaced by loans carrying a lower interest rate of 8%. Two years later SEC acquired total control of Porta.

Anyone who distributes his wealth around investments in some 20 companies must be limiting the risk. But equally he may be reducing the prospect of a good overall return. So it is with 73-year-old inveterate gambler Bob Morton who is reputed to be as keen on horse and greyhound racing (he and his son Charles own 50% of Henlow Racing) as he is on speculating on the fortunes of companies.

But last week he was on the receiving end of the equivalent of a stewards' enquiry when the Takeover Panel reprimanded him quite severely for a series of breaches while seeking to build a substantial shareholding in Armour Group without making an outright bid as required.

What was most surprising about the reprimand was that Morton is a mature chartered accountant who has been in business for a long time and would be expected to know the rules, or at least who to consult to find out

about them.

At the publicly-listed Armour Group, where Morton is chairman, the aggregate shareholdings of his family and connected companies (a "concert party" in stock market jargon) exceeded the 30% threshold that would require any further share acquisitions to be accompanied by a general offer to all shareholders.

Morton disregarded that rule and the Panel was unequivocal in its condemnation: "The Executive considers that the failure by Mr Morton to make an offer under Rule 9 in compliance with the Code in connection with the purchases of shares in Armour by Mr Morton's four sons in June and August 2011, and the associated breaches of Rule 5 and Rule 2, were serious breaches of the Code."

The background to these breaches was that certain investors who had participated in a public share placing by Armour in February

2011 wanted to sell their shareholdings and invited Morton to buy them. He declined to do so because the size of the existing shareholdings under the control of members of the Morton concert party was such that he would have been obliged to make an offer for the rest of the Armour shares in issue.

Claiming to be under a misapprehension that his adult sons would be regarded by the Panel as independent of him (and not part of his concert party), Morton grasped the opportunity to take advantage of the favourable share price by arranging for about 6.8 million Armour shares to be purchased in the names of the four sons. Separately, one of Morton's sons Charles purchased 385,174 shares.

But the Takeover Panel said that Morton already knew that the trusts set up for the benefit of three of his four sons would form part of his concert party because they had been described as such in an earlier circular. On this basis 39.1% of the voting rights were already held by the concert party before the event, necessitating an outright bid

The four sons' purchases resulted in each becoming interested in 1.8 million Armour shares which collectively augmented the voting rights of the pre-existing interests of Morton's concert party by 7.4%. Morton made gifts of cash to each of his sons to cover the cost of the share purchases.

The Panel's executive was particularly aggrieved that neither Morton nor his sons consulted it nor sought advice regarding the implications of these share purchases under the Code. Morton apologised for the breaches of the Code and agreed to make an offer for Armour.

"Nonetheless, Mr Morton's actions showed a disregard for the Code and his previous breaches of the Code must also be taken into consideration in determining the appropriate disciplinary sanction", the reprimand said. "Mr Morton is hereby criticised for his conduct in this case and his record of failing to comply with his obligations under the Code."

Described by the Takeover Panel as "an experienced investor who has been closely involved in several transactions subject to the Code", Morton's career started at the age of 16 when he is reported to have left school to train as an accountant – learning on the job and studying in the evening, rather than following the present-day route of going to university first.

He progressed to become a partner in a smallish firm in St Albans, trading as Morton Thornton, where he teamed up with a client to create a chain of car exhaust centre that were later sold on to Kwik Fit for a price said to have been a little under £11 million. Presumably that provided the nest egg from which his myriad investments have been fed.

Some have been successful. Some have not.

Morton's primary investment vehicle is called Hawk Investment Holdings and is registered in the Channel Islands tax haven where he lives for much of the time, although he gives a business address at Great Titchfield Street in London's West End. He has shared his largesse with his sons and his wife. As was evident from the Armour affair, each of the sons is the beneficiary of a trust that owns a personal company funded by Morton.

Among the more successful investments was a stake acquired by Morton and his sons in facilities manager Maclellan Group which they sold for £11 million in 2006. Also in 2006 the Morton family sold their shares in Systems Union Group for £23 million. More painful was the realisation of the Morton stakes in software developer Cryptic Software, accountancy firm RSM Tenon and marketing group Media Square, all of which became insolvent without

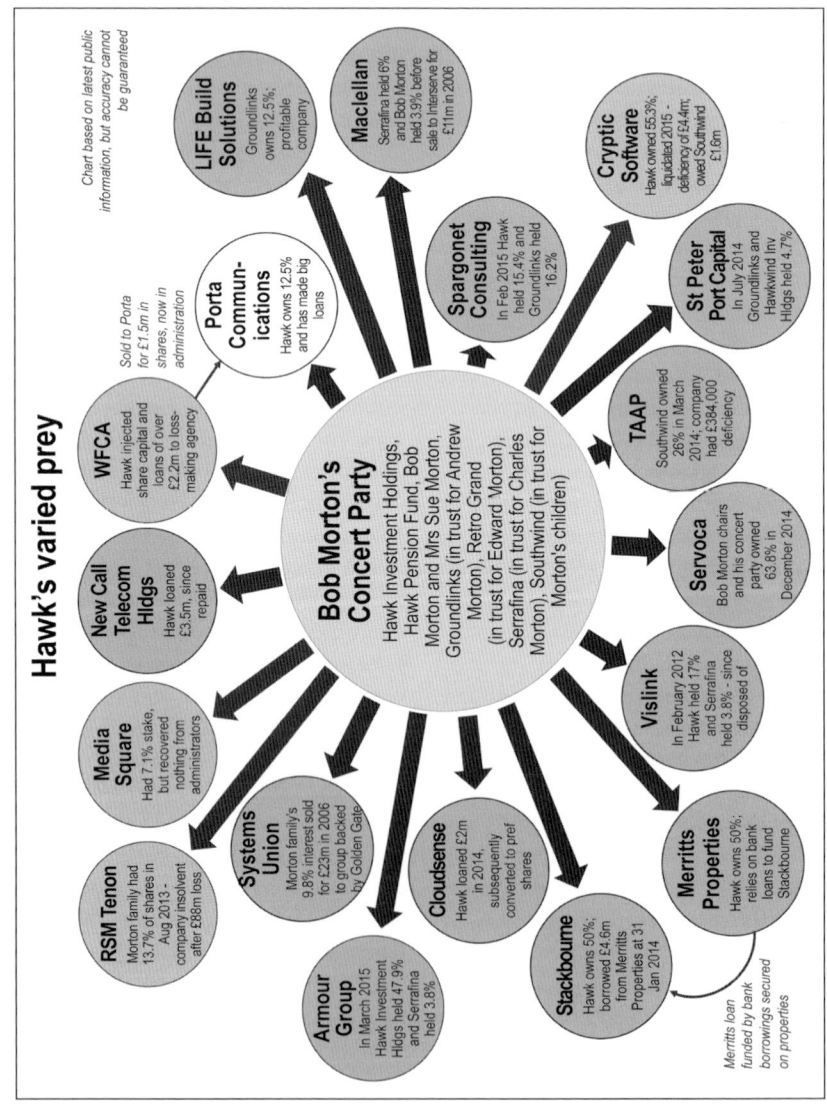

Hawk's varied prey

Chart based on latest public information, but accuracy cannot be guaranteed

Bob Morton's Concert Party
Hawk Investment Holdings, Hawk Pension Fund, Bob Morton and Mrs Sue Morton, Groundlinks (in trust for Andrew Morton), Retro Grand (in trust for Edward Morton), Serrafina (in trust for Charles Morton), Southwind (in trust for Morton's children)

LIFE Build Solutions — Groundlinks owns 12.5%; profitable company

Maclellan — Serrafina held 6% and Bob Morton held 3.9% before sale to Interserve for £11m in 2006

Cryptic Software — Hawk owned 55.3%; liquidated 2015 - deficiency of £24.4m; Southwind owned £1.6m

Spargonet Consulting — In Feb 2015 Hawk held 15.4% and Groundlinks held 16.2%

St Peter Port Capital — In July 2014 Groundlinks and Hawkwind Inv Hldgs held 4.7%

Porta Communications — Hawk owns 12.5% and has made big loans. Sold to Porta for £1.5m in shares, now in administration

TAAP — Southwind owned 26% in March 2014; company had £384,000 deficiency

WFCA — Hawk injected share capital and loans of over £2.2m to loss-making agency

Servoca — Bob Morton chairs and his concert party owned 63.8% in December 2014

New Call Telecom Hldgs — Hawk loaned £3.5m, since repaid

Vislink — In February 2012 Hawk held 17% and Serrafina held 3.8% - since disposed of

Media Square — Had 7.1% stake, but recovered nothing from administrators

Merritts Properties — Hawk owns 50%; relies on bank loans to fund Stackbourne. Meritts loan funded by bank borrowings secured on properties

RSM Tenon — Morton family had 13.7% of shares in Aug 2013 - company insolvent after £88m loss

Systems Union — Morton family's 9.8% interest sold for £23m in 2006 to group backed by Golden Gate

Cloudsense — Hawk loaned £2m in 2014, subsequently converted to pref shares

Stackbourne — Hawk owns 50%; borrowed £4.6m from Merritts Properties at 31 Jan 2014

Armour Group — In March 2015 Hawk Investment Hldgs held 47.9% and Serrafina held 3.8%

offering any material return to Morton and his companies.

Advertising agency WFCA was threatening to go the same way, but Morton was able to sell it to Porta Communications in exchange for shares before the balloon burst, as indeed it did soon afterwards.

Morton had been pumping more cash into WFCA from his offshore company Hawk Investment Holdings before the sale and this debt was carried over to Porta Communications. Today Morton has a shareholding of 12.5% in Porta along with the Hawk loans. Morton acquired his first 4% tranche of shares in Porta through Hawk in November 2011, just after the controversial Armour bid. Hawk also starting lending money to Porta in 2011, both before and after the WFCA merger.

The need for cash became increasingly serious as Porta was trading at a substantial loss. In 2011 it lost nearly £0.5 million and the result would have been twice as bad without a windfall currency gain on disposal of a subsidiary. In 2012 the group lost almost £5 million. In 2013 it lost £2.5 million. By the end of 2013 Hawk

had lent Porta about £2.7 million – or so it appeared — and by May 2014 Bob Morton had increased his family share stake to 14.1%.

In fact a company associated with Bob Morton had lent an additional £2.3 million to Porta Communications by December 2013, but it was described as being "from a third party" in Porta's accounts for that year. That "third party" was a company called Retro Grand that is owned by the trustees of a trust for the benefit of Morton's son Edward – a member of Morton's concert party.

The full note about the loans from Retro Grand stated: "During 2013, the company obtained three new short term loan facilities with a total face value of £2,300,000 from a third party Retro Grand Limited for working capital needs. Subsequent to the year end, and following successful completion of the February 2014 placing, on 18 March 2014 the company has repaid all of its Retro Grand loans and related interest."

Porta was still trading at a loss halfway through 2014 and the full year's results will be awaited with some interest.

26
Grayling's Growing Pains

The Rector of Gravesend, the Reverend Canon Selwyn Gummer, had three children – Mark, John and Peter. Mark and Peter both became entrepreneurs, starting their own companies. John pursued a career in politics, becoming chairman of the Conservative Party. He is probably best known as a former Minister of Agriculture and latterly Secretary of State for the Environment.

Brother Peter has also been a long-serving member of the Conservative Party and is most famous for creating the global public relations consultancy Shandwick that was eventually sold to the US marketing network The Interpublic Group (see chapter 15). But that was not the end of Peter's love affair with public relations. After a transition period he left Shandwick and created a new public relations business known as Huntsworth.

It came as something of a surprise to learn that Peter Gummer had toyed with following his father into the priesthood after graduating from Cambridge with a degree in moral science and theology. But he chose journalism. Instead of spreading the Gospel, he opted for spreading other people's gospels. Today he sits in the House of Lords as Baron Chadlington of Dean. Dean is also the constituency home of the former Prime Minister David Cameron.

This chapter tells how Lord Chadlington sought to replicate Shandwick by building Huntsworth into a global practice. In doing so he acquired a number of companies that would eventually operate under the "Grayling" global brand. As a case study it illustrates yet again how the responsibilities of leadership can become entwined with ego.

Lord Chadlington: on a mission to spread the gospel

Too often in this book we read of entrepreneurs who find themselves in leadership roles for which they are not ideally equipped. Being a brilliant marketing or communications professional deserves respect and admiration, but it does not always translate into someone who has the appropriate skills to direct a large business successfully and profitably.

Despite his apparent success in building the Shandwick business, Chadlington's ambition to build another profitable global public relations brand under three successive divisional chief executives verged on a financial disaster. The original report, published in *Marketing Services Financial Intelligence* in May 2015, explored the events of the first 10 years of Chadlington's reign at Huntsworth and exposes some of the management shortcomings during that period.

After an expensive series of acquisitions, Huntsworth had resolved to rationalise its diverse portfolio of companies. On the face of it, such action would seem entirely sensible – until one looks at the accounting consequences. In 2009 the group reported a loss of £8.6 million after rationalisation costs in excess of £25 million. Among those costs was a £9.1 million charge for the impairment of intangible assets like goodwill that irritated Lord Chadlington and his finance director Sally Withey so much that they invited me to discuss it with them. I have to confess that I felt some sympathy for their view, as *Marketing Services Financial Intelligence* reported at the time:

> The rationalisation costs comprise a mixture of actual expenditure and asset write-downs of which £9.1 million is the result of a seemingly bizarre accounting rule. The £9.1 million

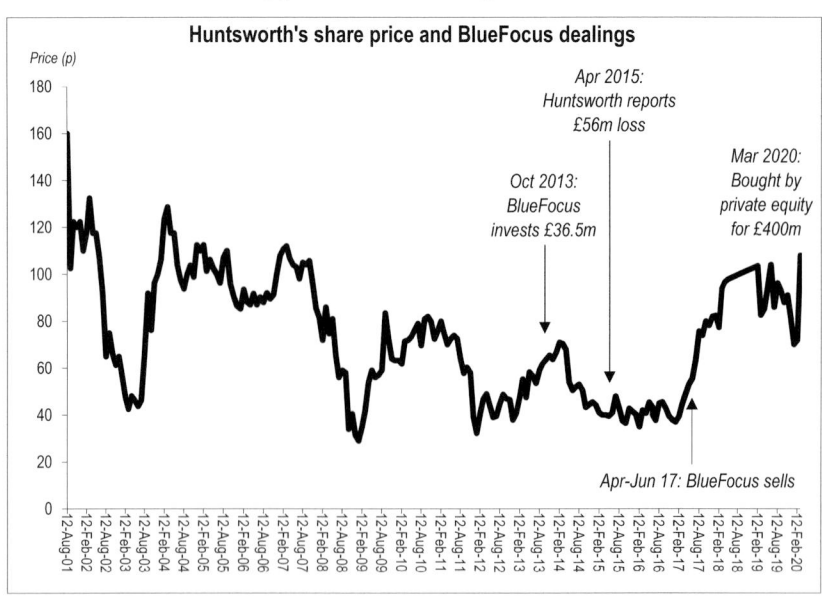

charge for "asset impairment" is required because the group's activities have been rationalised under just four brand names and so many of Huntsworth's subsidiaries' names are no longer being used. According to Huntsworth, the accounting rule-makers take the view that any part of the amount paid to acquire those subsidiary businesses that has been attributed to intangible assets like goodwill will no longer have any value, prompting the chunky impairment charge.

But if businesses previously carried on by two or more companies have been merged into one, surely common sense would dictate that the impairment review would be applied to the combined businesses? If as a result it can be demonstrated that in aggregate the future cash streams expected to be derived from the merged businesses are sufficient to support the book value of the intangible assets inherited, how can it be argued that any diminution in those asset values will have occurred? Whether or not some of the companies cease to trade in their own right is irrelevant.

Huntsworth may not have done itself any favours by describing its strategic rationalisation as anything to do with "brands". That implies the company names were more important assets than the resources harnessed within them. We delude ourselves if we believe that the actual brand name of a people business represents anything other than the reputation, skills and fee-earning capability of the people it employs[1].

After recording a massive £56 million loss in 2014, a new management team took over with Paul Taffe as chief executive and Derek Mapp as chairman. Profits returned in 2017 and the Chinese shareholder BlueFocus Communications took the opportunity to dispose of its 19.5% shareholding in two tranches. The aggregate sale proceeds totalled nearly £33 million, showing a loss of about £3.6 million and leaving any prospect of a profitable long-term strategic alliance in tatters.

Huntsworth found a buyer for the entire company in 2020 in the shape of a US private equity fund managed by Clayton Dubilier & Rice that offered £400 million in cash for Huntsworth's shares. That price represented a multiple of almost 20 times Huntsworth's much improved post-tax profit in 2019.

Yet another UK public company had surrendered its independent listing on the London stock market and fallen under US private ownership. So now let's go back to the beginning...

---

1. *Writing in 1989 the author suggested that, in a "people" business, the largest "unseparated" asset contained within the value of goodwill that normally arises on acquisition of an entity is not the entity brand value nor the residual goodwill but the unmeasured profit-earning capability of the productive employees. See "What's in a Name? Accounting for the brand name of a people business", Accountants Magazine, July 1989.*

In 2009 Huntsworth, the stock market listed public relations group, spent nearly £9 million on the much trumpeted strategic restructuring and rebranding of its business into four divisions. Of these, the biggest was the global public relations brand Grayling which accounted for 51% of the group's revenue.

The other three divisions were the financial communications agency Citigate, an integrated health agency Huntsworth Health and a "multi-specialist" consumer consultancy Red.

In the same year there was a £9 million write-off, reflecting the diminution in value of existing brands and goodwill that had been attributed to companies that would no longer trade under their own independent identities.

"Our strategic branding initiative has provided the group with the ability to win global clients and represents a key opportunity for growth", chief executive Lord Chadlington announced at the time.

The initial results looked encouraging as the group reported a much improved post-tax profit of £17.5 million in 2010. But that level of profit was never achieved again.

Five years later it is clear and that the strategy, or the manner of its implementation, has not worked. A few weeks ago the Huntsworth group reported a £56 million loss after writing down the value of its Grayling business by £65 million and, in doing so, wiping out all the profit earned since 2010.

As we shall see, there is growing evidence that the Grayling globalisation plan was at risk from the outset, despite the efforts of three successive chief executives to make it work.

Before Lord Chadlington's arrival on the Huntsworth board in 2000, it had been a struggling publicly-listed marketing group, perhaps better known under its former name of Holmes & Marchant. Soon it offered Lord Chadlington a seductive opportunity to begin replicating the Shandwick empire that he had previously created and sold to The Interpublic Group in 1998. Asked by *Marketing Services Financial Intelligence* whether he had consciously aspired to create another Shandwick

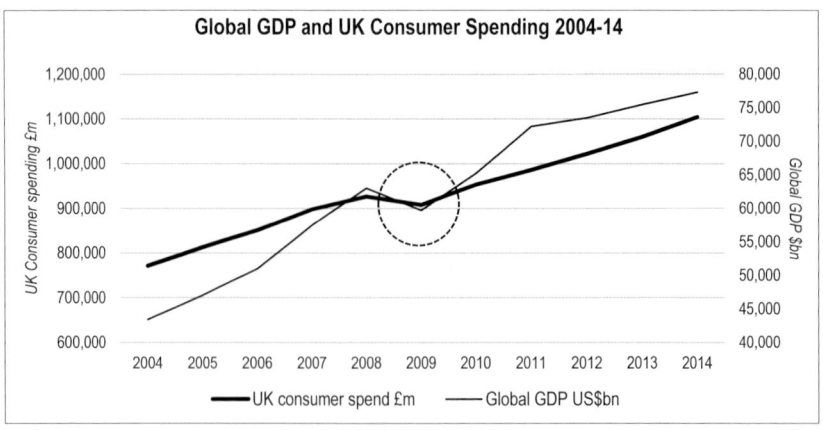

with global coverage, Lord Chadlington declined to comment. However, former colleagues recalled a number of occasions when Chadlington would reflect upon and make comparisons with his Shandwick experiences.

Grayling had offices in the UK and a modest presence in the Far East, Brussels and New York when it was acquired by Huntsworth from the French group Havas in 2004, along with 60% of a small financial agency Hudson Sandler.

On the same day as Huntsworth bought Grayling it also acquired the Swiss-based European public relations business Trimedia Group. Then, in 2005, Lord Chadlington's ambition was fuelled further by the seemingly overpriced acquisition of the Incepta Group, bringing with it a number of additional agencies that included the Citigate financial business, to be followed by an early bout of expensive restructuring.

The initial payment for Grayling alone was £10 million and the Grayling management was given a 30% stake that Huntsworth could buy back at a multiple of 8 times post-tax profits, less original cost, after four years. Those managers received a chunky £2.4 million on selling back the first 20%

Incepta Group's principal subsidiaries acquired by Huntsworth

Name	Country of incorporation /operation	Class of business[3]
Citigate Dewe Rogerson Limited	England	FCC
Citigate Public Affairs Limited	England	FCC
Citigate DVL Smith Limited [1]	England	FCC
Citigate Communications Limited	England	FCC
Citigate MARCHCom Limited [1]	England	FCC
Citigate Albert Frank Limited [1]	England	Adv
Finex Communications Group plc [1]	England	MS
Dynamo Marketing Limited [1]	England	MS
Hauck Research Services Limited [1]	England	MS
JKD Communications Limited [1]	England	MS
Karen Earl Sponsorship Limited [1]	England	MS
Park Avenue Productions plc	England	MS
The RED Consultancy Group Limited	England	MS
Redmandarin Limited [1]	England	MS
Citigate Lloyd Northover Limited [1]	England	MS
Citigate Publishing Limited [1]	England	MS
Incepta Online Limited [1]	England	H
Citigate SMARTS Limited [1]	Scotland	FCC, Adv, MS
Citigate Northern Ireland Limited	N Ireland	FCC, MS
Citigate Holdings GmbH	Germany	H
Citigate Dewe Rogerson GmbH	Germany	FCC
Citigate SEA GmbH & Co KG [1]	Germany	Adv
Citigate Demuth GmbH	Germany	FCC, Adv, MS
Hoffman Schalt Werbeagentur GmbH [1]	Germany	Adv
Citigate Gramma AB	Sweden	FCC
Citigate Training & Internal Communication Srl	Italy	Adv
Citigate Gunpowder Srl	Italy	MS
Citigate Sanchis SL	Spain	FCC
Citigate First Financial B.V	Netherlands	FCC
PR Force Netherlands B.V	Netherlands	FCC
PR Force Public Relat'ns & Press Relat'ns NV	Belgium	FCC
Incepta Group Inc	•USA	H
Citigate Inc	USA	
Citigate Albert Frank[1]	USA	Adv, MS
Citigate Sard Verbinnen Inc [2]	USA	FCC
Citigate Cunningham Inc	USA	FCC
Citigate Dewe Rogerson Inc (trading as Citigate Financial Intelligence)	USA	FCC
Citigate Global Intelligence & Security, LLC	USA	FCC
Citigate Hudson Inc [1]	USA	FCC
Citigate Broad Street Inc	USA	MS
Citigate Markowitz & McNaughton, Inc.	USA	FCC
Cosmic Blender, Inc.	USA	MS
Citigate Asia Limited	Hong Kong	
Citigate Dewe Rogerson	Hong Kong	FCC
Citigate Lloyd Northover [1]	Hong Kong	MS
Citigate Albert Frank Limited [1]	Hong Kong	Adv
Citigate Dewe Rogerson i.MAGE pte Ltd	Singapore	FCC
Citigate Su Yeang Design Pte Ltd [1]	Singapore	MS
Citigate Dewe Rogerson Communications Private Limited	India	FCC
Citigate South Africa (Pty) Limited [1]	South Africa	FCC,Adv,MS

1. Sold to Media Square in 2005; later sold on to MSQ Partners by Media Square administrators. 2. Sold to management in 2006. 3. Key: FCC = Financial & Corporate Communications; Adv = Advertising; MS = Marketing Services; H = Intermediate holding company.

tranche in 2008, and a further £2.1 million in 2010. The biggest individual participant was Nigel Kennedy who had a 4.5% shareholding but left his post as chief executive officer in 2009.

Kennedy's replacement was Michael Murphy, one of Lord Chadlington's associates from the Shandwick era who had been lured with his company Hatch Group into the expanding Huntsworth empire to take charge of Trimedia.

The restructuring hullabaloo of 2009 may have appeared to be a common sense rationalisation of the myriad companies that had been bought into the Huntsworth fold. But it was more than that.

In 2007 Huntsworth had pitched for the British Airways business with Lord Chadlington leading the charge. But most of the business went elsewhere, although Grayling was able to oust Edelman from Asia Pacific amidst the loser's cries of unfair fee-cutting. Did this mean that Huntsworth could still not achieve the global clout previously experienced by Shandwick?

Worse was to come: group results for the first half of 2009 were down by 80% when compared with the equivalent period in 2008 as severance payments and property rationalisation costs lopped £5.3 million off the pre-tax profit.

Perhaps it was time for a bold new initiative to cheer up investors. If so, the creation of a global public relations business under the Grayling brand from a number of subsidiaries dotted around the world could offer an ideal solution. It might also make global pitches for clients like British Airways easier to win in the future as would prove to be the case when Grayling added the European business to its roster in 2011.

The only snag was that Lord Chadlington's bold new initiative came as almost as big a surprise to many of those inside Huntsworth as it did to investors outside. A number of executives who were in the company at the time have since

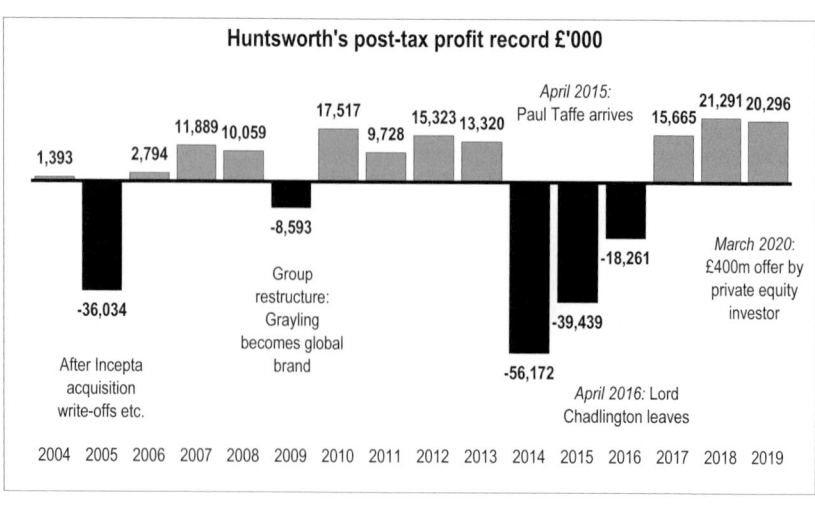

Huntsworth's post-tax profit record £'000

1,393   2,794   11,889 10,059   17,517   9,728   15,323 13,320   April 2015: Paul Taffe arrives   15,665   21,291 20,296

-8,593

Group restructure: Grayling becomes global brand

-36,034

After Incepta acquisition write-offs etc.

-56,172

-39,439

-18,261

March 2020: £400m offer by private equity investor

April 2016: Lord Chadlington leaves

2004 2005 2006 2007 2008 2009 2010 2011 2012 2013 2014 2015 2016 2017 2018 2019

Michael Murphy: hired to run Grayling in 2003   *Pete Pedersen: parachuted in to turn Grayling round*   *Lord Chadlington: global dream shattered?*

expressed astonishment at the speed at which the plan was conceived and implemented.

What's more, it soon became clear that Huntsworth's purse strings were not as elastic as its ambitions. Managers found themselves unable to spend the money they felt necessary to win clients and deliver a global service.

Since acquiring Grayling, Huntsworth had spent £90 million on acquisitions in cash and in borrowings taken over with the acquired companies – even after deducting the cash generated by selling off some of the Incepta businesses. On top of that were the restructuring costs incurred in 2009. By the end of that year the Huntsworth balance sheet included net debt of £49 million and outstanding acquisition payments of £32 million. Its short-term liabilities exceeded readily realisable assets by £15 million and it would be understandable if there was a preoccupation with paying the bills rather than investing further sums in Grayling.

And however stressful the winds of change may have been within the company, they were as nothing when compared with the cold economic blasts from without, as 2009 witnessed a serious drop in global and domestic economic activity. Yet Grayling was still nowhere close to a global network — counting roughly 50 disparate staff in North America and not many more in Asia Pacific. It was essentially a very strong EMEA (Europe, Middle East and Africa) network parcelled up as a global firm.

Doubtless Murphy and his colleagues did their best to implement the restructuring plan and the group reported a welcome boost to profits in 2010, but thereafter Grayling's post-rationalisation performance did not go too well.

Some former executives claim there was a tension between the group's desire to keep margins close to 20% while at the same time seeking new business, facing fee-discounting pressures from big-spending global clients, and needing to hire and/or retain heavy-hitting account handlers around the world. The client appeal of the business also continued to fall between two stools – on the one hand it did not have sufficient size to compete adequately for some large global clients and, on the other hand, some smaller clients were turned off by the new global structure.

In 2011 the group's profit dropped by an alarming 40%. That disappointing performance was attributed in part to a slower than anticipated lead time in converting some of Grayling's recently won global accounts into real revenue streams, despite expanding its hold on the British Airways business to embrace Europe.

Huntsworth's performance was also hit by litigation and further restructuring costs after several projects were cancelled "without warning and very late in the year". The litigation related to alleged breaches of contract by former employees, although it is not thought that those departures came from the Grayling network or contributed to the cutback in client projects awarded to that part of the Huntsworth group.

The group acknowledged that the globalisation and re-branding of its main divisions was taking longer than expected to yield results. Lord Chadlington would devote more of his time to "managing and soliciting multi-office client relationships" — presumably taking more of a hands-on role in Grayling than its chief executive Michael Murphy might have anticipated — while Chadlington's close colleague, the formidable chief operating officer and finance director Sally Withey, would take more responsibility for the day-to-day management of the group's business.

In the first half of 2012, it looked as though the Grayling medicine was beginning to work. Its profit and profit margins improved. But beneath the surface Grayling's senior managers had become increasingly unsettled. A number of Murphy's team were frustrated by a perceived lack of investment, the constant pressure to achieve target profit margins and the interventions of group management. Several had already resigned.

But by July 2012 further cracks were beginning to appear in the Grayling management structure. Murphy resigned, but agreed to move into the role of non-executive chairman as soon as a successor could be appointed. The announcement bore the hallmarks of an unexpected crisis, not least because a suitable internal candidate had not been identified to succeed Murphy. As a consequence Lord Chadlington and Sally Withey became even more directly involved than might otherwise have been the case.

Adding to the impression that the company was trying to put a positive gloss on a situation that clearly was neither going quite to plan nor likely to endear Huntsworth to its investors, chartered accountant Joe McHale was brought on to the parent company board as a non-executive director.

Fortunately 2013 appeared to be showing some real progress. The group reported better margins and a 58% increase in post-tax profit in 2012, along with plans to raise an additional £36 million in share capital from the Chinese public

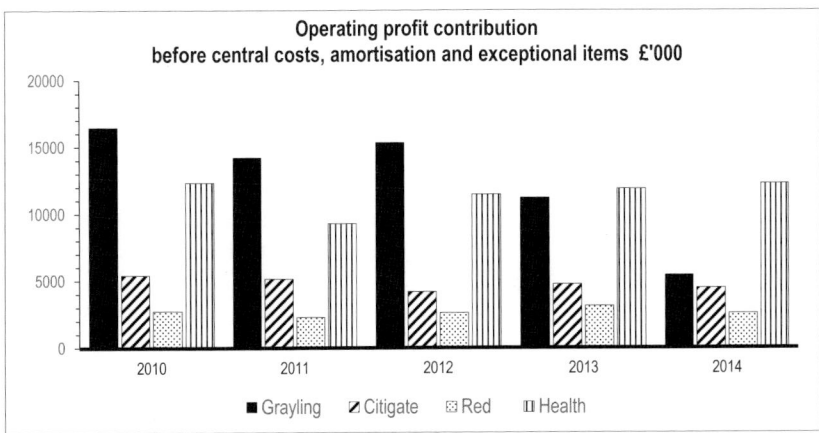

relations company BlueFocus Communication Group. Today it is hard not to ponder whether the apparent improvement in performance was a pre-requisite for the delivery of Chinese money.

Grayling's new chief executive Pete Pedersen was appointed in July 2013 amidst signs of more problems to come. Huntsworth revealed an 18% fall in profit for the half year to 30 June and the Chinese capital injection was being delayed – apparently due to procedural bureaucracy that is not uncommon in that country.

In the absence of a chief executive Grayling's revenue had slipped by more than 6% (7.2% if acquisitions were excluded) and the operating margin had fallen from 20.2% to 13.5% — that was before central costs, restructuring and amortisation charges.

The practice of reporting divisional performance before allocating any central, non-recurring or exceptional costs is questionable in itself. Those costs are real and someone has to pay for them. It is a different matter when monitoring perfor-

mance for internal purposes, in that it is arguably unfair and potentially demotivating to include within the results of a division any of those items that do not fall under the control or influence of divisional management. But it is confusing to shareholders if the measurement of divisional performance does not take account of such exceptional costs as they clearly have an impact on the return on the funds invested in each division.

Grayling's new chief executive Pete Pedersen would have his work cut out to fulfil his brief to reverse the revenue decline, expand the business into under-represented markets and exploit the benefits of the new relationship with the BlueFocus Communication Group in China. Inevitably Pedersen made changes. He abolished the centralised unit that had been set up by Murphy to work on major new client pitches — a unit that has since been partially re-established — and spent money on a further restructuring of the network.

"Grayling is continuing its transition from a business principally reliant on single office clients to one where the client base is increasingly multi-office or global", the company said, but added that the expected decline in single office client revenues had been exacerbated by client budget reductions in the difficult markets in many of the areas where Grayling was operating.

By the end of 2013 Grayling revenues had fallen by 6.4% compared with 2012 and the blame was being laid at the door of "European markets".

However, some of that decline may also have been attributable to the loss of clients that previously had been big fishes in a local pool and now felt like smaller fishes in a much bigger global pool. Grayling had also decided not to retain or pitch for a number of clients with small budgets. Whatever the reasons, Huntsworth's post-tax profit fell by another 13%.

Perhaps anticipating difficult questions from shareholders, Huntsworth secured the services of Lord Myners as prospective chairman. But the appointment survived only four months. In the meantime, at the 2014 annual meeting, 32% of voting shareholders expressed disapproval of the board remuneration policy put forward for their approval.

The extent of that opposition may have been fuelled by the fact that executive directors Lord Chadlington and Sally Withey were contractually entitled to an inflation-proof basic salary irrespective of performance. On top of that each executive was entitled to performance-related bonuses up to a maximum of 125% of basic salary.

It emerged that Huntsworth's two-man remuneration committee, comprising John Farrell and Joe MacHale, had been engaged in "protracted" discussions with the executive directors about alternative approaches and policies, but the directors had resisted any change in their contractual terms. MacHale and Farrell both left the board while Lord Chadlington and Sally Withey were able to look forward to pay packets of up to £2.2 million and £1.5 million respectively, despite the declining profits.

Within a month of the annual meeting, Huntsworth issued a profits warning. In a cryptic note, the company said: "First half results will be below market expectations. The board is reviewing the second half year and, while there is work to do, we believe that the second half will show improvement over the first half year." It is hard to believe that the board had not become at least vaguely aware of the prospect of the underperformance by the time the annual meeting was taking place a few weeks earlier.

The group's post-tax profit for the half year was £4.3 million, down from £6.4 million earned in the corresponding period of 2013. Grayling revenues were down 4.9% on a like-for-like basis to £36.5m with margins of 7.9%. The company conceded that Grayling's performance was "disappointing" in the UK and Europe.

A search had begun for a successor to Lord Chadlington as chief executive, by then aged 72, with the intention that he would continue as chief executive officer until a successor could be appointed after which he would remain at the group as a senior adviser.

The remaining months of 2014 were marked by the departure of chairman Lord Myners and the arrival of additional non-executive directors, including Derek Mapp as chairman. It was also announced that, after months of sick leave due to a back injury, Sally Withey would be leaving the company. By January 2015 Grayling had lost its latest chief executive Pete Pedersen within two years of his appointment and without any immediate replacement. On 7 April, Lord Chadlington's successor arrived in the form of Paul Taaffe. Three days later the group announced its biggest ever loss.

27
MDC: Why Didn't the Dogs Bark?

I first became acquainted with the Canadian marketing group MDC Partners in June 2004 when *Campaign* magazine asked me to interview Chuck Porter. I knew very little about Porter, or his advertising agency Crispin Porter & Bogusky, but apparently his Colorado agency had been bought by MDC and Porter had been charged with the task of raising the company's profile as it pursued the ambition of its principal shareholder and chairman Miles Nadal to conquer the advertising world.

MDC was on the acquisition trail and Chuck Porter thought the company had a novel and highly appealing offer:

"We're not really looking to buy agencies", Porter told me. "MDC is really much more in the partnership business. The philosophy of MDC is to do essentially 50/50 deals. The numbers may be slightly different but essentially we're looking to partner with smart people and to provide the resources for them to grow faster.[1]" In effect MDC sought substantial minority shareholdings in thriving agencies, presumably hoping to be able to take control at a later date. The theory was that the leadership team of the target agency would remain motivated to build the business, rather than walk away after a few years and start afresh.

There had long been a desire to find a way whereby entrepreneurial founders of marketing agencies would be able to realise value from their investment while retaining some form of control over the business, particularly where the owners were averse to seeking a public flotation of the company's shares with its attendant scrutiny.

Miles Nadal: "expenses improperly paid"

Private equity funds were still unheard of and even well-known agencies that were committed to retaining ownership among managers and staff

1 *Campaign, 4 June 2004*

eventually resorted to selling to a global group. More recently, the Business Growth Fund has been established by the clearing banks with the aim of meeting the need for a partial realisation (see chapter 30). So at the time MDC's proposition was certainly appealing. But, as we shall see, it had its drawbacks too. Miles Nadal spent too much on partial acquisitions and found that his bankers wanted him to mortgage the assets of those partially-acquired companies as security. That is not something that lawyers acting for the minority shareholders would normally encourage.

But the biggest drawback was Nadal himself. He had built up his marketing empire over 35 years to achieve annual revenues of $1.2 billion and in doing so accumulated losses of $492 million. At their peak MDC's net borrowings reached $924 million. Constantly boasting of the group's success while simultaneously announcing a stream of losses, it transpired that Nadal had treated some of the company's assets as his own to satisfy his private needs. Why investors and the group's bankers tolerated the situation remains a mystery.

The account that follows documents the creation of MDC under Nadal's leadership, culminating in his enforced departure in 2015 under the shadow of an ongoing SEC investigation (MDC's shares were listed in the US on the NASDAQ stock market). Two years later the SEC imposed a five year ban on Nadal acting as an officer of various classes of company registered with the Commission. Nadal was also fined $5.5 million. In Canada, the Ontario Securities Commission banned Nadal from holding positions of director or officer of any public company until May 2022.

Since publication of the original report in *Marketing Services Financial Intelligence* in August 2015, MDC has continued to experience an erratic performance.

Nadal was succeeded by Scott Kauffman who had been the company's chairman since 2006, but Kauffman's tenure was short-lived. In September 2018, MDC announced a search for a new chief executive to succeed him. Perhaps more significantly, the company announced that it had decided "to explore and evaluate potential strategic alternatives, which may result in — among other things — the possible sale of the company".

Six months later a US investment fund called Stagwell Group invested $100 million and installed its chairman and managing partner Mark Penn as MDC's chief executive. Stagwell Group's investments included The Harris Poll and several other opinion research companies. Mark Penn was a former Burson Marsteller chief executive and acted as adviser to the Democratic Party in the United States and to the UK's former Prime Minister Tony Blair. Penn's first company Penn & Schoen was sold to WPP in 2001.

Stagwell's investment in MDC comprised $50 million in common shares and $50 million in non-voting convertible preference shares. As a result Stagwell owned approximately 19.5% of the outstanding common equity of MDC. Assuming the full conversion of the preference shares, Stagwell would then own approximately 29.2% of MDC's equity share capital. However, if Goldman Sachs also converted the preference shares it acquired in 2017, the Stagwell equity stake would be reduced to 24.8%.

Stagwell's motives became clearer in June 2020 when it made a proposal for a "potential business combination". That proposal was formalised in a merger scheme announced on 22 December 2020 that would result in Stagwell and associates holding 79% of the combined businesses.

Reporting the group's results for 2020 in March 2021, the historic trend continued[1] with another loss - this time of $243 million after making a $93 million provision for asset impairment and restructuring. No more detailed explanation was forthcoming. *Plus ca change, plus c'est la meme chose.*

However, the merger was not without dissenters. In an attempt to calm opposition, Stagwell proposed various governance improvements to provide "increased protection to MDC minority shareholders". The improvements would include the appointment of four independent directors to the board of the merged group, namely former WPP finance director Paul Richardson, former US Secretary for Transportation Rodney Slater, Ballmer Group's chief operating officer Brandt Vaughan, and lawyer and former US trade ambassador Charlene Barshefsky who already serves as an independent director of Stagwell.

I n July 2015 the Canadian marketing group MDC Partners, whose shares are listed on stock exchanges in Toronto and New York, parted company with its chairman and chief executive Miles Nadal.

The parting had been a long time coming and was prompted by an investigation by the US Securities and Exchange Commission that, in the words of MDC, lead to the discovery of "expenses that were improperly paid". As a result, Nadal agreed to repay expenses of $10.5 million[2] paid to him or to his offshore company

1. See chart on page 330

2. All references to dollars in this chapter are to US dollars unless otherwise stated.

Nadal Management. In addition Nadal was required to refund amounts paid on account of incentive bonuses between 2012 and 2015 that totalled $10.6 million. "Mr Nadal is not eligible for any compensation payments or severance", the company added just in case there might be any doubt.

Nadal's departure may not prove to be the final chapter in a saga of questionable financial practices, trading losses and misleading announcements, but it is certainly an important one.

From his behaviour it is hard not to believe that Nadal regarded MDC as his own property. For example, *Marketing Services Financial Intelligence* reported in November 2007 that, despite its loss-making history and heavy level of debt, MDC had approved a payment of $3.5 million that enabled Nadal to refund an amount of $2.7 million previously loaned to his management company and written off as "irrecoverable". Later, in 2012-3, shareholders were expressing concern about further loans made to Nadal by the company and these were repaid.

A long time before that, in January 2005, *Marketing Services Financial Intelligence* was drawing attention to MDC's accounting eccentricities: "MDC Partners has been forced to take a more prudent view of how it recognises income from various financial transactions following a review of its accounting policies by its new auditors KPMG", the report said, explaining that the accounting changes had knocked $6.7 million off profits previously reported for the nine months to 30 September 2003, a period that originally had relied on gains of $47.5 million from asset disposals to turn an operating loss into a post-tax profit of $20 million.

The timing of the recognition of revenue and profit from various financial transactions was among a total of eight accounting policies that were corrected as a result of the KPMG review.

At the same time as rewriting its accounts to 30 September 2003, MDC reported its results for the nine months to 30 September 2004 in which a potential loss of $8 million was offset by a net gain of $14.9 million from the sale of MDC's residual 20% stake in Custom Direct. It would not be unreasonable to question the role of the company's financial officers in relation to accounting shortcomings, and changes have been made. But as time has passed it has also become clear that Nadal's personal influence permeated every corner of MDC and beyond.

Nadal could always look on the bright side. Entrepreneurs seeking a buyer, along with bankers, investment analysts and journalists, all seem to have fallen under his spell, accepting his ever-optimistic pronouncements. Indeed, Nadal created a new language for describing the company's recurring losses.

In 2009 MDC declared "strong results" for the nine months to 30 September, namely a profit of $36,000. "We are thrilled with our best in class financial performance in the third quarter", Nadal said. In July 2010 MDC was "very pleased" with a $16 million half year loss. By October 2010 MDC's "unique" model was...another loss. A rare and modest profit was reported for the final quarter of 2010 and by April 2011 an overenthusiastic Nadal was trumpeting MDC's "terrific" start to 2011 with more losses and more debt.

In May 2012 Nadal called another massive $26 million loss "solid results". In July 2012 he claimed the company had "performed well" with a $46 million loss. In November 2012 MDC was "very pleased" with another quarter's loss.

By February 2013 Nadal was celebrating "a record year" by losing $85.4 million. And so the trend continued, punctuated only occasionally by a modest profit, until losses of $492 million had accumulated by 30 June 2015.

Was it Nadal's personality or his lifestyle, or both, that won such unwavering support for such a wavering balance sheet year after year? He remains an enigma.

Nadal had a lavish expense account with the company along with trappings of wealth and power that included an executive jet. Laudatory personal profiles appeared in magazines like *Lifestyle* and *Canadian Business.* And his well-publicised philanthropy towards the Jewish Community Centre in Toronto may also have enhanced his credentials. Why didn't anyone realise that Nadal's favourable image was being financed indirectly by the company's clients and bankers?

By 30 June 2015, the company was reliant on a mixture of net borrowings of $707 million, prepaid billings to clients of $157 million and deferred acquisition obligations of $221 million. Past losses had already wiped out shareholders' funds. On

From Marketing Services Financial Intelligence: November 2007

MDC's bigger CPB stake adds to debt burden

Continued from page 61-1: conversion rights as the terms are based on a share value of Can$14.07 whereas its current share price is wallowing at Can$9.20.

Despite its loss-making history and heavy level of debt, MDC has approved a new deal with its chief executive Miles Nadal. The deal included what can only be described as a "golden hello again" payment of $3.5 million that enabled him to repay an amount of $2.7 million previously loaned to his management company and written off as irrecoverable.

Nadal's annual package now starts with a basic salary of $950,000 plus bonus of up to 250% of basic salary plus an annual $500,000 to cover pension and health arrangements.

top of that the group was potentially liable to pay out another $148 million if minority shareholders in subsidiary companies decided to exercise their right to require MDC to buy their shares.

It wasn't as if Nadal was poorly paid. His remuneration in 2014 alone totalled $16.8 million, of which $11.7 million was in bonuses and $2.3 million was in stock awards. How the chief executive of a loss-making company could qualify for such large bonuses and stock awards defies comprehension.

The remuneration package also included $0.5 million as a fixed expense allowance and a benefit of $91,038 from the personal use of a company aircraft. That benefit included use by members of Nadal's family which in future he would reimburse. Surprisingly, the company also paid costs of $263,000 incurred in selling a proportion of Nadal's shareholding in MDC last year.

No wonder the company has asked for $21 million to be repaid in respect of expenses and bonus advances received during the last six years.

Aside from the refunds agreed with Nadal, the SEC enquiry prompted MDC to implement a series of "remedial steps to improve and strengthen the company's internal controls and procedures regarding travel, entertainment and related expenses".

Those remedial steps included the adoption of new policies for private aircraft usage, travel and entertainment, the hiring of a senior vice president responsible for internal controls and compliance and the hiring of a director of compliance and risk management, both reporting to the audit committee. There would also be quarterly reviews of how well the company's executive officers were complying with travel and expense reimbursement policies.

In June 2015 MDC announced that it was replacing the chairmen of its compensation committee and audit committee, and removing any management directors from the board... apart from its influential chairman and chief executive Miles Nadal.

How did MDC — this maverick marketing monolith, this formulation of froth — come about?

Nadal's entry into entrepreneurship is reported to have taken the form of a photographic business he started in 1980. From this he created Multi Discipline Communications by investing in direct marketing, communications and printing businesses. The printing activities focussed on security products like cheques, postage stamps, boarding passes, lottery and sports tickets.

In 1986 Nadal was able to merge his business with that of a publicly-listed mining company Branbury Exploration, renaming the merged company MDC Corporation.

The next decade was spent borrowing and buying. By 1996, MDC's net borrowings had grown from almost nothing to $142 million, almost double the funds provided by shareholders. And much of that money had been spent on expanding the security printing division. That division provided the lion's share of profit in 1996 — $8.6 million out of a total $12.3 million, but that was before charging interest of $6.4 million on MDC's burgeoning borrowings.

In 1998 Nadal decided to rebrand the communications division as Maxxcom and to spend increasing amounts on expanding that part of the group. Many of the target companies – like Source Marketing – were located in the United States rather than Canada. MDC also acquired the US-based personalised cheque and greeting card printer Artistic Greetings.

By the end of 1998 MDC's borrowings had escalated to $268 million - almost double the level recorded at the end of 1996. Total assets employed in the security printing division had tripled in that period while those in the marketing division were about to explode also. The profit earned in 1998 represented a pre-tax, pre-interest return of 11.2% on the average funds employed during that year – not a great reward relative to the risks involved, bearing in mind that MDC's borrowing costs were ranging between 6% and 12.4% at the time. The return on shareholders' funds was 6.7%.

As the decade drew to a close and MDC continued its acquisition spree, it became clear that its debt mountain was not sustainable.

In 1999 alone the company had acquired an 80% stake in the Minneapolis marketing agency Colle & McVoy, 50.1% of call centre operator Accent Marketing Services and 70% of the Atlanta agency Fletcher Martin Associates, plus top-up investments in other part-owned subsidiaries. It

also bought the advertising agency Allard-Associates in Canada and merged it into what is now Allard Johnson Communications.

But the economy was cooling down and it was time to focus on reducing MDC's borrowings. Attempts were made to sell the Regal Cards & Gifts business although it took longer than anticipated. At the same time Nadal was preparing to sell a minority shareholding in the entire Maxxcom marketing division by means of an initial public offering planned for 2000.

Even after a number of disposals and the sale of part of Maxxcom in 2000, the group's net borrowings remained in excess of $340 million. And while the group declared a profit of $21.7 million, this was only after including a $50.3 million gain realised from the business disposals and the public issue of Maxxcom shares. Whichever way one looks at it, without the asset disposals MDC would have traded at a loss in 2000 and would have been nursing an even bigger pile of debt at the end of that year.

Matters got worse in 2001. The group lost $99.2 million after incurring an assortment of exceptional charges totalling no less than $295 million. The secure printing division alone lost $86 million, thereby placing a big question-mark over Nadal's earlier enthusiasm for investing in this sector.

Some $40 million of the year's loss arose when the group at last succeeded in selling its Regal Greetings & Gift business. There were also write-downs of $67 million in the value of goodwill attributed to other subsidiaries.

The group amended its less than prudent practice of deferring "customer acquisition costs" arising in the pursuit of sales of direct-to-consumer cheque printing, and made further provisions for asset write-downs, redundancies and onerous lease obligations.

The pressure was on to realise more cash and, if possible, to find some exceptional gains against which to offset the exceptional losses.

Some relief was found in the disposal of the Canadian cheque printer Davis & Henderson, although the sale proceeds were spread over two years. There was another benefit too: MDC was able to apply the $62 million gain on disposal of the first tranche to reduce the year's overall loss.

While MDC's priority was to reduce its borrowings in a fairly unfavourable economic climate, Nadal remained eager to expand its Maxxcom subsidiary. In January 2001 Maxxcom acquired 49% of the award winning advertising agency Crispin Porter & Bogusky based in

Miami, Florida, reflecting a relatively uncommon investment strategy that had two great attractions.

Firstly, and to MDC's credit it maintained a beneficial sense of co-ownership between the agency's leadership team and its buyer for several years ahead – in contrast to the more conventional agency takeover which gave 100% ownership at the outset albeit with prospect of further deferred purchase payments based on future performance.

"What distinguishes Maxxcom from its competitors in the marketing communications industry is Perpetual PartnershipTM", MDC explained. "Maxxcom acquires between 51% and 80% of highly successful companies led by entrepreneurs who are committed to continuing to grow their businesses. Maxxcom then provides the resources – business and strategic planning services, human resource management, merger and acquisition advisory services, and capital – that these companies need to accelerate their growth rate."

The second benefit to Maxxcom was that the deal structure reduced

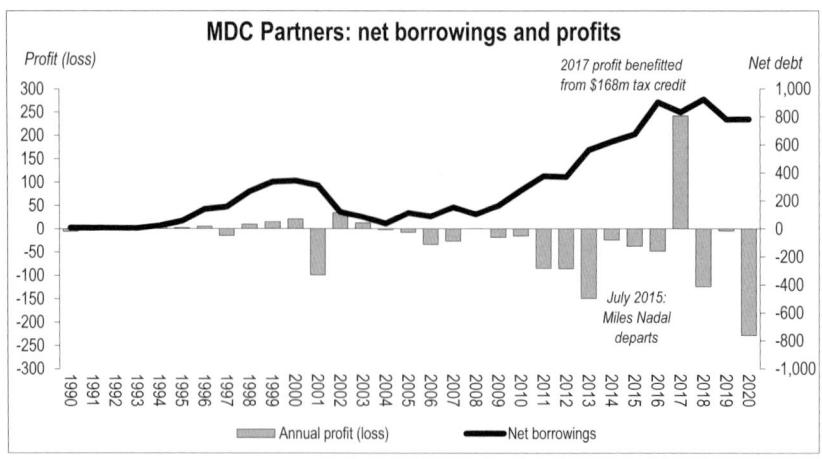

MDC Partners: net borrowings and profits

Profit (loss) / Net debt

2017 profit benefitted from $168m tax credit

July 2015: Miles Nadal departs

Annual profit (loss) — Net borrowings

its initial cash outlay, although the initial acquisition of shares would normally be accompanied by an option for either party to increase the MDC shareholding by several instalments until it reached 100% at a later date. By December 2005, there were minority shareholdings in 18 out of 26 subsidiaries. But the partial acquisition formula had disadvantages too: for as long as the previous shareholders retained a stake in their company, they would be reluctant to grant MDC or Maxxcom the right to pledge the company's assets as security for group borrowings.

Meanwhile MDC's efforts to reduce those borrowings continued into 2002 with further asset realisations. Five companies were sold along with the balance of Davis & Henderson, bringing in much needed cash of $187 million, plus an equally useful $106 million gain from the disposals to help the group return to profit. In 2003 $128 million gross was received from the sale of 80% of cheque supplier Custom Direct. Out of the proceeds MDC was able to redeem loan notes of $86.4 million.

But despite the welcome reduction in debt and finance costs, the profit would not last.

In 2003 MDC bought back the public shareholding in Maxxcom by means of a share exchange: "MDC's future lies with marketing services", Nadal proclaimed, marking the start of another 10 years investing in businesses that rarely offered any material financial return for MDC shareholders. There were several reasons.

First, a large slice of profits

earned by operating subsidiaries was soaked up very quickly by so-called "corporate costs" – typically around $20 million per annum. Apparently this related to group personnel like the chief financial officer and the chief executive officer, together with their office costs. A massive rise in corporate costs in 2013 included a $57.8 million cash pay-out to Nadal under the company's "stock appreciation" scheme plus an additional $9.6 million bonus because the stock price had hit specified targets.

Secondly, as acquisitions continued there was a resurgence in borrowings and a rise in interest rates that lead to increasing finance costs, reaching $100 million in 2013. Among acquisitions was a 60% stake in the US advertising agency Kirshenbaum Bond + Partners that involved a $20.7 million cash payment in 2004 and a 61% stake in the marketing strategy consultancy Zyman Group that required a cash outlay of $52 million in 2005.

Thirdly, the group's policy of leaving a sizeable minority shareholding with the former owners of subsidiaries acquired by MDC meant that, if those subsidiaries earned any profit, a large slice would be reserved for their minority shareholders and would not be available to shareholders in MDC. Conversely – and sometimes to MDC's advantage – a proportion of a subsidiary's losses could be excluded from the group's results.

Early in 2004 MDC acknowledged that its ability to repay its long-term debt was partially dependent upon cash flows from its subsidiaries and that, as a number of those subsidiaries were not wholly-owned, they were subject to agreements that contained "certain restrictions on the payment of dividends, distributions and advances". At 30 June 2004, $8 million was held by subsidiaries in cash that could not be distributed to Maxxcom (and therefore to MDC).

The extent to which cash – or lack of it – was becoming a serious concern was well illustrated by the announcement that MDC's bankers would bring forward the termination date for the current credit facility to September 2004 from March 2005 and release the company from its quarterly repayment that would have become due in June 2004.

"The company is actively seeking to refinance the amounts owing on 30 September 2004 under its bank credit facility", MDC said, adding that a prospective lender was undertaking "due diligence" research.

However, if a definitive credit agreement could not be secured in time the company would be faced with the need either to seek alternative sources of financing or an extension to the current credit facility or to reach an agreement with certain shareholders of subsidiaries to permit the advance of their cash balances to Maxxcom in order to meet or amend its obligation under its existing credit facilities. "There is no certainty that such events will occur", the announcement concluded gloomily.

Seven days before the existing bank facilities were due to end, MDC succeeded in negotiating replacement facilities of $100 million for a period of three years from a syndicate led by JP Morgan Chase Bank.

There was a price to pay. The majority shareholders in Crispin Porter Bogusky agreed to permit its assets to be pledged as security for the new bank facilities. In addition MDC implemented a cash management programme with the majority of its subsidiaries whereby it gained access to any surplus cash. These measures, coupled with MDC's existing entitlement to 49% of profits plus a further 8.5% of profits in excess of $4.2 million, meant that MDC had a controlling financial interest in Crispin Porter. That enabled MDC to consolidate the results of Crispin Porter into its group accounts for the first time.

However, while these negotiations were going on, the company had failed to file its quarterly financial statements with the Securities & Exchange Commission "on a timely basis", putting it in breach of its borrowing covenants. Among other consequences, the Nasdaq Stock Market commenced steps to suspend listing of MDC's shares.

In due course the breaches were waived as part of the new banking deal, but the cause of the filing delays soon became clear. MDC had appointed KPMG as new auditors at the start of 2004 and a wide range of contentious accounting issues had emerged as a result, necessitating the revision of earlier financial statements in a negative direction. MDC also told the SEC that it had identified "material weaknesses in its internal control over financial reporting".

Significant internal work and

analysis would be required to complete the annual financial report for
the year 2004 and other disclosures
within the prescribed period without
unreasonable effort and expense.

The SEC maintained an interest
in the financial statements filed by
MDC over the next decade – a period
in which MDC lost $444 million of
which $361 million was attributable
to the cost of its borrowings.

In October 2014 it emerged that
the SEC had been asking questions
about the presentation of MDC's
financial affairs in press releases and
regulatory filings. The questions
related to eight separate aspects of
MDC's financial reporting, ranging
from the use of the term "free cash
flow" to the measurement and presentation of deferred and contingent
acquisition payments.

MDC agreed not to use the
term "free cash flow" to describe
profit as adjusted by the company to
exclude interest, tax, depreciation,
amortisation and various other items
such as deal costs and losses from
discontinued activities.

"We note that this measure as
currently presented excludes line
items that are of an operating nature",
the SEC observed. "Accordingly, we
do not believe that it is appropriate
to refer to this measure as 'free cash
flows'." MDC also agreed to provide
a detailed definition and complete
reconciliation of this unofficial
measure to the post-tax profit measured in accordance with accounting
regulations.

In one sense the horse had bolted
before the stable door had been
closed. Three months before the

SEC's enquiries became public – and
immediately after one of only three
financial quarters in the preceding
five years that had yielded a profit
– Nadal had sold 40% of his MDC
shareholding for $81 million. That
valued the loss-making company at
about $1 billion.

As the SEC's enquiries continued,
the first signs of their extent emerged
when the company announced the
pending refund of $8.6 million
paid to or on behalf of the group's
chairman and chief executive Miles
Nadal or his company Nadal Management over a six year period.

The announcement was accompanied by news of a further $32 million
loss, the removal of chief accounting
officer Michael Sabatino into a new
role working on special projects, the
assumption of his responsibilities by
chief financial officer David Doft
(appointed after the accounting
"corrections" of 2007), and a 30%
slump in MDC's share price.

The company said that the SEC's
enquiries were still in progress and
included a review of how MDC had
been accounting for goodwill arising
from acquisitions. Inevitably US law
firms saw the opportunity to initiate
class actions against the company.

With the damaging SEC
enquiries continuing, MDC's board
decided it was time to blow the
whistle and on 20 July 2015 Nadal's
reign came to an end.

His valedictory remarks included
the words: "MDC Partners is an
exceptional organization." Certainly
MDC is exceptional, but not necessarily in the way that Nadal sought to
depict.

*M&C Saatchi shares ownership of each individual agency with its executives.
It was a factor contributing to the recent overstatement of the group's profits.*

28
Motivation at M&C Saatchi

We first came across the marketing group called M&C Saatchi in chapter 13. Having expanded into a multinational business that is listed on the Alternative Investment Market of the London stock exchange, like many other companies in the sector it has had to grapple with how best to motivate executives of businesses that it has acquired or started up.

This chapter tells of an innovative share ownership scheme devised by M&C Saatchi which genuinely sought to give executives at its operating subsidiaries a continuing sense of ownership, of how accounting rules eventually portrayed the scheme as a financial burden that in fact was entirely imaginary and how three major accountancy firms seemed to have different views about the most appropriate financial presentation.

During all the years that I have had dealings with "people businesses" — mainly in the creative industries — I have become acutely aware of two challenges that can arise when the time comes for ownership to pass from the founding generation.

First there is the difficulty of maintaining the agency's independence and retaining its key personnel while, at the same time, achieving a reasonably priced exit opportunity for the founders. As readers will already have deduced, it is not as simple as it sounds. Even the advent of private equity investors has often done no more than delay the inevitable sale to an established large global group.

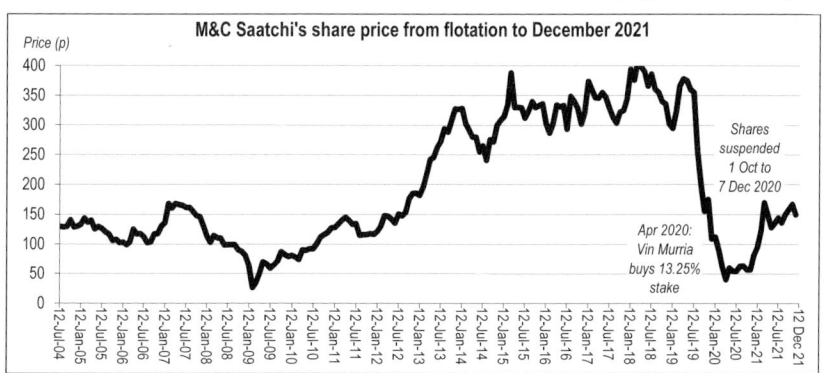

Secondly, if sold to an established group, the continuing management team can quickly become unsettled if their agency loses the sense of partnership that tends to evolve in a first generation employee-owned company — a cultural characteristic that is particularly prevalent among successful creative businesses. Senior employees may also become unsettled by having to report to another, remote and much larger organisation. Not surprisingly, many of the most ambitious among them soon develop a desire to seek another outlet for their talent.

Against that backcloth, I was intrigued by the innovative executive share participation scheme introduced at subsidiaries of M&C Saatchi – so much so that I asked to meet up with the company and explore the scheme in greater detail. The outcome, first published in *Marketing Services Financial Intelligence* in March 2016, forms the substance of this chapter.

By coincidence or otherwise the scheme was introduced at around the same time as the group announced that it had agreed to a management buy-in at its main UK subsidiary – London based M&C Saatchi (UK). That plan involved making about 30% of the subsidiary's shares available to five members of its management.

Three years later we were to learn that the group had been hit by a massive accounting controversy and that the focus of attention was on the London based agencies and central group services. PricewaterhouseCoopers (PwC) was engaged to conduct an investigation and warnings emerged of substantial downward adjustments to past profits. The Financial Reporting Council also initiated an investigation[1]. While the investigations continued, the group's audited results for 2019 remained outstanding. As a consequence, trading in the company's shares on the Alternative Investment Market (AIM) was suspended at a price of 57.4p on 1 October 2020[2].

My initial concern was about whether any of the accounting adjustments might have stemmed from attempts by participants in the share scheme to maximise the apparent performance of their subsidiaries, and thereby enhance the value of their shares before they were exchanged for shares in the parent company. To date the company has vigorously denied that any of the accounting adjustments arose from such activities and no specific evidence has emerged to suggest this was the case.

---

1. *On 21 January 2022, M&C Saatchi announced that The Financail Conduct Authority had closed its investigation of the company and that no enforcement action would be taken.*

2. *The suspension was lifted on 7 December 2020 when audited accounts were published.*

Nevertheless, the restatement of the group's accounts for the half year to 30 June 2018 showed that income was overstated and expenditure understated in that period. Consequently, if the accounting errors had not been discovered, one would have expected any valuation of shares in the companies affected by the restatement to have been overstated also. In response to my enquiries, the company said:

> "Those companies responsible for the adjustments were loss-making and, as such, there was and is no possibility of any individual within those companies benefitting whether via share options or bonus payments."

That statement misses the point. There can be no assumption that the affected companies would have continued to be loss-making or that any continuing overstatement of profits would not have had a favourable impact on any future share valuation to the benefit of the shareholders. Even if that were not the case, this question remains: were senior executives tempted to overstate results of some subsidiary companies with the aim of boosting their share rewards even if those efforts proved to have been in vain because losses in those subsidiaries continued?

Meanwhile another surprise was on its way. In December 2019 three non-executive directors "stepped down" from the board – Lord Dobbs (Conservative Party speech-writer, author and former adviser to Lady Thatcher), Sir Michael Peat (chartered accountant and former principal private secretary to the Prince of Wales and Duchess of Cornwall) and Lorna Tilbian (chairman of Dowgate Capital Stockbrokers). Co-founder Maurice (Lord) Saatchi resigned. By the end of 2020 all of the company's executive directors would have resigned apart from M&C Worldwide's chief executive officer Moray MacLennan who took on the role of group chief executive with effect from 1 January 2021.

Predictably, the December 2019 announcement had prompted the company's share price to plummet to its lowest level since January 2009, wallowing at about 10% of its peak value. Then, in April 2020, a parcel of 15,250,000 shares had been bought by Vinodka (Vin) Murria and family at an estimated cost of about £5.8 million. That cost was minuscule when compared with the £765 million that she and her fellow shareholders were reported to have received from the sale of Advanced Computer Software Group in 2015. No explanation was forthcoming as to why a troubled marketing group might have been of interest to a highly successful

Indian born and UK educated entrepreneur until 6 January 2022 when it was revealed that M&C Saatchi had received a "preliminary approach from AdvancedAdvT Limited, a vehicle connected with Vin Murria"[1].

Back in 2020, while investors were awaiting more information about the extent and cause of the prior years' accounting changes, M&C Saatchi had issued a reassuring statement about trading conditions and bank facilities. One welcome source of increasing income was identified as the group's relatively new World Services division led by Marcus Peffers who was previously chief operating officer at M&C Saatchi (UK).

M&C World Services' activities are described as "tackling some of humanity's most challenging and important problems, in fragile states and developing countries" with the aim of harnessing the "power of cutting-edge marketing, communications and creativity, so that they become key tenets of behaviour change activity throughout the International Development sector". Seemingly, much of its early income was prepaid which will have been helpful to cash flow. M&C Saatchi World Services reported a post-tax profit of £5.8 million for 2018 before allowing for any remuneration or profit share payable to the partners. According to filings with the Registrar of Companies, Peffers was the only individual partner in the business, alongside M&C Saatchi International, and may have been sharing in as much as 20% of the division's profits.

It was not until September 2020 that M&C Saatchi began to reveal the extent and nature of accounting failures, but even then the newly appointed auditors PwC were not expected to provide a clean bill of health when their work was eventually completed.

In a provisional announcement, the company said that it had incurred a loss attributable to M&C Saatchi shareholders of £11.8 million in 2019 and that its previously reported profit of £8.3 million in 2018 had been revised downwards to a loss of £14 million (later amended to £13 million). If the interests of minority shareholders in subsidiaries were to be included, the downward movement in its 2018 results became £23.9 million. When the audited accounts were published on 8 December 2020, they were accompanied by this statement from PwC:

---

1. . *When the stock market opened on 6 January 2022, shares in M&C Saatchi were trading at 197.50p compared with 35.70p before Vin Murria made her initial purchase in April 2020. The January 2022 approach was met by a counter bid from Next Fifteen Communications Group but both offers failed to gain sufficient support and lapsed in October 2022.*

Because of the significance of the possible impact of our inability to obtain sufficient appropriate audit evidence over the opening balances, as described in the "Basis for disclaimer of opinion/qualified opinion" section below, we have not been able to obtain sufficient appropriate audit evidence to provide a basis for an audit opinion on the Group's loss and cash flows. Accordingly, we do not express an opinion on the Group's loss and cash flows for the year ended 31 December 2019.

The company confirmed that previous years' accounts had overstated income and understated costs. It also reported a 5% fall in revenue in the Americas, with post-tax profits there down from £3.1 million to £1.3 million, due principally to losses at the Los Angeles agency that has since been closed. But it was not just revenue that was in short supply. So too was adequate financial information, as the company has now admitted:

There was substantial turnover of finance staff based in such subsidiary which resulted in poor record keeping and a lack of financial information for 2019. The group finance team has adequate information to confirm the 2019 closing balance sheet for the Los Angeles subsidiary, including revenue cut-off between 2019 and 2020, but is unable to confirm the opening balance sheet for 2019 given the lack of financial records.

Nevertheless, the net effect of financial misstatements arising from poor book-keeping was relatively modest. By far the biggest cause of the restated results was the revised treatment of put options granted to executives of subsidiaries under the various share schemes. Under those schemes, employees in operating companies had an option (a "put option") to exchange their shares for shares in the publicly listed parent after five years and the group had the right to buy in the employees' shares at any time after eight years.

How M&C Saatchi's accounts were transformed

Year ended 31 December	2019 Audited £'000	2018 Restated £'000	2018 Reported £'000
Billings	561,426	603,652	609,610
Cost of sales	-304,991	-353,348	-354,237
Revenue (gross income)	256,435	250,304	255,373
Amortisation of intangible assets	-2,865	-4,730	-4,427
Impairment of tangible and intangible assets	-11,084	-4,167	-2,869
Gain on revaluing Saatchinvest start-ups	-	1,584	1,584
Other operating costs	-242,134	-227,187	-225,453
Operating profit (loss) before deferred acquisition payments and put option costs	352	15,804	24,208
Cost or revaluation of deferred consideration and put options	-16,449	-19,144	-7,440
Notional finance costs on above	-3,100	-3,344	-911
Operating profit (loss) after deferred acquisition payments, put option costs and related finance charges	-19,197	-6,684	15,857
Other finance income (costs)	-2,520	-855	-1,084
Share of associates/JV results and gain on disposal	13,210	2,151	2,825
Taxation	-3,256	-7,587	-6,635
Minority interests	-33	-121	-2,708
Profit (loss) after tax	-11,796	-13,096	8,255

As we shall see, the revised accounting treatment of the put options exposed a confusing mixture of interpretations of the rules over several years by several major firms of accountants acting as advisers or auditors. In essence the issue revolved around whether in each case the shares under option had been acquired simply as an investment or as a component of an employee's remuneration.

Most such share schemes are governed by a collection of accounting rules known as international financial reporting standards (IFRS) 2, 3 and 9. M&C Saatchi now takes the view that the wrong accounting treatment was applied to some of the shares that were subject to put options, being shares in subsidiaries that were retained by employees at the time of acquisition. There was also an incorrect interpretation of the accounting treatment applicable to some other shares subject to put options.

The changes in accounting treatment dented the previously reported results for 2018 by £15 million — £13 million now shown as extra staff costs and £2 million in finance charges — albeit none of those costs involved any cash outflow. The change also added £10.6 million to the loss incurred in 2019.

The accountancy firm **BDO** is understood to have been involved initially in advising the company on the share participation arrangements and their accounting presentation. BDO had also been providing an internal audit function at M&C Saatchi since 2014. In 2018 the company's accounts were audited by **KPMG** and given a clean opinion, implying that the firm was happy with the treatment of put options that year. The subsequently restated results for 2018 were audited by PwC. On completing the 2019 audit its was agreed that PwC would not seek re-election for the

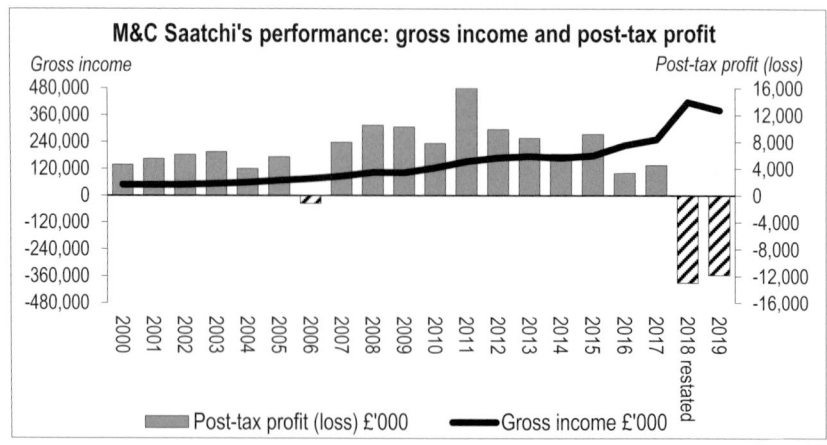

M&C Saatchi's performance: gross income and post-tax profit

ensuing year and BDO was appointed in its place.

While acknowledging that the primary responsibility for the accuracy of accounts rests with a company's directors, it is rare for two different accounting treatments to be acceptable to different auditors and KPMG may have some explaining to do. This is not the first occasion in the history of accounting when major reputable firms of accountants have come to different judgements.

At M&C Saatchi there were three principal circumstances in which put options were granted, two of which are particularly relevant here.

First, they arose on the acquisition of subsidiaries when some of the shares were retained by the vendors. An option was granted over those shares that enabled the holder to sell them after a specified period at a value that would have reflected any improvement in financial performance during that period

Secondly, put options were granted over new shares in other subsidiary companies that had been issued to managers with the aim of injecting new momentum into the business. Those shares would have been issued for cash at their fair value under the share ownership scheme that is described at some length later in this chapter.

In both of the above scenarios, the exercise of the put options by the minority shareholders would usually result in their shares being exchanged for shares in the parent company with an equivalent value, thereby creating a ready market for their subsequent conversion into cash.

The accounting presentation prescribed for any benefit derived from minority shareholdings retained by employees after their company has been sold depends on whether the consideration payable on disposal of that shareholding represents a "transaction that remunerates employees or former owners of the acquiree for future services"[1]. If so, the cost would be charged as employee remuneration and would not be associated with the sale of the shares. Whether or not the consequent dent in reported profits would have been eligible for corporation tax relief remains unclear and is likely to have been influenced by how the payment was to be treated for tax purposes in the hands of the recipient.

Guidance[2] provided by the International Accounting Standards Board (IASB) on the accounting presentation suggests that the net proceeds derived from a minority shareholding might be most

1. *See International Financial Reporting Standard (IFRS) 3, paragraph 52(b)*
2. *For the full text see IFRS 3, guidance paragraph B55, of which this is only a summary*

appropriately treated as remuneration if, among other things:

(a) it results from an arrangement in which the consideration for the shares will be forfeited if employment terminates;

(b) the option holder is committed to remaining in the company's employment at least until the expiry of the option exercise period;

(c) the core remuneration is materially lower than that enjoyed by comparable key employees in the company[1];

(d) other selling shareholders who do not continue their employment with the company are entitled to a lesser payment per share for their minority shareholdings than those who continue in employment;

(e) the formula for calculating the consideration for the minority shareholdings is based on a specified percentage of profits (similar to a bonus) rather than a multiple of earnings;

In a subsequent interpretation, issued in January 2013, the IASB said that example (a) above meant that "an arrangement in which contingent payments are automatically forfeited if employment terminates would lead to a conclusion that the arrangement is compensation for post-combination services rather than additional consideration for an acquisition, unless the service condition is not substantive".

The circumstances itemised under paragraphs (a) to (e) above in which payments to acquire a residual minority shareholding are to be treated as remuneration apply equally to deferred payments made under an acquisition agreement that provides for all of the target company shares to be acquired at the outset but for some of the purchase price to be paid later and geared to future financial performance (i.e., an "earn-out" arrangement).[2]

M&C Saatchi's preliminary accounts for 2019 stated that "the *put option* is dependent upon the holder's continued employment by the group". If that note were to be interpreted literally, it would mean that after departure the employee would cease to have the right to sell the shares on the terms contained in the option but instead would remain a shareholder (in effect, on similar terms to any other outside shareholder) unless an individual arrangement could be entered into. However, the evidence suggests that, notwithstanding the wording of the note in the 2019 preliminary accounts, employees who had held shares in some of the operating companies that were subject to a put option after five years were *compelled* to

---

1. *Arguably the test should go further and establish that the core remuneration is not materially lower than that enjoyed by persons performing a comparable role in a similar business.*

2. *See IFRS3 "Business Combinations", paragraphs 55(a)-55(h)*

dispose of those shares if they decided to leave the company in the meantime. This was not an "option" at all, but instead a contractual obligation to sell. In the opinion of KPMG that obligation was sufficient to require the benefits derived from such shares to be treated as remuneration rather than a return on the employee's investment.

Nevertheless, to add to the confusion, M&C Saatchi now says that some of the put options granted over minority shareholdings in acquired subsidiaries should not have been treated as remuneration but instead should have been treated as deferred payments for shares held at the time of acquisition. It all depended on the nature of the agreement in each specific case.

M&C Saatchi has also decided that any financial benefit derived from put options exercised over minority shareholdings acquired under the share scheme introduced for executives of operating subsidiaries should be treated as remuneration on the basis that those options were "dependent on the holders' continued employment".

Originally it was judged that those shares were purchased by employees as an investment on arm's length terms similar to those that would have applied to any outside investor. No additional services were provided by the employees beyond those rewarded at market rates by their core remuneration. No evidence has been provided to suggest the shares were obtained at a concessionary price. The purchase of the shares may have been funded by loans, as was the case at an Australian subsidiary, but otherwise there is no indication that the company had provided a benefit to those employee shareholders. And, if the shares were to be deemed to be remuneration, would HM Custom & Revenue allow any loss in value to be offset against other taxable income as one might expect?

The fundamental matter of principle underlying the accounting presentation of the shares that were subject to the put options is this: were those shares really offered to employees as an additional form of reward for services rendered or were they offered in order to create or maintain a sense of co-ownership – with all the risks and rewards that go with it and on which the culture of such creative businesses tends to rely?

On the understanding that, in most cases, the shares were issued for a material financial consideration there seems little doubt that their purpose was to extend a sense of genuine ownership among the most important members of those creative businesses. They were not conceived, for example, as a means of providing a tax efficient form of profit-sharing, even if share ownership can offer favourable tax outcomes when compared with normal earnings.

Even the obligation to offer back the shares on ceasing to be employed is not in itself a convincing justification for treating the shares as quasi remuneration. In my experience many marketing agencies have made it a condition of shareholding (whether by founders or subsequent arrivals) that the shares should be offered for sale back to other employees (or to the company) on departure. The reason is not because the shares are intended to provide some form of remuneration for employment, but because privately owned creative businesses seek to maintain their independence and culture by retaining control of ownership among those engaged in the business. The ability to control ownership is a fundamental characteristic of a private company. The obligation to surrender the shares does not change their nature as an investment with attendant risks throughout their ownership – risks that would never apply to conventional rewards from employment.

Furthermore, in the absence of a potential pathway to exit, why would anyone with any sense – employee or otherwise - spend their own cash to acquire a minority shareholding in a private company?

What we are witnessing is the influence of the academic wing of the accountancy profession, seeking to make rules that are far removed from reality. While acknowledging that accounts need to reflect the substance of financial transactions rather than simply their legal form, the boffins at the International Accounting Standards Board have taken that principle one step further.

Now they are adopting a concept that I call "as if" accounting[1] – a concept that reflects neither substance nor form, but simply hypothetical scenarios, to arrive at a presentation of their own liking.

As a result M&C Saatchi has now been obliged to present an arrangement that was introduced for entirely laudable business purposes as if it was something else: as if the benefits (or otherwise) of

---

1. *The concept, of "as if" accounting gained unwitting support in the nineteen seventies when a coalition of Government, public utilities, academics and accountants combined to develop "Current Cost Accounting" during a period of high inflation that put pressure on businesses to retain more of their profits so as to ensure they had an adequate capital base. Put over-simply, this aim was to be achieved by calculating profits "as if" all purchases had been transacted at prices prevailing at the reporting date rather than at the date of the actual transactions. The difference between the reported profit and the actual profit was set aside as an additional reserve. By adopting this accounting method, it was also hoped to avoid criticism of higher prices that flowed through to higher profits under the historic accounting concept, while at the same time minimising pressure from shareholders for bigger dividends. The initiative survived for only two years as inflation waned and corporation tax remained wedded to the historic accounting concept.*

share ownership by persons who happen to be employees were in substance a method of remuneration for their services as employees. That may have offered a tax benefit to the company as HM Revenue & Customs' approach tends to follow the accounting rules in the absence of any other over-riding regulations.

The IASB's love affair with "as if" accounting does not end there. At M&C Saatchi and many other companies it also ventures into the balance sheet presentation of acquisitions that leave some of the vendors with a residual minority shareholding that is subject to put and call options exercisable on separate future dates. Depending on the circumstances, the rule-makers may require the acquisition of the subsidiary to be treated as a single purchase of 100% of the target company — as if the put option was nothing more than a deferred component of the total acquisition price (and some have argued that this is indeed the substance of the transaction). As a result the put option is shown as a committed liability in the balance sheet from the outset,

The accounting treatment prescribed for such minority interests involves estimating what the future exchange value of the shares will be when the put option is exercised and adding that to the initial outlay. As this transaction will occur some years later than the creation of the option, part of the exchange value will be treated as a payment for that extended credit and charged as a finance cost over the life of the put option, leaving the balance to be recorded either as employment costs spread over that period or as an additional cost of the acquisition, depending on how the arrangement has been interpreted under IFRS rules.

However, the estimated exchange value applicable to the put option will vary as the years pass and the actual financial performance of the subsidiary has an impact upon it. Any such change in the estimate of the eventual exchange value will also be shown as a finance charge in the profit and loss account.

There is an alternative argument that such options reflect nothing more than *intentions* and there is no certainty that they will be exercised (even though in most, but not all, circumstances, they are). Meanwhile the substance of the minority shareholder's continuing ownership interest remains unchanged - often demonstrated by an undertaking by the new majority owner not to pledge assets of the company to secure borrowings to the wider acquiring group. This safeguard would be unnecessary if 100% ownership had already passed as would be the case with a conventional earn-out arrangement. Further evidence that the minority shareholders retain legal ownership in substance as well as form, that the put and call options have a commercial purpose and that their exercise represents a discrete transaction, can be found in these characteristics:

1. The options allow minority shareholders in a private company to have the certainty of a future exit opportunity if they wish to exercise it, thereby avoiding the devaluation that otherwise would almost inevitably affect those shares.

2. The options allow the majority holder(s) to know that they can deliver 100% ownership of the company on a future sale without being held to ransom by a minority shareholder.

On that basis it would be premature to treat the minority shareholdings as having been acquired until the options have been exercised. In the meantime such potential obligations would be reported in a note among other "contingent liabilities", as indeed was the situation before the IASB intervened.

The massive charges relating to put options that have been included in M&C Saatchi's profit and loss account bear no relationship to any cash expended, but simply arise from book-keeping transfers between the profit and loss account and other categories of shareholders' funds — transfers that seemingly are intended to show the "cost" of some notional economic benefit provided to the company by reason of those employees' shareholdings, despite the fact that over time the only financial consequences would be an increase in share capital and a corresponding reduction in retained profits appearing on the balance sheet. So, overall, shareholders' funds would remain unchanged.

Self-evidently, the accounting treatment of certain types of share scheme is both complicated and contentious. At M&C Saatchi the outcome was a bizarre accounting presentation that bears no resemblance to the underlying facts or the financial consequences of the arrangement. Worse still, it undermines a much-needed means of enabling young entrepreneurs to share ownership of the businesses they manage.

This is how M&C Saatchi's share scheme evolved...

Emblazoned across an early page of M&C Saatchi's website is a statement (opposite) that could easily be dismissed as a gimmicky attempt to distinguish the M&C Saatchi agency from others. But there is justification. At M&C Saatchi, the publicly-listed parent company shares the ownership of each individual agency with its executives, whereas at other marketing groups the most that is normally offered to the senior exec-

"If you own something, you care more: our managers have equity in their business"

utives of individual agencies is the opportunity to share ownership in the group with other group shareholders.

So it should have come as no surprise to learn a few weeks ago that senior executives at M&C Saatchi's London agency were to acquire personal shareholdings in that business.

Of course the case for employee share ownership can be argued either way. Most groups justify taking and keeping 100% ownership of all their businesses on two grounds: first, that by offering options or other stakes in the parent company, the executives in subsidiary companies are better motivated to collaborate with partner agencies in the group, rather than operate within their own silos. Secondly, it has been claimed that the parent company owes it to its shareholders to acquire the maximum slice of profit earned by each subsidiary.

Various fudges have been experimented with, such as issuing share options in the parent company the number of which are calculated by reference to the performance of the individual subsidiary.

Others have tried phantom share options – a concept that is little more than a profit sharing scheme wrapped up as something else. And there lies the rub: what, if anything, is to be gained by handing out real shares in the subsidiary, rather than some other form of financial inducement?

Finance director Jamie Hewitt[1] is in no doubt about the merits of the M&C Saatchi model: "To us, it's integral to what we do. I think it was a reaction to old Saatchi (the Saatchi & Saatchi agency from which M&C Saatchi's management is derived) where it was buy and build, acquisitions, earn out and debt. We wanted to do the exact opposite, which was avoid debt and to get the organic route working properly. It was important to have the managers of the individual operating entities owning equity. We've done it geographically

1. On 21 Septemeber 2018 it was announced that Jamie Hewitt had decided to leave the company. He left on 31 March 2019 and was succeeded by Mickey Kalifa who in turn resigned in January 2022.
2. David Kershaw left the company at the end of 2020.

Former chief executive David Kershaw[2]: negotiated with UK managers

Former finance director Jamie Hewitt: very happy with share ownership model

in terms of our expansion and we've done it in terms of diversification."

So M&C Saatchi's recent decision to share the ownership of the London agency with its senior executives is simply a continuation of a policy that was well entrenched when the company first came to the stock market in June 2004 (see chapter 13). And, as we shall see, executive share ownership brings with it an obligation to ensure there is adequate succession planning.

The M&C Saatchi model adds weight to the argument that share ownership builds commitment to the business that enhances value not just for the shareholding executives but for shareholders in the group as a whole.

It is too early to conclude whether acquisitive "people businesses" in the marketing sector have collectively woken up to the benefits of leaving partial ownership with the managers of acquired companies or, as at M&C Saatchi, are ready to offer share ownership to executives of subsidiaries after their acquisition. But it may prove significant that WPP left 20% of Essence Digital Group's shares with the management when it was acquired in November 2015 unless this was simply an alternative form of "earn-out" arrangement.

So why is the practice not more widespread? There are a number of reasons, some of which are attributable to nothing more than short-termism among investors and short-sighted greed among the parties. It has not been unusual to hear acquisitive public companies explain that their shareholders want to maximise the immediate return on their investment – as if buying 100%

will produce a bigger rate of return on their investment than buying 80%.

What those companies probably mean is that they want to grow their businesses in absolute terms as quickly as possible (perhaps to feed egos more than for any other reason) and reckon they can motivate the executives of acquired companies in other ways – hence the proliferation of parent company share ownership (and "phantom share") schemes geared to the performance of the individual subsidiaries.

But such schemes do not reinforce positive ownership behaviours at the subsidiary level. Instead they encourage participating executives to pursue performance targets imposed from above that are potentially at the expense of the long-term health of the particular business they manage.

There can also be more plausible technical difficulties in offering share ownership at the subsidiary level, especially to executives who have not held shares in the company previously. If not structured carefully, share ownership can give rise to adverse tax charges on participants — particularly if shares are issued below the market price because the prospective buyers cannot afford to pay more.

However, such risks have sometimes been avoided by "freezing" the value of the company at the point of participation, allocating it to existing shareholders, and issuing new shares to incomers at a nominal price on the basis that they only participate in the future value growth alongside the existing shareholders.

Essence Digital Group provides a recent example of this type of arrangement where a class of share entitles its holders to participate only in the company's value growth in excess of a specified amount – in that case £44 million. When **WPP** acquired the group, it not only left 20% of the shares with executives but updated the value growth threshold to £100 million.

At **M&C** Saatchi, there is a well-developed framework for the sharing of ownership with executives that the company believes avoids tax pitfalls and makes share ownership affordable. For established businesses that **M&C** Saatchi acquires it encourages the management to keep or acquire at least 20% of its shares, emphasising the tax benefit of holding at least 5% so as to qualify for lower capital gains tax rates under the Entrepreneurs' Relief rules when the time comes to sell:

"Initially it was an 80/20 model", explains Hewitt, "but where the executives excel they can get up to 30% or 40%. We'd like them to own these larger shareholdings because we think we get better growth and 60% of that business is much better for us. We're very happy with the model and we believe that, where we have less majority ownership, the better the growth we'll get."

A similar principle is applied to start-ups and new branches. According to Hewitt many start-ups were brought to them by people who had previously worked for one of the big global marketing groups: "They want to do something entrepreneurial, but they don't want to risk everything – they're sort of middle-aged, in their 40s, probably with a couple of kids at school. They want to be associated with a good name.They want someone to provide the working capital."

Participants acquire shares at their fair value at the time of purchase with a loan arranged by the company, but at the borrower's risk, that is repayable with interest out of future sale proceeds. "The borrowers are therefore fully at risk, which gives

How M&C Saatchi shares ownership in its businesses

Subsidiary	Primary location	Management shareholding
M&C Saatchi (UK)	London	In negotiation
M&C Saatchi LA	Los Angeles	6.0%
M&C Saatchi Marketing Arts	London	50.0%
M&C Saatchi (M) SDN BHD	Malaysia	20.0%
M&C Saatchi Sports & Entertainment Ltd	London	2.8%
Influence Communications Ltd	London	5.0%
M&C Saatchi Europe Holdings Ltd		4.0%
M&C Saatchi German Holdings Ltd		4.0%
M&C Saatchi Communications Pty Ltd	Australia	13.0%
M&C Saatchi Berlin GmbH	Germany	20.0%
Talk PR Audience Ltd	London	17.0%
FCINQ SAS	France	15.0%
Clear Ideas Consulting LLP	UK	12.5%
M&C Saatchi PR LLP (US)	US	35.0%
M&C Saatchi Mobile Ltd	London	10.0%
M&C Saatchi Sport & Entertainment Pty Ltd	Australia	49.0%
Talk PR Ltd	London	49.0%
M&C Saatchi UK PR LLP	UK	35.0%
M&C Saatchi Corporate SAS	France	29.8%
M&C Saatchi (Switzerland) SA	Switzerland	40.0%
Samuelson Talbot and Partners Pty Ltd	Australia	40.0%
M&C Saatchi Merlin Ltd	UK	45.0%
The Source (London) Ltd	UK	30.0%
Direct One SAS	France	20.0%
M&C Saatchi Brazil Cominicação Ltda	Brazil	40.0%
Lean Mean Fighting Machine Ltd	UK	39.9%

them a keen focus", Hewitt observes.

The shares can be sold at the holder's option at any time after five years from purchase. The company has the option to buy in the shares after a period of eight years, although that has proved to be an elastic deadline. If the employee leaves in the meantime, the shares have to be offered back immediately. Shares offered for sale by an employee of an M&C Saatchi subsidiary are exchanged for shares in the parent company, using a predetermined formula, and then those shares can be sold on the stock market.

The sale of an individual parcel of shares by an employee of a private company may be more difficult without the ready market for an executive's shares that a public company like M&C Saatchi is able to provide. Indeed the shareholding executive might have to resign to trigger a sale — hardly consistent with a scheme designed to maximise loyalty — or wait for the company itself to be sold.

However, it is sometimes possible for the company to lend money to an employee benefit trust that will then buy in the executive's shares.

Writtle Holdings is an example of a privately-owned company that has a similar philosophy to M&C Saatchi and has been contemplating how to offer a "buy back" facility to employee shareholders in the absence of an ability to exchange shares in a subsidiary for shares in a public company...yet (see Writtle in surprising slowdown). It may be a great idea for M&C Saatchi to have made it easy for shareholders in subsidiaries to realise their investments within the allotted time period, but will such benevolence encourage shareholders to cash in their shares and move on?

That is not always as easy as it may seem. While M&C Saatchi acknowledges the right of even the most important executives to be able to sell their shares and leave, the company expects adequate management succession to be in place before that time arrives.

"The exit mechanism is always subject to succession criteria". Hewitt explains. "If management are leaving, then they have to replace that management to our satisfaction. They have to have handed over, we would say, 75% of relationships by value.

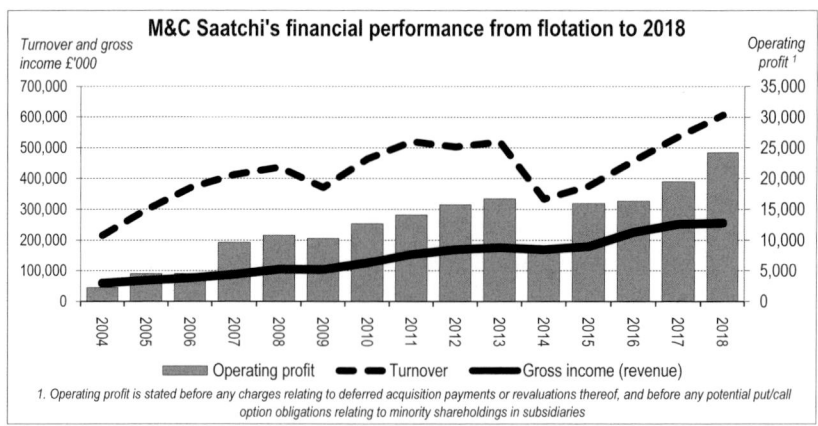

M&C Saatchi's financial performance from flotation to 2018

1. Operating profit is stated before any charges relating to deferred acquisition payments or revaluations thereof, and before any potential put/call option obligations relating to minority shareholdings in subsidiaries

BETWEEN THE BALANCE SHEETS

Forward-looking numbers have to be at least ahead of the ones they had last posted, although that's discretionary to our satisfaction."

In reality many senior executives who might have contemplated selling up and leaving do not do so, although some may sell a small portion of their shares. Hewitt says they're happy with the healthy dividend stream they receive on their shares, and with running their own business to a large extent: "They're enjoying it and fulfilling their potential."

Leaving aside the mechanics of the scheme, does it actually add value to the M&C Saatchi group? Hewitt points to the strong motivating effect and the shared objectives: "They're keen to optimise these businesses in terms of performance. So we don't have to debate budgets or when their bonuses are going to kick in. In terms of the balance sheet, they understand the importance of working capital. They want the dividend so they're going to make sure they're paid on time and they're not spending huge amounts of capital expenditure. So it's self-fulfilling. They want to manage as well."

Another example of how the M&C Saatchi scheme can benefit all parties can be found in Australia where the agency underwent a torrid period in 2011 after losing some major accounts like Qantas, ANZ and Westfield. The founding executives Tom Dery and Tom McFarlane had each acquired a 10% shareholding in the Australian agency in 2010, funded by loans. But in 2014 they realised their shareholdings, moving on to group roles and allowing a new management team to be appointed that has its own share stake in the agency, headed by Jaimes Leggatt.

Since the new management has been in place they have retained a major account Optus and picked up the Woolworth account which is the second largest account in Australia in terms of spend. Hewitt says the ownership stake has given the new team an additional appetite: "They are hungry and, when you meet them, they're excited about the business. They want to move it forward. It's more dynamic. We could see a change in pace."

Listening to Hewitt, it is hard not to believe that M&C Saatchi's model is one that many other companies should be following. So why don't they?" I don't know why it doesn't appeal to them. It's building something for the long-term, which we think will become much more robust. Equity ownership changes the psychology. It's an important distinction from phantom shares and the like.

"We found that to be the case too with the new set-up for the London agency. We looked at various other routes, but the team wanted to own actual equity and I think that's what makes a difference. So we've put in place a mechanism whereby they have loans to buy those shares at fair value. However, we have the right to call in those shares if it doesn't work out. They accepted that.

"We are convinced our model is working. Investors who have been with us long-term get it and appreciate that it's building something that we think will maintain aggressive growth".

In pursuit of global ambitions, Japan's marketing group lost sight of domestic operations - where over-billing and dubious employment conditions prevailed

29

Dentsu's Daring Dash

I n pursuit of global ambitions, Japan's biggest marketing group seemed to lose sight of its domestic operations where over-billing, false reporting and dubious employment conditions resulted in the resignation of the group's chief executive officer Tadashi Ishii.

Interestingly, the three chapters in this book that focus on Dentsu provide a composite picture of the challenges it had to face. In chapter 6 we read of the group's painful attempts to break out of its domestic bubble as it came under threat from other global competitors. After a series of local acquisitions, the group eventually formed a strategic partnership with the global network Bcom3 Group (Leo Burnett, D'Arcy and Starcom Mediavest) that resulted in Dentsu gaining a 21% stake in the US based group in 2002. That deal unravelled when Publicis bought Bcom3 Group in its entirety in 2007, after which Dentsu appears to have become increasingly disenchanted with the relationship and sold all but 2% of its stake to Publicis in 2012 (see chapter 7).

Then chapter 23 told how Dentsu took the bolder step of acquiring Aegis Group outright, devolving much of the day-to-day management of the group's global operations to the Aegis chief executive Jerry Buhlmann. In July 2013 Buhlmann became only the second non-Japanese executive officer at Dentsu. He retired as chief executive of Dentsu Aegis Network in December 2018. This

Resigned: Dentsu's chief executive officer Tadashi Ishii.

chapter, first published on January 2017, describes how with Buhlmann's help Dentsu made an aggressive attempt to achieve a genuine global status and, in doing so, appears to have lost sight of its domestic operations where its business practices slipped below acceptable standards.

More recently hints have began to emerge that some of the acquisitions may not have produced the juicy returns anticipated.

To anyone who understood some of the more bizarre rules

Jerry Buhlmann: former chief executive officer of Dentsu Aegis Network

of accountancy and was prepared to delve into the accounts of the group's Dentsu Aegis Network subsidiary, signs of under-performance were appearing in 2018. Under the headline "Lower expectations from acquisitions added 30% to Dentsu Aegis Network's 2017 profit", *Marketing Services Financial Intelligence* reported that those accounts included £91.7 million of "finance income" that was due solely to a downward revision of deferred acquisition and put option obligations:

> Those revaluations reflect a lowered assessment of future profit flows from past acquisitions. But quirky accounting rules require such downward revaluations to be added to the reported profit for the current year.
>
> Instead of simply adding any deferred acquisition payments (like earn-outs) to the cost of the investment when the payments are made, the International Accounting Standards Board requires companies to estimate the present value of future payments at the time the acquisition takes place (including potential obligations under put and call options).
>
> The impact of any subsequent revaluation is required to be reported as a positive or negative component of the acquiring company's profit in the year the revaluation is made.

In February 2020 news arrived from Australia and China that was even more disconcerting. Dentsu announced that it would be making a provision of ¥70 billion (almost £500 million) for the impairment of goodwill arising on past acquisitions in those regions, prompting a loss of ¥80.9 billion (£563 million) for 2019. Dentsu was rather coy about the identity of the underperforming agencies.

In Australia Dentsu had bought a 51% stake in the Australian advertising agency Belgiovane Williams Mackay (BWM) in 2015. But the biggest acquisition there was probably Mitchell Communications, acquired for £207 million in 2010. There was a note of caution when *Marketing Services Financial Intelligence* reported the deal at the time:

> As previously reported here, the deal could prove a valuable strategic development as over half of Mitchell's revenues come from digital activities and the group had no net debt at its June 2009 balance sheet date.
>
> However, Aegis has paid a substantial price for a business on the other side of the world that has hitherto been heavily reliant on the leadership of 67-year-old Harold Mitchell and his son Stephen who is chief executive.
>
> Mitchell senior will retain a sizeable shareholding in Aegis for at least two years and take on the role of chairman of Aegis Group's Asia Pacific business, but will that be enough to maintain the momentum necessary to justify the purchase price?

Aegis had also been active in China before the Dentsu takeover, buying OMP, Beijing Catch Stone Advertising, Beijing Adsit Technology and search marketing company PinZhong (known as Pzoom). In addition, Aegis had acquired part ownership of the Chinese ad agency Charm Communications while Dentsu itself had also been investing in China.

In August 2020, Dentsu announced a "comprehensive review and accelerated transformation program" involving every region. The aim was to create a more efficient organization by:

- simplifying the business for both clients and operations;
- permanently lowering operating expenses;
- enhancing the efficiency of its balance sheet; and
- maximising long-term shareholder value.

In December 2020 Dentsu issued a further announcement that made grim reading:

> The accelerated transformation will fully integrate the brand portfolio, moving from 160+ brands to six global leadership brands within two years. This transformation program will initially be led by our largest markets which cover over 80% of Dentsu International's revenue, but will include all markets. The transformation will also include all service lines, functions and central teams.
>
> The transformation will result in an approximate 12.5% reduction in total headcount across Dentsu International, subject to local regulations. The estimated cost for FY2020 and FY2021 Q3 and Q4 at Dentsu International is expected to be approximately £640 million (¥87.6 billion). £410 million (¥56.1 billion)

will be recognized in the fiscal year ending December 31, 2020 and the remainder will be recognized in the fiscal year ending December 31, 2021. More than £400 million (¥54.7 billion) of related cost reductions from personnel and other sources is expected to be saved on an annual basis from the end of FY2021.

After two years of losses and extensive rationalisation plans, it was inevitable that questions would be asked about the sustainability of the value attributed to goodwill arising from the stream of past acquisitions. Dentsu said that it would be reviewing the book value of goodwill before the year-end (March 2021), taking into account the unprecedented impact on revenues of the COVID-19 pandemic and the "continued uncertainty in the operating environment". The outcome made further depressing reading:

> This review has resulted in a decision to record a goodwill impairment amounting to ¥140.3 billion in the fourth quarter by recalculating the net present value of Dentsu International with a conservative view. An impairment loss was also recognised in Japan, bringing the total impairment charge for the fourth quarter to ¥142.1 billion.

The impairment provision, when added to restructuring costs of ¥78 billion, pushed Dentsu into a ¥160 billion (£1.1 billion) loss for 2020.

Eager to shore up its balance sheet, the group announced that it was exploring the possibility, of a sale and leaseback of its

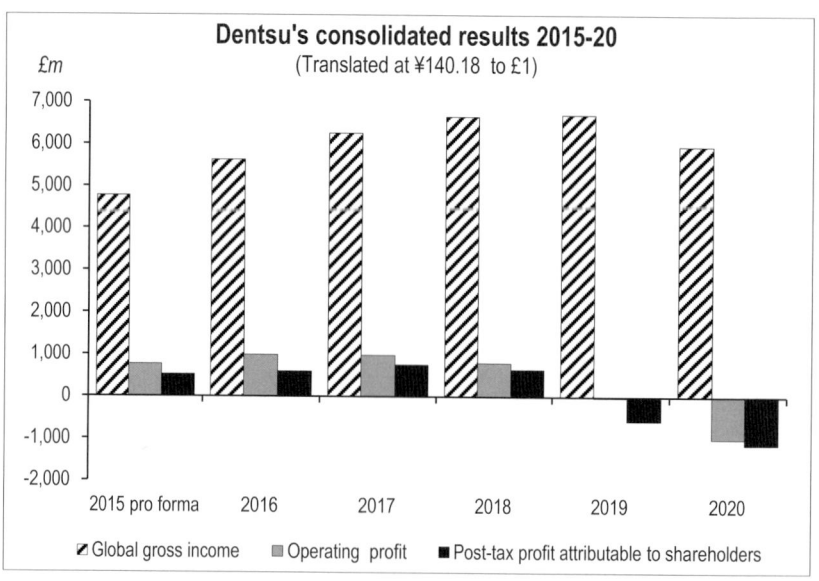

Dentsu's consolidated results 2015-20
(Translated at ¥140.18 to £1)

£m

Global gross income | Operating profit | Post-tax profit attributable to shareholders

2015 pro forma | 2016 | 2017 | 2018 | 2019 | 2020

headquarters building in Tokyo. Then, in March 2021, Dentsu said it would sell two property assets – comprising an athletic facility, garden and training centre - to an undisclosed third party for an undisclosed amount, albeit generating a gain on the sale of approximately ¥30 billion (£195 million). "The sale will improve capital efficiency, further strengthen the financial structure, and secure funds to invest for growth", the company explained. In June 2021, Dentsu announced the planned sale and leaseback of its headquarters building was expected to realise a ¥89 billion (£578 million) gain to bolster its results for 2021.

One of the lessons to be drawn from the Aegis experience is that major global development strategies often take a long time to execute. Aegis began its current global expansion strategy some 20 years ago when it entered into its strategic alliance with Bcom3 Group. Only now can it claim to have a credible global business that offers all the mainstream services a client may desire. Even so, there are sure to be further hiccups in the future.

Any company that expands quickly runs the risk of casualties or setbacks along the way. That does not necessarily invalidate the strategy, but it highlights the need for executives who can maintain the desired strategic direction while minimising any collateral damage. It also highlights the need for lots of capital.

At Dentsu, the stresses of fast expansion were compounded by the day-to-day stresses imposed on its employees in Japan. As if to acknowledge its management shortcomings, late in 2020 Dentsu brought in Wendy Clark from the Omnicom subsidiary DDB Worldwide to become Dentsu Aegis Network's global chief executive officer in succession to Jerry Buhlmann, while Tim Andree retained the chairman role. The network was renamed Dentsu International. But, as we learned in chapter 23, Clark's tenancy did not last long.

In September 2022 Dentsu confirmed earlier rumours that it would "transition to a new globally integrated leadership structure" whereby the Dentsu International brand would be collapsed into a single global network and Clark's job would be eliminated.

Sixty-five-year-old Tadashi Ishii proved to be an adventurous leader of the Japanese marketing group Dentsu after taking charge as chief executive officer in April 2011.

Within months of his promotion he was involved in the unravelling of the relationship with Publicis Groupe – a product of Dentsu's earlier alliance with Bcom3 before that group was acquired by Publicis in 2002. The unravelling put £535 million into

Dentsu's coffers and removed the obligation to gain Publicis approval for future investments or commercial liaisons with competitor companies.

Thus the stage was set for a transformational deal with Aegis Group that offered the prospect of creating a truly global business providing international media buying coverage as well as a substantial enhancement of Dentsu's digital marketing and media businesses.

Dentsu understood media. After all, the agency had been part of a wider Japanese media-owning group almost from its inception in 1901. However, in 1938 the Japanese Government had insisted that Dentsu should be freed from media control and today just two Japanese media groups have shareholdings, namely Kyodo News with 6.6% and Jiji Press with almost 6%.

Aegis Group's former chairman John Napier had made no secret of his desire to sell or break up the business. Dentsu obliged with a near £3.2 billion offer in March 2012.

The deal was completed in March 2013 and thereafter London would provide a headquarters for Dentsu's international ambitions under the guise of the Dentsu Aegis Network (or DAN). So it is somewhat ironic that Dentsu's current management crisis revolves around shortcomings in its domestic operations rather than in its overseas acquisitions.

To put the Aegis deal into perspective, along with a host of other acquisitions initiated during Tadashi Ishii's reign, it is helpful to turn the clock back to the beginning of this century when, in November 2001, Dentsu sought a listing for its shares on the Tokyo stock exchange. Prior to that time the group had been little more than a powerful domestic advertising agency, and a very profitable one.

In 2001 Dentsu's operating profit margins exceeded 20%, helped by relatively low staff costs. Those margins would have been the envy of most global competitors, as would have been its intimate relationship with Japanese media owners. As *Marketing*

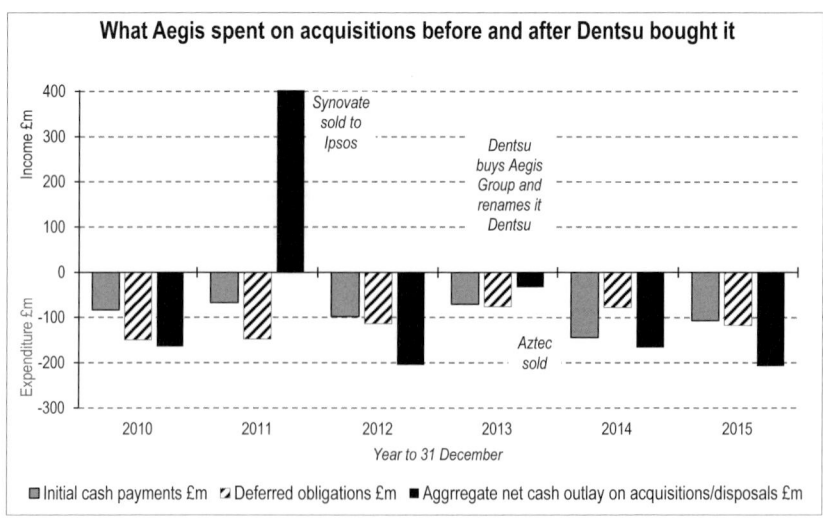

What Aegis spent on acquisitions before and after Dentsu bought it

Services Financial Intelligence noted at the time, Dentsu's output per employee — in terms of revenue handled — was double that achieved by the top US and European groups. "On the face of it, Japanese profit margins benefit from harder-working Japanese employees", the publication observed – an observation that now seems rather prescient in the wake of the recently embarrassing revelations about the group's employment conditions.

But while Dentsu's past record of domestic profitability had been impressive, attempts to create a more global footprint had enjoyed very limited success. And as the years passed its domestic clout was coming under increasing attack from abroad (see chapter 6).

In October 2001, immediately prior to its stock market debut, Dentsu announced that it would close its loss-making CDP agency in London, allowing for redundancy costs of almost £1.5 million and a £7.6 million loss on surrendering its lease. The remnants of CDP were merged with Dentsu's existing UK agency Travis Sully and continued to trade until relaunched under the McGarryBowen banner in 2012.

Meanwhile, on the global stage, Dentsu had acquired a 21% stake in the newly-created Bcom3 Group that owned Leo Burnett Worldwide (and through it a minority share in Bartle Bogle Hegarty) and The MacManus Group. Then, in 2008, Dentsu acquired the lively creative agency McGarryBowen, also in the United States.

Dentsu's revenue showed steady growth after its stock market debut, but sadly its post–tax profit remained stuck in an increasingly unexciting groove. In 2009, trading took a turn for the worse as the economic climate hardened. Revenue and operating profits slipped. And the group suffered a £313 million write-down in the value of its investments.

Despite (or, perhaps, because of) the falling revenue and profit, Dentsu began to take a far more outward-looking stance under the leadership of its new chief executive officer Tadashi Ishii. Its ambitions were boosted in March 2012 when it bid for Aegis, a deal that took a year to complete but would bring chief executive Jerry Buhlmann into the Dentsu management team.

Between March 2013 and 31 December 2015, Dentsu Aegis Network spent about £400 million in cash on acquisitions, net of receipts. Its total commitment to new acquisitions during that period, when deferred purchase payments are taken into account, was closer to £600 million.

Those acquisitions included a majority stake in the Italian digital marketing company Simple Agency, a 51% shareholding in Australian marketing group Oddfellows Holdings, the US experiential marketing group MKTG for which the group paid $52 million in cash, and a 51% stake in Australian advertising agency Belgiovane Williams Mackay (BWM) that had been previously sold back to its management by the financially stressed Enero Group.

Dentsu also paid a massive $979 million to acquire the Maryland-based CRM, digital, and search agency Merkle, along with a string of smaller deals in locations ranging from London to Brazil.

Not content with that, Dentsu bought out the Publicis stake in the Razorfish joint venture, acquired the business-to-business marketing agency Gyro Communications and then bought the UK contract publisher John Brown Media Group. It also expanded its McGarryBowen creative network.

By December 2015, the Dentsu group revenue had reached £16.8 billion, but its operating profit had grown less impressively to £506 million – or 10.7% of gross income, the lowest operating profit margin since the company's shares were admitted to the Tokyo stock market in 2001.

As the business was growing, so the value of the Yen was declining. Consequently many of the overseas acquisitions were costing more, even though past acquisitions offered the prospect of better yields on translation into Yen. When Dentsu reported its results for

the six months to September 2014, its profit had declined by 72%. The currency impact alone had substantially increased the charge for amortisation of goodwill arising from acquisitions like Aegis Group, although the cash impact was negligible.

Towards the end of 2014 the company decided to raise a large amount of capital by transferring major property assets in Tokyo to an unnamed Japanese Corporation to "utilise management resources and strengthen the financial structure through the reduction of assets owned by the Dentsu Group".

The cash proceeds helped fund further acquisitions and added £153 million to the group's 2014 profit for the shortened nine month period to 31 December 2014, conveniently offsetting a 14.6% decline in operating profit in the period.

A further £280 million or thereabouts was raised in 2016 by

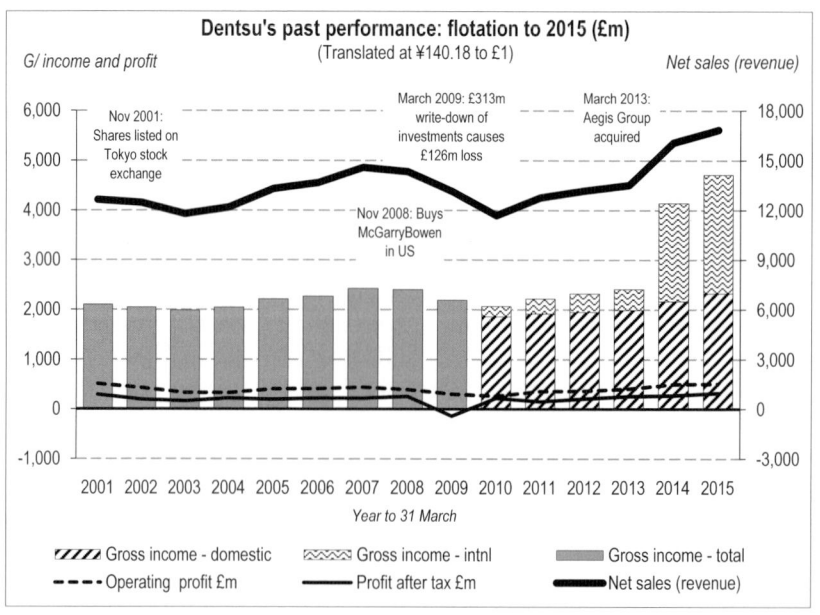

selling 30% of its shareholding in the Japanese recruitment business Recruit Holdings at a prospective profit of about £212 million[1] .

In January 2015, Dentsu offered early retirement arrangements to up to 300 employees and decided to change its company pension scheme from a defined benefit plan to a financially less onerous defined contribution plan, subject to Japanese government approval. The premature shedding of 300 staff had been made possible by "the promotion of asset efficiency and other structural reforms".

The preoccupation with improving efficiency and profitability seems to have had more widespread implications. We now know that management expectations were leading to working conditions that were to have very damaging consequences.

In December 2016 Dentsu announced substantial reforms to its employment conditions following the suicide of a female employee who was reported to have been working 105 extra hours in a month, but the company declined to estimate the cost implications.

_____

[1] *Dentsu enjoyed a further £1.3 billion gain from the sale of most of its residual Recruit shareholding in 2020.*

The drive for greater efficiency and profitability may also have played its part in influencing working practices in the supply and billing of digital advertising in Dentsu's home territory.

In September 2016 the group had announced an investigation into, among other matters, discrepancies in advertising placement periods made either consciously or by human error, failure of placement, and false reporting regarding performance results or achievements. The company had also detected incidents where invoices did not reflect actual results, resulting in unjust overcharged billing.

As at 22 September 2016, 633 suspicious transactions had been identified with an aggregate value of ¥230 million (£1.75 million) and the number of advertisers concerned totalled 111. In 14 cases fees had been charged without any advertisement being placed.

To make matters worse Dentsu later announced that it would miss the 31 December deadline it had previously set for reporting on those irregularities.

By the time the report appears, chief executive Tadashi Ishii will have handed on this particular poisoned chalice to his successor.

GlobalData's chief executive and controlling shareholder sold to the public company a collection of businesses he had previously bought privately.

30
Gleaning the Gains at GlobalData

This is a story about someone who built a very successful business twice, and in doing so highlighted what appeared to be a material gap in current company regulation, namely the absence of any obligation upon a public company to inform its shareholders about any gain or loss accruing to its chief executive and dominant shareholder from acquiring businesses personally and later selling them on to that public company.

The public company in this story is called GlobalData. It is run by a very bright and experienced entrepreneur, Mike Danson. As we shall read, most of his success has been derived from creating companies whose business is the collection of market data about various industries and packaging it for onward sale, usually by subscription. The company reported a record post-tax profit of £24.9 million for 2021, no mean feat in the midst of a coronavirus pandemic.

This chapter traces the development of GlobalData and the businesses it has acquired from Danson. In doing so I have examined published accounts and other public documents to see whether it might have been possible for anyone — minority share-holder or outsider — to ascertain what, if any, gain may have been derived by Danson from selling his privately-owned businesses on to the public company. It was a frustrating exercise.

In the process I discovered mistakes in financial report-ing by the privately-owned companies, less than comprehensive (albeit legally compliant) disclosures, and a somewhat liberal interpretation of the *UK Corporate Governance Code.* None of this is to imply any unlawful or improper intent. But, as we shall see, it poses questions about transparency and accountability – about how much information anyone might reasonably expect to glean about a company's financial affairs from an examination of its published financial statements.

Born in Chorley, near Wigan, to

GlobalData's chief executive Mike Danson

parents who were both teachers, Danson graduated in law from Oxford University and then took a job in management consultancy before starting his first business. Now he appears regularly in *The Sunday Times* rich list - reaching number 119 in 2021 with a fortune estimated at £1.4 billion.

Alongside ownership of the majority of GlobalData, Danson has used some of his accumulated wealth to support other ventures close to his heart. He set up The Danson Foundation at St Anne's College, Oxford, with his wife Helen to help support students achieve their potential, regardless of background, by offering a wealth of opportunities through the funding of Oxford bursaries, an internship scheme and incubator start-up projects.

More recently he bought at least 25% of the share capital in Lenagan Investments - the company owning the Wigan Warriors rugby league team that had accumulated losses in excess of £5 million by November 2019. He has also bought a controlling stake in the *New Statesman* and one of his companies bought the *Press Gazette* (once known as the *UK Press Gazette*) in 2009 when it faced closure after having been rescued from administration in December 2006. Between them, New Statesman and New Statesman Media Group had accumulated losses of £32 million by the end of 2019 (the latest figures available at the time of writing), funded almost entirely by interest-free loans from Danson.

The particular focus of this chapter is on the sale of a collection of Danson's privately-owned businesses to the public company GlobalData for almost £100 million on 25 April 2018. On closer examination I discovered this was not the first occasion when a transaction of this nature had occurred. In 2016 Danson had sold another parcel of companies to the public group for £67 million.

At the time of writing, Danson owned about two-thirds of GlobalData's shares. He also still owned a personal controlling stake in a number of other companies, some of which have continued to be parties to transactions with the public company as this extract from GlobalData's 2019 accounts explained:

> Corporate support services are provided to and from other companies owned by Mike Danson, principally finance, human resources, IT and facilities management. These are recharged to companies that consume these services based on specific drivers of costs, such as proportional occupancy of buildings for facilities management, headcount for human resources services, revenue or gross profit for finance services and headcount for IT services. The net recharge made from GlobalData Plc to these companies for the year ended 31 December 2019 was £556,100 (2018: £490,400).

Danson's practice of assembling a collection of companies privately

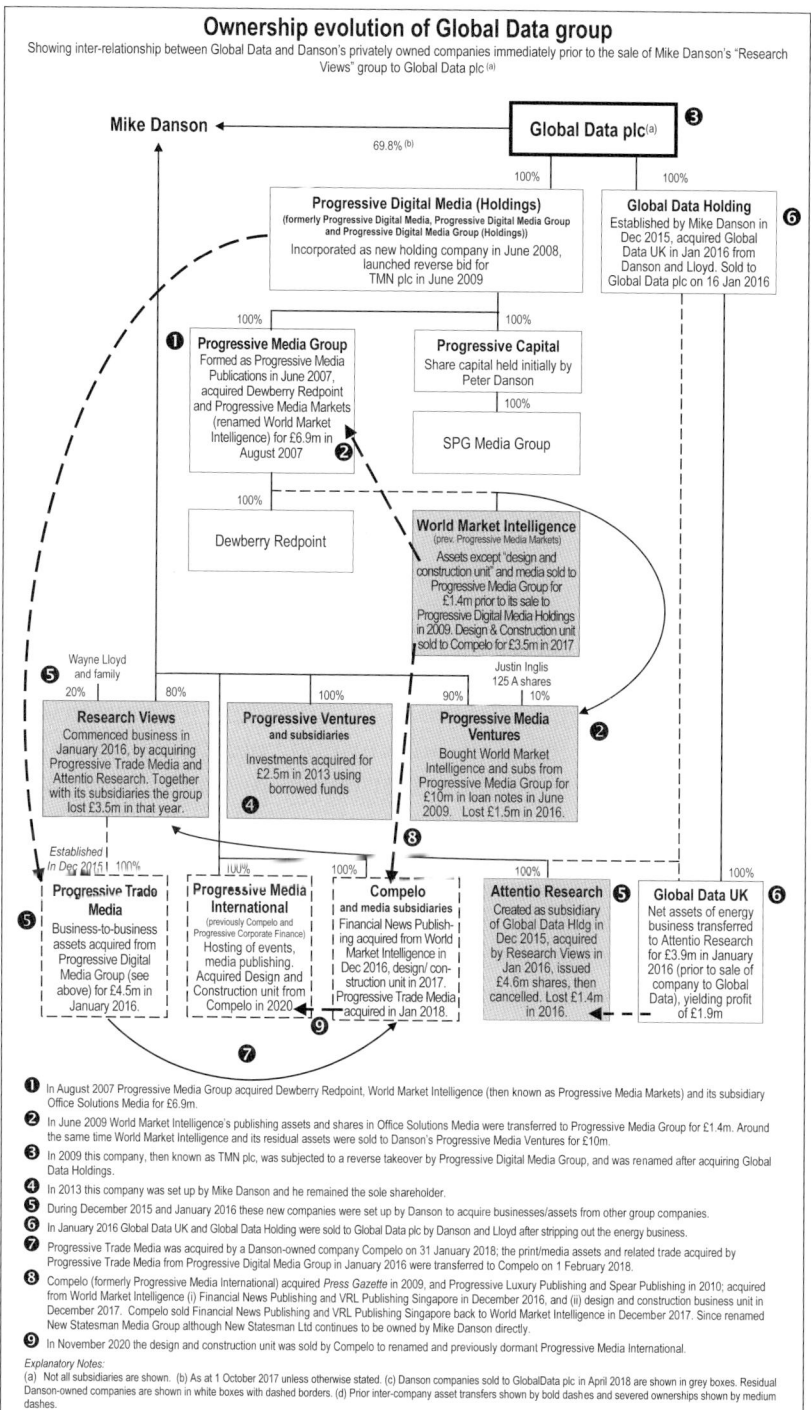

Ownership evolution of Global Data group

Showing inter-relationship between Global Data and Danson's privately owned companies immediately prior to the sale of Mike Danson's "Research Views" group to Global Data plc [a]

Mike Danson ←

69.8% [b]

Global Data plc [a] ❸

100%

100%

Progressive Digital Media (Holdings)
(formerly Progressive Digital Media, Progressive Digital Media Group and Progressive Digital Media Group (Holdings))
Incorporated as new holding company in June 2008, launched reverse bid for TMN plc in June 2009

Global Data Holding ❻
Established by Mike Danson in Dec 2015, acquired Global Data UK in Jan 2016 from Danson and Lloyd. Sold to Global Data plc on 16 Jan 2016

100%

100%

Progressive Media Group ❶
Formed as Progressive Media Publications in June 2007, acquired Dewberry Redpoint and Progressive Media Markets (renamed World Market Intelligence) for £6.9m in August 2007 ❷

Progressive Capital
Share capital held initially by Peter Danson

100%

SPG Media Group

100%

Dewberry Redpoint

World Market Intelligence
(prev. Progressive Media Markets)
Assets except "design and construction unit" and media sold to Progressive Media Group for £1.4m prior to its sale to Progressive Digital Media Holdings in 2009. Design & Construction unit sold to Compelo for £3.5m in 2017

Wayne Lloyd and family ❺
20%   80%

100%

Justin Inglis
125 A shares
90%   10%

Research Views
Commenced business in January 2016, by acquiring Progressive Trade Media and Attentio Research. Together with its subsidiaries the group lost £3.5m in that year. ❹

Progressive Ventures
and subsidiaries
Investments acquired for £2.5m in 2013 using borrowed funds ❹

Progressive Media Ventures ❷
Bought World Market Intelligence and subs from Progressive Media Group for £10m in loan notes in June 2009. Lost £1.5m in 2016.

❽

Established in Dec 2015   100%

100%

100%

100%

100%

Progressive Trade Media ❺
Business-to-business assets acquired from Progressive Digital Media Group (see above) for £4.5m in January 2016.

Progressive Media International
(previously Compelo and Progressive Corporate Finance)
Hosting of events, media publishing. Acquired Design and Construction unit from Compelo in 2020.

Compelo
and media subsidiaries ❽
Financial News Publishing acquired from World Market Intelligence in Dec 2016, design/construction unit in 2017. Progressive Trade Media acquired in Jan 2018.
❾

Attentio Research ❺
Created as subsidiary of Global Data Hldg in Dec 2015, acquired by Research Views in Jan 2016, issued £4.6m shares, then cancelled. Lost £1.4m in 2016. ◄

Global Data UK ❻
Net assets of energy business transferred to Attentio Research for £3.9m in January 2016 (prior to sale of company to Global Data), yielding profit of £1.9m

❼

❶ In August 2007 Progressive Media Group acquired Dewberry Redpoint, World Market Intelligence (then known as Progressive Media Markets) and its subsidiary Office Solutions Media for £6.9m.

❷ In June 2009 World Market Intelligence's publishing assets and shares in Office Solutions Media were transferred to Progressive Media Group for £1.4m. Around the same time World Market Intelligence and its residual assets were sold to Danson's Progressive Media Ventures for £10m.

❸ In 2009 this company, then known as TMN plc, was subjected to a reverse takeover by Progressive Digital Media Group, and was renamed after acquiring Global Data Holdings.

❹ In 2013 this company was set up by Mike Danson and he remained the sole shareholder.

❺ During December 2015 and January 2016 these new companies were set up by Danson to acquire businesses/assets from other group companies.

❻ In January 2016 Global Data UK and Global Data Holding were sold to Global Data plc by Danson and Lloyd after stripping out the energy business.

❼ Progressive Trade Media was acquired by a Danson-owned company Compelo on 31 January 2018; the print/media assets and related trade acquired by Progressive Trade Media from Progressive Digital Media Group in January 2016 were transferred to Compelo on 1 February 2018.

❽ Compelo (formerly Progressive Media International) acquired Press Gazette in 2009, and Progressive Luxury Publishing and Spear Publishing in 2010; acquired from World Market Intelligence (i) Financial News Publishing and VRL Publishing Singapore in December 2016, and (ii) design and construction business unit in December 2017. Compelo sold Financial News Publishing and VRL Publishing Singapore back to World Market Intelligence in December 2017. Since renamed New Statesman Media Group although New Statesman Ltd continues to be owned by Mike Danson directly.

❾ In November 2020 the design and construction unit was sold by Compelo to renamed and previously dormant Progressive Media International.

Explanatory Notes:
(a) Not all subsidiaries are shown. (b) As at 1 October 2017 unless otherwise stated. (c) Danson companies sold to GlobalData plc in April 2018 are shown in grey boxes. Residual Danson-owned companies are shown in white boxes with dashed borders. (d) Prior inter-company asset transfers shown by bold dashes and severed ownerships shown by medium dashes.

and then parcelling them up for sale to the public company is entirely lawful as long as the consideration has been declared and, where appropriate, the value of the consideration reviewed and deemed fair by an independent party. Nevertheless, the shareholders in the public company may never know whether Danson derived a personal gain (or suffered a personal loss) from such transactions or whether they could have benefited by also participating in those transactions alongside Danson if they had been given the choice.

And there is another question: should an executive with a controlling share stake in a public company be permitted to retain ownership of businesses that trade or compete with that company or which may create a diversion from his primary obligation to work for the benefit of the public company?

In advocating that a public company should be obliged to inform its shareholders about any gain or loss accruing to an executive director and material shareholder from acquiring businesses personally and later selling them on to that public company, there will be some who respond that this will impose an unreasonable administrative burden on the person involved. But is that really true? Presumably a similar calculation will be required for the completion of the individual's tax return? And if the individual resents having to disclose the information publicly, the solution is simple: sell the privately owned businesses to a third party rather than to the public company. Better still, ensure that any privately owned businesses that are engaged in activities similar to those of the public company are divested or sold to the public company itself when the owner first acquires a shareholding and directorship in that public company, thereby enabling the financial outcome to be shared between all shareholders.

Over the years there have been a number of well publicised situations (some of which are recounted elsewhere in this book) that have prompted lawyers and stockbrokers to recommend that such potential conflicts are removed before a company seeks a share listing on the London Stock Exchange. Typically those privately owned companies are transferred into the public group or they are disposed of to a third party. However, there are exceptions: M&C Saatchi's founders formed a partnership that owned its Golden Square headquarters for a number of years.

The account that follows dates back to 2007 when Danson sold his original market intelligence business Datamonitor to Informa, a public company describing itself as a leading interna-

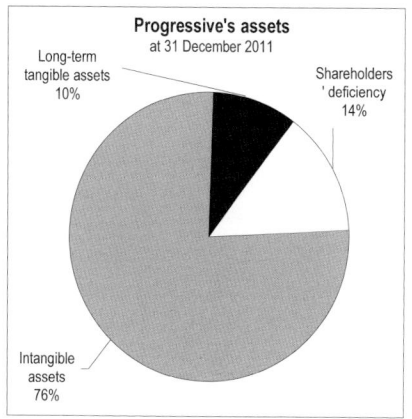

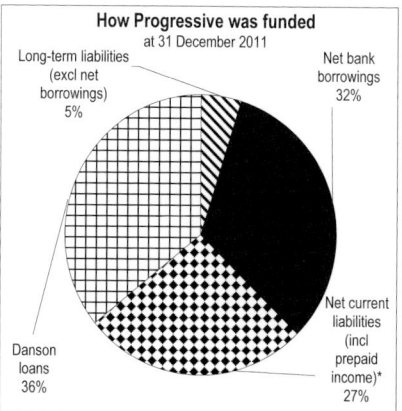

tional intelligence, events and scholarly research group. Using some of his share of the £510 million proceeds, Danson re-entered the market intelligence industry by acquiring a series of businesses many of which are owned by GlobalData today. The acquisition vehicles were funded principally by Danson loans.

A year later, in 2008, Danson packaged up his new acquisitions under a new holding company called Progressive Digital Media Group and reversed it into a public company called TMN Group. Thereafter TMN adopted the Progressive name which was later changed to GlobalData.

By the end of 2020 — the period covered by the accompanying narrative — the enlarged GlobalData group boasted assets (net of short-term liabilities) of £369 million of which £242 million was in the form of intangible assets, reflecting the excess of acquisition prices paid by GlobalData for companies — previously Danson-owned or otherwise — over the net book value of the assets acquired. By this time GlobalData had also accumulated losses of a little under £2 million since coming under Danson management, but had succeeded in raising additional share capital to fund the business that enabled the group to replace most of Danson's personal loans.

Back in 2011 the group's balance sheet had been fairly weak (see chart). Its long-term assets (mainly intangible) had a book value of £28.3 million and were being financed predominantly by net bank borrowings of £10.7 million and short-term loans of £11.8 million from Danson. Other short-term liabilities exceeded readily realisable assets by £8.8 million. Shareholders' funds were in deficit by £4.6 million. In other words, at that time a large proportion of GlobalData's long-term assets were being funded by a mixture

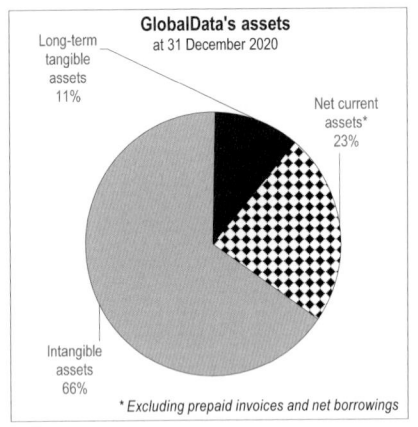

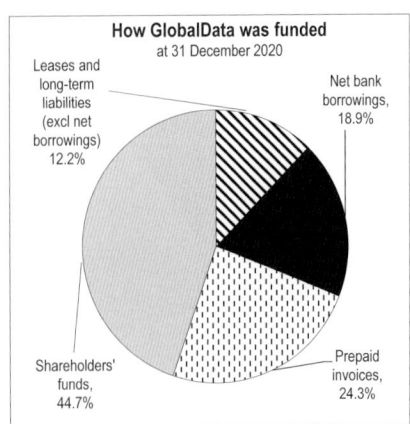

of short-term creditors and short-term loans from Danson. It is widely recognised that long-term assets are best financed principally by long-term finance such as permanent share capital, and that short-term liabilities should be matched by readily realisable assets. Otherwise the company might find itself unable to pay all of its bills when they fall due.

GlobalData[1] was not alone in relying on credit from suppliers and prepaid subscriptions to provide some of the capital to fund its longer-term assets. Indeed, it is important to acknowledge that one of the benefits of subscription based businesses like GlobalData is the positive cash flow that they can generate, minimising the need for outside finance whether from shareholders or banks. However, it is equally important to ensure that the cash flow benefit is used primarily for the purpose for which it was intended - the delivery of the services covered by the subscriptions. If, instead, those funds were to be tied up in the purchase of long-term assets or in financing loss-making activities[2], alternative sources of finance would be required. And, if additional outside funding were not available, a company might be tempted to use new subscription receipts to pay for the cost of servicing other people's previous subscriptions so as to delay the day when pressure might otherwise mount on its working capital if, for example, its revenue were suddenly to decline.

At the end of 2020 (the latest date for which accounts were

---

1. *References to Global Data in this chapter should be interpreted as including the predecessor parent company of the group Progressive Digital Media Group plc and its subsidiaries unless the context implies otherwise.*

2. *Salutary examples of customers' funds being applied in this way can be found in the Government reports on the collapse of Pinnock Finance Company in 1967 and of Court Line in 1974.*

BETWEEN THE BALANCE SHEETS

available at the time of writing) GlobalData had prepaid subscription income of £74.7 million. On average about 82% of its income was being applied to meet operating costs, suggesting that about £61 million of the prepaid subscription income would be absorbed in this way. Fortunately, the company had £65.4 million available in cash and other readily realisable assets at that time – seemingly sufficient to cover the related operating costs.

Back in 2011 creditors had faced a separate potential threat. With Danson's loans being repayable on demand, rather than forming part of the long-term capital, they would have ranked alongside all the other ordinary creditors if the company failed, thereby diluting those creditors' potential claims. However, such potential fears were allayed when Danson wrote a letter undertaking not to seek repayment of his loans for a period of 12 months from the 31 December 2011 "to ensure that the directors could prepare the accounts on a going concern basis". That allowed the loan to be shown as longer term.

As *Marketing Services Financial Intelligence* observed at the time: "Given the frail balance sheet, it seems surprising that Danson has not provided more comfort to ordinary creditors by converting some of his debt into permanent share capital." The group responded in 2012 by raising almost £20 million in additional share capital that helped restore its balance sheet to a healthier state. At the same time Danson agreed to convert almost all of his remaining loans to the company into shares.

Danson had previously withdrawn £6.5 million of the £18.8 million loans he had made to GlobalData after the company raised additional bank borrowings. The new share issue substantially reduced the balance of those bank borrowings and also provided some cash for future expansion. And future expansion there was, but mainly in the shape of businesses acquired from Danson himself, as recounted below. By 31 December 2018, 89% of Global Data's assets were intangible – mostly goodwill arising from the most recent acquisition of the Research Views Group from Danson.

On the face of it the GlobalData balance sheet looked healthy enough with some 52% of the group's assets financed by shareholders' funds (see chart) – not unusual for an expansive company and much improved from 2011. But only a very small proportion of those shareholders' funds was derived from cash subscribed for shares or from retained profits.

The vast majority — £97.3 million - was derived from two

simple paper transactions reflecting the excess of the price paid to acquire Danson's companies (the Research Views Group and GlobalData Holding) over the nominal value of GlobalData shares issued as consideration, sometimes known as a "premium" or "merger reserve". The higher the value placed on those companies, the bigger the amount shown as shareholders' funds - and the better the ratio of shareholders' funds to net borrowings ("gearing"). Put another way, if the value placed on those acquisitions were to diminish, GlobalData's balance sheet would be materially weakened.

Given the potential controversy that might have accompanied publication of my report, and mindful of the advice Charles Raw had given in connection with the publication of the report I had produced on Excess Holdings in 1971 (see chapter 2), I sent a draft to the company in May 2018, having first compiled a file of supporting evidence. GlobalData's lawyers complained on behalf of the company and Danson himself that it contained "very significant inaccuracies" without specifying what was alleged to be inaccurate, save to assert that there had been "no wrongdoing on the part of our client". Invited to elaborate on several occasions, the lawyers did not respond. By raising questions in this chapter there is no intention to allege any unlawful or improper behaviour by GlobalData or Mike Danson, but simply to prompt a debate about whether there should be a review of the current regulation of transactions between related parties. In this context I have referred in my preface to a number of proposals for improved disclosure – some arising from this chapter – that were first recommended to the Government in 2018.

Coincidently, it was not long before changes were afoot among GlobalData's senior financial personnel and improvements were being introduced to the company's corporate governance regime.

On 3 October 2019, the company announced the appointment of Sally Johnson as chief financial officer in place of Graham Lilley who was a long-serving member of staff and had held the top position since his predecessor Simon Pyper left in 2017. Johnson had held a number of senior financial positions within the Pearson global publishing group since joining in 2000. Apparently Lilley had "decided to step down" but would remain in post until his successor arrived. However, the succession never took place.

GlobalData announced in January 2020 that Sally Johnson would not be joining the company after all. Pearson had offered her the top job of group chief financial officer to fill the void left by the impending departure of Coram Williams. "We have mutually agreed that she will now remain at Pearson", GlobalData confirmed. "Until further notice Graham Lilley, GlobalData's chief financial officer will continue in his role." Two months later, GlobalData expressed pleasure that Lilley had "committed to the business long-term and will continue in this role permanently".

Among the corporate governance enhancements introduced by the company in 2020 was the creation of a "Related Party Transaction (RPT) Committee", comprising four non-executive directors charged with ensuring that "there are adequate controls in place to provide assurance that any transaction which is or may be a related party transaction in nature is conducted on terms which are arm's length and reasonable".

Further board changes were announced early in 2021. Chairman Bernard Cragg would retire at the April annual general meeting and be replaced by Murray Legg, a non-executive director and former partner in the accountancy firm PricewaterhouseCoopers. Legg would hand over the role of audit committee chairman to a newly-appointed non-executive director Catherine Birkett, chief financial officer at GoCardless. In its annual report for 2020, published in March 2021, the company acknowledged that it had failed to comply with several requirements of the *UK Corporate Governance Code*[1], namely:

- As a result of the chairman's time served as a director, and his participation in the employee share option scheme (with vesting targets based on time rather than company performance), along with the senior independent director Peter Harkness' time served with the company, they were not considered to be independent under provisions 9, 10 and 19 of the *Code*. Nevertheless, the company claimed that the individuals had demonstrated independence in practice and that the chairman's independence of character and judgement had not been impaired.
- During 2020 the company did not engage with the workforce using a method prescribed by the *Code*, the company was therefore in non-compliance of provision 5 of the *Code*. However, the company announced that the new remuneration committee chair Annette Barnes would undertake the additional role of designated non-executive for the workforce.
- The company did not have a policy in respect of post-employment shareholding requirements and as a result did not comply with provision 36 of the *Code*. The company promised to address this in 2021.
- In non-compliance with provisions 40 and 41 of the *UK*

1. *Financial Reporting Council "UK Corporate Governance Code 2018"*

Corporate Governance Code, the remuneration committee had not engaged with employees and shareholders when setting remuneration because it was considered sufficient to review benchmark reports when setting executive remuneration.

When the 2021 annual general meeting took place, over 19% of the votes were cast against receiving the company's annual report and accounts for 2020, and the audit report thereon[1]. Some 12% of votes were cast against the reappointment of long-serving senior independent director Peter Harkness, a former deputy editor of the Birmingham based *Sunday Mercury*. By the time the 2022 annual meeting arrived, the share price had fallen by 34%.

In February 2022 GlobalData's board announced its intention to "reduce and eventually eliminate the number of related party transactions and wind down the service agreements that are currently in place". Meanwhile the abovementioned Related Party Transactions Committee would oversee related party transactions and review them to "ensure that the transactions are in the best interest of GlobalData and its stakeholders, and that the transactions are recorded and disclosed on an arms-length basis". However, there was no suggestion that the committee would be required to review past transactions, leaving unanswered the question of what, if any, financial gain was derived by Mike Danson from the acquisition of businesses in a personal capacity and their subsequent onward sale to the public company, or whether such a transaction by a director of GlobalData was most likely to have promoted the success of the public company "for the benefit of its members as a whole[2]" compared with the outcome if those businesses had been acquired by GlobalData in the first place. And there has been no hint that the law will be changed to require any such disclosure in future.

So let us turn the clock back to the transaction that prompted my interest in the financial affairs of GlobalData...

On 26 February 2018 the publicly-listed market intelligence provider GlobalData announced that it was in advanced discussions concerning the possible purchase of various businesses that had been

---

1. *Shareholders were also asked to pass resolutions that retrospectively authorised unlawful distributions made to, or for the benefit of, shareholders between 2018 and 2020 totalling £60 million, after (i) having incorrectly treated as distributable reserves the funds set aside to acquire shares for employees of subsidiaries, (ii) having insufficient other reserves available for distribution, and (iii) having failed to file accounts to demonstrate that sufficient distributable profits were available. To provide sufficient distributable reserves, Court approval was subsequently obtained to convert the £164 million "premium" derived from shares issued to vendors of Global Data Holding and Research View into distributable reserves.*

2. *See Companies Act 2006, ss.170-177. and p.375.*

acquired by the company's chief executive and controlling shareholder Mike Danson and a number of other minority shareholders. The purchase price for the collection of businesses was almost £100 million. Two months later, on 25 April, the transaction was completed with shareholder approval.

What the shareholders were not told was the amount of profit, if any, that may have accrued to Danson personally from the trans-action. GlobalData is listed on the Alternative Investment Market of the London Stock Exchange and will have had to complete a series of procedures to demonstrate that the transaction was being conducted at arm's length between the related parties, bearing in mind that Danson was the controlling shareholder in both parties to the deal.

The transaction also raises a wider question of whether external shareholders in GlobalData should have had the opportunity to partic-ipate in any capital gain that may have accrued to Danson and which arguably would have been shared with all GlobalData's shareholders if the various businesses had been acquired directly by GlobalData without any intermediate ownership by Danson's private companies.

In other words, the question is not about whether the deal terms were at arm's length (or whether previous similar deals had been valued at arm's length), for which safeguards are already provided. It is about whether company law should be amended to prohibit a dominant shareholding executive in a public company from owning other private companies engaged in the same industry and selling them on to the public company at a later date without any obligation to disclose the profit or loss accruing to him/her from the sale as a result of that period of private ownership. For the avoidance of doubt, there is no suggestion that Danson or GlobalData have failed to comply with existing law or that there

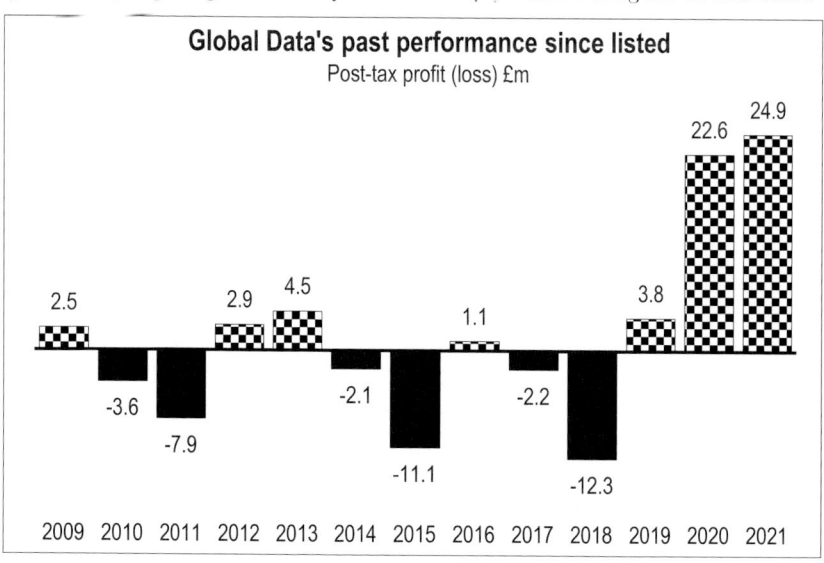

Global Data's past performance since listed

Post-tax profit (loss) £m

2.5 -3.6 -7.9 2.9 4.5 -2.1 1.1 -11.1 -2.2 -12.3 3.8 22.6 24.9

2009 2010 2011 2012 2013 2014 2015 2016 2017 2018 2019 2020 2021 has been any wrongdoing.

The situation is complicated not only because Danson had a controlling interest in each of the three companies that have just been acquired by GlobalData but also because those companies had previously acquired various businesses from Danson and his associates. Furthermore, on this and previous occasions Danson had extracted some businesses from companies prior to their sale to GlobalData or its predecessor public company.

Against this backcloth another, more general, question arises: would it have been more desirable for all of the businesses that were being managed directly or indirectly by the same person to have belonged to a cohesive group – public company or not?

In Danson's case there are some contrary arguments insofar as at that time his privately-owned companies could conveniently be allocated into two separate categories – (i) those engaged in activities complementary to those of the public company and (ii) those less allied to the activities of the public company and in which Danson had perhaps invested for more altruistic or philanthropic purposes, such as the *New Statesman*.

As we shall see, many of the businesses engaged in data collection and related activities were sold on to the public company in 2016 and 2018 at an undisclosed profit or loss. It could be argued that, if any of those privately owned companies had been under-performing in the years that preceded sale to the public company, GlobalData's shareholders will have been relieved of the associated risk

and the potentially adverse impact on its share price that would have occurred if those companies had been bought by GlobalData at the outset.

This can be well illustrated by taking a look at another of Danson's private companies – Compelo – that had chalked up losses of £16 million by the time that the Research Views Group was sold to GlobalData.

If the Compelo companies had been included in that deal (which they were not) and continued to incur losses, those losses would have reduced the value of GlobalData shares, including those held by Danson himself. Bearing in mind that those shares were being traded at a price/earnings multiple ranging between 30 and 40 at the time of the Research Views Group deal, it almost certainly would have been in the financial interests of all shareholders to exclude loss-making companies from that deal and for Danson to continue to support them personally.

Furthermore, if any financial gain were to accrue to Danson from having revitalised and sold any under-performing companies he had retained, that might be viewed as a fair reward for taking the risk. On the other hand, GlobalData's minority shareholders might have preferred to have shared in the risks and rewards of owning all of Danson's companies, given a choice.

At the time of writing, GlobalData was not obliged to tell shareholders about the amount of any prospective or actual gain (or loss) accruing to Danson personally from selling businesses to GlobalData. All that the regulations required was for the company to disclose the financial consideration involved, that Danson was a party to the various transactions and that each has been independently valued and reviewed for fairness.

Marketing Services Financial Intelligence sought confirmation from the Financial Conduct Authority (FCA) – the organisation charged with overseeing the conduct of public companies in the United Kingdom – that there was no regulatory obligation for a public company to disclose a gain or loss accruing to a shareholding director from the sale of a private company owned by that director to the public company:

"There's nothing in the FCA's securities regulatory framework nor in the applicable accounting standards that requires this specific piece of information", a spokesperson said[1].

"As you state, there will be disclosure of the quantum of the transaction but not specifically the gain for the director. For premium listed companies, if the transaction is significant then there may also be extra notification or even shareholder approval requirements in LR11 that apply, but again the gain of the individual director is not part of the package of required disclosures even then."

Company law is equally silent on the subject of disclosure. The Companies Act 2006 simply requires a director to act "in the way he considers, in good faith, would be most likely to promote the success of the company for the benefit of its members as a whole". In doing so the director must exercise independent

judgement and must avoid a situation in which he has, or can have, a direct or indirect interest that conflicts, or possibly may conflict, with the interests of the company.[2]

Typically companies are already obliged to disclose benefits provided to directors[3] in the form of salary, bonus and long-term incentive schemes, along with contributions towards directors' pension schemes and gains derived from the exercise of share options. So why not disclose any benefit derived from the sale to the company of companies previously acquired privately?

Taking into account Danson's dominant shareholding it may come as no surprise to learn that, on occasions when resolutions were put to GlobalData's shareholders in connection with the acquisition of assets from (and the disposal of assets to) Danson's private companies, holders of less than 10% of shares in issue voted against or abstained.

Oblivious of the amount of any personal gain (or loss) made by Danson, the minority shareholders were either content with the proposals as presented or they recognised that the outcome was inevitable. After all, their share price had increased six-fold since 2009 and a rosy future seemed to lie ahead, despite GlobalData having accumulated losses of about £16 million in the same period.

Danson is undoubtedly a successful businessman, having founded

1. *Email from Financial Conduct Authority dated 9 May 2018, reconfirmed 21 July 2021*

2. *See Companies Act 2006, ss.170-177.*

3. *See s.412, Companies Act 2006 and The Large and Medium-sized Companies and Groups (Accounts and Reports) (Amendment) Regulations 2013 SI 1981.*

Datamonitor and made a lot of money from its sale to a UK public company Informa for approximately £510 million in 2007[1]. He owned about 25% of the shares at the time.

Seven years later Informa announced that it had written down the price paid for "certain information assets...which were acquired as part of the Datamonitor acquisition in 2007" by no less than £202 million. Shortly afterwards GlobalData[2] would buy back some of those Datamonitor businesses for £25 million.

Presumably the Datamonitor sale proceeds provided at least some of the funds that Danson later invested in creating the GlobalData group. Indeed, selling and buying individual businesses appears to have become something of a habit – more particularly when Danson was the controlling shareholder in both the seller and the buyer.

Just before Danson had completed the sale of Datamonitor to Informa in July 2007, a new company had been set up that would form the foundations of today's GlobalData business. Initially this company was called Progressive Media Publications. It was formed by Peter John Danson, who was also the first director.

It would not be unreasonable to ponder whether Peter Danson is related to Mike Danson as he continues to hold directorships of various companies owned by Mike. According to documents filed at Companies House, Peter Danson was born in September 1965 and lives in Lostock, near Bolton in Lancashire – not very far from Mike Danson's birthplace.

But it was not possible to trace a public record of anyone called Peter Danson or Peter John Danson having been born in the UK in 1965. That may say more about the quality of form filling by employees of Danson companies than anything else, as eventually a birth certificate was found for someone called *John Peter* Danson. Lo and behold, he was born on 19 September 1965 and his parents lived in Standish on the outskirts of Wigan.

While our search of public records continued, we took a more direct approach. I wrote to both Peter and Mike Danson asking whether, and if so how, they might be related to each other. I received no response. But then, as luck would have it, we located a copy of Mike Danson's birth certificate and, yes, he is the brother of Peter.

Our research would have been made even more difficult if a change in company law, enacted in 2006, had been retrospective in its effect. That legislation now excuses companies from disclosing the residential addresses of directors at Companies House or anywhere else[3], although

---

1. *The Informa offer document dated 14 May 2007 stated that Michael Danson would remain with Datamonitor as its Chief Executive Officer for a period of twelve months from completion on 31 July 2007 and that certain non-compete covenants within his service agreement would cease to apply after the expiry of one year following the termination of his employment.*

2. *References to GlobalData should be interpreted as including the predecessor parent company of the group Progressive Digital Media Group plc and its subsidiaries unless the context implies otherwise.*

3. *See ss.165, 240-242, Companies Act 2006. A service address - like the company's registered office – must be provided instead.*

the addresses must be recorded in a register kept by the company that is not available for public inspection. Why such privacy should be afforded to people running companies that already enjoy the privilege of being able to limit their liability to creditors is difficult to comprehend. Surely the understandable desire to stamp out abusive use of personal data should not have been taken that far?

Reverting to the evolution of GlobalData, within months of Progressive Media Publications' incorporation all of its shares were transferred from Peter to Mike Danson and the name was changed to Progressive Media Group. Mike Danson did not take a seat on the board until 3 June 2009 – a few days after brother Peter departed and just before certain Datamonitor non-compete restrictions were due to expire. Throughout this period the second director was a long-standing Datamonitor colleague Simon Pyper.

Days after Danson sold Datamonitor in July 2007, Progressive Media Group had taken its first step towards building today's GlobalData group. It acquired World Market Intelligence and Dewberry Redpoint from Wilmington Group for £6.9 million in cash. The deal was financed by loans from Danson.

World Market Intelligence incurred a £1.3 million loss in 2008 after incurring various restructuring costs. It would have lost money again in 2009 if it had not recorded gains of £4.1 million on disposal of various assets to other Danson companies — its Foots Cray property was sold to Estel Property Investments and some

of its other assets were sold to its parent Progressive Media Group.

In June 2009, Danson was planning to gain a stock market listing for his expanding Progressive Media Group by way of a reverse takeover by a company called TMN Group. As part of this deal, World Market Intelligence's publishing assets and its shareholding in Office Solutions Media were transferred to Progressive Media Group for £1.4 million.

However, the World Market Intelligence company itself and its residual assets remained under Danson's personal control, having been sold to another newly-created company called Progressive Media Ventures for £10.8 million[1], yielding a profit of £6.3 million on its £4.5 million cost.

Danson owned 90% of Progressive Media Ventures' shares and provided a loan to fund the purchase.

Surprisingly, this sizeable transaction was overlooked when Progressive Media Ventures' 2009 accounts were being prepared. Belatedly the acquisition appeared as a "prior year adjustment" in 2010 and was promptly written down by £6 million without any further explanation.

Thus the framework had been established for two parallel business empires — on the one hand, the publicly-listed Progressive group (soon to be named GlobalData) and, on the other hand, a collection of companies owned personally by Danson.

It is some of those privately owned companies that GlobalData acquired from Danson and his associates in April 2018 - namely the aforementioned Progressive Media Ventures,

1. *See chart on page* 365.

along with Research Views, Progressive Ventures and their respective subsidiaries, together described at the time as the "Research Views Group". They included several businesses that had been specifically excluded from earlier sales of companies by Danson to the public company group.

So let's take a closer look at the three companies acquired by GlobalData in 2018, starting with Research Views itself.

Prior to its sale to GlobalData, Danson owned 80% of the company, the balance being held by another GlobalData executive Wayne Lloyd and his family. Lloyd runs Global-Data's American businesses.

Research Views had started trading on 20 January 2016. Its purpose appears to have been to acquire certain businesses that Danson wished to exclude from the public company at that time, namely Progressive Trade Media and Attentio Research.

Research Views had acquired Progressive Trade Media from the public company on 19 January 2016. Immediately prior to its acquisition Progressive Trade Media had purchased "certain print/media assets and related trade" from elsewhere in the public company group. Progressive Trade Media's activities were described as "hosting of events and both digital and printed media publishing". The acquired assets were mainly debtors.

According to Progressive Trade Media, its newly acquired assets cost £4 million net, although the public company's accounts showed the sale proceeds as £4.5 million - financed by a £4.6 million interest-bearing vendor

loan repayable by annual instalments starting in January 2018. Whatever the correct figure may have been, the same assets had already been written down by £6.2 million in 2015 in advance of the disposal (the write-down having been reflected in the public company's results for that year).

Research Views paid a nominal sum of £1 for Progressive Trade Media, with its newly acquired assets and related £4.6 million liability. Progressive Trade Media reported a loss of £2.4 million in 2016.

The reasons given by the public company for disposing of Progressive Trade Media were that "revenue from these assets has already been in decline for a number of years" and that the assets were "non-core" to the public company. Certainly it could be argued that those activities were peripheral to the main-stream business of gathering and selling market intelligence carried on by GlobalData. And offloading the loss-making company to Research Views might have done wonders for GlobalData's share price.

The transfer of the trade and assets to Progressive Trade Media in January 2016 formed part of a wider package of transactions involving the public company. Among those transactions was the sale by Danson and his associate Wayne Lloyd to the public company of GlobalData Holding and its sole operating subsidiary, the healthcare business information provider GlobalData UK, at a valuation of £66.5 million[1].

The completion of this package of transactions was to prompt a rather

1.. *See also p.380.*

important question in 2018 when the public company GlobalData announced that it was acquiring the Research Views Group[1]. Did this mean that GlobalData would be reacquiring the "non-core" businesses that it (and/or its predecessor group parented by Progressive Digital Media Group) had sold to Progressive Trade Media before it was acquired by Research Views?

Marketing Services Financial Intelligence put that question to Global Data's chief financial officer who declined to comment. Later the proposition was put more explicitly to Global Data's lawyers and it elicited a very firm denial, albeit no further information was volunteered.

---

1. All references to "Research Views Group" relate collectively to Research Views, Progressive Media Ventures, Progressive Ventures and their respective subsidiaries at the relevant time.

So what had happened to the trade and assets acquired from the public company group in 2016 on which Progressive Trade Media had been founded? In the absence of any reference to the matter in the circular sent to GlobalData shareholders, a clue might have been found by a particularly inquisitive shareholder in the unlikely event that he or she had examined Research Views' accounts for 2016. A note on its goodwill accounting policy referred to the acquisition of some unidentified assets from the public company in January 2016 that were all "disposed of in 2017 to Compelo Limited".

What were those assets? Who owned Compelo? And what value was attached to the disposals? Why wasn't there any reference to the acquisition of those assets in Compelo's own accounts in 2017? And why wasn't a

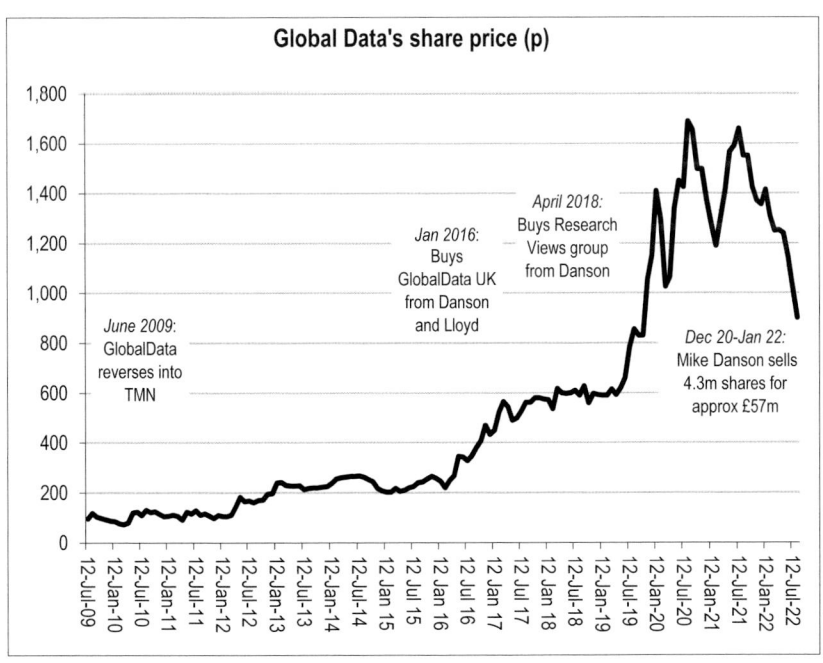

Global Data's share price (p)

June 2009: GlobalData reverses into TMN

Jan 2016: Buys GlobalData UK from Danson and Lloyd

April 2018: Buys Research Views group from Danson

Dec 20-Jan 22: Mike Danson sells 4.3m shares for approx £57m fuller explanation of such a post balance sheet event provided as a separate item in Research Views' 2016 accounts as would appear to be required[1] by accounting rules? The reason is quite simple: the note was wrong.

It was not until several months after GlobalData had acquired the Research Views Group in 2018, and I had asked whether in doing so it had reacquired the assets it had previously sold to Progressive Trade Media, that any firm evidence could be found of Research Views having divested those assets to Compelo. That evidence appeared in September 2018, when Research Views published its 2017 accounts. They included this brief note about a post balance sheet event:

> On 31 January 2018 the company disposed of its 100% investment in Progressive Trade Media Ltd to Compelo Ltd.

This was confirmed in December 2019, when the 2018 accounts of Research Views included this note:

> Progressive Trade Media was disposed of in the period at nil cost as part of a corporate reorganisation.

Thus the earlier reference to the disposal taking place in 2017 was simply untrue. Maybe Research Views had every intention of disposing of the assets in 2017, but forgot to complete the accounting formalities. Whatever the explanation, the various companies moved swiftly to ensure that Progressive Trade Media had indeed been transferred to Compelo

before Research Views was sold to GlobalData in April 2018.

Meanwhile further research had revealed that Compelo was another Danson-owned private company.

At different times the name Compelo has been attached to three separate companies belonging to Mike Danson. This particular Compelo began life as Progressive Media International in August 2007 and was initially owned by Peter Danson[2], but has been wholly owned by Mike Danson since 2011. It appears to have been the vehicle into which Danson has channelled some of his substantial wealth in order to support various worthy ventures, many of them loss-making. It adopted the name Compelo on 8 February 2017 and has changed its name twice more since then. At the time of writing, it is called New Statesman Media Group.

Making sense of that company's early activities from its accounts was not straightforward. Its accounts for the year to August 2009 were filed as a dormant company called Progressive Media International, showing just £100 in unpaid share capital and a similar amount due from its initial shareholder Peter Danson.

By March 2011, the company had had second thoughts. It produced unaudited amended accounts for the same period to August 2009 showing that, if indeed the company had been dormant during that time, it must have been sleep-walking. Those amended accounts showed that the company had acquired publishing

---

1. See UK Financial Reporting Standard 102, section 32 "Events after the End of the Reporting Period" which requires disclosure of (a) the nature of the event, and (b) an estimate of its financial effect or a statement that such an estimate cannot be made.

---

2. The company's 2011 annual return failed to disclose the disposal of shares by Peter Danson.

rights costing £133,053 — presumably those of the *Press Gazette* — and had lost £66,275. Mike Danson had lent the company an interest-free loan of £75,000.

In the following years Compelo engaged in buying and selling a number of companies - often from and to other Danson-related companies.

The company acquired Progressive Luxury Publishing and its subsidiary Spear Publishing in 2010. In December 2016 it acquired Financial News Publishing and its subsidiary VRL Publishing Singapore from Danson-owned World Market Intelligence for £1.2 million (non-cash) financed by a loan from Danson. Then, on 31 December 2017 - and for no apparent reason - Compelo sold Financial News Publishing and its subsidiary VRL Publishing Singapore back to World Market Intelligence for the amount it had previously paid for them, just before World Market Intelligence was included in the Research Views Group package of businesses sold to GlobalData in April 2018. Also on 31 December 2017 Compelo acquired a "design and construction business unit" from World Market Intelligence for £3.5 million.

But nowhere in Compelo's 2017 accounts was there any mention of any assets being acquired from Research Views, as had been claimed in Research View's own accounts.

We now know why: it was not until one month later, in January 2018, that Compelo acquired the entire share capital of Progressive Trade Media. That company's trade,

assets and liabilities were transferred to Compelo itself at book value on the following day.

Having established that Mike Danson owned Compelo as well as the majority of the public company GlobalData, who was actually managing Compelo while it was buying and selling all these businesses?

Danson had not occupied a board seat since 2012. Indeed, he appears to have made a deliberate attempt to devolve the day-to-day management, and to distance the board membership, of his privately-owned companies from that of the public company. He had also appointed a nine-partner Hull-based firm of auditors called Smailes Goldie to act for the private companies whereas Grant Thornton[1] audited GlobalData.

Among the directors Danson appointed to his private companies at various times were Ken Appiah, Simon Pyper and Peter Danson. None of them appear to have a direct relationship with the public company GlobalData today, but all of them have historical connections with Danson and GlobalData.

Appiah, a certified accountant, is a long-term Danson acolyte who was finance director of Progressive Digital Media from 2005 until 2010 when it was transformed into the public company that is now GlobalData. More recently he has held board positions among a variety of Danson-

---

1. In April 2020, Deloitte replaced Grant Thornton as group auditors. According to GlobalData this was because of "the length of Grant Thornton's current tenure". The 2019 profit was restated to reflect downward adjustments of £3.2m.

owned businesses, but has not been a director of the public company.

Simon Pyper was associated with Danson between 2005 and December 2017, having been chief financial officer alongside Danson at Datamonitor before serving him in a similar capacity at what is now GlobalData. He resigned all his roles in 2017.

Peter John Danson, brother of Mike, appears on the board of a number of Danson's companies and was the first director of Progressive Media Group which is now part of GlobalData.

Immediately prior to its sale to GlobalData in 2018, Research Views had been managed by Ken Appiah and Simon Pyper. Under their management Research Views had acquired a subsidiary called Atten-

tio Research. Attentio's sole assets comprised the "energy business unit" that had been extracted from another Danson company GlobalData UK shortly before that company was sold to the public company for £66.5 million as part of the January 2016 package of transactions referred to earlier[1].

Prior to its sale, GlobalData UK had been owned personally by Mike Danson, Wayne Lloyd and members of Lloyd's family. Incorporated a few months before the sale of Datamonitor to Informa, Peter Danson was the first director and Mike Danson provided 80% of the £5 million share capital. The company supplied business information services in the UK and beyond, including the

1. See page 378.

Extract from Research Views' 2018 annual report

DIVIDENDS: On 3 April 2018 the Company received a dividend of £1 million from a direct subsidiary undertaking. On the same day Research Views Limited paid a dividend of £1 million to its shareholders. The dividends were issued as part of the corporate reorganisation (note 9) prior to the purchase of Research Views Limited and its subsidiaries by GlobalData Pic. At the date of issuing the dividend the director considered the distributable reserves position, however this did not take into consideration the associated legal and professional fees incurred as part of the restructuring activity. Following consideration of these costs distributable reserves were found to be insufficient to cover the dividend issued of £1 million and thus did not comply with the requirements of the Companies Act 2006. The legal and professional fees incurred were for the benefit of the Group as a whole and therefore the directors feel it is a reasonable position to pass on these costs to GlobalData UK on the basis that the reorganisation and associated legal costs arising from this took place for the purpose of the GlobalData Pic acquisition of Research Views and its subsidiaries under the new corporate structure. The Directors have also considered the external creditor position as at 31 December 2018 and are satisfied that the dividend did not have any adverse impact on any external suppliers or employees. Therefore, these costs will be recharged in 2019. The recharge of costs will provide Research Views Limited with sufficient distributable reserves to issue the dividends and settle the amounts due back from shareholders reported within debtors as at 31 December 2018.

United States, Singapore and India. GlobalData UK had accumulated losses of £11.7 million by the time it was sold to the public company in 2016, although the Attentio business had been reporting profits.

According to GlobalData UK the assets of its energy business unit had been sold to Attentio for £3.9 million. At about the same time Attentio issued a solitary share at a hefty premium of £4.6 million in settlement of a loan of £4.6 million owed by the company to GlobalData UK. There is no obvious reason why GlobalData UK would have been owed that amount from the newly-formed Attentio unless it arose primarily from financing the acquisition of the energy business unit.

On 19 January 2016 the Attentio share was cancelled and the premium was converted into distributable reserves that were applied to offset a trading loss of £1.4 million incurred by Attentio Research in that year.

More recently the public company had cited the addition of the energy industry to the group's offering as a benefit of the Research Views Group acquisition. No mention was made — indeed there was no obligation to make mention — of the fact that the energy business could have been acquired by the public company when it acquired GlobalData UK in 2016 instead of being transferred to Attentio Research immediately beforehand.

On top of the accounting mistakes already identified in the course of this chapter, it emerged that Attentio Research and Research Views were caught up in a mistake of their own just before they were sold to GlobalData in 2018.

On 3 April that year Attentio paid a dividend to Research Views of £1 million. Research Views then declared a dividend of £1 million itself but overlooked the fact that its distributable reserves were insufficient to cover that amount. Thus the dividend declaration was unlawful (see extract opposite). However, to remedy the position the group's parent company agreed to pick up the bill for some reorganisation costs incurred by Research Views in 2018 and thereby replenish that company's reserves.

The third company in the Research Views Group acquisition package was Progressive Ventures. It had invested £2.5 million in acquiring one or more unidentified subsidiary companies in 2013. Their trading performance is unknown.

Progressive Ventures itself files "micro accounts" with no details of its subsidiaries and no indication of whether any of them have traded at a profit or at all. Danson owned 100% of this company and presumably lent it the £2.5 million needed to purchase the various unknown subsidiaries.

According to the Companies Acts, a company is permitted to file "micro accounts" if it satisfies two of three size criteria. It may be argued that the law is deficient in permitting a company to be excused from filing anything more than micro accounts when it is one of a collection of companies that are under common control and which, if structured as a conventional group under a single holding company, would be sufficiently large in aggregate to have to disclose more information.

With ownership of so many of Danson's businesses moving to and fro, it is difficult to be absolutely sure about the effect that would have had on any attempt to ascertain the original cost of the businesses and privately-owned companies sold to the public company GlobalData for almost £100 million in 2018.

Research by *Marketing Services Financial Intelligence* suggested that they would have been acquired originally at a cost of a little over £16 million. However, that figure is no more than an estimate based on such evidence as could be found. Hence the need for better and fuller disclosure in financial statements when parties related to a public company are involved in a transaction of this nature. When approached by *Marketing Services Financial Intelligence*, GlobalData declined to confirm or comment upon the cost of those businesses or to deny that Danson had derived a personal gain from the transaction.

In 2016 — the latest year for which audited figures were available at the time — those same businesses appear to have lost about £5 million between them, excluding any profit earned, or loss incurred, by unidentified subsidiaries of Progressive Ventures.

More pertinent was the announcement on 29 March 2018 that the aggregate profit earned in 2017 by all the companies being acquired was £2.1 million before charging interest, depreciation, amortisation and tax (EBITDA) and before allowing for anticipated cost savings of £1 million per annum. GlobalData had already indicated that the target companies

earned aggregate "pro forma" revenue of £27 million in that year.

Whilst it has proved impossible to ascertain with certainty the cost of the various businesses comprising the Research Views Group that were sold by Danson and his associates to GlobalData in the deal approved on 25 April 2018, the terms of the sale were spelt out more clearly.

The consideration comprised almost 16 million shares whose price stood at about 610p on completion, valuing the transaction at roughly £96 million (the value was about £90 million when the deal was first announced). On top of the value attaching to the sale shares, Danson was repaid net loans of £8.4 million.

Put simply, even at a value of £90 million GlobalData would have paid a multiple of at least 29 times the most recent EBITDA (as adjusted for future synergistic savings) of the various businesses being acquired or over three times their latest revenue.

Implicit in such a strong valuation is not only the expectation of stable income that tends to flow from a subscription based business but also significant growth potential. So the minority shareholders will have been reassured by the fact that the valuation had been subjected to scrutiny by a "leading global firm of accountants" and that the transaction had been recommended by the company's "independent" directors after consulting its advisers N+1 Singer.

The committee of independent directors was chaired by accountant Bernard Cragg who at the time was GlobalData's 63-year-old executive chairman and had been a close colleague of Danson for many years, working alongside him at Datamonitor between 2003 and 2007 (latterly as chairman) until it was sold to Informa[1]. Cragg had joined the GlobalData board originally as a non-executive director and assumed the role of non-executive chairman in 2015. The role was upgraded to executive chairman in 2016.

Following the Research Views Group acquisition, GlobalData's 2018 annual report acknowledged that "as the chairman is an executive director and participates in the company's employee share option scheme he is not considered independent" but added that this "does not influence the chairman's independence of character and judgement".

According to the 2014 edition of the *UK Corporate Governance Code* which applied at the time when Cragg was appointed chairman of GlobalData, the board was required to determine not only whether the chairman was independent in character and judgement but also whether there were relationships or circumstances which were likely to affect, or could appear to affect, the director's judgement[2]: "The board should state its reasons if it determines that a director is independent notwithstanding the existence of relationships or circumstances which may

appear relevant to its determination, including if the director:

- has been an employee of the company or group within the last five years;
- has, or has had within the last three years, a material business relationship with the company either directly, or as a partner, shareholder, director or senior employee of a body that has such a relationship with the company;
- has received or receives additional remuneration from the company apart from a director's fee, participates in the company's share option or a performance related pay scheme, or is a member of the company's pension scheme;
- has close family ties with any of the company's advisers, directors or senior employees.
- holds cross-directorships or has significant links with other directors through involvement in other companies or bodies;
- represents a significant shareholder; or
- has served on the board for more than nine years from the date of their first election."

At the time when Cragg became chairman in 2015 it is not clear whether he had been an "employee" of the group despite his long association with Danson. He had been a non-executive director, for which he appears to have received a £50,000 fee, and he owned 140,000 shares. If, after comparing this and any other relevant information with the criteria listed above, the board decided that there were no relationships or circumstances that could affect Cragg's

1 *Bernard Cragg stood down as chairman of GlobalData on 20 April 2021 and was succeeded by Murray Legg*

2. *See The UK Corporate Governance Code (September 2014), paragraphs A.3.1 and B.1.1. Similar requirements were incorporated into the 2018 edition of the Code. Paragraph B.1.1 also states that every annual report should identify each non-executive director who may be regarded as independent by reference to the criteria listed.*

judgement, there would have been no need to offer any further evidence of independence.

Furthermore, the chairman was only required to meet the above independence criteria on appointment. Thereafter "the test of independence is not appropriate in relation to the chairman", the *Code* stated, taking no account of the possibility that Cragg's chairmanship role would become executive in the following year. It was not until 2018 that the board acknowledged Cragg's lack of independence and then dismissed the notion that this might impair his judgement.

According to the circular sent to shareholders on 29 March 2018, existing shareholders (apart from Danson and Wayne) will have suffered a dilution of approximately 15.6% to their existing ordinary share interests in the company as a result of the Research Views Group acquisition.

What the circular omitted to explain was the gain (or loss) accruing to Danson and his associates from selling those businesses to the public company. That information would appear to have been relevant and potentially very helpful to GlobalData's shareholders.

As the purchase price was settled entirely by the issue of GlobalData shares, Danson received no immediate cash benefit apart from the loan repayment. But he will have received a substantial majority of the consideration shares, thereby enhancing the value of his GlobalData shareholding and increasing the prospect that he may choose to sell at least some of his shares in the not too distant future[1] .

All in all, there is evidence to suggest that GlobalData's minority shareholders may have missed out on a share of what seems to have been a substantial gain in value enjoyed by Danson from acquiring businesses in a personal capacity and selling them on to the public company at a later date when compared with the outcome if instead those businesses had been bought by the public company in the first place.

To enable shareholders to have a clearer picture, there would appear to be a strong case for exploring whether company law should impose higher standards of disclosure and/

Some Danson private companies
At 30 November 2020

Compelo Media Ltd
New Statesman Ltd
New Statesman Media Group Ltd
Progressive Trade Media Ltd
Progressive Luxury Publishing Ltd
Spear Publishing Ltd
Progressive Media Publishing Worldwide Ltd
Progressive Media Asset Management Ltd
Sisyphus Media Ltd
Progressive Broadcasting Ltd
Estel Property Group Ltd
Progressive Media International Ltd

---

1. *Between December 2020 and January 2022 Danson sold 4.3 million shares – a very small proportion of his total 79 million holding – for over £57 million. GlobalData's share price had more than doubled from the 547.5p price prevailing immediately before the Research Views group acquisition was announced on 24 February 2018, and at one stage had soared to three times that price. But by July 2022 it had fallen back to 900p.*

or limit the ability of public company directors to own material shareholdings in private companies engaged in a similar industry.

Can value be realised from a private business without giving up control? This chapter considers how The Business Growth Fund may provide an answer

31
Private Equity: Is there a Better Way?

Anyone who has the stamina to have read this far into the book might be wondering why people ever start businesses in the marketing industry, particularly if the founders have ambitions to remain involved for the long term and would like to be able to realise a decent amount for their shares without necessarily having to sell out to another marketing group.

And yet there have been some fine examples of successful businesses and talented businessmen and women. Indeed arguably it is the very success of the business that makes it hard for the founders to realise full value for their shares. Potential investors tend to associate the continuity of a successful track record with continuity of employment by at least some of the founders, even if only for a few more years. Wanting their cake as well as eating it, most investors attempt to buy 100% of the business as well as getting the vendors to sign up for a further length of service as employees of the acquirer – not always an easy relationship.

Without that continuity of service the agency has less appeal and will command a lower price for its shares. Indeed it may not find a buyer at all. Earlier chapters have described a few arrangements aimed at solving this dilemma. However, there has been little appetite among corporate investors for buying out minority or larger shareholdings for the long term without a guarantee of 100% ownership in the end.

Thus there is a gap in the market for anyone willing to finance the acquisition of less than 100% of a company's shares on a relatively indefinite basis. That gap is one version of what has become known as an "equity gap" – a gap in the availability of funds for entrepreneurs who wish to sell a minority of their company's shares and perhaps also need additional funds to enable their business to expand.

One marketing company that has managed to realise a capital reward for its founding investors, without selling out, is Mother. Over the years Mother has come across several opportunities to invest in infant businesses that have subsequently prospered to such an extent that it has been possible to sell them at a healthy profit after divesting them from the Mother group. That profit has probably alleviated any pent-up pressure from founders to realise some of their investment in Mother itself. As this strategy evolved, Mother's long-serving group finance director Matt Clark gradually devoted more of his time to the development of other new ventures under the umbrella of Mother Ventures, while keeping a watching brief on the core agency.

Clark played a key role in developing a number of stand-alone investments, supported by Mother finance and management expertise, that included the fashion marketing business Wednesday Agency Group and the digital agency Poke. Both were sold subsequently – to BBDO and Publicis Groupe respectively – for a sizeable profit. But it is not every agency founder who would wish to venture into such uncharted territory and accept the risks that may be involved.

The report that accompanies this chapter reflects on the way in which marketing businesses have been financed and on how their founders have sought to turn their hard work into financial rewards. I won't repeat any of that commentary here beyond drawing attention to chapter 18 which reviewed the role of private equity capital and the issues that have been faced. Sometimes private equity is a perfect panacea that allows founders to realise some value while retaining control of the business in private hands for a few more years. Sometimes it is definitely not. Suffice it to say that, as an adviser, it has often been a challenge.

Even the words "private equity" can be misleading. There is privacy by comparison with a company listed on the stock exchange, but the notion that the founders and their successors will continue to retain the privacy that comes with independent indefinite management control is rather fanciful.

Private equity investors are interested first and last in making money from buying and then selling their stake, normally within about five years. So they will seek to ensure that the management signs up to a similar agenda, meaning that their loyalty will usually shift from thinking about the long-term future of the business and its loyal employees to sharing in the maximum payout when it is sold.

The term "equity" is also misleading. True, the investor acquires a shareholding and to that extent it has an equity stake. But almost without exception the vast majority of capital injected by private equity investors is in the form of loans. It is more readily extracted if and when the need arises. It is more tax-efficient. And it offers the opportunity, by taking a charge over the recipient's assets, to obtain some protection from the risks to which genuine equity is exposed.

In chapter 18 there is a table listing 28 private equity investments in the marketing sector between 1990 and 2017[1]. The total invested was over £1 billion. All but two of the companies disclosed a breakdown between equity and debt invested. Of those giving a breakdown, on average 60% of funds invested was in the form of debt, 5% was in preference shares and 35% was in genuine equity shares.

In other words, most of the investments were highly geared, dependant on debt that was often subject to commercial rates of interest. The debt and related interest was tolerable in good times, but when trading conditions deteriorated, the debt would sometimes be called in and the notion of equity (permanent risk capital) was totally absent. On other occasions the debt and related interest would be carried forward in the hope of a full recovery when the shares were sold.

Small wonder then that, in August 2020, as the economy lurched into recession under the weight of coronavirus and companies found it hard to keep afloat, *The Financial Times* reported that private equity funds were begging the Government to hand out rescue packages to the debt-laden companies in which they had invested[2]. More likely than not, banks were disinclined to add more debt to the existing pile created by private equity investors without cast iron security, and there was nothing left to secure. There was already too much debt and not enough equity.

According to the *Concise Oxford Dictionary*, one interpretation of the word "equity" means "being fair and impartial". In the context of company ownership, one would expect that to mean fair rights and rewards of ownership. But with private equity investors, they will often be able dictate the timing and terms of eventual sale by inserting an appropriate clause in a shareholders' agreement. That is understandable, given that the private equity fund is investing a large amount of money and has an obligation to provide a payback to its investors within a specified time horizon. But it makes it difficult for any management shareholders to pursue a

---

1. See page 215

2 The Financial Times, 17 August 2020

different course if they believe that may be in the longer-term interests of the company, its clients and/or employees.

When I came across digital marketing agency Zone, its management appeared to have found a financial partner with a different philosophy. In 2014 it had attracted investment from the Business Growth Fund — a new name to me, supposedly with a new *raison d'être*. It invested alongside the founders of privately-owned companies, encouraging wider share ownership and enabling partial realisations without any pressure to sell the business.

A little later I discovered Four Communications Group – a company that describes itself as an "integrated marketing agency" offering services spanning advertising, creative, branding, PR, public affairs, behaviour change, media planning, media buying, marketing, performance, social analytics, content, web, digital marketing, video and animation, search engine optimisation, events, crisis management, corporate social responsibility, sponsorship, partnerships and training.

It too had partnered with BGF to enable the partial realisation of shareholdings without disturbing the day-to-day ownership or management framework. It all seemed almost too good to be true. So I met with BGF, Four and Zone to find out more and we published the following account in 2017. Shortly thereafter, Zone was acquired by Nasdaq-listed professional services company Cognizant. James Freedman left in 2019 and has involved himself in a new start-up called YUUP – a digital marketplace based in Bristol that he chairs.

Having started out hoping that BGF would offer a long-term means of funding ownership transition from one management generation to another, the evidence now suggests that it is more suited to facilitating partial or interim realisations of value – either for all shareholders or for an individual shareholder who wishes to exit before the rest of the founding management

I n the nineteen eighties marketing agencies were created with twin aspirations. First, they wanted to be famous and recognised for the quality of their work. Secondly, they wanted to get rich. Those aspirations are probably as relevant today as they were then. But when it comes to getting rich, the options have narrowed.

In the nineteen eighties, many of the home-grown agencies offered their shares for sale on the stock market. It was called "going public" although today it is more commonly described as an "IPO" (meaning an initial public offering). The share offer provided the founding owners

Table 1: Marketing companies that were publicly listed at 1 January 1990

Company name	Year admitted	First year's Profit[1]	Exit Year	Last profit[7]	Notes	Reason
Abbott Mead Vickers	1985	1,270	1999	424	2	Bought by Omnicom
Addison Consultancy Group	1985	694	1988	(362)	3	Marketing businesses divested after losing money; refocused on research.
BNB Resources (formerly Charles Barker)	1986	966	2007	(5,557)	5	Went into administration with estimated £88m deficiency after failure of acquisitions and declining revenue.
Broad Street Group	1986	502	1991	(2,427)	6,7	French group BDDP took 100% control in March 1991.
Brunning Group (subsequently The Birkdale Group and The 10 Group)	1961	n/a	2003	(1,181)		Several management teams attempted to turn business round, but eventually all marketing subsidiaries were divested and company liquidated in 2004.
Clarke Hooper	1986	528	1992	(1,391)	13	Business sold to Abbott Mead Vickers, company liquidated in 1994.
Geers Gross	1969	n/a	1991	563		Bought by Publicis after death of co-founder Bob Gross.
Gold Greenlees Trott (later GGT Group)	1986	829	1998	(87,678)		Omnicom came to rescue after costly acquisition of French BDDP followed by client losses and closure of US subsidiary.
Holmes & Marchant Group (Huntsworth since1999)	1985	690	2000	(7,070)	8	Shareholder supported management buy-in.
KLP Group		Not available	1993	(526)		Ceased trading in 1993 after substantial losses.
Lopex	1986	1,547	1990	3,753	9	Havas outbid Incepta, but losses followed.
Lowe Group (previously Lowe Howard Spink & Bell)	1984	1,284	1990	15,155	10	Interpublic uplifted its 35% minority shareholding to 100%, allowing founders to realise an estimated £8m.
Osprey Communications	1984	136	2001	(129)	11	Reversed into Ten Alps (became Zinc Media Group).
Paragon Communications	1987	442	1990	844	12	Sold to Shandwick plc (now part of Interpublic).
Saatchi & Saatchi Company (became Cordiant Communications Group)	1975	355	2003	(233,600)	14	Saatchi & Saatchi divested in 1997, bought by Publicis in 2001; overpaid for Lighthouse group and other acquisitions. Rump sold to WPP in July 2003.
Shandwick (renamed International Public Relations)	1985	Not known	1998	4,477		Bought by Interpublic – founder Lord Chadlington sold 9.6m shares .
TMD Advertising Holdings	1985	276	1991	1,894		Aegis acquired 70.1% not already acquired via Carat.
VPI Group (formerly Valin Pollen Intnll)	1984	597	1991	4,402	15	Administrator appointed after company hit by fraud at US acquisition The Carter Organisation bought for $76m.
Wight Collins Rutherford Scott (Holdings) (later became Aegis Group)	1984	625	1992	(28,400)	4	Costly expansion caused losses; French fines under competition law; agency sold to Havas, media buying bought by Dentsu.
WPP	1985	1,101		Still listed		

Notes: 1. Profit £'000 after tax and minority interests but before cost of flotation. 2. Profits stated after substantial goodwill amortisation charges. 3. Formed from merger of Addison Page and Chetwynd Streets in 1986; initial profit relates to Chetwynd Streets; recruitment, advertising, PR and design businesses divested in 1988-89, leaving Taylor Nelson research business that merged with Sofres in 1998 and was acquired by WPP in 2008. 4. Expanded internationally, then acquired Carat, sold off non-media businesses in 1992, renamed rump as Aegis Group (later sold to Dentsu). 5. Originally Charles Barker, specialised in recruitment and recruitment/financial advertising, made costly acquisitions while core business declined – sold to Penna by administrators. 6. Broad Street Associates reversed into Stanelco in 1986, followed by name change and disposal of Stanelco's non marketing operations; later sold on to GGT Group and thereafter broken up – part to management and part to TBWA/Omnicom. 7. Profit/loss excludes any abnormal gain on disposal of subsidiaries, debt restructuring etc. 8. Lord Chadlington mounted a management buy-in and acquired 4.9 million shares in 2000, thereafter expanding the group as a public relations business. 9. Last profit reported here was subsequently adjusted down by a £993,000 property provision. 10. Profit includes £2.7m gain on sale of Lowe Bell Communications to Chime. 11. Company initially an investment trust listed on stock exchange, transformed by acquisitions in 1984; pre-exit loss is after crediting £1.2m from disposal of business. 12. Sale met strategic interests of shareholders, among whom the founder held 24.3%. 13. Pre-exit loss relates to main operating subsidiary only. 14.Flotation achieved by reverse takeover of Compton UK Partners - first year's profit stated after Compton merger costs, office move and redundancies. 15. Last accounts prepared.

Sources: Fintellect research, Marketing Services Financial Intelligence and Companies House.

with an opportunity to realise some of the value they had created while at the same time remaining in the driving seat if that was what they wanted.

By the end of that decade, there were 20 publicly-listed marketing agency groups (see Table 1). Only WPP remains on the stock market today.

Nearly all of the rest were sold to, or rescued by, even bigger companies – mainly foreign. A few failed altogether.

Many of the entrepreneurs involved bemoaned the costs and external pressures imposed on public companies. Analysts and journalists had to be kept happy. Profit trends had to be consistently upwards.

Our research confirms that many of the companies that chose the public flotation route failed to survive as independent businesses, but most of their founders had banked a healthy gain along the way. Our research also confirms that many of those companies faced challenging times after going public, and that many of the difficulties arose from over ambitious and/or inexperienced managers who were ill-prepared for their new environment.

Even after the initial flotation, several founders retained substantial shareholdings and took advantage of subsequent takeover bids to relinquish any residual management roles and realise the remainder of their shares, sometimes — but not always — at a favourable price.

During their short-lived heyday the publicly-listed groups were encouraged by the City to grow faster by making acquisitions, fuelled by an influx of cash introduced by American investment banks that had arrived in the UK. The experience was entirely new to many of the incumbent managements and often ended in tears as the acquirers made some expensive mistakes and their fair-weather investment bankers turned tail, heading back across the Atlantic with as much of their precious cash as they could retrieve.

After the flush of fresh-faced newcomers had begun to retreat from the stock market, a new breed of marketing entrepreneur took their place. These were mainly people with a marketing background who sought to imitate Sir Martin Sorrell by acquiring relatively inactive "shell companies" with an existing stock market listing and using them to "buy and build" a marketing group from almost nothing (see adjacent table).

Thus the focus of these people has been on collecting businesses rather more than on building on the solid foundations of their existing successful marketing agency. Sir Martin Sorrell's giant WPP[1], now the biggest marketing group in the world, is an excellent example, while on a smaller

Marketing companies listed on the London stock exchange in 2017

Be Heard Group, Cello Group, Communisis, Crossrider, dotDigital Group, Ebiquity, GlobalData, Huntsworth, Jaywing, M&C Saatchi, Matomy Media Group, Next Fifteen Communications Group, Porta Communications, Reach4Entertainment Enterprises, St Ives, The Mission Marketing Group, WPP, Zinc Media Group

1. Sir Martin Sorrell left WPP in April 2018

scale was the more recently-launched Be Heard Group, headed by Peter Scott[1].

But even some of these public companies — like Creston and Chime Communications — found the going less than appealing and later opted to accept offers from private equity investors to buy them out of public ownership. In doing so they have tacitly acknowledged that control of the company would eventually be sold on.

The home-grown buy-and-build groups that remained on the stock market joined the collection of established global players — like WPP, Omnicom, Publicis, Interpublic, Havas and Dentsu — in offering a prospective exit route for the founders of first generation marketing agencies. But the opportunity for those agency founders to realise a sizeable slice of the value they had created, while still retaining an element of control of their business, remained as elusive as ever.

In the UK, only M&C Saatchi appears to have seriously embraced the notion of continuing management co-ownership (see chapter 28). Crispin Porter & Bogusky tried something similar in the United States until the ideal was impaired by the agency's subsequent takeover by the controversial Canadian group MDC Partners (see chapter 27).

It is therefore not surprising that most of today's entrepreneurs who run marketing agencies start out with the sole ambition of selling their business to an existing trade buyer. Along the way, a few have embraced

offers from private equity investors to acquire an interim minority shareholding on the implicit understanding that the business (and therefore management control) will be sold on within about five years.

The option of retaining control within the management team over a long period of time is rarely considered.

Nevertheless, many of those entrepreneurs have longer term ambitions for their businesses that they would like to fulfil before looking for an exit. Building a business — whether by acquiring a bigger range of skill sets, reacting to technological change or taking advantage of opportunities overseas — needs cash. Without access to the stock market for long term capital or to the coffers of a bigger group that already has access to the stock market, there are few places to go for that cash. Clearing banks are nervous about how much they lend to private companies and for how long, and about how those funds can be secured. In a nutshell, it can sometimes be hard to expand and for the founders to retain ownership control at the same time.

But the arrival on the scene in 2011 of BGF - the Government sponsored Business Growth Fund - seemed to offer a way to achieve such an aspiration. To observers a little long in the tooth, BGF had some similarities to earlier post-war government-sponsored entities like the Industrial & Commercial Finance Corporation. Its aim was to fill an "equity gap" by supplying expansion capital to entrepreneurs whose privately owned businesses were too small to access the public stock markets.

It is proving to be a useful provider of interim finance for expanding businesses and for those companies where the founders prefer to remain in management control when one of their number wishes to depart before the others.

BGF is backed by five of the UK's main banking groups — Barclays, HSBC, Lloyds, RBS and Standard Chartered — and has up to £2.5 billion with which to make long-term equity investments. BGF has already invested in several marketing agencies, including Palmer Hargreaves in the Midlands, public relations group FCG Worldwide (better known as Four Communications) and digital agency Zone.

Typically the BGF investment has been used to fund the partial realisation of shares held by one or more of the founding partners, but only where the continuing management has the ambition and ability to build the business further and thereby add value to BGF's investment (as well as to their own), with the aim of realising a healthy financial gain at a later date.

BGF invested £10 million in Four's parent company FCG Worldwide in 2015. Half of that amount was invested in ordinary shares, giving BGF a 30% holding, and the other half was provided in the form of an unsecured 10% loan note that becomes repayable in four half yearly instalments starting on 30 June 2021.

The BGF shareholding also carries preferential rights to participate in future capital realisations

and to a cumulative dividend of 10% of net profits earned in each year starting from January 2021.

At Zone, BGF purchased 22% of the share capital for £6 million in 2014. Of that amount, £3 million went to shareholders and £3 million went on to the balance sheet. The shares entitled BGF to a preferential dividend of 3%. From 1 January 2020, BGF will be entitled to share in 8% of post-tax profits or, if higher, 10% of the capital BGF has subscribed. Thus the minimum dividend would amount to £600,000 per annum.

"We gave them a six-year plan to 2020", explains one of Zone's founders, chief executive James Freedman. "We felt that the focus would be on the UK and Europe. We had already made a couple of acquisitions in terms of Public Zone and Auros that had helped us go from revenue of around £10 million in 2013 to almost £15 million in 2014. So that was a huge endorsement that showed we knew how to do it and we were profitable."

We had no bank facility. So we had been very careful and cautious. It had taken us a long time from 2000 — it was brick-by-brick — and BGF knew that we were committed long-term. I think the fact that we'd previously had another successful business that we'd sold also showed them that we could do it."

Four Communications also had a track record of paying for acquisitions out of the company's cash flow before BGF arrived on the scene: "We did the first acquisition right at the beginning of 2011 and thereafter all the way through to 2015", group chief executive Nan Williams recalls. "We just did one a year, making four or five in total, and we just used our own cash. We always had plenty of cash because the business is very cash-generative."

As well as helping Four to expand on a bigger scale, the BGF investment allowed several senior managers to realise a portion of their shareholding value without the need to surrender control of the business through a sale, for example. As a result co-founder Christopher O'Donoghue was also able to retain much of his own shareholding — now just under 25% — when he retired after leading the group's development for the first 15 years. Similarly Zone's shareholders were able to realise some of their share value as a result of the BGF investment.

But did the BGF investment set these two companies on an irreversible pathway to eventual sale that would sacrifice any prospect of keeping ownership control with the management in the longer term?

The answer is "not necessarily, but probably". The Zone founders are entirely relaxed about the longer term prospect of a sale, but they wanted to fulfil their expansion plans first.

"We felt there was much further to go on the journey and that we liked our independence", says Freedman. "We were enjoying it. We always had million-pound-plus clients, even from the early days. We were in a small side street on the edge of Camden Town and it was fun to get to a bigger office and to see some success.

"We liked getting bigger — it was playing to our strengths and skills. And the stories around earn-outs and networks were largely bad. There were a few exceptions but they were very much the exceptions that prove the rule. It just felt there was a long road ahead for us and what else were we going to do apart from pocket the money? And neither I nor Marc nor anyone else wanted to go and sit on the beach — I mean, what's the point?

"The idea of building something that's sustainable is fun and challenging. I'm really a business guy. I'm not really a practitioner.

"I think that a lot of businesses in our sector tend to be founded by practitioners and they're very good practitioners, brilliant planners, brilliant creatives, brilliant suits. But it doesn't necessarily mean they like the business side of it. I really do enjoy the business side of it. I really enjoy challenges. I get very disappointed if we don't achieve a margin target, or if we can't get the revenue per employee — it's part of my motivation and competitive streak."

Reading between the lines, BGF always hopes for a profitable exit within a reasonable timeframe of five years or so. But there is nothing set in stone. "We cannot force a CEO or management team to exit against their will", says BGF's director of external affairs Jon Rhodes. Nevertheless BGF commonly structures its investments so as to motivate investee companies' managers to seek their own exit path in due course.

As already described, the FCG share structure is such that BGF will be entitled to a cumulative annual dividend of 10% of net profits from

1 January 2021 as it begins to receive repayment of the £5 million loan note. When that date approaches, if FCG's management are loathe to live with the BGF dividend commitment, they may feel motivated to seek an alternative investor or a sale. But the choice is theirs – they can continue with BGF if they wish, paying off the loan and sharing with them a slice of their profits.

Following the same model, Zone will be only too aware that BGF's 8% profit sharing requirement will take effect from January 2020, with a minimum annual entitlement of £600,000.

Even with share capital of £2.5 billion, there is a limit to the amount of money BGF has available to invest at any time and so it needs to rotate those funds if it is to meet future investment requests. Only by realising existing investments over time can it achieve that end.

"Any exit strategy is discussed and agreed with the full consent of the management team and only on terms that are in the best interests of the business", explains BGF's Jon Rhodes. "Typically, all shareholders will exit together. This could be to new and larger investors for the next growth phase, a public listing or a full or partial sale."

Does the prospect of a future sale put off acquisition targets or the recruitment of potentially high flying employees?

Zone's James Freedman doesn't think so: "I think that it's just about being open and transparent with them and kind of recognising that, at some point, we'll have to do something else. They've got share options. All the people we care about have got options. And I think that options are quite a good thing to do."

Nan Williams agrees: "We've been very clear with everybody from the start. But it tends not to be of relevance to people day-to-day. It just becomes part of the fabric really, as long as you don't let the culture become all about that."

So how do you stop a potential future sale from becoming part of the culture?

Williams ponders before responding: "Just hard work and

How BGF invested in Four and Zone*

	Four (FCG)	Zone
Initial investment total	£10 million	£6 million
Unsecured loan note element	£5 million	nil
Rate of interest or pref dividend	10% interest	3% divi
Loan repayments	Four half yearly instalments from 30 June 2021	Not applicable
Equity share element	£5 million for 30%	£6 million for 22%
Profit participation "holiday"	Five years	Five years
Subsequent cumulative profit share	10% of annual net profit from 2021	8% of annual net profit from 2020, or £600,000 if higher

Principal features only. Source: Companies House

THE FOUNDING OF FOUR

Four's chief executive Nan Williams (right) started work at Barclays International in 1984 on its graduate entry scheme after studying at Cambridge University. "I cannot for the life of me remember why", she says. "They sent you around the organisation doing everything. The last assignment was with the marketing department where I suddenly felt much more at home. And that's when I left to join Charles Barker."

Nan was at Charles Barker for 15 years before founding Four: "There were four of us originally – hence the company name - and we'd all one way or another been at Charles Barker — I had hired Ray Eglington and Tim Lewis as grad trainees there actually. They had gone off and done different things and eventually they persuaded me to set up and they'd join in. Andrew Jack had formed a separate business in media buying. We had the same chairman and the two companies came together to form the group.

"We were seven people when we started and, when Andrew's team came in, we had each grown to about 25 employees. It gave us a really good boost as we'd been clear from the beginning that we thought that the future direction was for integrated work — digital was just emerging. It was clear that PR was not going to stay as PR, and that media buying wasn't going to stay as media buying. These services were going to converge together. And so that was the plan at the beginning: to try and do something that used lots of the marketing disciplines.

"Originally, people would come to us for a PR programme and we would build the digital support into it. We'd do the branding around it. We'd create brochures or whatever. So we would do all those other pieces of work in support of a PR campaign. Now people come to us either just with a problem or they may come to us for an ad campaign. And we build other things around that. That said, some people just still come for PR.

"People would say: 'Why are you using your own money?' And we said: "Well we just do it nice and careful. We won't take on any debt and then we'll make it work and see how it goes. So we did that for a long time until about 2014."

THE ORIGINS OF ZONE

Zone's founder James Freedman (right) read classics at Cambridge University and then worked in the theatre: "I got a scholarship to do a masters degree in screen writing and screen directing at the University of California. I did the first year, then ran out of money."

Freedman moved to New York where he met his wife Anna Kissin. "I didn't really know what to do next, so we decided to move back to the UK. My father had a job with Manchester United as merchandising director. He called me: 'Someone has done an unofficial Manchester United magazine. Would you like to write an article for it?'

"We took over the magazine in 1993. Then we branched out into a whole raft of other publications — working with Arsenal, Chelsea, Roma in Italy, and the FA. We did videos, books and a whole range of things. By the end of the nineties, having started in a bedroom in Belsize Park, we had built a very profitable business, with the biggest selling sports monthly. It was the beginning of desktop publishing. In the end, we sold the publishing license to Future Publishing.

"The focus of the Zone idea was to take the editorial and design skills we had learned in magazine publishing and marry those with technology because the monthly magazine cycle was feeling a little bit outdated when you could go to a website and fan forums and get your football news hourly up to the minute. The internet was going to change the way in which customers interacted with media. If you could understand your customers like we had done with Manchester United, producing compelling content for them, that was a powerful proposition. And if you could underpin that with technology, that would be really good."

Zone started in 2000 and acquired a small IT consultancy run by Marc Parnell (now a Zone partner). "I had met him through work he'd done at Channel 4 and Channel 5. He was a mathematician who had done computer science. So it was a very good marriage." In the second half of the 2000s Zone hired Jon Davie (now chief executive), ten years younger than Freedman.

vigilance. Just character, I suppose. You have to keep at it. Mostly it's quite easy: staff very quickly get to like it here — it's a very sociable place. And people get promoted quickly. They have fun colleagues who do something completely different down the road, and they just like that. So staff fit in very quickly."

Following the BGF deal FCG has 16 people across the business with shares or share options. "We want to extend that to the other senior managers as well, so we're all in one boat together", Williams says. "It is really important to think what you're going to do, particularly if earn-outs come to an end and they've done well. We don't really want them buzzing off and just leaving us, however good the succession is, so you have to work on the succession.

"But you also have to work on something that means they feel they want to stay, and maybe do a different role. It would be great to think that, after (say) a three-year earn-out, there's something in place for people to take the business forward with us."

One of the often-cited justifications by those advocating a public share listing has been the ready market it provides for selling shares, thereby enabling acquisitive companies to offer shares as part of the purchase consideration. That provides a modest inducement for selling shareholders to remain committed to their new masters. It also eases the potential cash strain on buyers. But if private companies like Zone and FCG offer shares as part of the purchase consideration, the recipient may be more reluctant to accept them in the absence of an active and reputable market place in which to sell them later.

"That's definitely a concern",

Features of a typical BGF funding deal

- BGF invests in private and publicly listed companies across all sectors except regulated financial services.
- BGF has made many investments in family owned businesses and can co-invest alongside other funders.
- BGF Growth invests in businesses typically generating revenues of £5m to £100m.
- Businesses will usually have at least three years' trading history and have been profitable for at least two years in the preceding three.
- Initial investments are typically between £2m and £10m.
- Investments typically comprise a mixture of interest-bearing unsecured loan notes and equity shares.
- BGF will always take a board seat.
- BGF takes only a minority equity stake in its investee companies, rather than outright control.

James Freedman acknowledges. "But they may gain comfort from the knowledge that we've got BGF as an investor and they won't want to be there forever. The BGF investment is also a validation of the Zone share value by a third party that came in by acquiring a minority shareholding."

So far Four has not sought to use shares as part of an acquisition payment, although Nan Williams says she thinks many vendors would like to obtain some Four shares. There is a simple reason why shares have not been offered so far: BGF has a 30% holding in Four's parent company and, under the terms of that arrangement, the BGF shareholding has to be maintained at 30%. "If we start issuing more shares to other people, we would have to top BGF's shareholding back up", Nan Williams explains. "It's too complicated for my simple brain."

When competing in the acquisition market against the bigger publicly listed groups, where shares are readily offered and accepted (and sometimes yield taxation benefits), it would have come as no surprise to learn that Zone and Four sometimes felt they were at a disadvantage. And yet neither would have us believe that they have been seriously impeded in their ambitions so far.

So what are the strings that come attached to a typical BGF funding package? Does BGF demand a charge over assets to secure its loans? It says "no". Does BGF impose outside nominees on the investee company's board? Yes, it does.

"BGF will always take a board seat", the company says. Often the nominee will be the BGF executive who handled the investment deal.

"In addition, we usually introduce a chairman or other non-executive candidates who we believe can help the company to face the challenges that come with the next stage of growth", Jon Rhodes explains. "The management team of an investee company is typically introduced to three or more prospective chairmen before making a choice."

BGF claims that its Talent Network has more than 3,000 board level contacts across the UK in all sectors, helping it assess investment opportunities and sharing invaluable market insight. To date, over 100 chairman and non-executives have been appointed to investee company boards from that network.

"There are no hard and fast rules however", Rhodes adds reassuringly. "A company may already have a strong board, or the management team may have identified their own candidate. We can be flexible. The single most important outcome is ensuring the company has a board capable of taking it to the next stage."

Many private companies will be nervous about inviting in an outside investor in case it seeks to pursue it own undeclared ends in priority to those of the management shareholders. For example, a number of private equity investors have a policy of realising their shareholdings within a specified time horizon. Some will even demand the right to sell the company over its management's head if the realisation opportunity takes a long time coming.

At first glance the arrival of

private equity funds had already filled many of the interim funding needs of prosperous private companies. So how does the BGF proposition differ from a typical offer by a private equity investor?

"BGF is not a private equity firm, which typically focuses on leverage buyouts and controlling stakes in the business it invests in", argues Jon Rhodes, although perhaps he overstates that distinction. Private equity investors have certainly taken minority stakes in a number of marketing companies in recent years, as described in chapter 18.

Rhodes continues: "BGF invests off its own balance sheet and has a conservative approach to debt. We invest over a longer term and take a minority equity stake in our investee companies, rather than looking for outright control. We are not distracted by having to raise funds, nor are we under time pressure to make returns."

On the face of it, BGF's willingness to take a longer-term perspective is attractive, even if that involves sharing more of the profits with that institution to do so. Private equity investors will counter with the argument that they will often be prepared to sell their stake on to another private equity fund in order to achieve their desired exit within about five years, but that introduces an element of uncertainty at the outset. Equally attractive is BGF's willingness to provide some of the funding by loan without taking a charge over the company's assets as security.

Whether BGF pays as much for its investments as might be obtained from a trade buyer or a more conventional private equity investor remains a secret. It must be assumed that BGF would price a minority shareholding at less than could be obtained from an outright sale to a trade buyer or from a stock exchange placing that provides an unrestricted market for the shares. But the situation is less clear when considering conventional private equity offers: the choice may be influenced more by the specific features of each proposition.

Both Four and Zone appeared contented with BGF as a junior partner, and BGF seems happy occupying that role;

"BGF will only ever take a minority stake in a company: no more than 40% and typically around 25%", Rhodes says. "BGF is looking to build, not buy, businesses. This approach is arguably the strongest possible endorsement of a management team as they remain in control of their business."

Index

BETWEEN THE BALANCE SHEETS

BETWEEN THE BALANCE SHEETS

BETWEEN THE BALANCE SHEETS

M

BETWEEN THE BALANCE SHEETS

T